VISUAL QUICKSTART GUIDE

# America Online 3

FOR MACINTOSH

Maria Langer

Peachpit Press

Visual QuickStart Guide

**America Online 3 for Macintosh**

Maria Langer

**Peachpit Press**
2414 Sixth Street
Berkeley, CA 94710
510/548-4393
510/548-5991 (fax)

Find us on the World Wide Web at: http://www.peachpit.com

Peachpit Press is a division of Addison Wesley Longman



Editor: Kaethin Prizer
Copy Editor: Terry Wilson
Technical Editor: Stu Gitlow
Proofreader: Terry Wilson
Indexer: Deni Boyer
Cover Design: The Visual Group
Production: Maria Langer, Kate Reber

## Colophon

This book was produced with QuarkXPress 3.3 on a Power Macintosh 7100/66. The fonts used were Charlotte, Charlotte Sans, and Corinthian Bold from Letraset.

## Notice of Rights



## Notice of Liability



ISBN 0-201-68807-7

9 8 7 6 5 4 3 2 1

Printed and bound in the United States of America.

# Dedication

To Jeremy Judson,
with many thanks.

## Thanks!

To Kaethin Prizer for letting me put this book aside while the AOL software went through weekly revision cycles during its development phase. I think we both learned a valuable lesson while working on my two AOL books: it's better to let a book hit the stores a bit late than to revise a manuscript each time a software beta is updated.

To the rest of the folks at Peachpit Press for giving me a chance to write a *Macintosh* book about the online service I've been using for eight years.

To Terry Wilson, Stu Gitlow, and Deni Boyer for applying their copy editing, technical editing, indexing, and proof-reading skills. A special thanks goes to Stu for explaining some of the intracacies of AOL, which aren't very obvious to the user.

To the folks at America Online, including Howard Rosenman and Kathy Jonson. A special thanks goes to Jennifer Watson, Bob Strange, and Valerie L. Downey, for providing the keyword list I used as the basis for the one in Appendix D.

And to Mike, for his continuous moral support.

http://www.intac.com/~gilesrd/

# TABLE OF CONTENTS

Table of Contents

## Note from the Author

Writing a book about America Online is like shooting arrows at a target that won't stand still.

During the two months it took me to complete this project, I learned that the appearance and functionality of windows and dialog boxes on AOL can change at any time. That's because the AOL user interface is created by two pieces of software: the AOL 3 software this book was written about and the AOL server software that users connect to. While the server software changes don't usually add major features, they can change what appears in windows and what content is available to users.

Peachpit Press and I have done everything humanly possible to make this book up-to-date for the release of AOL 3 for Macintosh. If you find any differences between what you see on these pages and what you see on your monitor while using AOL, don't think you've bought the wrong book! You've just discovered an example of what I call "AOL Evolution"—a never-ending process of internal tweaking that makes AOL and its software the best it can be.

Maria Langer,
January 1997

# GETTING STARTED 1

## Introduction

America Online (or *AOL*) is an online service that offers access to a wide range of content and features. Its attractive graphic user interface, which makes it easy to use, has helped it become the largest commercial online service, with over 6 million subscribers or *members*. Even in its off-peak hours, there are at least 30,000 AOL members connected at once!

This Visual QuickStart Guide will help you navigate AOL and take advantage of its resources by providing step-by-step instructions, plenty of illustrations, and a generous helping of tips. Within these pages, you'll find everything you need to know to explore AOL, find the information and software you want, and make new friends.

This book is designed for page-flipping. Use the thumb tabs, index, or table of contents to find the topics for which you need help. If you're brand new to AOL, however, be sure to begin by reading at least the first three chapters. In them, you'll find important information about installing, using, and navigating AOL.

Your AOL membership opens a whole world of information, entertainment, and personal relationships—all accessible right from your computer. Think of this book as your guide for exploring this online world.

## About America Online

AOL is a commercial online service. Each member uses a personal computer, modem, standard telephone line (or Internet connection), and AOL software to connect to AOL's server. While connected or *online*, members can access any of AOL's content or features, including:

- Electronic mail and topical message boards
- Shareware, freeware, and commercial software updates
- Up-to-the-minute news, sports, weather, and stock quotes
- Online versions of popular printed publications and television shows
- Areas filled with information related to specific hobbies and interests
- Internet features like the World Wide Web, FTP, Gopher, and Usenet newsgroups

### ✔ Tips

- The above list is just a small sample of what AOL has to offer. As you explore AOL, you'll find far more features and content than what's covered in this book.
- As you read this book, you may find a few differences between what you see on your computer screen and what is illustrated in book figures. This is because of constant changes in AOL's content and features.

## About AOL Software

AOL's graphic user interface, which is discussed in detail in **Chapter 2**, comes from two sources:

- The AOL software provides standard interface elements and features.
- The AOL server transmits or *downloads* additional graphic elements and features as needed while a member is connected. It also tells AOL software what installed elements to display as content or features are accessed.

### ✔ Tips

- You must obtain and install AOL's software in order to access AOL.
- **Table 1** lists the system requirements for AOL 3 for Macintosh software. Make sure your system meets these requirements before trying it.
- This book covers version 3 of the AOL software, which includes many features not found in version 2.7 (the previous version, which may have been preinstalled on your Macintosh).

| America Online 3 for Macintosh |
|---|
| **Minimum System Requirements** |
| ■ 68030 or better CPU |
| ■ System 7.1 |
| ■ 8 MB physical RAM |
| ■ 15 MB free hard disk space |
| ■ 13", 256-color monitor |
| ■ 9600 bps modem |
| **Recommended System Requirements** |
| ■ 68040 or better CPU |
| ■ System 7.5.3 Revision 2 or later |
| ■ 16 MB RAM |
| ■ 15 MB free hard disk space |
| ■ 13", 256-color monitor |
| ■ 28.8K bps modem |

**Table 1.** *Minimum and recommended system requirements for AOL 3 for Macintosh.*

## To obtain AOL software by phone

Call 1-888-265-8002. This toll-free number will connect you to an orders representative so you can order the software.

### ✔Tip

- This toll-free number can be used from the US or Canada. AOL also has locations in other countries.

## To obtain an upgrade from a previous version

1. Connect to AOL using the version of AOL software you already have.
2. Choose Keyword from the Go To menu or press ⌘K.
3. In the Keyword dialog box that appears, enter the keyword UPGRADE (see **Figure 1**).
4. Click the Go button or press Enter.
5. A dialog box that asks whether you want to enter a free area appears. Click OK or press Enter.
6. In the upgrade window that appears, choose the appropriate options to locate and download the AOL 3 for Macintosh software.
7. Follow the instructions on screen to complete the download. You can then disconnect from AOL and install your new software.

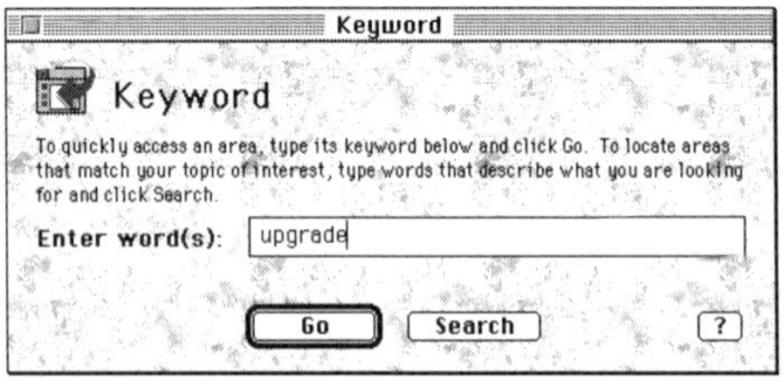


**Figure 1.** *Enter UPGRADE in the Keyword dialog box and click Go to go right to the upgrade area.*

### ✔ Tips

- To follow the above steps, you must already have an AOL account.
- Because the software upgrade is downloaded from a free area on AOL, there is no charge (other than applicable telephone company phone charges) to obtain it.

## About Installing the AOL Software

The AOL software has its own installer. When you launch the installer, it:

- Installs the AOL software and support files on your hard disk.
- Installs the AOL Scheduler program in the Startup Items folder inside your System folder.

Installation instructions and progress information appear on your screen as the software is installed.

## About Configuring the AOL Software

When you launch the software for the first time, dialog boxes and windows guide you to:

- Obtain a local access number to connect to AOL's server.
- Create a new account or enter existing account information.

### ✔ Tips

- If you're upgrading from a previous version, let AOL copy settings like your screen name, password, and preferences from the previous version. AOL does this automatically if it can find the previous version.
- Once you've upgraded from a previous version of AOL software and know you can successfully connect and use the system with the new version, you can delete the previous version and all of its files if desired.

## About Connecting to AOL

To take advantage of the content and features AOL has to offer, you must connect to the AOL server.

- Begin by launching the AOL software and displaying the Welcome or Sign On window (see **Figure 2**).
- Then configure the connection to use the desired screen name and location file and proper password.
- Finally, use the Sign On button to initiate a connection.

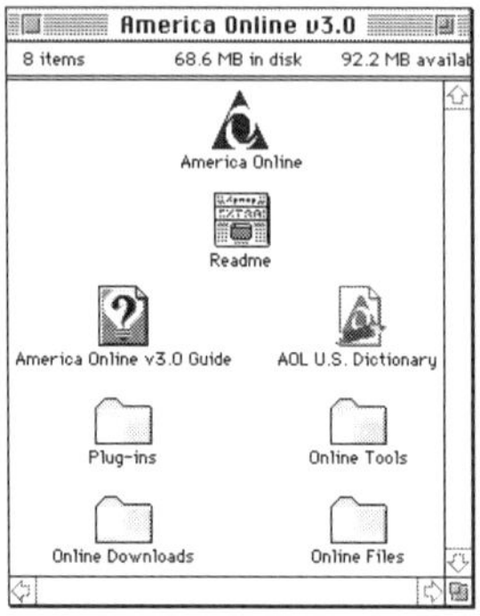


**Figure 2.** *Double-click the America Online application icon inside the America Online v3.0 folder window.*

## To run the AOL software & display the Welcome window

In the Finder, double-click the America Online application icon inside the America Online v3.0 folder window (see **Figure 2**).

A Welcome window like the one in **Figure 3** appears.

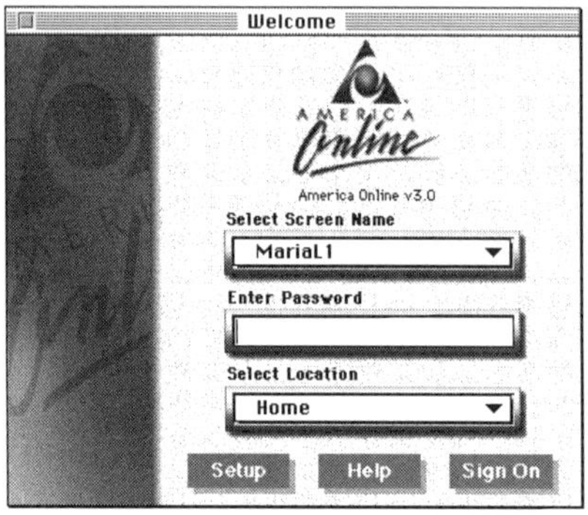


**Figure 3.** *Use the Welcome or Sign On window to set up a connection.*

### ✔ Tip

- If the AOL software is already running but the Welcome window is not displayed, choose Setup & Sign On from the Go To menu (see **Figure 4**) to display the Welcome window. If you're already connected, this command won't be available.

**Figure 4.** *Choose Setup & Sign On from the Go To menu to display the Welcome window. If you're already connected, this command won't be available.*

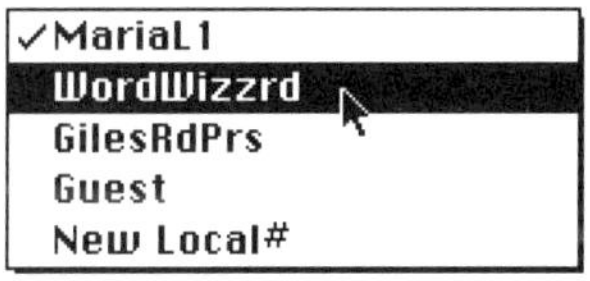


**Figure 5.** *Choose the screen name with which you want to connect.*

**Figure 6.** *When you enter a password, a bullet appears for each character you type, so type carefully!*

**Figure 7.** *A window like this keeps you informed about the progress of your connection.*

**Figure 8.** *When you connect, the Channels and Welcome windows appear.*

## To set up a connection

1. If the screen name with which you want to connect is not displayed in the Welcome window (see **Figure 3**), choose it from the Select a Screen Name pop-up menu (see **Figure 5**).
2. If the location from which you want to connect does not appear in the Welcome window, choose it from the Select Location pop-up menu.
3. In the Enter Password edit box, enter the password for the screen name you selected (see **Figure 6**).

### ✔ Tips

- Each AOL account can have up to five screen names. Creating additional screen names is covered in **Chapter 11**.
- Locations are discussed later in this chapter.
- You can store your password so you do not need to enter it each time you connect. Storing passwords is discussed in **Chapter 11**. Keep in mind, however, that anyone who has access to your computer can also access your AOL account if your password is stored within the AOL software.

## To connect to AOL

1. Once a connection has been set up in the Welcome window, click the Sign On button.
2. A connection window appears (see **Figure 7**) as the software attempts to connect to AOL.

### ✔ Tip

- You'll know you've successfully connected when the Channels and Welcome windows appear (see **Figure 8**). You'll hear a male voice say "Welcome!"

## To connect from a friend's computer

1. Launch the AOL software and display the Welcome window as discussed earlier in this chapter.
2. Choose Guest from the Select Screen Name pop-up menu (see **Figure 9**). The Enter Password edit box is grayed out in the Welcome window (see **Figure 10**).
3. If necessary, change the location file by choosing a different one from the Select Location pop-up menu.
4. Click the Sign On button.
5. Wait while the software connects to AOL.
6. Enter your screen name and password in the Guest Account Information window that appears (see **Figure 11**) and click OK or press Enter. You will be connected with your own screen name and password.

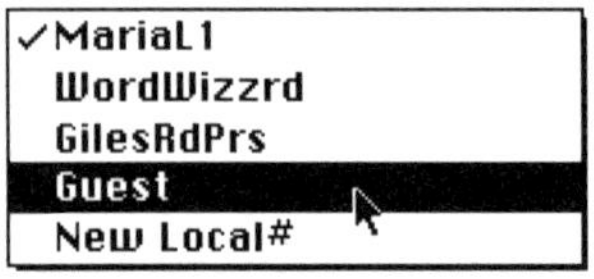


**Figure 9.** *To connect from a friend's computer, choose Guest from the Select Screen Name pop-up menu.*

**Figure 10.** *When you select Guest from the Select Screen Name pop-up menu, the Enter Password edit box is grayed out.*

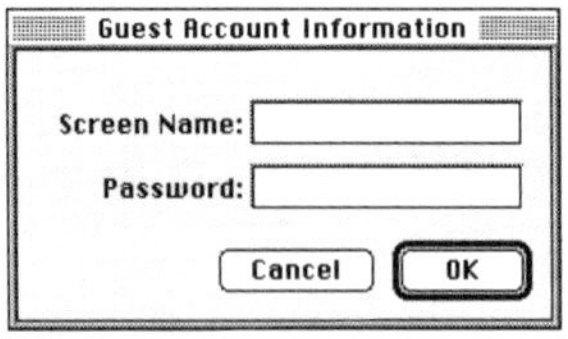


**Figure 11.** *Enter your screen name and password in a window like this.*

## ✔ Tips

- AOL automatically stores your screen name(s) in your copy of the AOL software. That's why you need to use the Guest screen name when connecting from someone else's computer.
- If you connect from someone else's computer using that person's screen name and password, you will not have access to your e-mail or other customized options.
- Locations are discussed later in this chapter.

## About Connection Problems

Although the AOL software is easy to set up and use, members occasionally have trouble connecting. Here are a few things to keep in mind if you have trouble connecting:

- Pay close attention to any error messages or windows that appear on screen. **Figures 12** and **13** show examples. Messages like these often tell you exactly what to do to solve the problem or where you can turn to find additional information about it.
- Watch the messages that appear in the connection window (see **Figure 7**) as they flash by. These messages can often tell you where the problem is occurring.
- If you're able to connect, but the connection is often broken unexpectedly, check to make sure you've selected the correct modem. Follow the instructions in the section titled "To change modem setup options" later in this chapter for details.
- If your telephone service includes call waiting, be sure to disable it before connecting to AOL. Failure to do so could result in broken connections. Follow the instructions in the section titled "To disable call waiting" later in this chapter for details.
- If you can't connect no matter what you try, call AOL Technical Support toll free at 1-888-265-8007 for assistance.

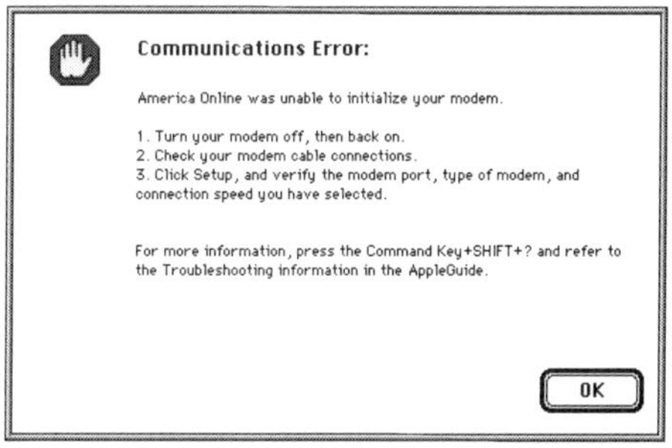


**Figures 12 & 13.** *Dialog boxes like these tell you about connection problems and offer instructions for correcting them or getting help.*

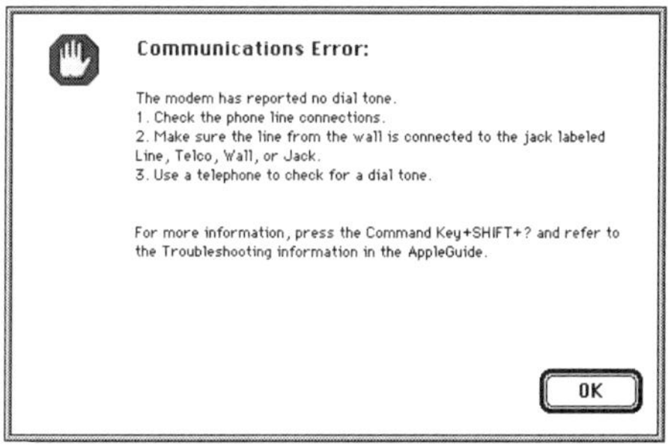

## About Locations

The AOL software automatically creates a *location file* named Home, which stores information required to connect to AOL. You can edit or create location files to set the following options:

- Change the name of the location so it's more meaningful to you.
- Change the network name, local access number, and modem configuration options.
- Add or remove dialing prefixes or commands to dial an outside line or disable call waiting.

### ✔ Tip

- Location files are especially useful for people who access AOL from a laptop computer while travelling.

## To create a location file

1. If necessary, choose Setup & Sign On from the Go To menu to display the Welcome window (see **Figure 3**).
2. Choose New Location from the Select Location pop-up menu (see **Figure 14**).
3. In the New Location dialog box that appears (see **Figure 15**) modify the default location settings.
4. When your changes are complete, click the Save button.
5. In the standard Save As dialog box that appears, enter a name for the location and save it into the Online Files folder (see **Figure 16**).
6. The new location appears selected in the Select Location pop-up menu in the Welcome window (see **Figure 17**).

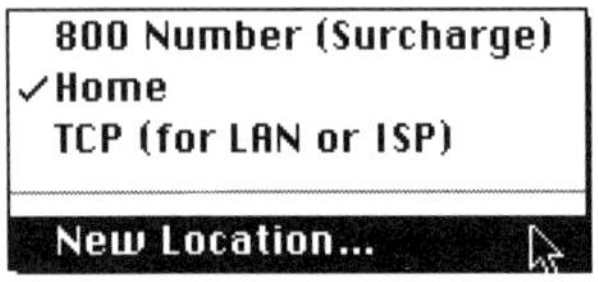


**Figure 14.** *Choose New Location from the Select Location pop-up menu.*

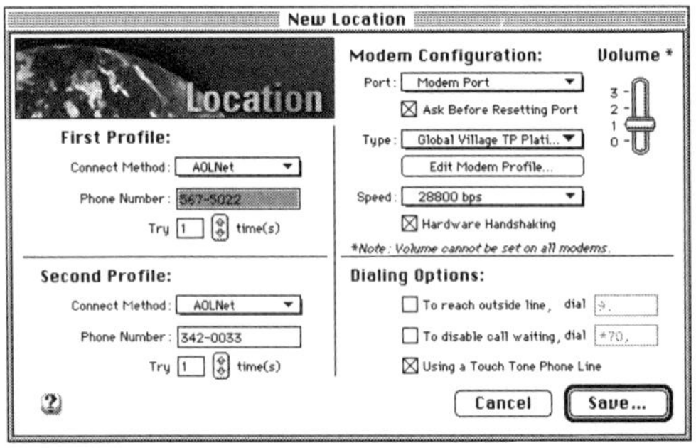


**Figure 15.** *Use the New Location dialog box to set networks, phone numbers, modem configuration, and dialing options.*

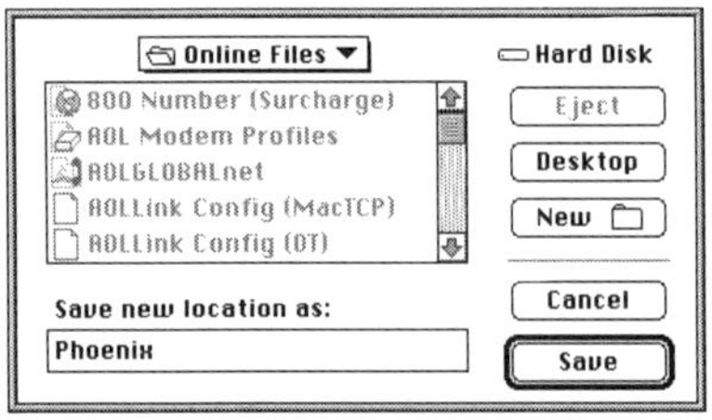


**Figure 16.** *Use a standard Save As dialog box to save the location file settings.*

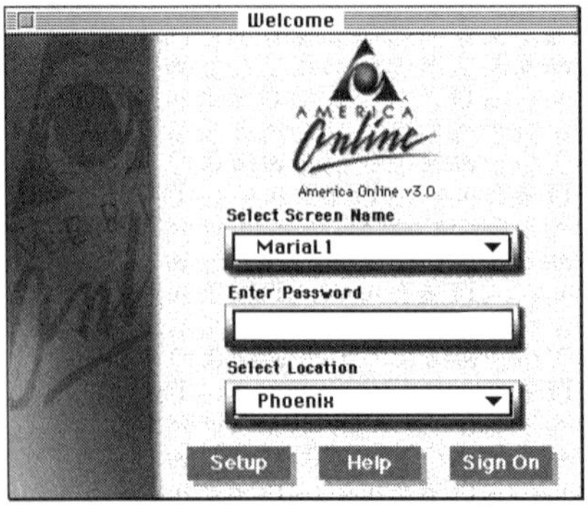


**Figure 17.** *The location you created appears selected in the Select Location pop-up menu.*

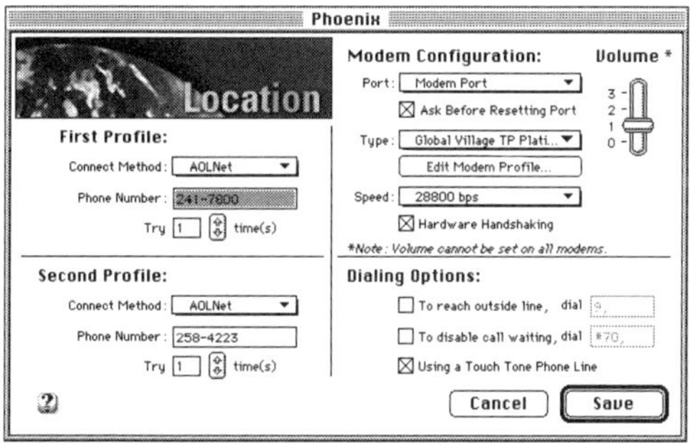


**Figure 18.** *Use a dialog box like this to change settings for an existing location.*

## To edit a location file

1. If necessary, choose Setup & Sign On from the Go To menu to display the Welcome window (see **Figure 17**).
2. Choose the location you want to edit from the Select Location pop-up menu.
3. Click the Setup button in the Welcome window.
4. Use the dialog box that appears (see **Figure 18**) to modify the location's settings.
5. When your changes are complete, click the Save button.

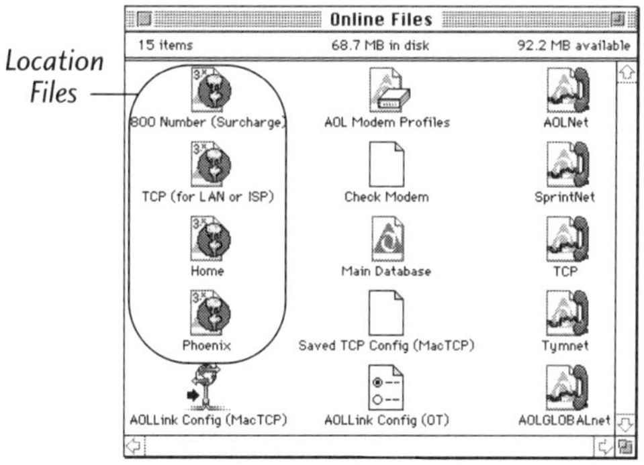


**Figure 19.** *To delete a location file, simply drag its icon to the Trash in the Finder.*

## To rename a location file

1. If the America Online software is running, quit.
2. In the Finder, locate and open the Online Files folder inside the America Online v3.0 folder (see **Figure 19**).
3. Click the name of the location file you want to rename. When an edit box appears around the name, make changes as desired and press Return to accept them.

## To delete a location file

1. If the America Online software is running, quit.
2. In the Finder, locate and open the Online Files folder inside the America Online v3.0 folder (see **Figure 19**).
3. Drag the file for the location you want to delete to the Trash.
4. Empty the Trash.

## ✔ Tip

- Quitting the America Online software is discussed later in this chapter.

## To get a local access number for a location

1. If necessary, choose Setup & Sign On from the Go To menu to display the Welcome window (see **Figure 17**).
2. Choose the name of the location for which you want to get a local access number from the Select Location pop-up menu.
3. Choose New Local# from the Select Screen Name pop-up menu (see **Figure 20**).
4. Click Sign On. A connection window appears as AOL dials an 800 number with your modem.
5. A Welcome window like the one in **Figure 21** appears. Enter the telephone area code for the location in the edit box and click Continue or press Enter.
6. In the Choose a Local Access Telephone Number dialog box that appears next (see **Figure 22**), scroll through the list of numbers until you find one that's local (or closest) to you. Click it once to select it and then click the Select Phone Number button.
7. A similar dialog box for a second choice access number appears next (see **Figure 23**). Scroll through the list of numbers until you find another one that's local (or closest) to you. Click it once to select it and then click the Select Phone Number button.
8. In the Confirm Your Access Number Choices dialog box that appears next (see **Figure 24**), make any necessary changes to the access numbers you selected. Then click Continue.

After you confirm the first and second choice numbers, the modem disconnects from AOL's special 800 number. The phone numbers and corresponding network name are copied to the location file for the location you specified in step 2.

**Figure 20.** *Choose New Local # from the Select Screen Name pop-up menu.*

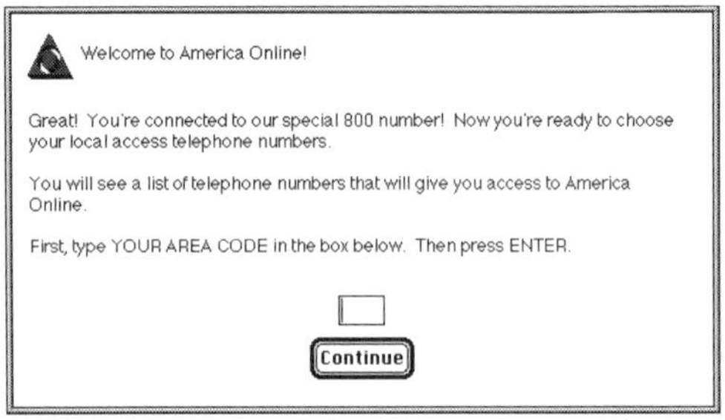


**Figure 21.** *Once you've connected to AOL's toll-free number, you can enter your area code to begin a search for local access numbers.*

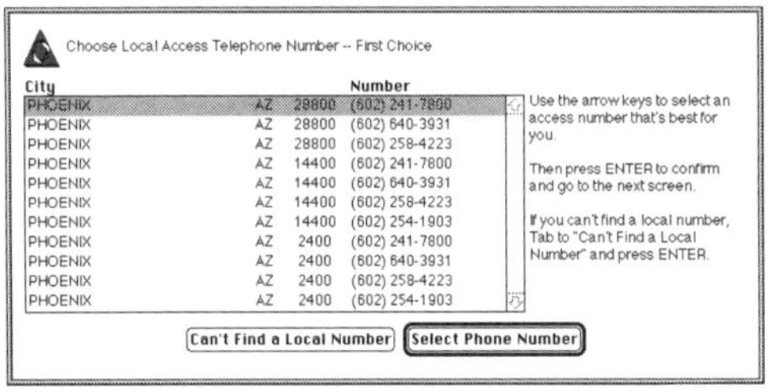


**Figure 22.** *Scroll through the access numbers in this dialog box to find one that's local to you.*

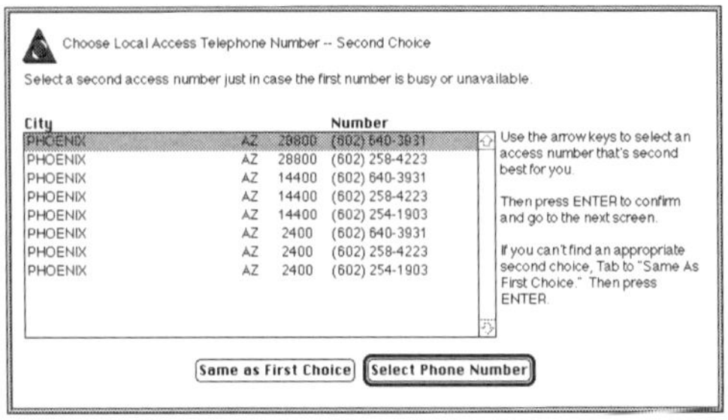


**Figure 23.** *Choose a second local access number in this dialog box. If there's only one local number, you can click the Same as First Choice button.*

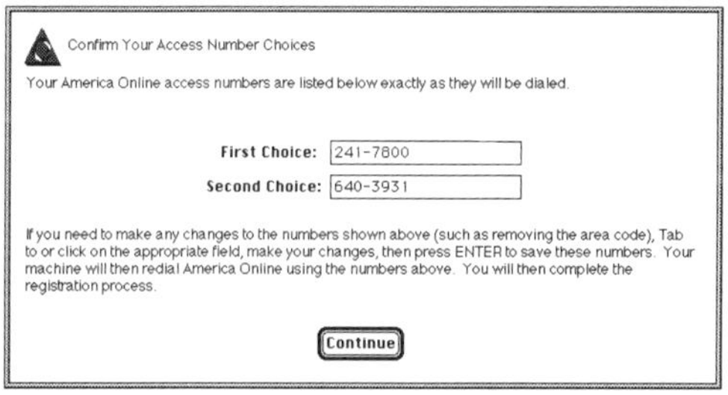


**Figure 24.** *This dialog box gives you a chance to make any last-minute changes to the access numbers you've selected.*

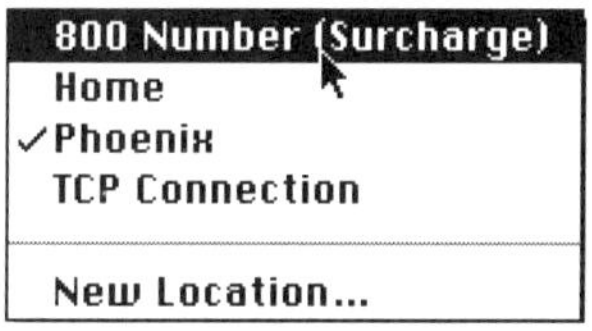


**Figure 25.** *If there's no local number for you and you don't mind paying a surcharge, you can connect with a toll-free number.*

## ✔ Tips

- Steps 5 through 8 are identical to the steps you must perform when configuring the AOL software for first-time use.
- If no local numbers appear in the Choose Local Access Telephone Number—First Choice dialog box (see **Figure 22**), click the Can't Find a Local Number button to enter a different area code and try again.
- You can click the Same as First Choice button in the Choose Local Access Telephone Number—Second Choice dialog box (see **Figure 23**) to use one phone number for both your first and second choices.
- AOL offers toll-free number access for an additional $6 per hour (in the US; more in Canada). Use this as a last resort if you cannot find a local number in your area. To connect with a toll-free number, choose 800 Number (Surcharge) from the Select Location pop-up menu (see **Figure 25**).

## To enter a dialing prefix

1. If necessary, choose Setup & Sign On from the Go To menu to display the Welcome window (see **Figure 17**).
2. Choose the name of the location for which you want to enter a dialing prefix from the Select Location pop-up menu.
3. Click the Setup button in the Welcome window.
4. In the dialog box that appears (see **Figure 18**), turn on the check box before the "To reach an outside line," edit box (see **Figure 26**).
5. Enter the prefix you want to dial, followed by a comma, in the edit box.
6. Click the Save button to save your changes.

## ✔ Tips

- A dialing prefix is any number or series of numbers that must be dialed before an access number.
- Dialing prefixes are often used to dial an outside line from within an office building or hotel.
- The comma you include in the prefix represents a pause. You may enter as many commas as you like to change the length of the pause.
- You can disable a dialing prefix by turning off the check box in step 4 above.

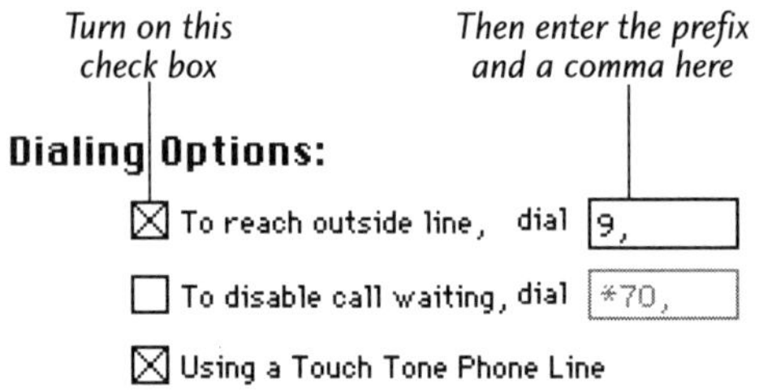


**Figure 26.** *After turning on a check box, you can enter a dialing prefix for the location.*

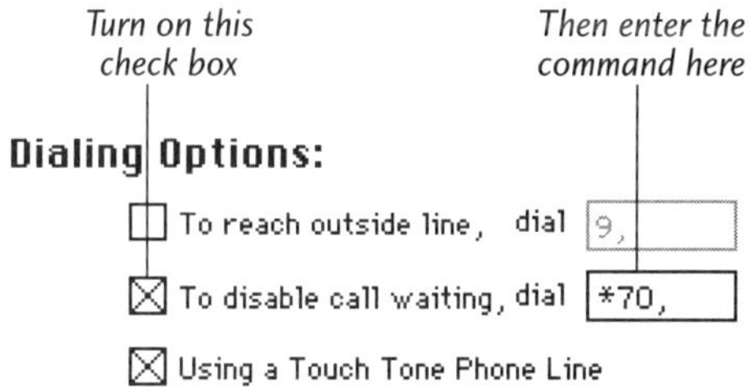


**Figure 27.** *Disabling call waiting is usually as easy as turning on a check box.*

## To disable call waiting

1. If necessary, choose Setup & Sign On from the Go To menu to display the Welcome window (see **Figure 17**).
2. Choose the name of the location for which you want to disable call waiting from the Select Location pop-up menu.
3. Click the Setup button in the Welcome window.
4. In the dialog box that appears (see **Figure 18**), turn on the check box before the "To disable call waiting" edit box (see **Figure 27**).
5. If necessary, edit the command in the edit box.
6. Click the Save button to save your changes.

## ✔ Tips

- Call waiting uses a tone or clicking sound to signal you about incoming calls while you are on the phone with another caller. Because this tone may cause modem connections to disconnect, it's a good idea to disable call waiting before using your modem.
- If you do not subscribe to a call waiting service, do not follow the steps on this page to disable it.
- The command automatically entered in the edit box in step 5 above is the one most commonly used to disable call waiting. Check with your local phone company to make sure this is the right command for you.
- The comma you include in the call waiting command represents a pause, which is usually required to wait for a dial tone. You may enter as many commas as you like to change the length of the pause.
- When you use a command to disable call waiting, it is only disabled during the current phone call. The next time you make a call without dialing the command, call waiting is enabled again.

## To change modem setup options

1. If necessary, choose Setup & Sign On from the Go To menu to display the Welcome window (see **Figure 17**).
2. Choose the name of the location for which you want to change modem setup options from the Select Location pop-up menu.
3. Click the Setup button in the Welcome window.
4. In the dialog box that appears (see **Figure 18**), make changes in the Modem Configuration area (see **Figure 28**) as follows:
   - ▲ To change the modem port, choose a port from the Port pop-up menu.
   - ▲ To change the modem make and model, choose an option from the Type pop-up menu. Most popular modem brand names are included in this menu. If your modem is not among those listed, try choosing Hayes Basic.
   - ▲ To change the modem maximum speed, choose a speed from the Speed pop-up menu.
   - ▲ If your modem operates at 9600 bps or faster and has a hardware handshaking cable, be sure to turn on the Hardware Handshaking check box.
   - ▲ To change the speaker volume of the modem, slide the Volume control up (louder) or down (softer) as desired.
5. Click Save to save your changes.

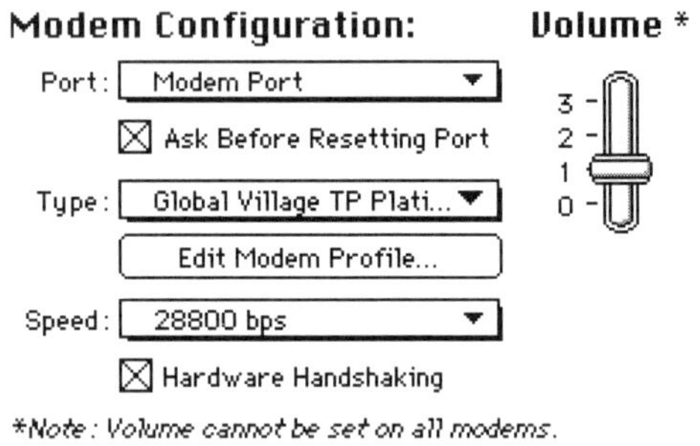


**Figure 28.** *Set options in the Modem Configuration area for a location file to fine-tune your modem setup.*

### ✔ Tips

- Do not make changes to your modem setup unless you are having trouble connecting to or staying connected to AOL. Remember the golden rule of software configuration: "If it ain't broke, don't fix it."
- If your modem is not among those listed in the Type pop-up menu and Hayes Basic doesn't work, you can create a custom modem profile by clicking the Edit Modem Profile button. To utilize this feature, however, you must be prepared to enter complete modem strings that vary from modem to modem. Check the manual that came with your modem for help.

**Figure 29.** *To properly disconnect from AOL, choose Sign Off from the Go To menu.*

**Figure 30.** *AOL confirms that you really do want to sign off.*

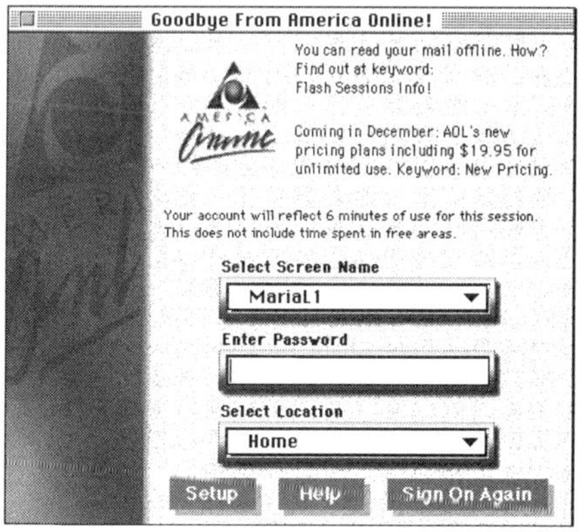


**Figure 31.** *The Goodbye window confirms that you've disconnected and lets you sign on again.*

**Figure 32.** *If you're idle too long, a dialog box like this will appear. If you don't click Yes, you'll be disconnected.*

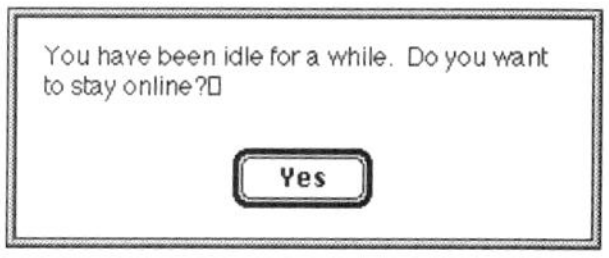


## About Disconnecting & Quitting from AOL

When you're finished accessing AOL's content and features, use the Sign Off command to disconnect. This stops the billing clock and frees up your modem for other use.

## To disconnect from AOL

1. Choose Sign Off from the Go To menu (see **Figure 29**).
2. In the Sign Off? window that appears (see **Figure 30**), click the Sign Off button.

## ✔ Tips

- You'll know you've successfully signed off when the Sign Off? window is replaced by a Goodbye from America Online! window (see **Figure 31**). You'll hear a male voice say "Goodbye!"
- You can also disconnect from AOL by choosing Quit from the File menu (see **Figure 33**). Click the Sign Off button in the Quit? window (see **Figure 34**) to disconnect.
- After a certain period of inactivity on your connection, AOL will display a dialog box like the one in **Figure 32**. If you fail to click the Yes button (because you've stepped away, for example), you'll automatically be disconnected.
- Once you've disconnected from AOL, you can continue to work with its software. **Chapter 10** discusses a number of features you can use while offline.

## To quit the AOL software

1. Choose Quit from the File menu (see **Figure 33**).

   *or*

   Press [⌘][Q].
2. If you are still connected to AOL, a Quit? window like the one in **Figure 34** appears. Click the Quit button to sign off and exit the software.

   *or*

   If you are not connected to AOL, the AOL software simply quits.

**Figure 33.** *To quit the AOL software, choose Quit from the File menu.*

### ✔ Tips

- You can also quit the AOL software by clicking the Quit button in the Sign Off? window (see **Figure 30**).
- Once you quit the AOL software, you cannot continue to work with it.
- Quitting the AOL software when you're finished using it frees up RAM for other applications you may want to run on your computer.

**Figure 34.** *Use the Quit? window to sign off and quit the AOL software at the same time.*

# AMERICA ONLINE BASICS 2

## About the AOL Interface

AOL has the same basic interface components found in many of your other Macintosh applications in that you:

- Access commands through menus, shortcut keys, and buttons.
- View information in windows, many of which can be moved, resized, or closed.
- Specify information in dialog boxes.

This chapter discusses AOL basics, like interface components and the way you use them.

### ✔ Tips

- If you're new to Macintosh computers, be sure to read this chapter thoroughly. It discusses many concepts and techniques that you'll use over and over while working with AOL and other Macintosh software.
- Even if you've been using a Macintosh for a while, be sure to at least skim this chapter. There's information here about specific AOL features—like the toolbar, artwork and features, and SmartArt—that you won't want to miss.

## The AOL Screen

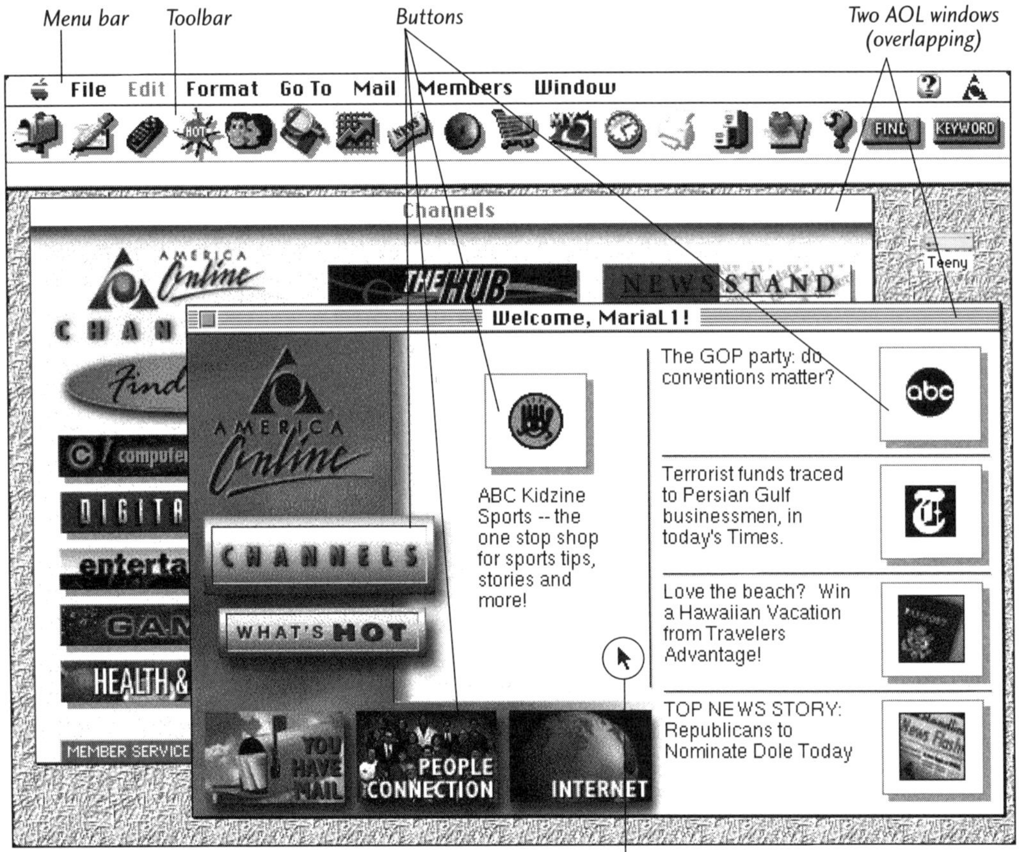


**Figure 1.** *The AOL screen.*



## Key to the AOL Screen

**Menu bar**

The menu bar gives you access to many of AOL's commands.

**Toolbar**

The toolbar offers buttons to access commonly used AOL commands and features.

**AOL Windows**

All of AOL's features and content appear in windows.

**Buttons**

Buttons give you access to AOL's content and features.

**Mouse Pointer**

Use the mouse pointer to select options, choose menu commands, and click buttons. When the mouse pointer is over a button, it often looks like a pointing finger.

## About the Mouse

The mouse is used extensively when working with AOL.

- Click buttons to access features and commands.
- Click list items to select them.
- Double-click list items to open them.
- Drag over text to select it for editing or formatting.

## To use the mouse

There are four basic mouse techniques:

- *Pointing* means to position the mouse pointer so that its tip is on the item to which you are pointing (see **Figures 2** and **3**).
- *Clicking* means to press the mouse button once and release it. You click to select a list item, choose a menu item or button, or position the insertion point when preparing to enter text.
- *Double-clicking* means to press the mouse button twice in rapid succession. You double-click to open a list item.
- *Dragging* means to press the mouse button down and hold it down while moving the mouse. You drag to resize a window or select multiple text characters.

**Figure 2.** *The mouse pointer looks like an arrow when it's pointing to a menu.*

**Figure 3.** *The mouse pointer looks like a pointing finger when it's pointing to a button.*

## ✔ Tip

- A track ball or track pad works a bit differently from a mouse. Instead of moving the mouse to move the mouse pointer, you roll the track ball or move your finger along the track pad. Otherwise, operation is the same.

## About Menus

AOL's menus include commands for working with AOL features and going to specific places on AOL.

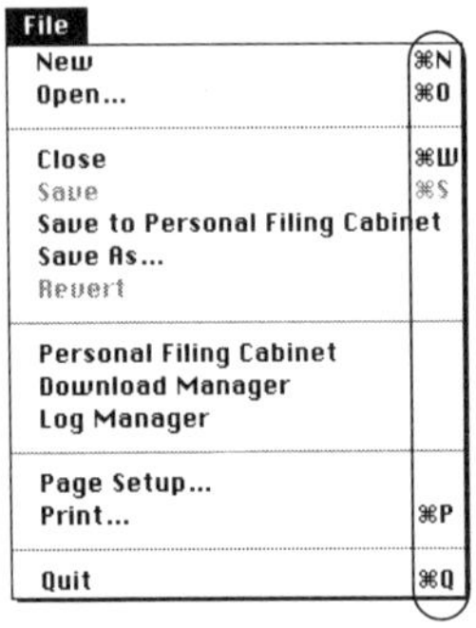


**Figure 4.** *AOL's File menu. Many of its commands can be accessed through the use of shortcut keys.*

### ✔ Tips

- Menu commands followed by an ellipsis (...) (see **Figures 4**, **5**, and **6**) display a dialog box to set options before completing the command.
- Menu commands followed by the Command key symbol and a letter, number, or symbol (see **Figure 4**) can be selected with shortcut keys.
- Menu commands that are gray cannot be selected (see **Figure 5**).
- Consult **Appendix A** for illustrations of AOL's menus and a list of shortcut keys.

**Figure 5.** *AOL's Edit menu, shown here with gray commands. The available commands vary based on what is selected or active.*

### To choose a menu command

1. Position the mouse pointer on the name of the menu that includes the command you want to use.
2. Press and hold down the mouse button. The menu drops down (see **Figure 4**).
3. Move the mouse pointer down the list of commands until the one you want is selected (see **Figure 6**).
4. Release the mouse button.

### To use a shortcut key

1. Hold down the modifier key (usually (⌘)) for the shortcut you want to use.
2. Press the letter or number for the shortcut. For example, to use a shortcut key for the Print command, press (P) while holding down (⌘).

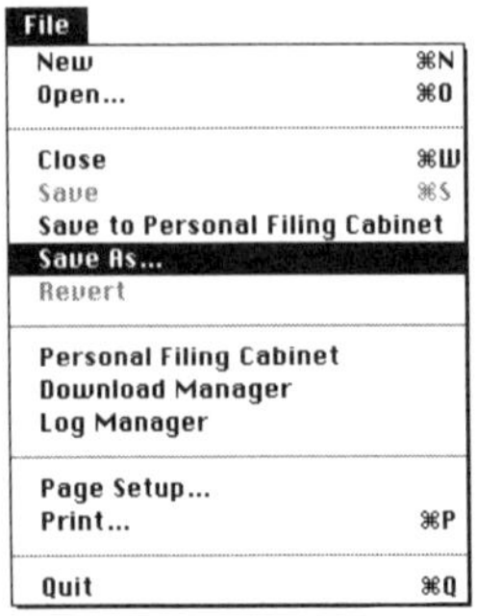


**Figure 6.** *To choose a menu command, use your mouse to display the menu, drag down until the command you want is selected, and release the mouse button.*

### ✔ Tip

- You can learn shortcut keys by looking at the keystrokes indicated beside menu commands (see **Figure 4**).

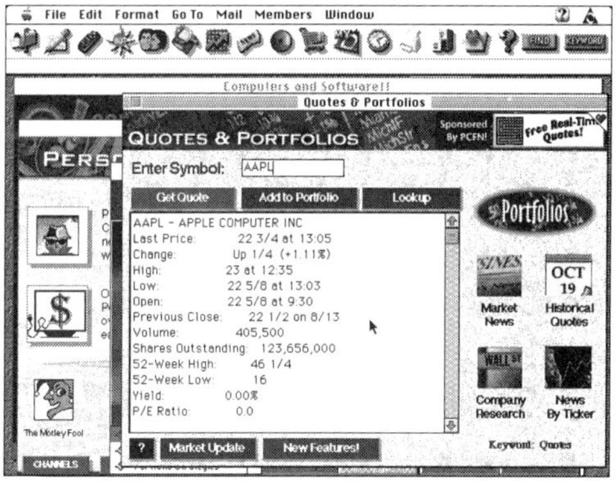


**Figure 7.** *Each window you open remains open until you close it.*

**Figure 8.** *You can find a list of all open windows at the bottom of the Window menu.*

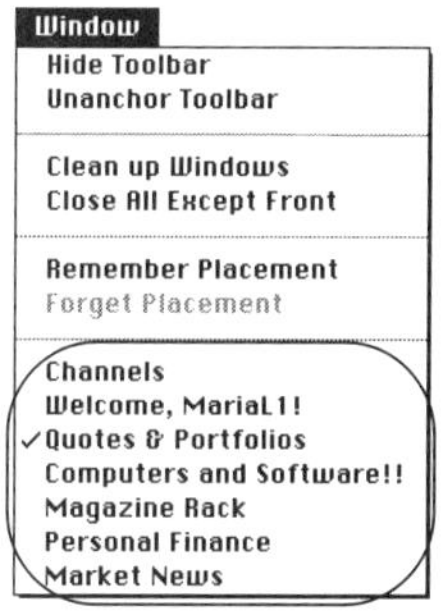


## About AOL's Windows

AOL's features and content appear in windows. Each window you open remains open until you close it.

Here are a few things you can do with open windows:

- Switch from one window to another.
- Move, close, zoom, or resize a window.
- Remember the size and/or location of a window.
- Neatly arrange windows.

## ✔ Tips

- If you keep opening windows without closing any of them, your screen will soon be cluttered with overlapping windows (see **Figure 7**).
- You can find a list of all open windows at the bottom of the Window menu (see **Figure 8**).
- Keeping multiple windows open makes it quick and easy to switch back and forth between specific areas.
- When you enter a free area, the windows for all other areas are hidden. Consult **Chapters 3** and **11** for more information about using free areas on AOL.

## To switch from one window to another

Click on any visible part of the window you want to view.

*or*

Choose the name of the window from the list at the bottom of the Window menu (see **Figure 8**).

### ✔ Tips

- A check mark appears in the Window menu beside the active (topmost) window's name (see **Figure 8**).
- If there are more windows open than can fit on the Window menu, a triangle appears at the bottom of the menu to indicate that there are additional items (see **Figure 9**). Drag over the triangle to display items not listed above.

**Figure 9.** *If there are too many items on the Window menu to display them all, a triangle appears at the bottom of the menu.*

## To move a window

1. Position the mouse pointer on the window's title bar (see **Figure 10**), press the mouse button down, and drag.
2. When the window's outline is in the desired position, release the mouse button.

## To resize a window

1. Position the mouse pointer on the window's size box.
2. Press the mouse button down and drag.
3. When the right and bottom borders of the window are in the desired position, release the mouse button.

### ✔ Tip

- If a window does not have a zoom box or size box (see **Figure 10**), the window cannot be resized.

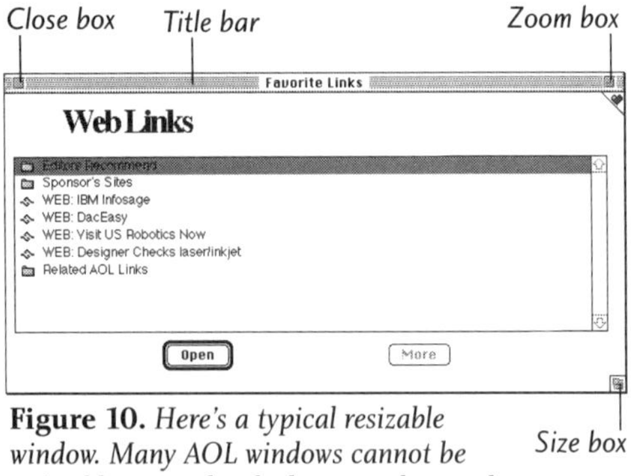


**Figure 10.** *Here's a typical resizable window. Many AOL windows cannot be resized because they lack a zoom box and size box.*

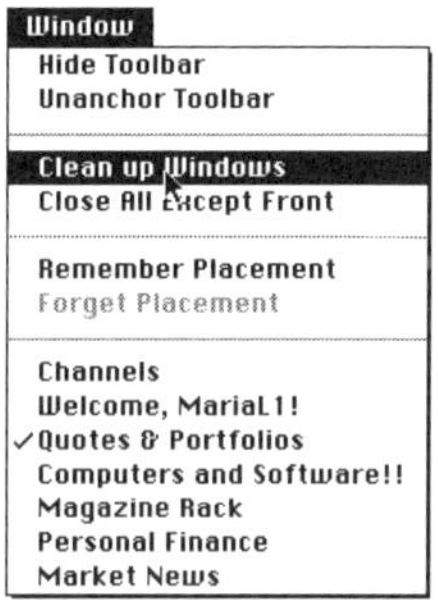


**Figure 11.** *Choose Clean up Windows from the Window menu…*

## To zoom a window to fill the screen

Click the window's zoom box (see **Figure 10**). The window resizes to fill the screen.

### ✔ Tip

- Not all of AOL's windows can be zoomed to fill the screen. If there is no zoom box (see **Figure 10**), the window cannot be resized.

## To return a zoomed window to its regular or custom size

Click the window's zoom box (see **Figure 10**). The window returns to its original or custom size.

### ✔ Tip

- A custom size is the size you make a window by dragging its size box. Resizing a window is discussed on the previous page.

## To neatly arrange windows

Choose Clean up Windows from the Window menu (see **Figure 11**). The windows are neatly arranged on your screen (see **Figure 12**).

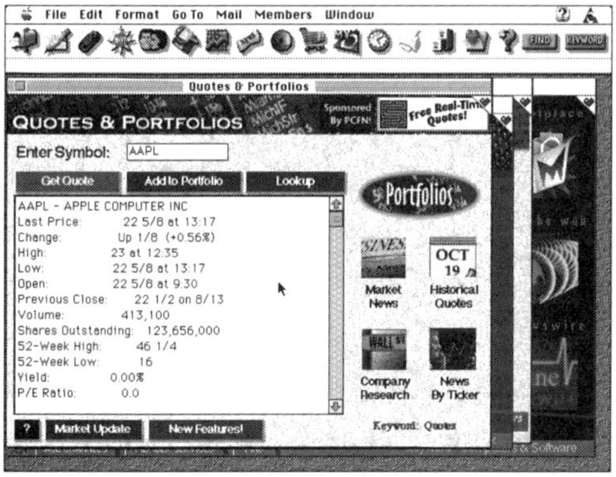


**Figure 12.** *…to neatly arrange all open windows on your screen.*

## To remember a window's position

Choose Remember Placement from the Window menu (see **Figure 13**).

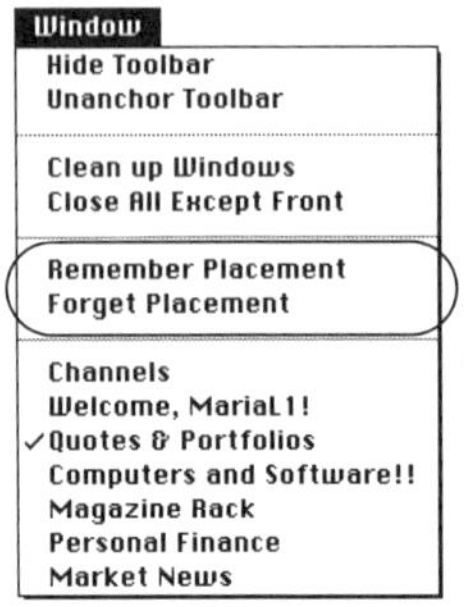


**Figure 13.** *The two Placement commands on the Window menu let you remember or forget a window's placement on screen.*

### ✔ Tips

- When you use the Remember Placement command for a window, each time AOL opens that window, it positions it the way it was when you chose the command.
- To reset the window to its default position, choose Forget Placement from the Window menu (see **Figure 13**). This command is only available if the window position has already been remembered.

## To close the active window

Choose Close from the File menu (see **Figure 14**).

*or*

Press [⌘W].

*or*

Click the window's close box (see **Figure 10**).

**Figure 14.** *To close the active window, choose Close from the File menu.*

## To close all windows except the active window

Choose Close All Except Front from the Window menu (see **Figure 15**). All windows except the active window close.

**Figure 15.** *To close all windows except the active window, choose Close All Except Front from the Window menu.*

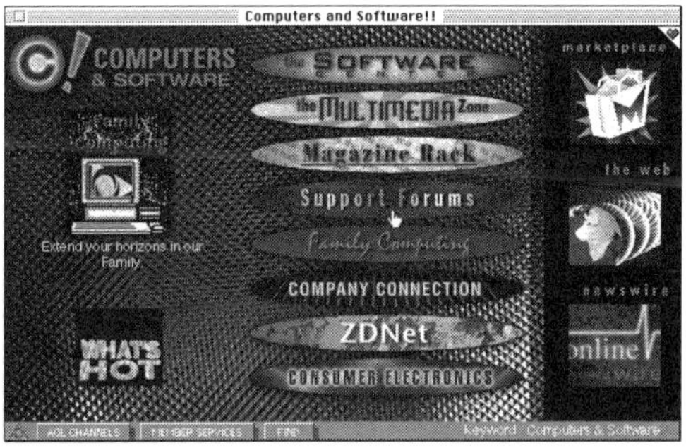


**Figure 16.** *The Computers & Software channel window displays a slick-looking screen full of clickable buttons.*

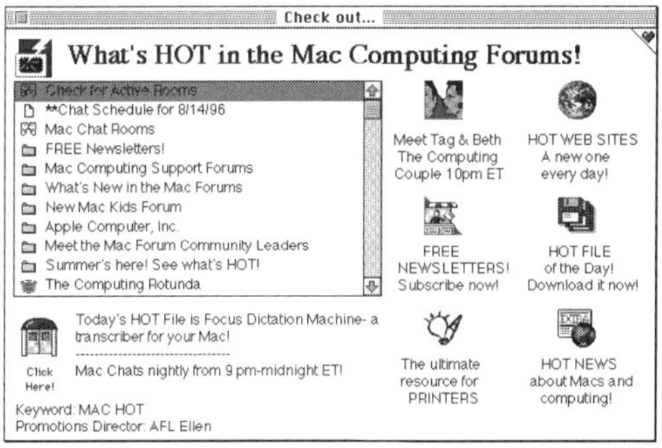


**Figure 17.** *The What's Hot in the Mac Computing Forums window combines a scrolling list of options with graphic buttons.*

| | |
|---|---|
| | File or Document icon—displays information. |
| | Folder icon—displays another list of items. |
| | File Library icon—displays a list of downloadable files or information about a specific downloadable file. |
| | Link icon—opens another AOL feature or area or links to the Internet. |
| | Message Board icon—opens a message or bulletin board. |
| | Chat icon—opens a chat or conference room window. |

**Table 1.** *Some icons commonly found in AOL lists.*

## About Buttons & Lists

Many AOL windows include buttons and lists to access features and content. **Figures 16** and **17** show two examples.

### To use a button in a window

Click the button once. A window for the item appears.

#### ✔ Tips

- If you're not sure whether an item is a clickable button, position the mouse pointer over it. If it's a button, the mouse pointer will turn into a pointing finger.
- Don't double-click a button. A single click is all that's needed to access the feature linked to it.

### To open an item in a list

Double-click a list item to select and open it. A window for the item appears.

#### ✔ Tips

- Sometimes a window containing a list of items will also include an Open button. Clicking the Open button will open the selected list item.
- The icon to the left of a list item often indicates the type of item it is. See **Table 1** for a summary of some commonly found icons.

## About Dialog Boxes

In addition to windows that provide information and allow data entry, AOL also displays standard Macintosh dialog boxes. Dialog boxes commonly appear for one of three reasons:

- To provide information (see **Figure 18**).
- To let you set options before completing a task (see **Figure 19**).
- To ask you to confirm that you really want to perform an action that cannot be undone (see **Figure 20**).

**Figure 18.** *This dialog box tells you that AOL has completed a task.*

### ✔ Tips

- When a dialog box appears, you must dismiss it by clicking one of its command buttons before you can continue working with AOL.
- You can often click a command button within a dialog box by pressing a keyboard key:
  - ▲ Press [Enter] to choose the default button (the button with the bold border around it: OK in **Figure 18**, Print in **Figure 19**, and Delete in **Figure 20**).
  - ▲ Press [Esc] to choose the Cancel button, if present (see **Figures 19** and **20**).
- You can press [Tab] to move from one edit box to another within a dialog box. This often works in AOL's windows, too.

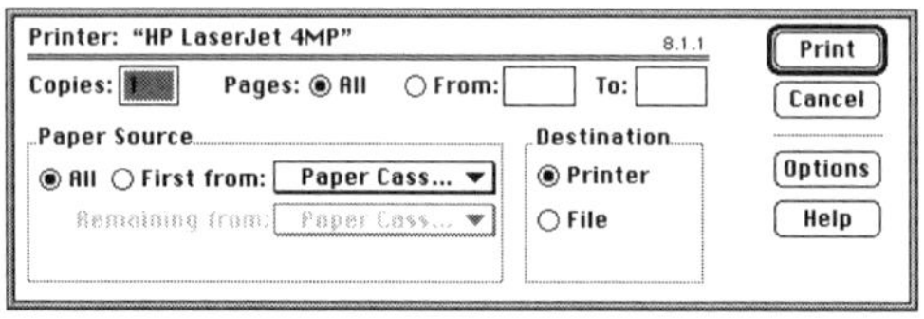


**Figure 19.** *This Print dialog box lets you set print options before completing the Print command.*

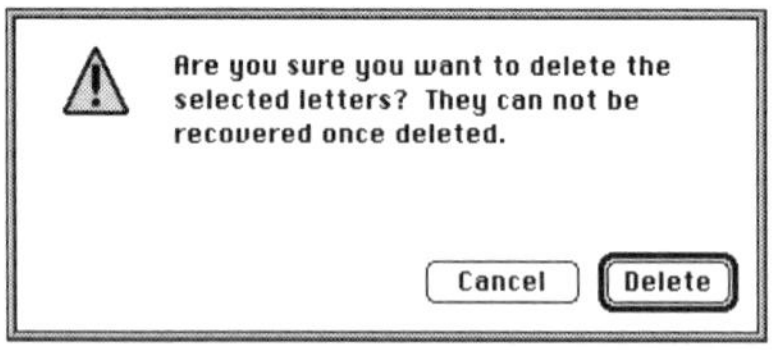


**Figure 20.** *Before performing an action that cannot be undone, AOL often asks for confirmation with a dialog box like this one.*

## About the Toolbar

AOL's toolbar (see **Figure 21**) offers a whole row of buttons you can use to access AOL features and content.

**Figure 21.** *AOL's toolbar offers access to many features and areas.*

**Figure 22.** *When you point to a toolbar button, its name and description appear in the area beneath the toolbar.*

### ✔ Tips

- When you point to a toolbar button, the button's name and description appear in the area immediately below the toolbar (see **Figure 22**).
- Although you can use some buttons regardless of whether you are connected to AOL, you must be connected for most buttons to work.
- Consult **Appendix B** for a complete reference to AOL's toolbar buttons.

## To use a toolbar button

Click the toolbar button once. A window for the feature or item appears.

### ✔ Tip

- Don't double-click a toolbar button. A single click is all that's needed to access the feature or item linked to it.

Using AOL's Toolbar

## To hide the toolbar

Choose Hide Toolbar from the Window menu (see **Figure 23**). The toolbar disappears.

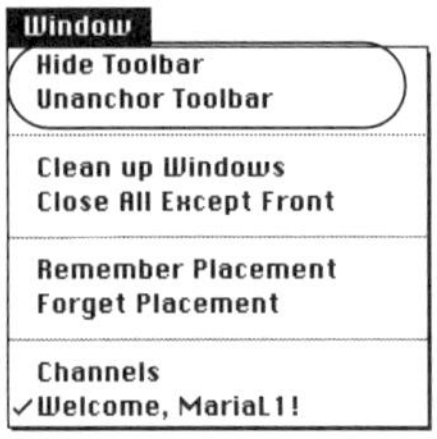


**Figure 23.** *The Window menu includes two commands to work with the toolbar.*

### ✔ Tip

- Another way to hide the toolbar is to click the toolbar's close box when it is not anchored (see **Figure 24**).

## To redisplay the toolbar

Choose Show Toolbar from the Window menu. The toolbar reappears.

## To move the toolbar

1. Choose Unanchor Toolbar from the Window menu (see **Figure 23**). A title bar appears on the toolbar (see **Figure 24**).
2. Drag the toolbar's title bar to reposition the toolbar as desired.

**Figure 24.** *When you unanchor the toolbar, a title bar appears on it. Use the title bar to move the toolbar around the screen.*

## To re-anchor the toolbar

Choose Anchor Toolbar from the Window menu. The toolbar's title bar disappears and the toolbar returns to its normal position near the top of the screen.

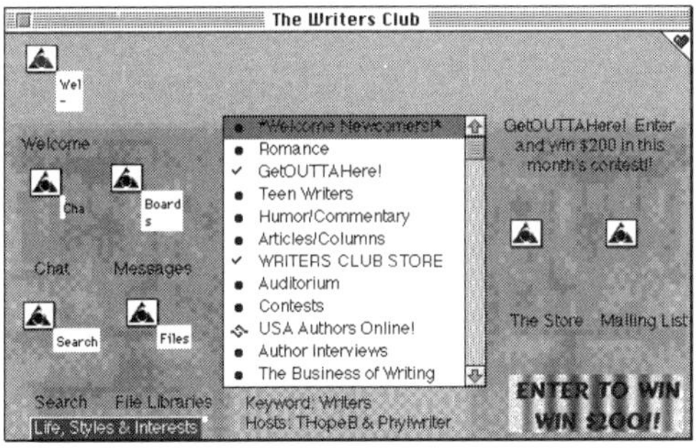


**Figure 25.** *When you first open a window, only a skeleton of its options may appear.*

**Figure 26.** *One by one, graphic elements appear until the window has been completely drawn.*

## About AOL Art & Features

AOL's graphic user interface and features are provided two ways:

- Standard, commonly used art and features are part of the AOL software.
- Additional art and features are downloaded from AOL's server to your computer when you need them.

## ✔ Tips

- Downloaded art and features are stored on your computer's hard disk in AOL's art database so you only need to download them once.
- You can specify a maximum size for the art database in Graphics preferences, which are discussed in **Chapter 11**.

## About SmartArt

*SmartArt* is an AOL feature that enables you to access buttons and list items in a window before the window has been completely drawn. This makes it possible to use an area's features immediately, as soon as the window opens.

## ✔ Tip

- When you first open a window, you may only see a skeleton of its options (see **Figure 25**). Although you can click buttons and choose list items immediately, if you wait, the rest of the window's graphic elements will fill themselves in, one by one, until the window is complete (see **Figure 26**).

# NAVIGATING AMERICA ONLINE 3

## About Navigation Tools

AOL offers a wide range of features—far more than what you first see when you connect. The AOL software offers a number of navigation tools you can use to get from one area to another:

- Welcome and Channel windows
- Menu commands
- Keywords
- Favorite Places

This chapter tells you how to use each of these navigation tools to access AOL content and features discussed throughout this book. It also explains how to use the Find feature to get information and locate AOL content and features of interest to you.

### ✔ Tips

- The AOL software usually offers several ways to access each system feature. Use the methods you find quickest or easiest.
- In general, the buttons in AOL windows are handy for when you want to browse system features. But to get to a specific AOL location quickly, use toolbar buttons, menu commands, keywords, or favorite places.

## About the Welcome & Channel Windows

When you first connect to AOL, two windows appear:

- The Welcome window (see **Figure 1**) appears as the frontmost window. It offers access to featured areas on AOL, as well as the Mail Center, People Connection, and Internet.
- The Channels window (see **Figure 2**) appears beneath the Welcome window. It offers access to all of AOL's content, organized by category, as well as the Find feature.

**Figure 1.** *The Welcome window offers quick access to featured areas on AOL.*

### ✔ Tips

- The Welcome and Channels windows offer a great starting point for a leisurely browse through America Online's features.
- The Welcome window changes often—there's a good chance it will be different each time you connect to AOL.
- The Welcome and Channels windows are sometimes referred to as *menus* by the AOL software since they each offer a menu of options.
- Like the Channels window, many AOL forum windows have a *navigation bar* with three or more buttons for accessing AOL areas (see **Figure 2**).

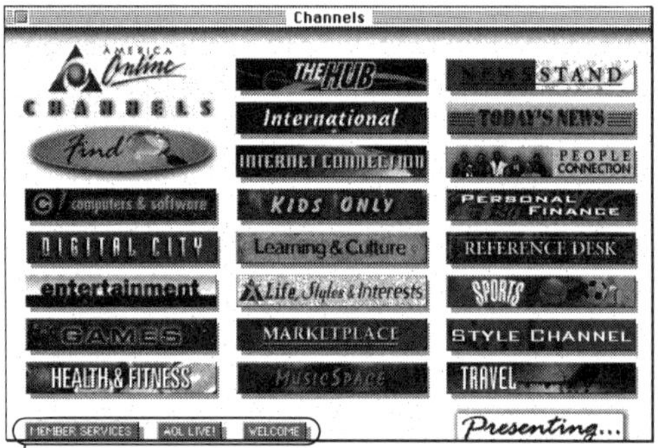


**Figure 2.** *The Channels window offers access to all features of AOL, organized by category.*

## To use the Welcome & Channels windows

1. Display the window which contains a button for the area or feature you want to access.
2. In the window, click the button for the area or feature to which you want to go.

### ✔ Tip

- Consult the next page for details about viewing the Welcome or Channels window.

**Figure 3.** *The Go To menu offers commands to view both the Welcome and Channels windows.*

**Figure 4.** *If the Welcome or Channels window is open, you can view it by choosing it from the Window menu.*

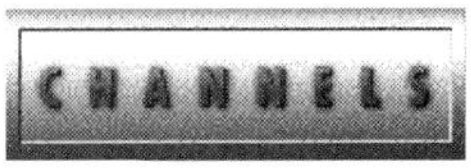


**Figure 5.** *The Channels button on the Welcome window displays the Channels window.*

## To view the Welcome window

Connect to AOL. The Welcome window appears automatically.

*or*

Choose Welcome Menu from the Go To menu (see **Figure 3**).

*or*

Click the Welcome button at the bottom of the Channels window (see **Figure 2**) or any other window in which it appears.

*or*

If the Welcome window is hidden behind other windows, click any part of it or choose Welcome from the Window menu (see **Figure 4**) to bring it to the front.

### ✔ Tip

- Your screen name is always part of the Welcome window's name on the Window menu.

## To view the Channels window

Choose Channels from the Go To menu (see **Figure 3**).

*or*

Click the Channels button on the toolbar.

*or*

Click the Channels button on the Welcome window (see **Figure 5**).

*or*

Click the Channels button at the bottom of any other window in which it appears.

*or*

If the Channels window is open but hidden behind other windows, click any part of it or choose Channels from the Window menu (see **Figure 4**) to bring it to the front.

## About Navigation Commands on AOL's Menus

While all of AOL's menus include commands for working with AOL features, certain menus offer commands that take you to specific places on AOL:

- The Go To menu (see **Figure 3**), which is customizable, comes preconfigured with ten popular AOL destinations: What's Hot, Discover America Online, Sign on a Friend, Top News, Stock Quotes, AOL Live, Internet Connection, Reference Desk, Entertainment, and Marketplace.
- The Mail menu (see **Figure 6**) offers access to the Mail Center, as well as the Offline Mail Drawer window. Consult **Chapter 4** for more information about e-mail and Mail menu commands.
- The Members menu (see **Figure 7**) offers access to the Member Services area, as well as preference options and the Member Directory. These areas are discussed in **Chapters 11** and **8** respectively.

### ✔ Tips

- Consult **Appendix A** for illustrations of all of AOL's menus.
- Consult **Chapter 2** for instructions on how to use menus and shortcut keys.

**Figure 6.** *Use commands under the Mail menu to access the Mail Center and the Online Mailbox.*

**Figure 7.** *Use commands under the Members menu to access Member Services, preference options, and the Member Directory.*

**Figure 8.** *Choose Edit Go To Menu from the Go To menu.*

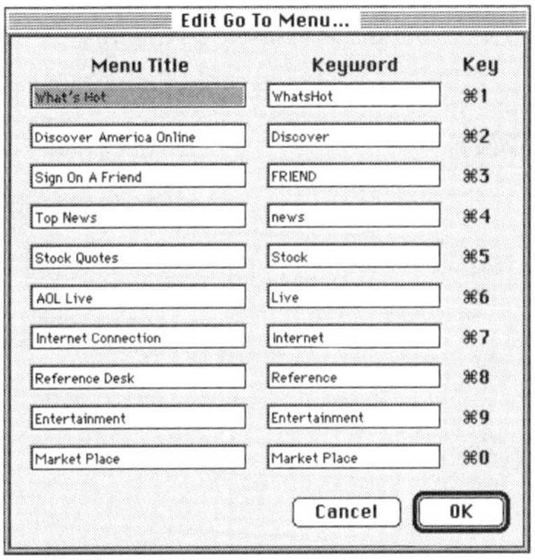


**Figure 9.** *The Edit Go To Menu dialog box lists the commands at the bottom of the Go To menu.*

**Figure 10.** *To edit a command, change the command's name and keyword.*

**Figure 11.** *The bottom of the Go To menu lists popular places on AOL—including places you specify.*

## About Editing the Go To Menu

The Go To menu can be customized to include up to ten of the locations you visit most often on AOL. The locations you specify appear at the bottom of the menu.

### ✔ Tips

- Each location on the bottom of the Go To menu has its own shortcut key, making it accessible right from the keyboard.
- You do not need to be connected to AOL to edit the Go To menu.

## To edit a Go To menu location

1. Choose Edit Go To Menu from the Go To menu (see **Figure 8**).
2. In the Edit Go To Menu dialog box that appears (see **Figure 9**), make changes as necessary to the Menu Title and Keyword edit boxes for the entry you want to change (see **Figure 10**).
3. Click OK or press Enter.

**Figure 11** shows the Go To menu with the change from **Figure 10**.

### ✔ Tip

- You must know the Keyword for the location you want to add to the Go To menu. Keywords are discussed later in this chapter.

## To remove a location from the Go To menu

1. Choose Edit Go To Menu from the Go To menu (see **Figure 8**).
2. In the Edit Go To Menu dialog box that appears (see **Figure 9**), select the contents of the Menu Entry edit box for the entry you want to remove and press Delete to delete it. Do the same for the contents of the Keyword edit box for the entry. **Figure 12** shows the Edit Go To Menu dialog box with the Top News command deleted.
3. Click OK or press Enter.

**Figure 13** shows the Go To menu with the change from **Figure 12**.

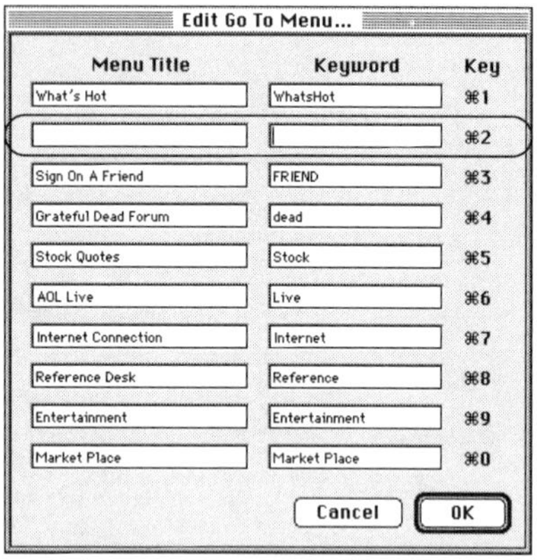


**Figure 12.** *Removing an entry from the Go To menu is as simple as deleting it.*

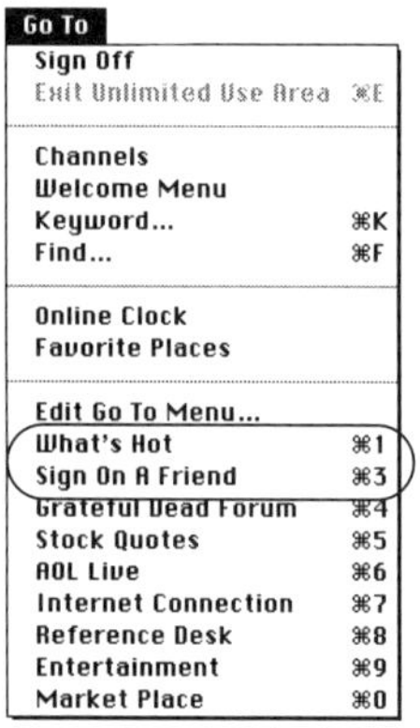


**Figure 13.** *Here's the Go To menu with the Discover AOL item removed.*

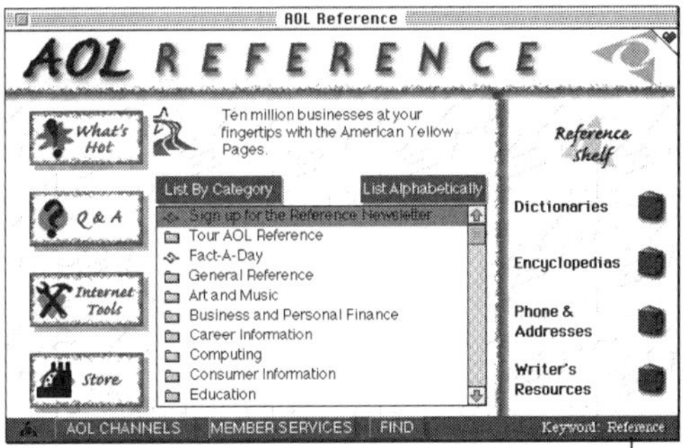


**Figure 14.** *An area's Keyword is usually displayed within the area's main window.*

*Keyword*

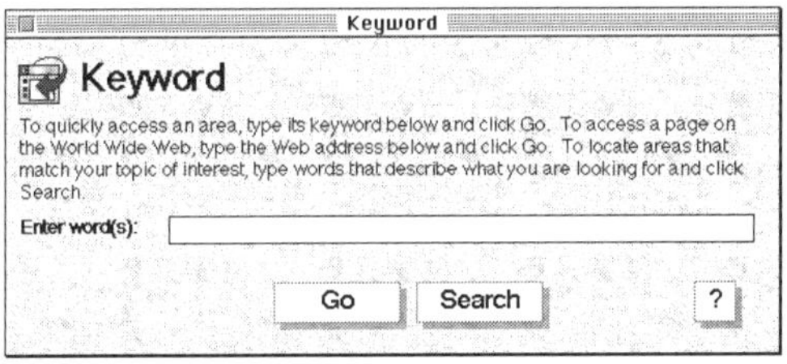


**Figure 15.** *Enter an area's keyword in the Keyword dialog box and click Go.*

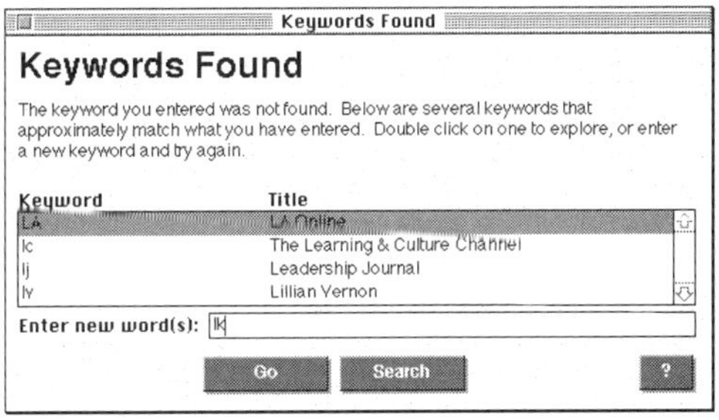


**Figure 16.** *If the keyword you enter is not valid, AOL displays a list of similar keywords.*

## About Keywords

Most AOL areas have *keywords* associated with them. A keyword is a word or phrase that, when entered into the Keyword dialog box, instantly transports you to the appropriate area.

### ✔ Tips

- Although not as quick and easy to use as shortcut keys, keywords offer a fast way to navigate between AOL areas.
- An area's keyword is usually displayed in the area's main window. (See **Figure 14** for an example.)
- Consult **Appendix D** for a comprehensive listing of AOL's areas and their keywords.
- Many areas have more than one keyword. Use the keyword you find easiest to remember.
- Keywords are not case-sensitive.

## To use a keyword

1. Click the Keyword button on the toolbar.

   *or*

   Choose Keyword from the Go To menu.

   *or*

   Press [⌘][K].
2. In the Keyword dialog box that appears (see **Figure 15**), enter the keyword for the area to which you want to go.
3. Click Go or press [Enter].

### ✔ Tip

- If you enter a keyword that does not exist, AOL displays the Keywords Found dialog box (see **Figure 16**) which lists areas with similar keywords. You can enter a different keyword or double-click an item in the list to go to the area you want.

Using Keywords

## About Favorite Places

The Favorite Places feature is just that: a list of your favorite places on AOL. You build a list of favorite places as you browse AOL. Then, when you want to return to an AOL location, simply double-click its entry in the Favorite Places window (see **Figure 21**).

### ✔ Tips

- There is no limit to the number of favorite places you can keep track of on AOL.
- The Favorite Places window also includes folders to help you organize favorite places entries. Using folders in the Favorite Places window is discussed later in this section.

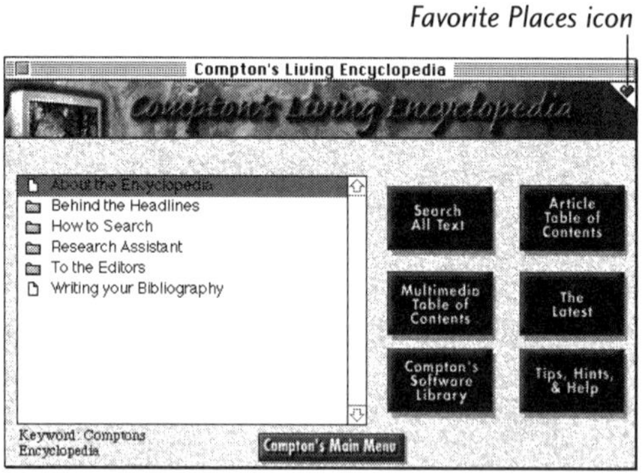


**Figure 17.** *Click the heart icon in the top right corner of a window to make that window one of your favorite places.*

## To add a favorite place while browsing AOL

1. Through normal navigation techniques discussed earlier in this chapter, display the window you want to add as a favorite place.
2. Click the heart icon in the top right corner of the window (see **Figure 17**).
3. A confirmation dialog box like the one in **Figure 18** appears. Make sure the "Add it to my Favorite Places" radio button is selected and then click OK or press Enter.

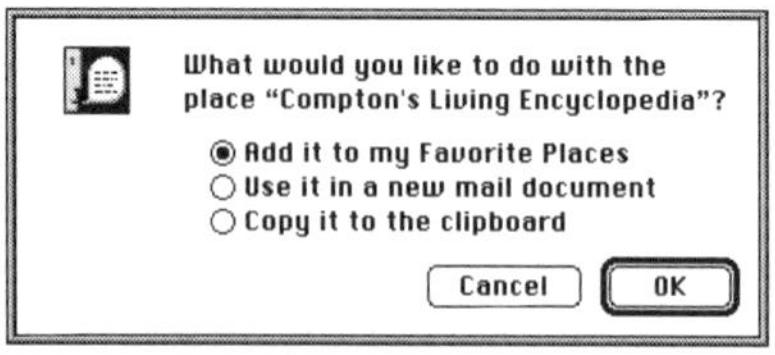


**Figure 18.** *A dialog box like this appears when you click a heart icon. Make sure "Add it to my Favorite Places" is selected and click OK.*

### ✔ Tip

- If a window does not have a heart icon in its top right corner, you cannot add it to favorite places.

**Figure 19.** *Choose Favorite Places from the Go To menu.*

**Figure 20.** *The Favorite Places window lists all of your favorite places.*

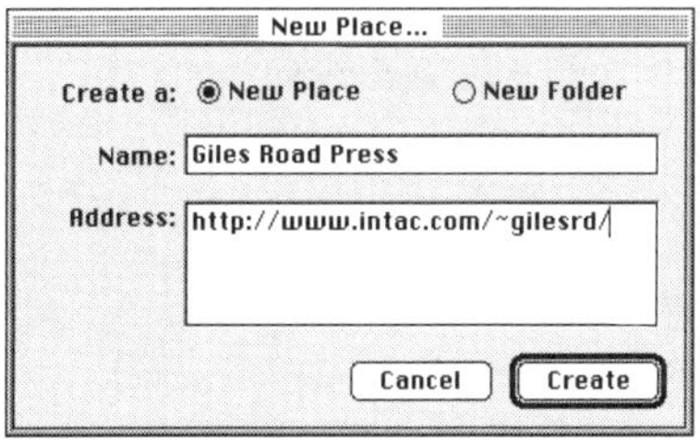


**Figure 21.** *Use the New Place dialog box to add a location to the Favorite Places window.*

## To open the Favorite Places window

Choose Favorite Places from the Go To menu (see **Figure 19**).

*or*

Click the Favorite Places button on the toolbar. 

The Favorite Places window appears (see **Figure 20**).

## To add a favorite place with the Favorite Places window

1. In the Favorite Places window (see **Figure 20**), click the New button.
2. In the dialog box that appears, make sure the New Place radio button is turned on. Then enter the name of the location in the Name edit box and the exact address of the location in the Address edit box (see **Figure 21**).
3. Click the Create button or press Enter.

The entry appears among the other items in the Favorite Places window (see **Figure 22**).

## ✔ Tips

- If you make an error while typing the address, the link to the location will not work.
- You can enter any location on the Internet or AOL in the address edit box. However, since locations on AOL have unusual and complex addresses (see **Figure 23** on the next page), it's very unlikely that you will know the correct address for an AOL location unless someone tells you.
- Consult **Chapter 9** for more information about the Internet.

## To modify a Favorite Place entry

1. In the Favorite Places window (see **Figure 22**), click once on the icon for the item you want to change.
2. Click the Edit button.
3. In the Edit Place dialog box that appears (see **Figure 23**), make changes to the name and address of the entry by editing the contents of the appropriate edit box.
4. Click OK or press Enter to accept your changes.

**Figure 22.** *To modify or delete a Favorite Places entry, begin by clicking the entry once to select it.*

### ✔ Tip

- Do not change the address of a favorite place unless it is incorrect and you know the correct address. Entering an incorrect address in the address edit box will prevent the favorite place link from working properly.

**Figure 23.** *You can modify any Favorite Places entry. As shown here, entries added for AOL locations may have complex addresses.*

## To rename a Favorite Place or Favorite Places folder

1. In the Favorite Places window (see **Figures 20** and **22**), click once on the name of the item you want to change. An edit box appears around the selected name.
2. Use standard editing techniques to change the contents of the edit box (see **Figure 24**).
3. Press Enter to accept your changes (see **Figure 25**).

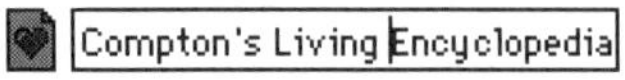


**Figure 24.** *When you click an entry name, an edit box appears around it. You can then use standard editing techniques to change it.*

**Figure 25.** *When you press Enter to accept your changes, the name of the item changes.*

### ✔ Tips

- Of course, you can also rename a Favorite Place or Favorite Places folder by selecting it and clicking the Edit button as discussed at the top of this page.
- Using folders to organize Favorite Places is discussed on the next page.

**Figure 26.** *Use the New Folder dialog box to create a Favorite Places folder.*

## To add a new folder to the Favorite Places window

1. In the Favorite Places window (see **Figures 20** and **22**), click the New button.
2. In the dialog box that appears, make sure the New Folder radio button is turned on. Then enter a name for the folder in the Name edit box (see **Figure 26**).
3. Click the Create button or press Enter.

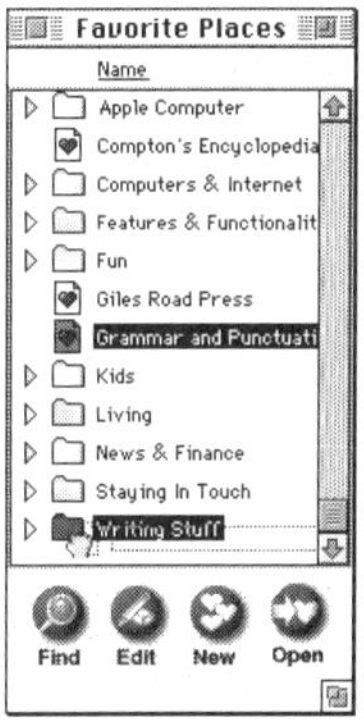


**Figure 27.** *To move an item into a folder, just drag it.*

## To organize favorite places with folders

1. In the Favorite Places window (see **Figures 20** and **21**), position the mouse pointer on an item you want to move into a folder, press the mouse button down, and drag toward the new folder.
2. When the intended destination folder becomes highlighted (see **Figure 27**), release the mouse button to drop the item inside it.

### ✔ Tips

- You can use this technique to place folders inside folders to further organize your favorite places.
- The Favorite Places window includes a number of predefined folders. You can use these folders as they are or rename or delete them as desired. Changing the name of a folder is discussed on the previous page. Deleting a folder is discussed on the next page.
- The Favorite Places window is displayed in an outline view with folder contents indented. To toggle the display of a folder's contents, click the triangle to the left of the folder name (see **Figure 28**).

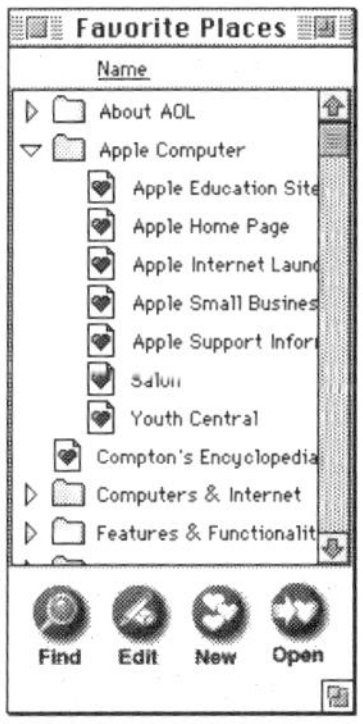


**Figure 28.** *Click the triangle to the left of a folder to show or hide its contents in outline view. In this example, the Apple Computer folder's contents are displayed.*

## To go to a favorite place

1. In the Favorite Places window, click the icon for the place to which you want to go to select it.
2. Click Open or press Enter.

*or*

In the Favorite Places window, double-click the icon for the place to which you want to go.

### ✔ Tip

- If you're not already connected to AOL, using the Favorite Places window to go to a favorite place automatically connects you.

## To delete a favorite place

1. In the Favorite Places window, click once on the name of the item you want to delete to select it.
2. Click the Edit button.
3. In the Edit Place dialog box that appears, click the Delete button.
4. In the confirmation dialog box that appears (see **Figure 29**), click Delete or press Enter.

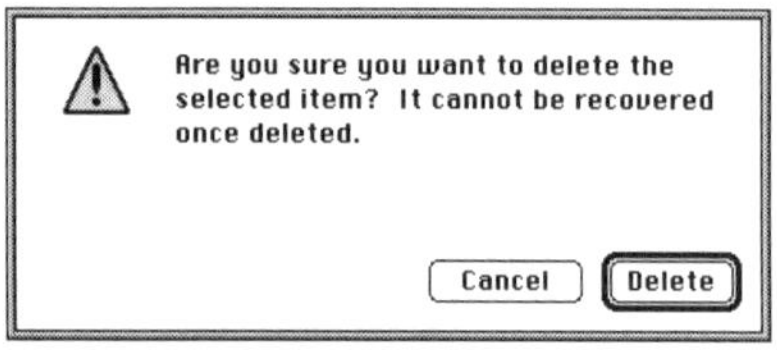


**Figure 29.** *AOL checks to make sure that you really do want to delete a favorite place before deleting it.*

### ✔ Tips

- You can also delete a favorite place or favorite place folder by selecting it in the Favorite Places window and then choosing Clear from the Edit menu. You'll still have to confirm the deletion in a dialog box like the one in **Figure 29**.
- When you delete a favorite places folder, the folder and all the items inside of it are deleted.

**Figure 30.** *Choose Find from the Go To menu.*

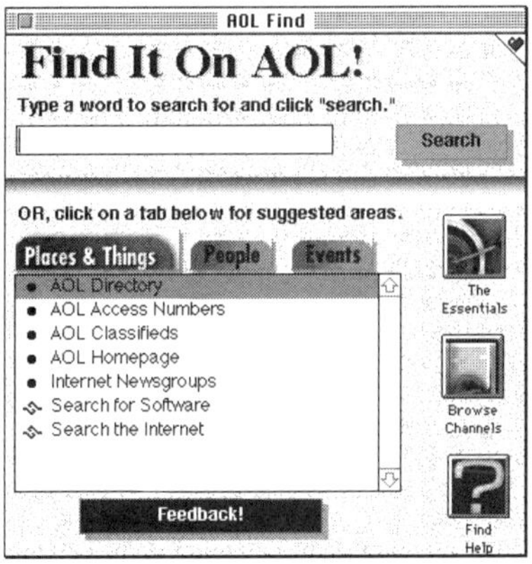


**Figure 31.** *Use the AOL Find window to search for or browse AOL's content and features.*

## About the Find Feature

The Find feature offers several ways to search through AOL's content and features to find just the information you're looking for:

- Enter a search word or phrase to locate areas covering a specific topic.
- Click a tab to browse suggested areas listed under Places & Things, People, or Events.
- Click a button to learn more about AOL Essentials, browse Channels, or get help for using the Find feature.

### ✔ Tips

- AOL's Find feature does not find every reference to a search word or phrase, but it's a good place to start when you're looking for content related to a specific topic.
- The Keyword dialog box (see **Figure 15**) offers a simpler find feature. You can enter a search word or phrase in its edit box and click the Search button to display a list of areas that contain that word or phrase. Keywords are discussed earlier in this chapter.

## To open the AOL Find window

Click the Find button in the Channels window (see **Figure 2**).

*or*

Click the Find button on the toolbar.

*or*

Choose Find from the Go To menu (see **Figure 30**).

*or*

Press ⌘F.

The AOL Find window appears (see **Figure 31**).

## To search for a specific topic

1. In the edit box near the top of the AOL Find window (see **Figure 31**), enter a word or phrase to describe the topic you want to find (see **Figure 32**).
2. Click the Search button.
3. In the AOL Search Results window that appears (see **Figure 33**), double-click an item that interests you to view a description of it (see **Figure 34**). Click the window's close box to close the description window when you're finished with it.
4. Repeat step 3 for each area that interests you.

## ✔ Tips

- When the Search Results window first opens, it displays only the first 20 matches (see **Figure 33**). Click the More button to display additional matches.
- Click an underlined "hot link" in an area description window (see **Figure 34**) to go to that topic in the area.
- Click the Go There button in an area description window (see **Figure 34**) to go to the area.
- Click the Related Areas button in an area description window to go to the main window for a related channel. For example, clicking the Related Areas button in **Figure 34** displays the Computers and Software channel's main window.
- If the topic you've entered cannot be found online, the Search Results dialog box will offer only one option: Search the Internet. This gives you access to AOL's Webcrawler search engine for searching the World Wide Web. The Internet is discussed in detail in **Chapter 9**.

**Figure 32.** *Enter a word or phrase to describe the topic you want to find, and click the Search button.*

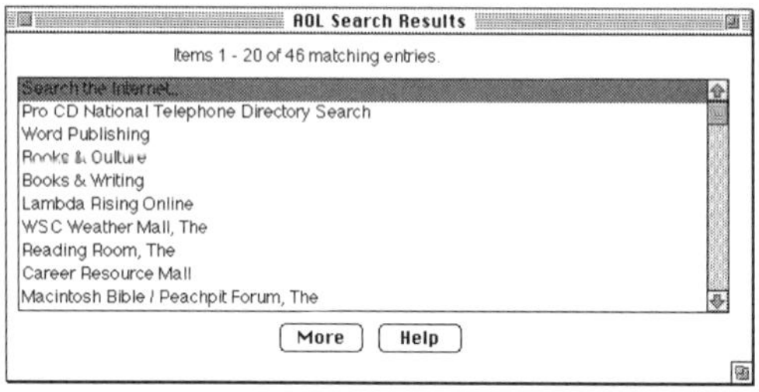


**Figure 33.** *The AOL Search Results window displays a list of areas related to the search word or phrase.*

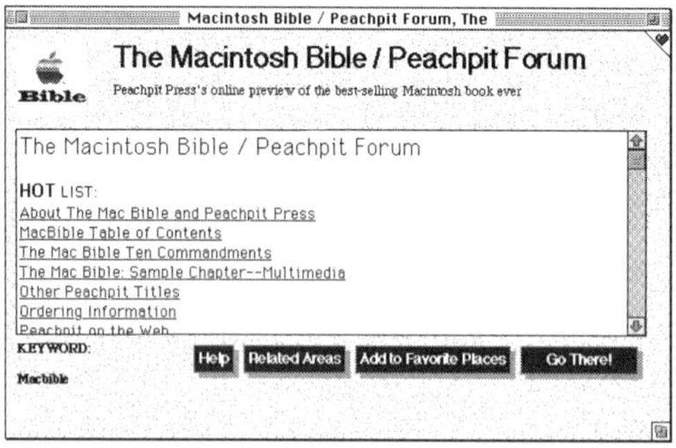


**Figure 34.** *Double-clicking an area in the AOL Search Results window displays a window with clickable links that take you to specific places within the area.*

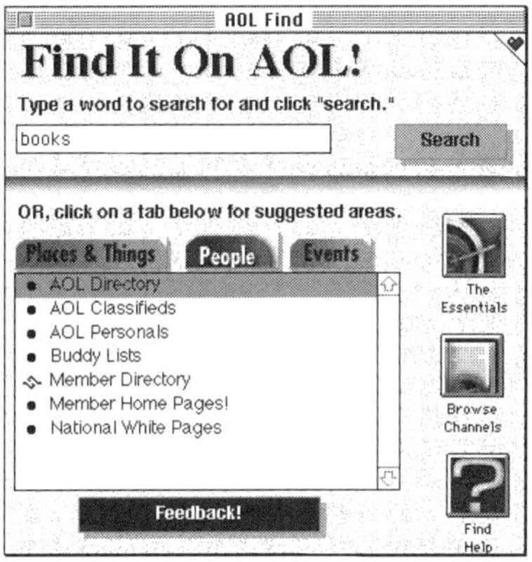


**Figure 35.** *The People tab gives you access to features for locating AOL members and other people.*

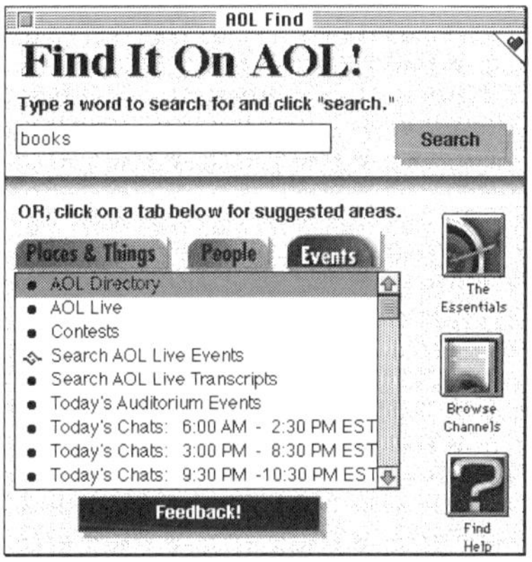


**Figure 36.** *The Events tab helps you find information about events and contests on AOL.*

**Figure 37.** *Click buttons in the The Essentials window to learn more about AOL features.*

## To browse suggested areas

1. In the AOL Find window (see **Figures 31**, **35**, and **36**), click the tab for the type of area you want to browse:
   - ▲ *Places & Things* (see **Figure 31**) lets you browse areas on AOL and Web pages on the Internet.
   - ▲ *People* (see **Figure 35**) lets you browse directories and other features to help you locate AOL members and other people.
   - ▲ *Events* (see **Figure 36**) lets you browse information about events and contests on AOL.
2. The scrolling list at the bottom of the AOL Find window displays a list of items for the tab you selected (see **Figures 31**, **35**, and **36**). Double-click the item that interests you to open it.

## To learn about "The Essentials"

1. In the AOL Find window (see **Figures 31**, **35**, and **36**), click the The Essentials button.
2. In the The Essentials window that appears (see **Figure 37**), click the button beside the topic for which you want more information.
3. Double-click list items in the subsequent windows to zero in on the information you want.

## ✔ Tips

- Click the Start button under Discover AOL in the The Essentials window (see **Figure 37**) to access online tutorials for using some of AOL's features.
- You may find it more cost effective to learn about AOL's features through options in the Member Services area, which is free. Member Services is discussed in **Chapter 11**.

## To browse channels

1. In the AOL Find window (see **Figures 31, 35, and 36**), click the Browse Channels button.
2. In the Channel Find window that appears (see **Figure 38**), use the Click Here to Select a Channel pop-up menu (see **Figure 39**) to choose a channel to browse.
3. Click the A-Z tab to display the channel's contents alphabetically (see **Figure 40**).

   *or*

   Click the By Topic tab to display the channel's contents by topic (see **Figure 41**).
4. Double-click an item to open it and explore its contents.

## ✔ Tips

- Until you select a channel from the pop-up menu as discussed in step 2 above, the scrolling list will remain empty.
- Another way to browse a channel is to open the Channels window and click the button for the channel in which you are interested. Opening and using the Channels window is discussed earlier in this chapter.

**Figure 38.** *The Channel Find window of AOL Find is a good place to start browsing channels.*

**Figure 39.** *Use this pop-up menu to choose a channel to browse.*

**Figure 40.** *Once you select a channel, the A-Z tab displays the channel's contents in alphabetical order.*

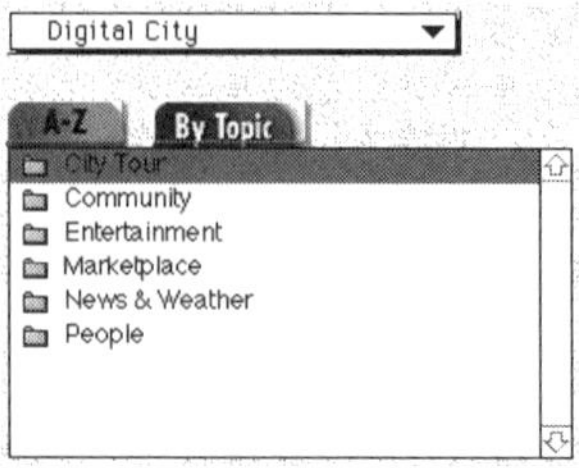


**Figure 41.** *Clicking the By Topic tab displays the channel's contents by topic.*

**Figure 42.** *Before letting you enter an unlimited use area, AOL warns you what will happen when you do.*

**Figure 43.** *One way to leave an unlimited use area is to choose Exit Unlimited Use Area from the Go To menu.*

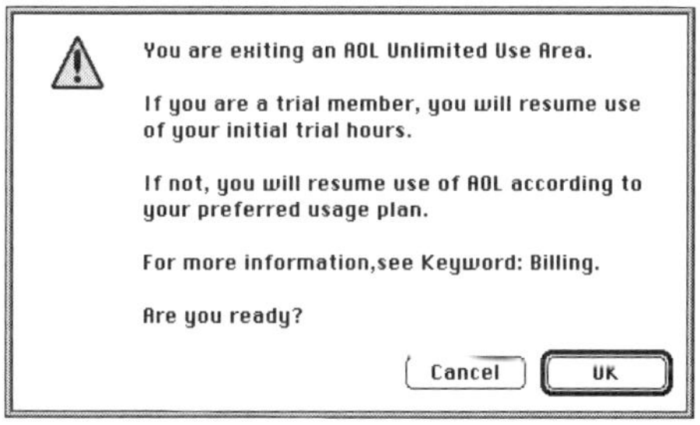


**Figure 44.** *AOL warns you again when you leave an unlimited use area.*

## About Unlimited Use Areas

AOL has several *unlimited use* areas that you can access free of charge no matter what billing plan you've chosen. Most of these are support areas that provide information about your account and assistance using AOL features. Member Services, which is discussed in **Chapter 12**, is an example.

### To enter an unlimited use area

1. Use one of the navigation techniques discussed earlier in this chapter to go to an unlimited use area.
2. In the dialog box that appears (see **Figure 42**), click OK or press Enter.

### ✔ Tip

- When you enter an unlimited use area, any chat or gateway windows you have open are closed and any file transfers or Internet activity is suspended.

### To exit an unlimited use area

1. Use one of the navigation techniques discussed earlier in this chapter to go to a regular area of AOL.

   *or*

   Choose Exit Unlimited Use Area from the Go To menu (see **Figure 43**).

   *or*

   Press ⌘E.
2. In the dialog box that appears (see **Figure 44**), click OK or press Enter.

### ✔ Tip

- When you exit an unlimited use area, any free file transfers in progress are suspended and hidden windows reappear. If you have selected a billing plan that keeps track of the time you spend online, the billing clock starts back up.

# EXCHANGING E-MAIL 4



## About E-Mail

*Electronic mail* or *e-mail* is a method of exchanging written messages between computer users. Using e-mail, you can communicate with anyone who has an e-mail address, including:

- Other members of AOL,
- Members of other online services like CompuServe or Prodigy, and
- People with e-mail accounts on the Internet.

AOL makes it easy to exchange e-mail with others, through the use of intuitive forms for reading and writing messages. This chapter teaches you everything you need to know about using AOL's e-mail features.

## ✔ Tips

- To send an e-mail message, you must know the recipient's e-mail address. Consult the next page for more information about e-mail addresses.
- AOL's Internet gateway is what makes it possible to exchange e-mail messages with people who are not AOL members.
- You can send the same e-mail message to more than one person. This is quicker and more cost effective than sending the same message multiple times.
- Generally speaking, e-mail is private. Under normal circumstances, the only people who have access to the contents of an e-mail message are the sender and receiver(s). Still, e-mail is not a recommended method for exchanging confidential information.

## About E-Mail Addresses

In order to send an e-mail message to someone, you must know his e-mail address. Use these guidelines to determine the correct e-mail address for the people with whom you communicate:

- The e-mail address for another AOL member is that member's screen name.
- The e-mail address for a member of another online service is that person's account name or number on the service followed by an "at" sign (@) and the domain name of the service. Consult **Table 1** for a partial listing of online service domain names.
- The e-mail address for someone with an e-mail account on the Internet is that person's account name followed by an "at" sign (@) and the domain name of his mail server.

| Service | Domain Name |
|---|---|
| AppleLink | applelink.apple.com |
| AT&T Mail | attmail.com |
| BIX | bix.com |
| CompuServe | compuserve.com |
| CONNECT | connectinc.com |
| Delphi | delphi.com |
| EasyLink | eln.attmail.com |
| GEnie | genie.geis.com |
| MCI Mail | mcimail.com |
| Microsoft Network | msn.com |
| Prodigy | prodigy.com |

**Table 1.** *Domain names for various online services.*

## About Your E-Mail Address

Your e-mail address varies depending on whether the person sending you mail is an AOL member or someone sending you mail through AOL's Internet gateway:

- Your e-mail address for messages coming from another AOL member is your screen name.
- Your e-mail address for messages coming to you through AOL's Internet gateway is your screen name (with any spaces omitted), followed by *@aol.com*.

## ✔ Tips

- When addressing a message to a member of another online service, be sure to remove any spaces or replace any commas with periods in the account name or number.
- The period character in an e-mail address or domain name is frequently referred to verbally as a "dot." So, for example, the domain name for AOL may be called "AOL-dot-com."
- The best way to get the correct e-mail address for someone with whom you want to exchange e-mail is to ask for it.

**Figure 1.** *The Mail Center offers access to incoming e-mail messages and general information about e-mail.*

**Figure 2.** *You can open the Mail Center window by choosing Mail Center from the Mail menu.*

**Figure 3.** *If you don't have any unread mail, you can open the Mail Center by clicking the Mail Center button in the Welcome window.*

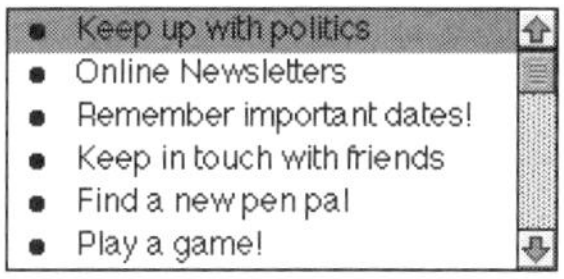


**Figure 4.** *The scrolling list inside the Mail Center window offers access to information about e-mail.*

## About the Mail Center

The Mail Center (see **Figure 1**) is where you can access all of your incoming mail and get general information about e-mail.

## To open the Mail Center

Choose Mail Center from the Mail menu (see **Figure 2**).

*or*

Click the Mail Center button in the Welcome window (see **Figure 3**).

*or*

Use the Keyword MAIL.

### ✔ Tip

- The Mail Center button appears in the Welcome window only if you do not have any unread mail. If you have unread mail, you'll see a You Have Mail button instead.

## To get more information about e-mail

1. Double-click the name of an item in the scrolling list within the Mail Center window (see **Figure 4**). An article containing information about the topic you selected appears.
2. When you're finished reading an article, click the close box on its window to close it.

### ✔ Tip

- Other buttons within the Mail Center window (see **Figure 1**) offer access to help and general information about e-mail.

## About Composing E-Mail

You write or *compose* an e-mail message with an intuitive form that includes fields for recipient address(es), subject, and message text (see **Figure 5**).

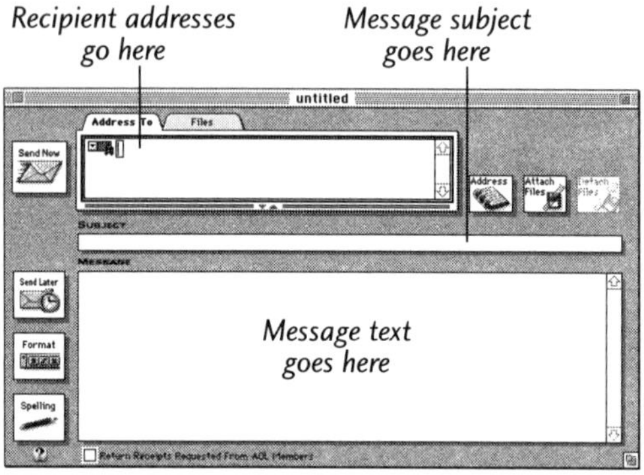


**Figure 5.** *Use a window like this to create an e-mail message.*

### ✔ Tip

- You may find it more cost effective to compose e-mail messages without being connected to AOL. Consult **Chapter 10** for information about working offline.

## To open a Compose Mail window

Choose Compose Mail from the Mail menu (see **Figure 6**).

**Figure 6.** *To open a Compose Mail window, choose Compose Mail from the Mail menu.*

*or*

Press [⌘][M].

*or*

Click the Compose Mail button on the toolbar.

*or*

Click the Compose Mail button in the Mail Center window (see **Figure 7**).

**Figure 7.** *If the Mail Center window is open, you can click the Compose Mail button to open a Compose Mail window.*

An untitled Compose Mail window appears (see **Figure 5**).

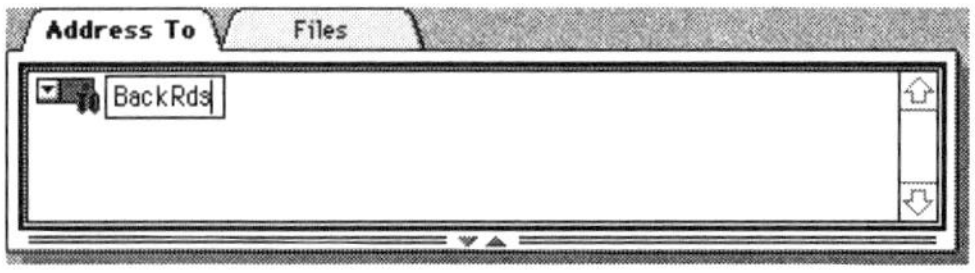


**Figure 8.** *Enter the e-mail address for the person to whom you want to send the message.*

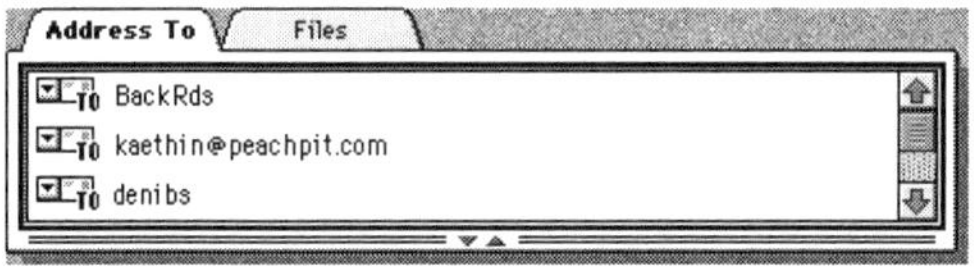


**Figure 9.** *Each addressee appears on a separate line in the Address To field.*

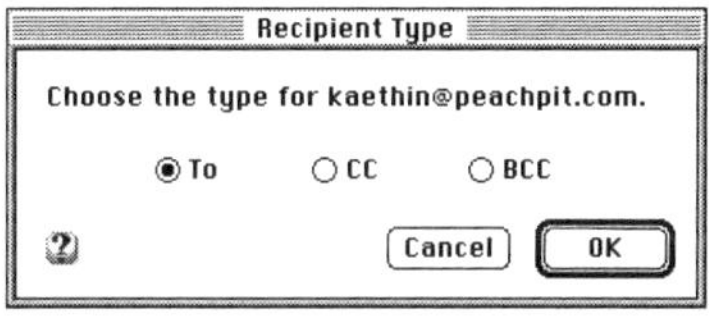


**Figure 10a.** *Use the Recipient Type dialog box to change the address type for an e-mail message recipient.*

**Figure 10b.** *You can also use the recipient type pop-up menu in the address area to change an address's recipient type.*

**Figure 11.** *In this example, each recipient is assigned a different address type.*

## ✔ Tips

- The name(s) of recipients who receive a carbon copy (CC) of an e-mail message appear in the message received by other recipients.
- The name(s) of recipients who receive a blind carbon copy (BCC) of an e-mail message *do not* appear anywhere in the message received by other recipients.

## To address an e-mail message

1. If necessary, click in the Address To field of the Compose Mail window to position an insertion point in a TO edit box inside it (see **Figure 5**).
2. Type in the address of the intended recipient (see **Figure 8**).
3. Press Return or ,.
4. Repeat steps 2 and 3 for each person to whom you want to send the message.

## ✔ Tips

- If the Address To field is not displayed in step 1 above, start by clicking the Address To tab to display it.
- When you address a message to more than one person, each person's e-mail address appears on a different line in the Address To field (see **Figure 9**).
- You can also use the Address Book button to address messages. Consult **Chapter 8** for more information about AOL's Address Book feature.

## To change a recipient's address type

1. Double-click the TO icon to the left of the recipient's name.
2. In the Recipient Type dialog box that appears (see **Figure 10a**), select the radio button for the type of addressing you want.
3. Click OK or press Enter.

*or*

Click the triangle to the left of the TO, CC, or BCC icon and choose the recipient type you want from the pop-up menu that appears (see **Figure 10b**).

**Figure 11** shows an example of each type of recipient in an Address To field.

## To give an e-mail message a subject

1. If necessary, click in the Subject field of the Compose Mail window to position an insertion point inside it.
2. Type in an appropriate subject for the message (see **Figure 12**).

**Figure 12.** *Use the Subject field of the Compose Mail window to give your message an appropriate subject.*

### ✔ Tips

- You can press Tab to move the insertion point from the Address field to the Subject field of a message.
- Make sure your message subject describes the contents of your message. Many people depend on message subjects to determine which messages they open first when their mailboxes are full of e-mail.

## To enter e-mail text

1. If necessary, click in the Message field of the Compose Mail window to position an insertion point inside it.
2. Type in the text for your message (see **Figure 13**).

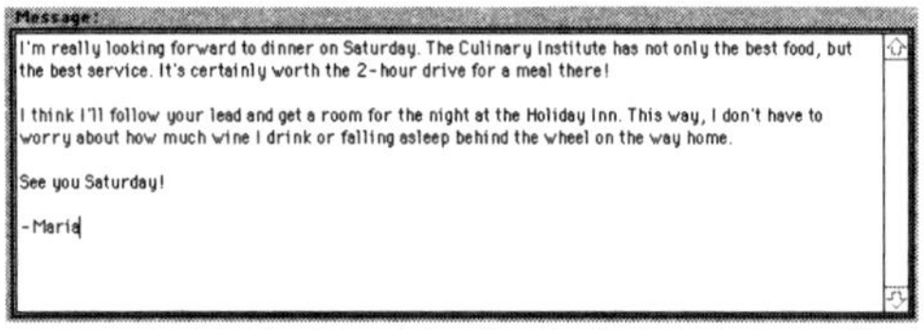


**Figure 13.** *Type your message into the body field of the Compose Mail window. This scrolling window can accept up to 32K of text for a single message.*

### ✔ Tips

- You can press Tab to move the insertion point from the Subject field to the Message field. Pressing Tab within the Message field, however, inserts a tab character in that field.
- The body field of the Compose Mail window is like a mini word processor (see **Figure 13**). Standard text entry and editing techniques apply.
- The body of an AOL message cannot exceed 32K in length. If you try to send a longer message, AOL will parse the message into segments that will be sent separately to the recipient(s).

**Figure 14.** *Click the Spelling button in a Compose Mail window to begin the spelling check…*

**Figure 15.** *…or choose Check Spelling from the Edit menu.*

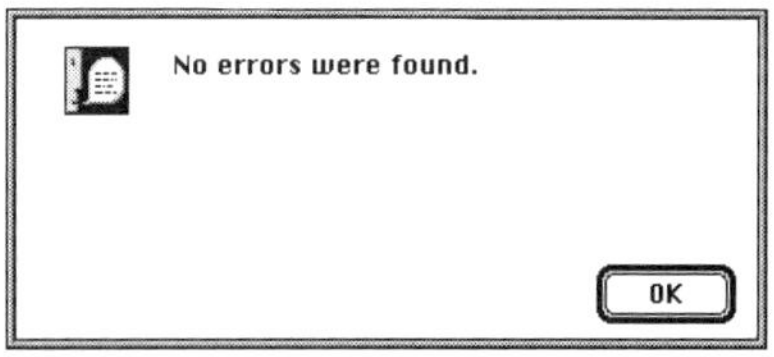


**Figure 16.** *If your spelling is perfect, AOL's spelling checker tells you.*

# About the Spell Checker

AOL includes a spelling checker you can use to make sure all words within an e-mail message are correctly spelled.

## To start a spelling check

1. Click in the Message field of a Compose Mail window to position an insertion point inside it.
2. Click the Spelling button in the Compose Mail window (see **Figure 14**).

   *or*

   Choose Check Spelling from the Edit menu (see **Figure 15**).

   *or*

   Press [⌘][=].

   The spelling check begins.
3. Follow the instructions on the next page to complete the spelling check.

## ✔ Tips

- AOL's spelling checker begins the check at the insertion point. To start checking from the beginning of the message, position the insertion point at the very beginning or end of the message.
- AOL may briefly display a Checking Spelling window to indicate that the spelling check has begun. This window disappears as soon as AOL finds a questionable word or completes the spelling check.
- If AOL completes the spelling check without finding any questionable words, it displays a dialog box like the one in **Figure 16**. Click OK or press [Enter] to dismiss it.

## To complete a spelling check

1. Start a spelling check as instructed on the previous page.
2. When the spelling checker encounters a word it does not recognize, it displays a dialog box like the one in **Figure 17**. You then have several options:
   - ▲ Click the Replace or Replace All button to replace this or all occurrences of the questionable word with the selected word in the Suggestions scrolling list.
   - ▲ Click the Skip or Skip All button to ignore this or all occurrences of the questionable word.
   - ▲ Click the Learn button to add the Questionable word to the list of acceptable words in AOL's dictionary.
   - ▲ Click the Cancel button to stop the spelling check.
3. Repeat step 2 for each questionable word AOL's spelling checker finds.
4. When the spelling check is complete, a dialog box like the one in **Figure 18** appears. Click OK or press [Enter] to dismiss it.

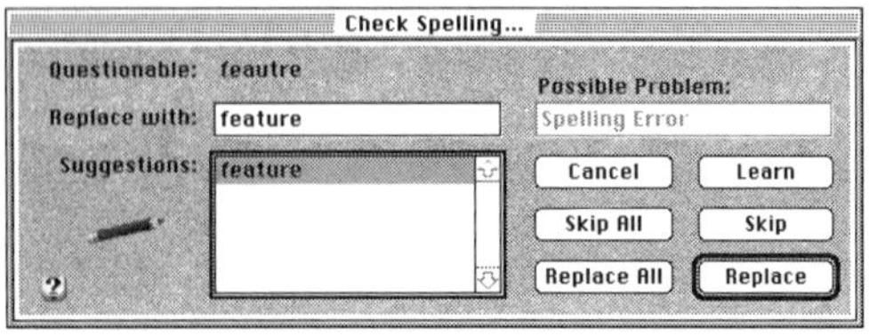


**Figure 17.** *The Check Spelling dialog box displays questionable words, one by one, so you can decide what to do about them.*

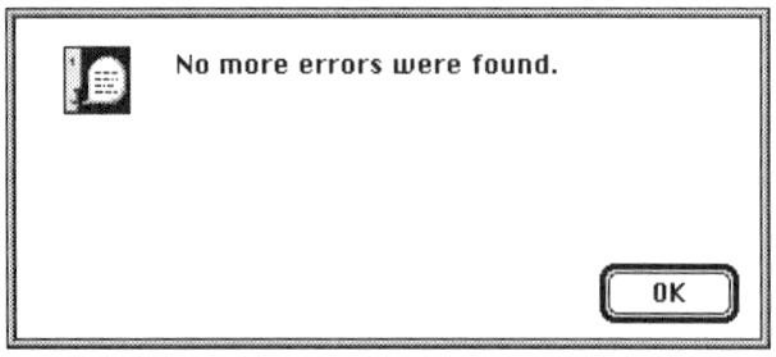


**Figure 18.** *When the spelling check is complete, a dialog box like this appears.*

### ✔ Tips

- ■ Do not click the Learn button unless you never want AOL's spelling checker to ask you about the questionable word ever again. Since the Learn button tells AOL to add the word to its internal dictionary, "learned" words are never questioned.
- ■ Do not depend on any spelling checker to check for typographical errors. If a typo spells a different, correct word—for example, *from* when you intended to type *form*—the spelling checker will not question it.

**Figure 19.** *The Format menu offers a number of submenus and commands for formatting the text of e-mail messages.*

**Figure 20.** *Choose Show Text Format Toolbar from the Format menu...*

**Figure 21.** *...or click the Format Text button in the Compose Mail window.*

## About Formatting E-Mail Message Text

Formatting is commonly used in word processing documents to help make text easier to read or to emphasize certain words or phrases. Nowadays, it's more common to see documents that include styled text than documents without it.

AOL's Compose Mail window supports a variety of e-mail message formatting options that you can use to help get your point across. Here's what you can do:

- Change the font of text characters.
- Change the size of text characters.
- Change the style of text characters to make them bold, italic, or underlined.
- Change the alignment of text.
- Change the color of the text and its background.

This section tells you how you can make any combination of these formatting changes three ways:

- Use commands under the Format menu (see **Figure 19**) when the Compose Mail window's Message field is active.
- Use formatting buttons on the Text Format toolbar (see **Figure 22**) that appears when you choose Show Text Format Toolbar from the Format menu (see **Figure 20**) or click the Format Text button (see **Figure 21**) in the Compose Mail window.
- Use shortcut keys for some text formatting options.

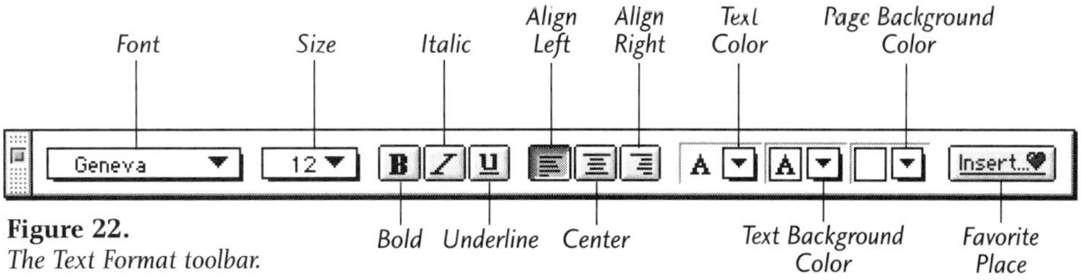


**Figure 22.**
*The Text Format toolbar.*

## ✔ Tips

- Although you can apply formatting to any e-mail message you compose, all formatting is lost if the message passes through AOL's Internet gateway to a recipient on another online service or the Internet—unless the recipient's e-mail system supports HTML tags. Don't waste your time formatting an e-mail message if none of the recipients is an AOL member.
- Formatting applied with AOL version 3 is lost when viewed earlier versions of the AOL software. Similarly, formatting applied with earlier versions of the AOL software is lost when viewed with AOL version 3.
- You must select the text you want to format (see **Figure 23**) before using a command, button, or shortcut key to format it.
- To quickly select all the text in an e-mail message, click in the Message field to activate it and choose Select All from the Edit menu (see **Figure 24**) or press [⌘][A].
- Like any form of written communication, e-mail can lose its effectiveness when text formatting is overdone. Don't get carried away when formatting your e-mail messages!

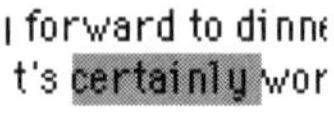


**Figure 23.** *You must select the text you want to format before applying the formatting.*

**Figure 24.** *To select all the text in a message, choose Select All from the Edit menu.*

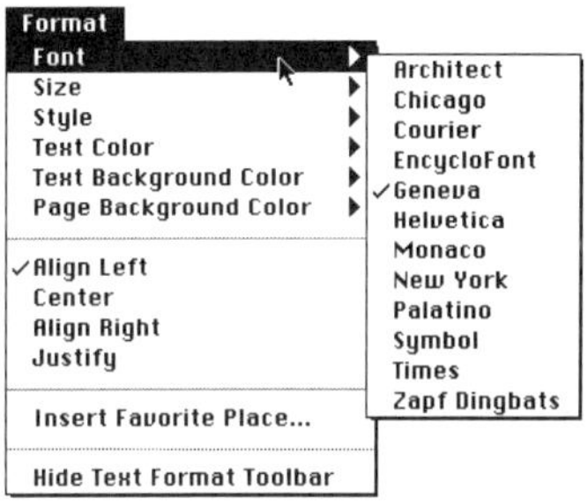


**Figure 25.** *The Font submenu under the Format menu lets you apply any installed font to the selected text.*

**Figure 26.** *Another way to change the font is by selecting a font from the Font pop-up menu on the Text Format toolbar.*

## To change character font

1. Select the characters whose font you want to change (see **Figure 23**).
2. Choose a font from the Font submenu under the Format menu (see **Figure 25**).

   *or*

   Choose a font from the Font pop-up menu on the Text Format toolbar (see **Figure 26**).

   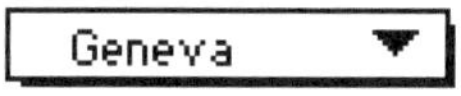
   

## ✔ Tips

- Only those fonts installed on your Macintosh will appear in the Font submenu (see **Figure 25**) or pop-up menu (see **Figure 26**).
- If you apply a font that the message recipient does not have installed on his computer, he will not see the text with the same font applied.

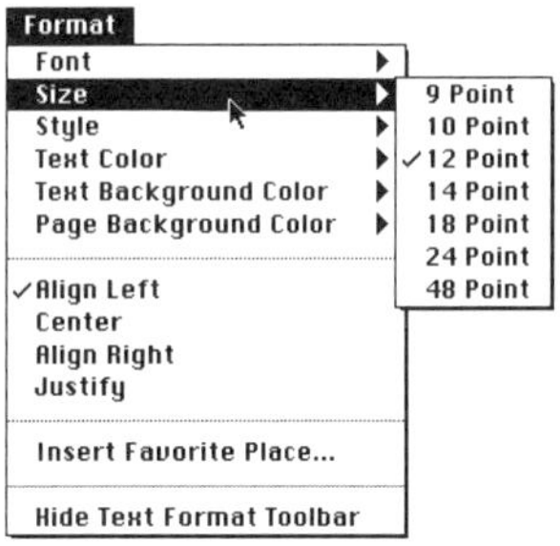


**Figure 27.** *The Size submenu under the Format menu offers commonly used character sizes to apply to selected text.*

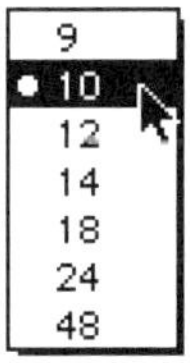


**Figure 28.** *Another way to change the font size is by selecting a size from the Size pop-up menu on the Text Format toolbar.*

## To change character size

1. Select the characters whose size you want to change (see **Figure 23**).
2. Choose a size from the Size submenu under the Format menu (see **Figure 27**).

   *or*

   Choose a size from the Size pop-up menu on the Text Format toolbar (see **Figure 28**).

   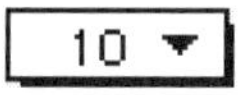
   

## ✔ Tip

- Character size is expressed in *points*. A point is 1/72nd of an inch.

## To change character style

1. Select the characters whose style you want to change (see **Figure 23**).
2. Choose a style from the Style submenu under the Format menu (see **Figure 29**).

   *or*

   Click one of the style buttons on the Text Format toolbar:

   ▲ Bold makes selected characters appear bold.

   ▲ Italic makes selected characters appear italic.

   ▲ Underline puts a single underline under selected characters.

   *or*

   Press a shortcut key for the style you want to apply:

   ▲ Press ⌘T for Plain text.

   ▲ Press ⌘B for Bold style.

   ▲ Press ⌘U for Underline style.

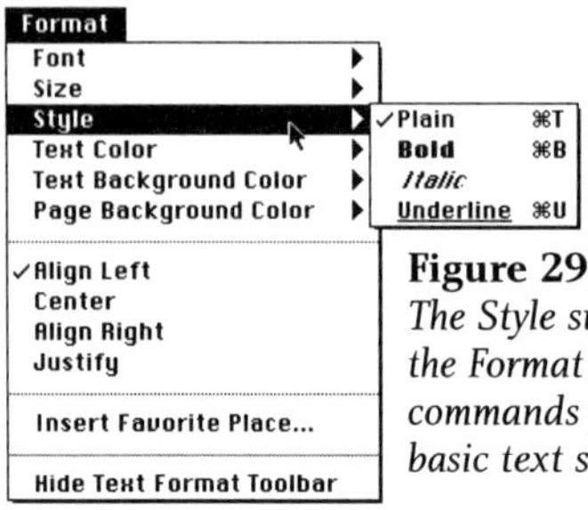


**Figure 29.** *The Style submenu under the Format menu offers commands for several basic text styles.*

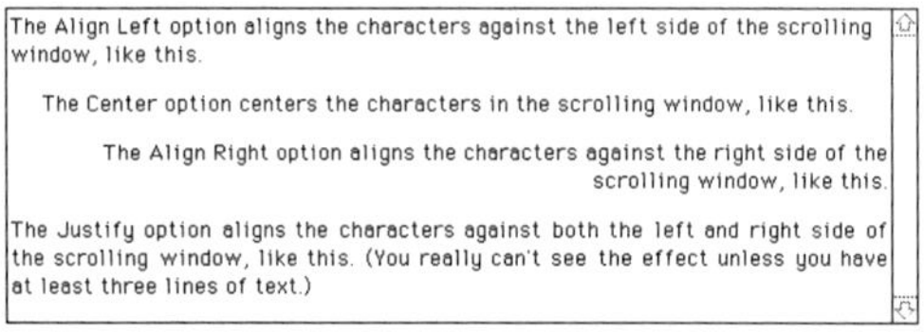


**Figure 30.** *Here's an example of the four alignment options: align left, center, align right, and justify.*

## To change text alignment

1. Select the paragraph(s) whose alignment you want to change.

   *or*

   Click anywhere in a paragraph whose alignment you want to change.
2. Click one of the alignment buttons on the Text Format toolbar:

   ▲ Align Left aligns characters against the left side of the scrolling window.

   ▲ Center centers characters in the scrolling window.

   ▲ Align Right aligns characters against the right side of the scrolling window.

   *or*

   Choose an alignment option from the Format menu (see **Figure 19**).

**Figure 30** shows an example of a Message field with each of the alignment options.

## ✔ Tip

■ Alignment options work on entire paragraphs. You cannot change the alignment of only part of a paragraph.

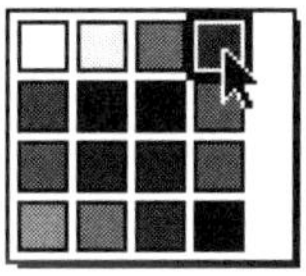

**Figure 31.** *The Text Color, Text Background Color, and Page Background Color pop-up menus on the Text Format toolbar all look like this.*

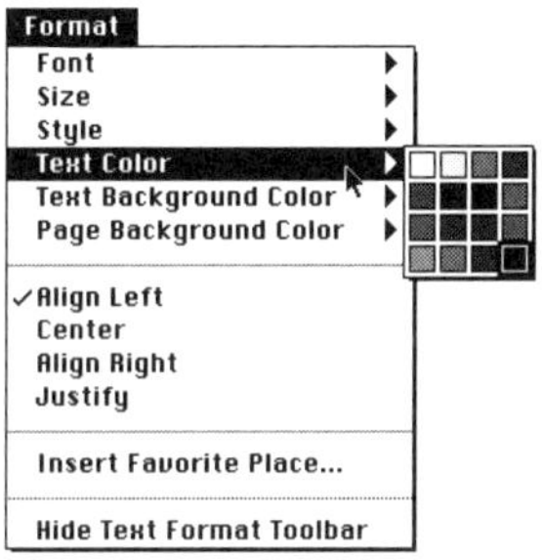


**Figure 32.** *You can choose a new color for selected text from the Text Color submenu under the Format menu. The Text Background Color and Page Background color submenus are similar.*

## To change the text or background color

1. Select the characters whose color or background color you want to change.
2. To change the color of selected text:
   - ▲ Choose a color from the Text Color pop-up menu on the Text Format toolbar (see **Figure 31**). 

     *or*
   - ▲ Choose a color from the Text Color submenu under the Format menu (see **Figure 32**).

   *or*

   To change the background color of selected text:
   - ▲ Choose a color from the Text Background Color pop-up menu on the Text Format toolbar (see **Figure 31**). 

     *or*
   - ▲ Choose a color from the Text Background Color submenu under the Format menu.

## To change the page background color

Choose a color from the Page Background Color pop-up menu on the Text Format toolbar (see **Figure 31**). 

*or*

Choose a color from the Page Background Color submenu under the Format menu.

## About File Attachments & Links

E-mail messages can include more than just text. You can also include:

- A *file attachment* is a file on your computer that you send via e-mail to the recipient of your message.
- A *hyperlink* or *hypertext link* to a favorite place is special message text that, when clicked by an AOL member reading the message, opens a location on AOL or the Internet.

**Figure 33.** *Click the Attach Files button to attach files to an e-mail message.*

## To attach a file to an e-mail message

1. Click the Attach Files button in the Compose Mail window (see **Figure 33**).
2. In the standard file dialog box that appears (see **Figure 34**), locate and select the file you want to attach.
3. If you want to automatically compress the file with StuffIt, turn on the Compress Attachments check box.
4. Click Attach or press Enter.
5. Repeat steps 1 through 4 for each file you want to attach to the message.

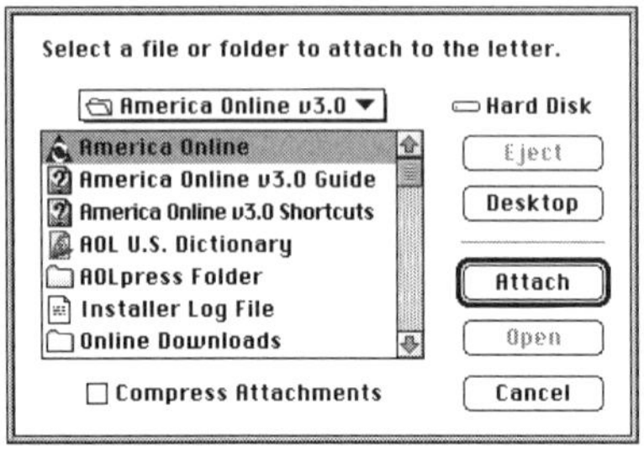


**Figure 34.** *Use this dialog box to select files to attach.*

## ✔ Tips

- Attached files appear in the Files tab at the top of the Compose Mail window (see **Figure 35**). A tiny disk icon appears beside the Files tab when a file is attached to a message.
- You can attach as many files as you like to a message. If you attach more than one file, the Compress Attachments check box in step 4 above is automatically turned on.
- File compression reduces the size of a file, making it quicker to send and receive. File compression and StuffIt are discussed in **Chapter 6**.

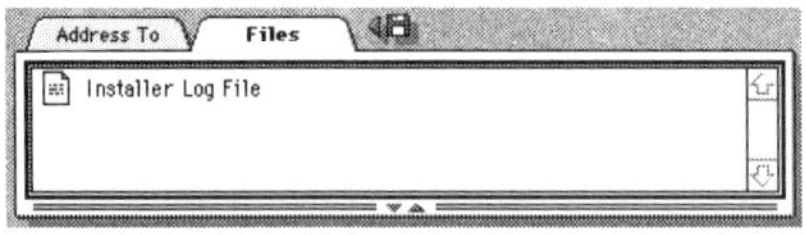


**Figure 35.** *Attached files appear in a list under the Files tab in the Compose Mail window.*

**Figure 36.** *Click the Detach Files button to detach a selected file from an e-mail message.*

## To detach a file from an e-mail message

1. If necessary, click the Files tab at the top of the Compose Mail window (see **Figure 35**).
2. Click on the name of the file you want to detach.
3. Click the Detach Files button (see **Figure 36**) in the Compose Mail window.
4. Repeat steps 2 and 3 for each file you want to detach from the message.

**Figure 37.** *You can turn selected message text into a hyperlink to a favorite place by choosing Insert Favorite Place from the Format menu.*

## To convert selected message text to a hyperlink

1. Type text that you want to make into a link into the body field of the Compose Mail window.
2. Select the text.
3. Choose Insert Favorite Place from the Format menu (see **Figure 37**).

   *or*

   Click the Insert Favorite Place button on the Text Format Toolbar.

4. In the Insert Favorite Place dialog box that appears, enter the complete URL (Uniform Resource Locator) for the link in the edit box (see **Figure 38**).
5. Click OK or press Enter.

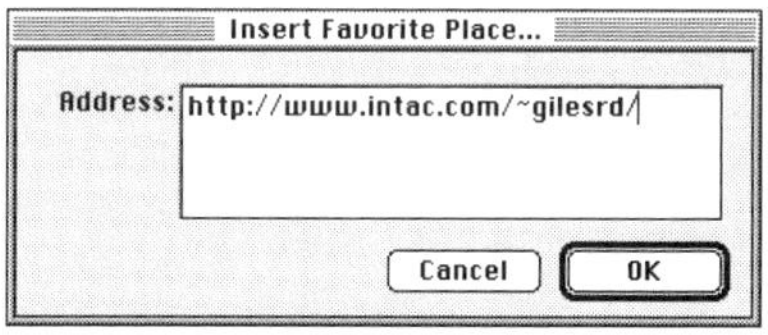


**Figure 38.** *Enter the URL for the link in the Insert Favorite Place dialog box.*

## To insert a hyperlink by typing

1. In the body field of a Compose Mail window, position the insertion point where you want the hyperlink to appear.
2. Choose Insert Favorite Place from the Format menu (see **Figure 37**).

   *or*

   Click the Insert Favorite Place button on the Text Format Toolbar.

3. In the Text edit box of the Insert Favorite Place dialog box, enter the text you want the message recipient to click to activate the link.
4. In the Address edit box, enter the complete URL (Uniform Resource Locator) for the link. When you're finished, the dialog box might look something like the one in **Figure 39**.
5. Click OK or press Enter.

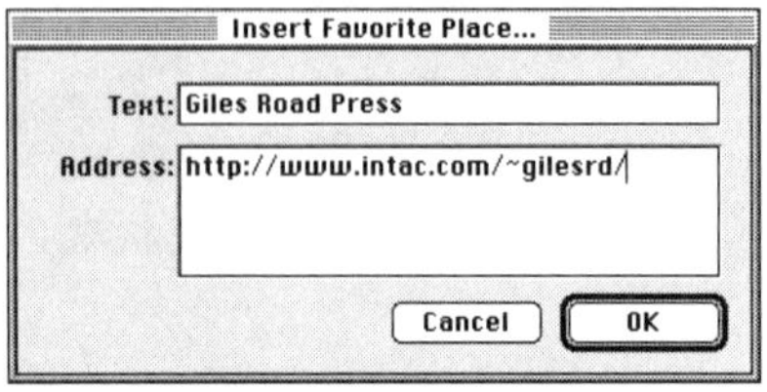


**Figure 39.** *The Insert Favorite Place dialog box lets you specify text for the link as well as the link's URL.*

**Figure 40.** *Choose Favorite Places from the Go To menu to open the Favorite Places window.*

## To add a hyperlink by dragging

1. Position the insertion point where you want the hyperlink to appear.
2. Choose Favorite Places from the Go To menu (see **Figure 40**).

   *or*

   Click the Favorite Places button on the toolbar.

3. Drag the icon for the Favorite Place link you want to use as a hyperlink from the Favorite Places window to the Compose Mail window (see **Figure 41**). When you release the mouse button, the link appears in the e-mail message (see **Figure 42**).

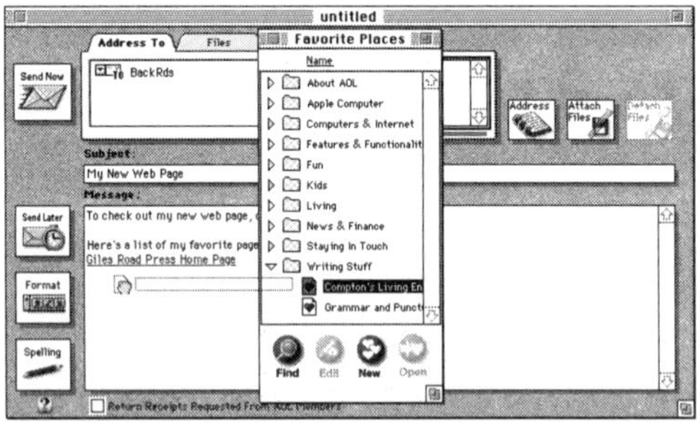


**Figure 41.** *You can drag an item from the Favorite Places window to the message window to create a hyperlink.*

### ✔ Tip

- You can also add a hyperlink to an e-mail message by dragging the heart icon in the upper right corner of an AOL window into a message window.

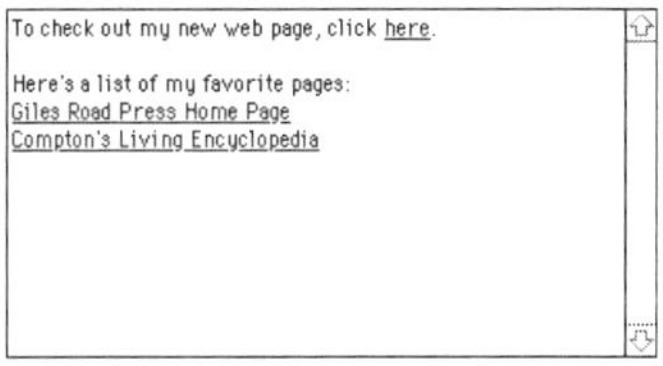


**Figure 42.** *Hyperlinks appear as underlined, blue text.*

**Figure 43.** *When a hyperlink is selected, you can choose Edit Favorite Place from the Format menu to change it.*

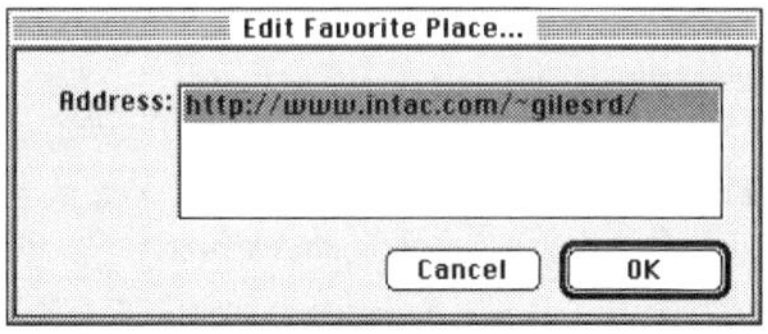


**Figure 44.** *Make changes to a hyperlink in the Edit Favorite Place dialog box.*

## ✔ Tips

- You can tell that text is a hyperlink because it appears in blue with an underline beneath it (see **Figure 42**).
- The URL you enter in the Insert Favorite Place dialog box can be for a World Wide Web page, FTP site, or any other location on the Internet. The Internet is discussed in **Chapter 9**.
- Consult **Chapter 3** for more information about Favorite Places.
- Hyperlinks can only be added to the Message field of an e-mail message. They cannot be included in the Address or Subject fields.

## To edit a hyperlink

1. Click anywhere in the hyperlink text.
2. Choose Edit Favorite Place from the Format menu (see **Figure 43**).

   *or*

   Click the Insert Favorite Place button on the Text Format Toolbar.

3. Make desired changes in the Edit Favorite Place dialog box that appears (see **Figure 44**).
4. Click OK or press [Enter] to accept your changes.

## To delete a hyperlink

1. Select the hyperlink text.
2. Press [Delete]. This deletes both the hyperlink and the text that was linked.

## About Return Receipts

AOL's return receipt feature can automatically notify you when an AOL member to whom you have sent a message has read that message. With this feature turned on for a specific e-mail message, you will receive a message like the one in **Figure 45** each time one of the message's recipients opens the message. This is a great way to keep track of when your e-mail is read.

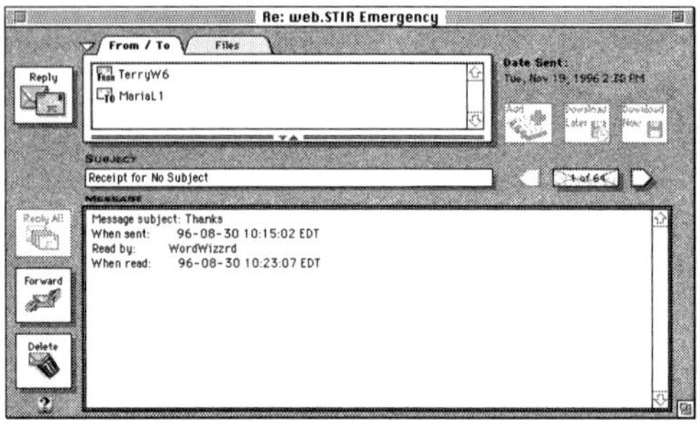


**Figure 45.** *When you request a return receipt, you'll get an e-mail message like this each time one of the message's recipients reads your message.*

### ✔ Tips

- The return receipt feature works for e-mail addressed to AOL members only. If one or more message recipients have e-mail addresses on services other than AOL or on the Internet, you will not be notified when they read the message.
- The message status feature, which is discussed later in this chapter, offers another way to track when messages are read.
- Reading incoming e-mail messages is discussed later in this chapter.

## To request a return receipt

Turn on the "Return Receipts Requested from AOL Members" check box (see **Figure 46**) at the bottom of the Compose Mail window.

**Figure 46.** *Requesting a return receipt is as simple as turning on a check box.*

## About Sending E-Mail

When you're finished composing and formatting an e-mail message, you must send it. Sending the message transfers it and any of its attachments from your computer to AOL's server. What happens to it next depends on how it is addressed:

- If the mail is addressed to another AOL member, that member's screen name is looked up in a database. If it's found, the message is stored for retrieval by the addressee.
- If the mail is addressed to someone on a system other than AOL, the message is sent through AOL's Internet gateway and routed to and stored on the system on which the addressee has an account.
- If the mail is addressed to several people with addresses on different online services, copies of the message are routed to and stored on the systems on which the addressees have accounts.

### ✔ Tips

- Although e-mail can take just seconds to reach a recipient's mailbox, it will remain unread until the recipient retrieves it. For this reason, you should not send time-sensitive e-mail messages to someone who checks for e-mail infrequently.
- If you close a Compose Mail window without sending the message, a dialog box like the one in **Figure 47** will appear. You have three options:
  - ▲ Click Save or press Enter to save the message as a file on disk.
  - ▲ Click Don't Save to close the window without saving the message at all.
  - ▲ Click Cancel to return to the Compose Mail window.

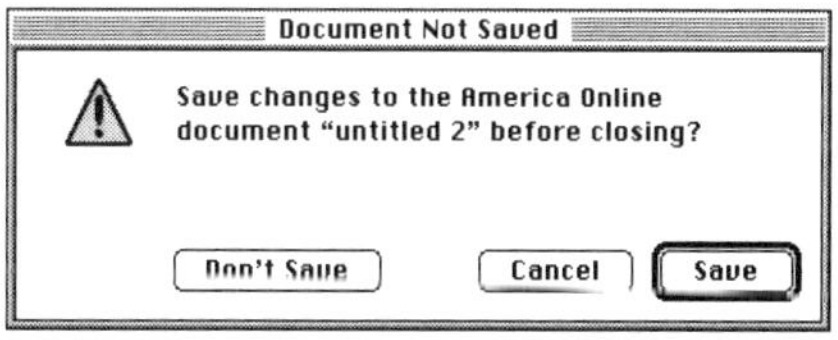


**Figure 47.** *If you try to close a message window without sending the message, you'll see a dialog box like this one.*

## To send an e-mail message immediately

1. Click the Send Now button (see **Figure 48**) in the Compose Mail window.

   *or*

   Press Enter.
2. A dialog box like the one in **Figure 49** appears, confirming that your e-mail message has been sent. Click OK or press Enter to dismiss it.

**Figure 48.** *To send an e-mail message immediately, click the Send Now button.*

**Figure 49.** *When you send a message, a dialog box like this appears to confirm that it has been successfully sent.*

### ✔ Tips

- You must be connected to AOL to use the Send Now button. If you are not connected, the Send Now button will be grayed out. Consult **Chapter 10** for more information about composing e-mail messages offline.
- If you attempt to send a message to an AOL member but have entered an incorrect screen name in the Address field, a window like the one in **Figure 50** appears. Click OK or press Enter, then re-address the message before attempting to send it again.

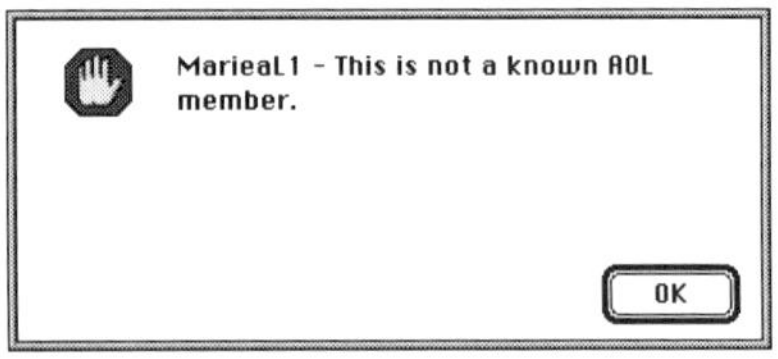


**Figure 50.** *If you incorrectly address a message, you may see a dialog box like this.*

## To send an e-mail message later

1. Click the Send Later button (see **Figure 51**) in the Compose Mail window.
2. A dialog box like the one in **Figure 52** appears, confirming that your e-mail message has been saved for later delivery. Click OK or press Enter to dismiss it.

**Figure 51.** *Click the Send Later button if you don't want to send a message right away.*

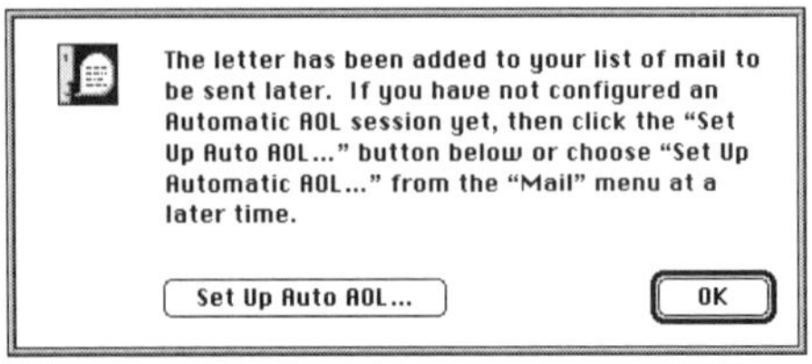


**Figure 52.** *When you click the Send Later button, a dialog box like this confirms that the message has been added to your list of mail to be sent later.*

### ✔ Tip

- Consult **Chapter 10** for more information about Automatic AOL sessions (also known as FlashSessions) and composing e-mail messages offline.

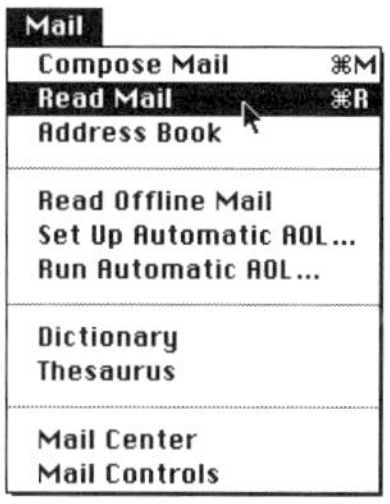


**Figure 53.** *Choose Read Mail from the Mail menu to open your online mailbox.*

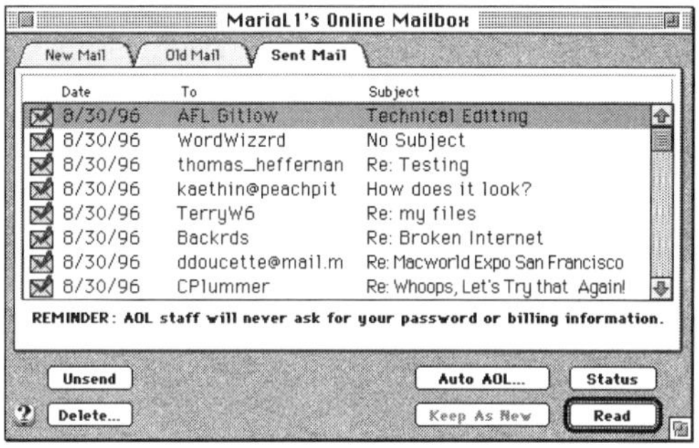


**Figure 54.** *The Sent Mail tab of the Online Mailbox window lists all the mail you've sent within the past 3 to 5 days.*

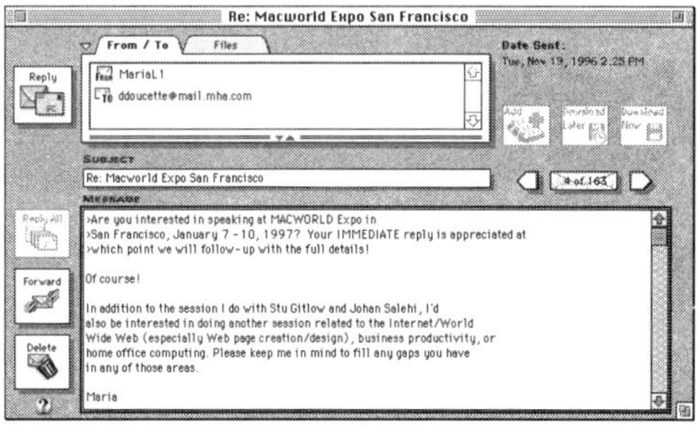


**Figure 55.** *Double-clicking an e-mail message you've already sent opens a window so you can read it.*

## To view a list of sent e-mail

1. Choose Read Mail from the Mail menu (see **Figure 53**).

   *or*

   Press [⌘R].
2. Click the Sent Mail tab. A list of all the messages you've sent appears in the Online Mailbox window (see **Figure 54**).

### ✔ Tip

- Sent mail remains in the Outgoing Mail window for 3 to 5 days from the date it was sent.

## To read an e-mail message you've sent

In the Sent Mail list of the Online Mailbox window (see **Figure 54**), double-click on the message you want to read.

*or*

Click once on the message you want to read and then click the Read button or press [Enter].

The message appears in a window like the one in **Figure 55**.

### ✔ Tip

- Reading e-mail is discussed in greater detail later in this chapter.

## To check the status of an outgoing e-mail message

1. In the Sent Mail list of the Online Mailbox window (see **Figure 54**), click once on the message you want to check and then click the Status button.
2. The status window that appears will tell you when the message was read (see **Figure 56a**) or that it hasn't been read yet (see **Figure 56b**). Click the window's close box to dismiss it.

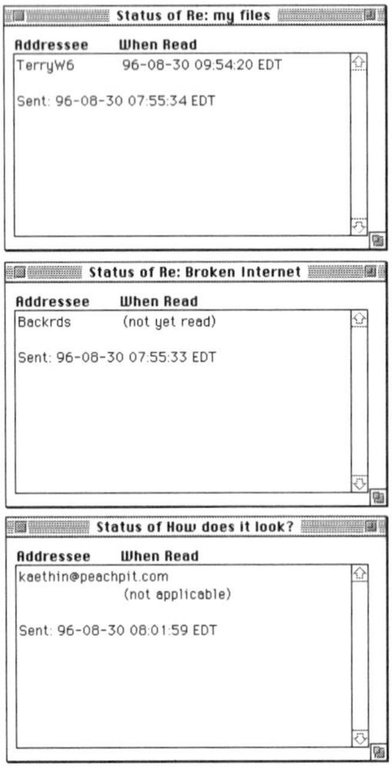


**Figures 56a, 56b, & 56c.** *When you check the status of a message you've sent, you'll see a status box like one of these if the message has been read (top), if it has not been read (middle), or if it is addressed to a user on another system or the Internet (bottom).*

### ✔ Tip

- There's no way to tell whether a message sent to someone on another service or the Internet has been read. If you try to check the status of such a message, the status window will look like the one in **Figure 56c**.

## To unsend a message

1. In the Sent Mail list of the Online Mailbox window (see **Figure 54**), click once on the message you want to check and then click the Unsend button.
2. In the confirmation dialog box that appears (see **Figure 57**), click Yes to unsend the message.
3. A dialog box confirms that the message has been unsent (see **Figure 58**). Click OK or press Enter to dismiss it.

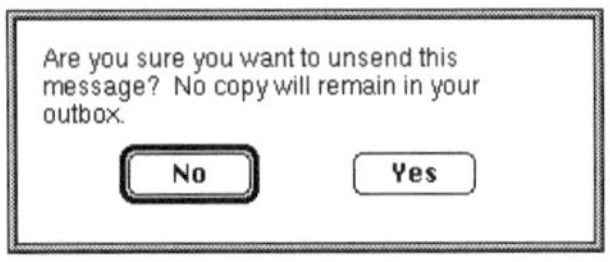


**Figure 57.** *Click the Yes button to unsend the selected message.*

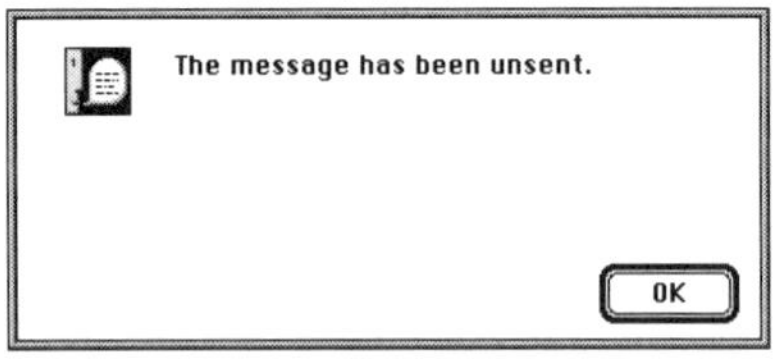


**Figure 58.** *A dialog box confirms that the message has been unsent.*

### ✔ Tips

- When you unsend a message, its intended recipient will never receive it.
- You cannot unsend a message that has already been read. If you try, you'll see a dialog box like the one in **Figure 59.**
- You cannot unsend a message that is addressed to someone other than an AOL member.

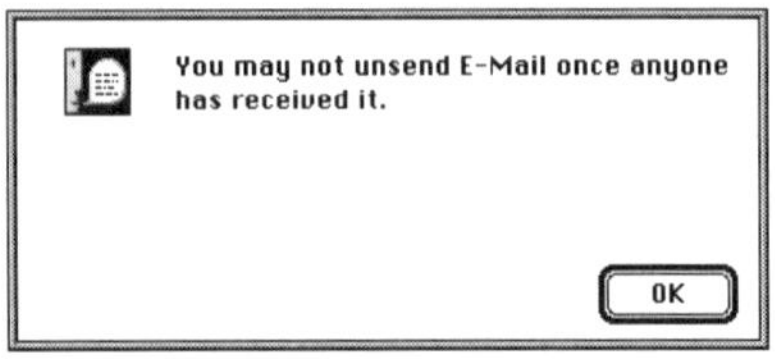


**Figure 59.** *If a message has already been read, it cannot be unsent.*

## About New E-Mail

When you connect to AOL and have unread mail in your mailbox, you're notified two ways:

- The Mail Center button on the Welcome screen appears as a You Have Mail button (see **Figure 60**).
- A male voice announces "You've got mail!"

**Figure 60.** *When you have unread mail in your mailbox, you'll see this button in the Welcome window.*

## ✔ Tips

- Incoming mail is considered "new mail" until read. If you don't read your mail during the current AOL session, you'll be reminded about it the next time you connect, even if no new additional messages have arrived in your mailbox since then.
- Unread mail remains on AOL's server for 35 days. After 35 days, the message is deleted—without you ever knowing the contents!
- You may find it more cost effective to read new mail without being connected to AOL. Consult **Chapter 10** about working with e-mail offline.

## To read new mail

**Figure 61.** *Click the Read New Mail button in the Mail Center window.*

1. Click the You Have Mail button in the Welcome window (see **Figure 60**).

   *or*

   Click the Read New Mail button in the Mail Center window (see **Figure 61**).

   *or*

   Click the New Mail button on the toolbar. 

   *or*

   Choose Read Mail from the Mail menu (see **Figure 53**).

   *or*

   Press ⌘R.
2. In the New Mail tab of the Online Mailbox window (see **Figure 62**), double-click the message you want to read or click it once and then click the Read button.
3. Read the message in the window that appears (see **Figure 63**).

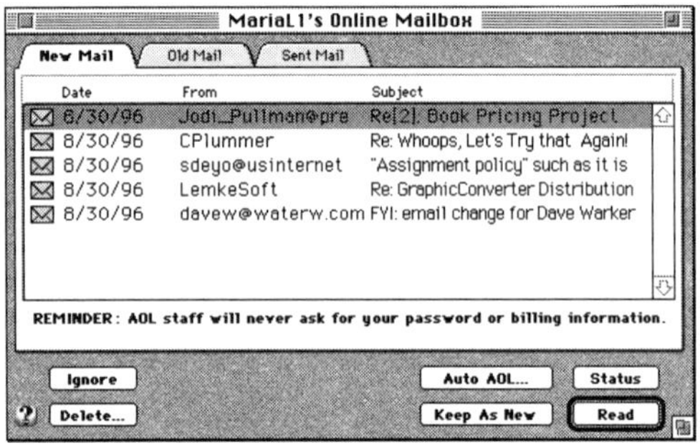


**Figure 62.** *The New Mail tab of the Online Mailbox window lists all your unread mail.*

### ✔ Tips

- If you select an unread message in the New Mail tab of the Online Mailbox window (see **Figure 62**) and click the Ignore button, it's marked as read.
- To delete a message, select it in the New Mail tab of the Online Mailbox window (see **Figure 62**) or open it (see **Figure 63**) and click the Delete button.
- You can click the triangular arrows to the right of the subject field in a message window (see **Figure 63**) or press the ← or → keys on your keyboard to read each of your new messages, one at a time.

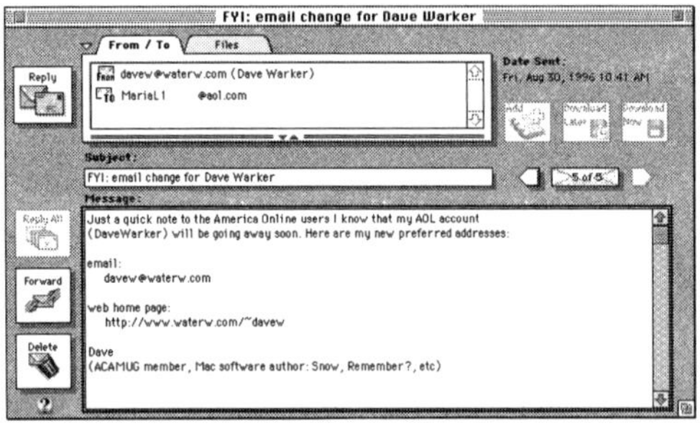


**Figure 63.** *You read incoming e-mail messages in a window like this.*

**Figure 64.** *Click the Download Now button to begin downloading a file attachment.*

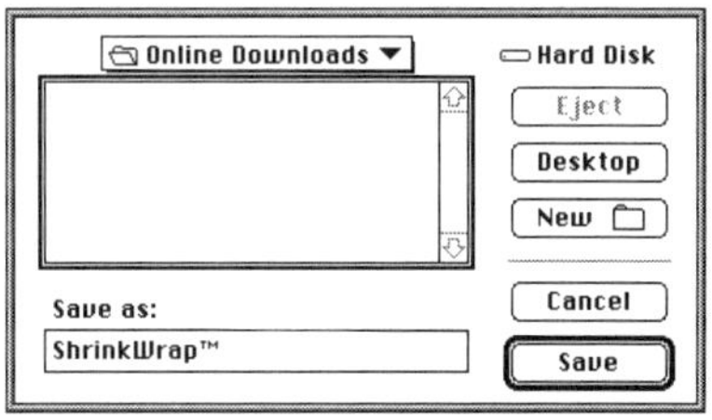


**Figure 65.** *Use a standard Save As dialog box to select a location for the file you are downloading.*

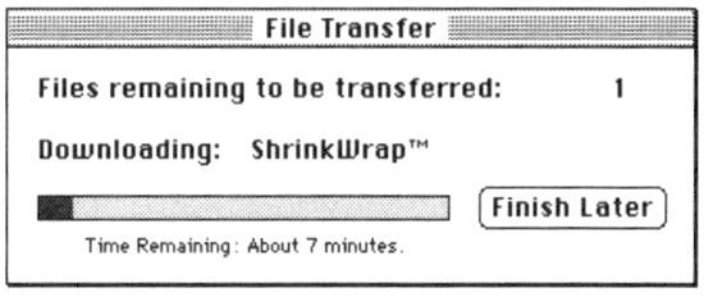


**Figure 66.** *The File Transfer dialog box reports the progress of the download.*

**Figure 67.** *The icons in a message list window indicate whether the message has been read (top), is unread (middle), or includes a file attachment (bottom).*

## To download a file attachment

1. Click the Download Now button (see **Figure 64**) in the message window.
2. In the standard Save As dialog box that appears (see **Figure 65**) specify a name and location for the file and click OK or press Enter.
3. A File Transfer dialog box appears to indicate the progress of the download (see **Figure 66**).
4. When the download is complete, a small dialog box tells you. Click OK or press Enter to dismiss it.

## ✔ Tips

- You can tell the difference between a message with a file attachment and one without a file attachment by its icon in a message list window (see **Figure 67**). A message with a file attachment includes a tiny floppy disk in its icon while a file without an attachment does not.
- If you prefer, you can click the Download Later button to download the file as part of a FlashSession. Consult **Chapter 10** for more information about FlashSessions.
- Consult **Chapter 6** for details about uploading and downloading files.

## To reply to an e-mail message

1. To reply to the individual who sent you the message, click the Reply button (see **Figure 68a**) in the message window or press Enter.

   *or*

   To reply to the sender and everyone who received a copy of the message (except blind CCs), click the Reply All button (see **Figure 68b**) in the message window.
2. A special Compose Mail window appears with the address(es) and subject already filled in (see **Figure 69**). Enter the text of your reply in the Message field of the window.
3. Click the Send or Send Later button as instructed earlier in this chapter to send the reply.

**Figures 68a & 68b.** *Click the Reply or Reply All button to reply to an e-mail message.*

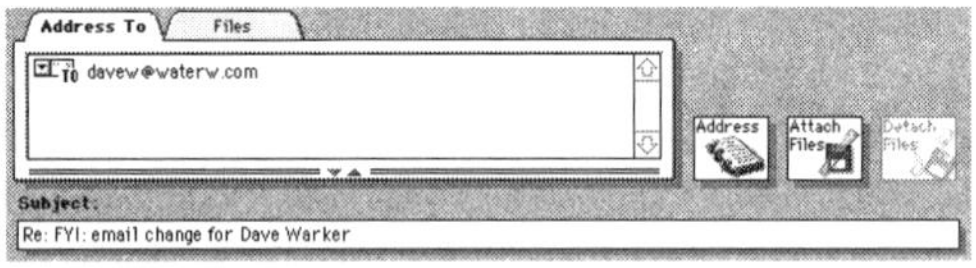


**Figure 69.** *When you click the Reply or Reply All button in a message window, AOL opens a Compose Mail window with the Address To and Subject fields already filled in.*

## To include quoted text in a reply

1. In the original message, select the text you want to quote (see **Figure 70**).
2. Click the Reply or Reply All button as instructed above.
3. A special Compose Mail window appears with the address(es) and subject already filled in. The text you selected is pasted into the reply's body field, along with a reference to the time and date the original message was written (see **Figure 71**).
4. Enter the text of your reply after the quote.
5. Click the Send or Send Later button as instructed earlier in this chapter to send the reply.

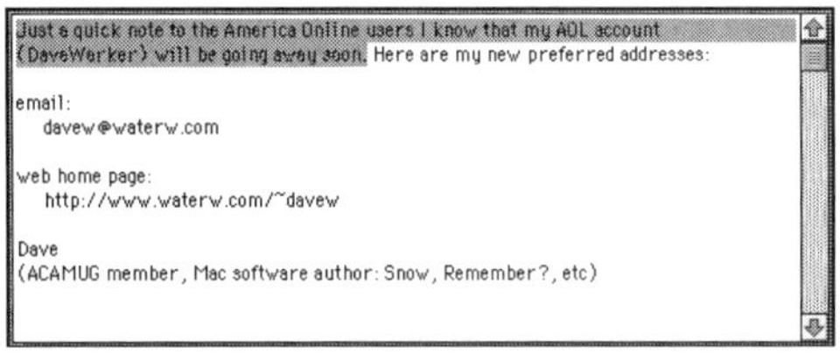


**Figure 70.** *To quote message text in a reply, begin by selecting it.*

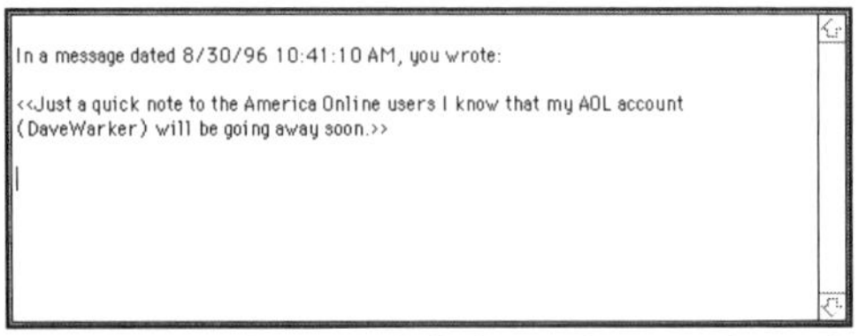


**Figure 71.** *When you click the Reply or Reply to All button, the selected text is pasted into the message body as a quote.*

**Figure 72.** *Click the Forward button to forward the contents of an e-mail message to someone else.*

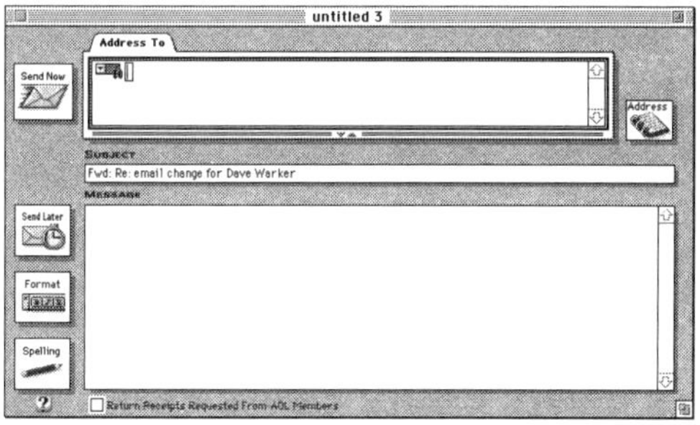


**Figure 73.** *When you click the Forward button, AOL opens a Compose Mail form with the subject already filled in.*

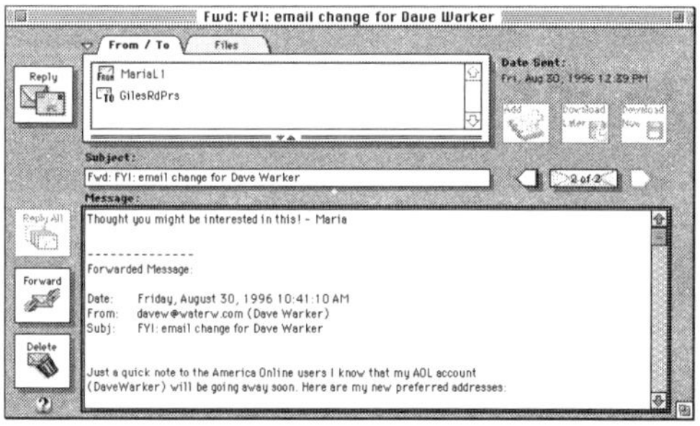


**Figure 74.** *The recipient of a forwarded message sees your comments, followed immediately by the text of the original message.*

## To forward an e-mail message

1. Click the Forward button in the message window (see **Figure 72**).
2. A special Compose Mail window appears with the subject already filled in (see **Figure 73**). Address the message as instructed earlier in this chapter.
3. Enter any text you want to appear before the forwarded message text in the body field of the message.
4. Click the Send or Send Later button as instructed earlier in this chapter to forward the message with your comments.

## ✔ Tips

- If you received the message as a Blind CC recipient, a dialog box will ask if you are certain you wish to forward it when you click the Forward button as instructed in step 1 above.
- The recipient of a forwarded message will see the comments you entered in the body field of the message, followed immediately by the text of the forwarded message (see **Figure 74**).
- When you forward a message that has a file attachment, the file attachment is automatically forwarded, too.

## To view a list of read e-mail

1. Choose Read Mail from the Mail menu (see **Figure 53**).

   *or*

   Press ⌘R.
2. Click the Old Mail tab. A list of all the messages you've read appears in the Online Mailbox window (see **Figure 75**).

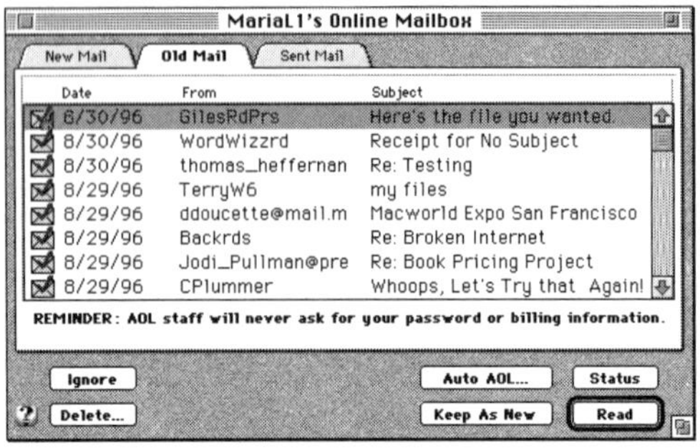


**Figure 75.** *The Old Mail tab of the Online Mailbox window lists all the mail you've read within the past 3 to 5 days.*

### ✔ Tip

- Read mail remains in the Old Mail window for 3 to 5 days from the date it was sent.

## To reread an e-mail message

In the Old Mail tab of the Online Mailbox window (see **Figure 75**), double-click on the message you want to reread or click it once and then click the Read button.

The message appears in a window like the one in **Figure 63**.

## To keep a read e-mail message as a new message

In the Old Mail tab of the Online Mailbox window (see **Figure 75**), click once on the message you want to keep and then click the Keep as New button.

### ✔ Tips

- You can distinguish between a new message and a read message by looking at the icon that appears to the left of the message in a list (see **Figure 67**). A read message's icon has a red check mark over it; an unread message has no check mark.
- When you keep a message as a new message, it is stored in your mailbox for up to 35 days from the date it was sent.

**Figure 76.** *Choose Save As from the File menu.*

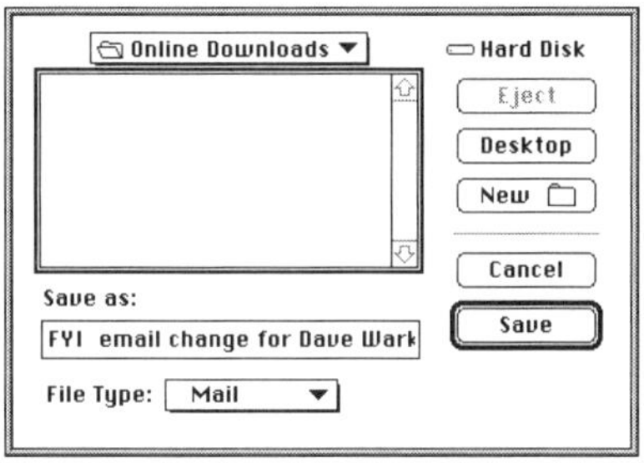


**Figure 77.** *Use a standard Save As dialog box to save the message.*

**Figure 78.** *To save an e-mail message as plain text, be sure to choose Text Only from the Mail pop-up menu.*

# About Saving & Printing E-Mail Messages

You can save or print the e-mail messages you send or receive on AOL. This makes it easy to keep copies of important electronic communication.

## To save an e-mail message

1. Open the message you want to save.
2. Choose Save As from the File menu (see **Figure 76**).
3. In the standard Save As dialog box that appears (see **Figure 77**), specify a name and location for the file.
4. To save the message as plain text, choose Text Only from the File Type pop-up menu (see **Figure 78**).
5. Click Save or press [Enter].

## ✔ Tips

- Once you've saved a message as a text file on disk, you can choose Open from the File menu or press [⌘O] to open it within AOL or any Macintosh application that can open plain text documents.
- You can also save an e-mail message to your Personal Filing Cabinet. The Personal Filing Cabinet feature of AOL is discussed in **Chapter 10**.
- E-mail messages saved as Mail with the Save As dialog box cannot be opened by AOL software versions prior to 3.0.

## To print an e-mail message

1. Open the message you want to print.
2. Choose Print from the File menu (see **Figure 79**).

   *or*

   Press ⌘P.

   *or*

   Click the Print button on the toolbar. 
3. In the Print dialog box that appears (see **Figure 80**), specify print options and click OK or press Enter.
4. While the document is being spooled to the printer, a small dialog box appears to indicate status. When it disappears, you can continue working with AOL.

**Figure 79.** *Choose Print from the File menu to print the contents of an open e-mail message.*

## ✔ Tips

- The appearance of the Print dialog box will vary depending on the printer you have selected in the Chooser. Consult the documentation that came with your Macintosh for more information about using the Chooser.
- A printed message includes the message header (Subj, Date, From, and To fields), followed by the message contents. A footer at the bottom of the page includes the print date, screen name, and page number.

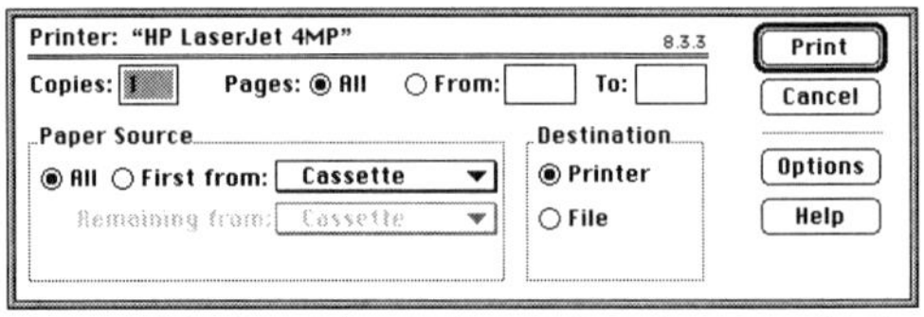


**Figure 80.** *Specify printing options in a standard Print dialog box.*

# USING MESSAGE BOARDS 5

## About Message Boards

AOL's message boards feature offers a way to exchange information and ideas with other AOL members who share your interests in specific topics.

Most AOL areas offer at least one message board. When you open a message board in an area that interests you, you'll find category or topic folders. Each folder can contain messages or folders for subcategories. This keeps the hundreds or thousands of messages in a message board organized so it's easy to find the messages that interest you.

Here are a few things you can do with AOL's message boards feature:

- Browse message boards to find topics and messages that interest you.
- Read messages.
- Locate messages based on the date posted.
- Post new messages.
- Create topic folders.
- Save or print messages.

### ✔ Tips

- AOL has two kinds of message boards. Standard message boards, which you'll find most often on AOL, store messages as separate readable files about specific topics. Threaded message boards, however, store messages and their responses together, so you can follow the "thread" of a message board conversation.
- AOL's message boards are similar in concept to Internet newsgroups. Consult **Chapter 9** for more information about the Internet.

## About Browsing Message Boards

Most of the areas on AOL have at least one message board. You browse message boards the same way you browse AOL areas—by using navigation tools to open areas, message boards, topics, and messages that interest you.

### ✔ Tips

- An area's message boards will include messages that relate somehow to the area's primary topic. For example, a message about changing the oil in a 1996 Ducati motorcycle would probably be found in an automotive or motorcycling area, not an area covering collectible cameras. Posting an off-topic message in a message board is a surefire way to make yourself very unpopular with that message board's regular participants.
- The content of AOL's message areas are protected by AOL's Terms of Service, which prohibits (among other things) the posting of offensive messages. You can read the Terms of Service while online for free by using a keyword of TOS.
- If you are concerned about your children reading messages that are inappropriate for their age group, you can use AOL's Parental Controls feature to limit their access. Consult **Chapter 11** for more information about parental controls.

**Figure 1.** *One way to go to an area's message board(s) is to click its Message Boards button.*

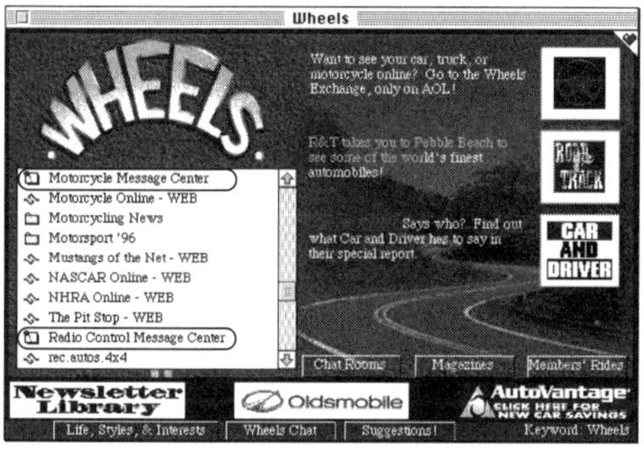


**Figure 2.** *In the Wheels area, many features, including message boards like these two, are included in a scrolling list.*

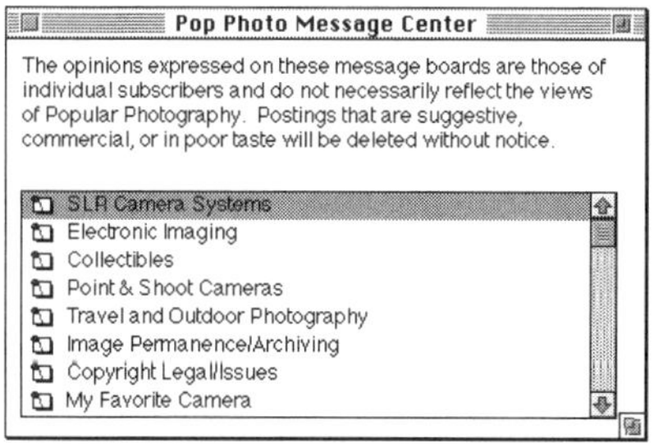


**Figure 3.** *Clicking a Message Boards button like the one in* **Figure 1** *may display a list of message boards within the area.*

## To go to an area's message board(s)

1. Use one of AOL's navigation tools to go to an area that interests you.
2. Click the area's Message Boards button (see **Figure 1**).

   *or*

   Double-click a list item displaying a message board icon before it (see **Figure 2**).

## ✔ Tips

- Not all areas include Message Board buttons on their main screens. Sometimes, you'll have to go deeper within an area to locate its message boards.
- Sometimes, when you click an area's Message Board button, a window with a list of message boards will appear (see **Figure 3**). To open a specific message board in the list, double-click it. A window like the one in **Figure 4** or **5** will appear.

## To browse a message board

1. If a message board window like the one in **Figure 4** appears, click the List Topics button. If a message board window like the one in **Figure 5** appears, skip to the next step.
2. In the topics window (see **Figure 5**), use the scroll bar to scroll through the list of topical folders.
3. To view a list of all the messages in a folder (see **Figures 6a** and **6b**), click the folder once to select it and click the List Messages button. You can then click the subject of the message you want to read to select it and click the Read Message button to open a message window containing the message (see **Figure 7a** or **7b**).

   *or*

   To read the first message in a folder, click the folder once in the topics window (see **Figure 5**) to select it and then click the Read 1st Message button to open a message window containing the message (see **Figure 7a** or **7b**).

### ✔ Tips

- To open any list item, you can simply double-click it.
- A short description of the message board appears near the top of the main message board window (see **Figure 4**) and list of topical folders (see **Figure 5**).
- A short description of a folder's topic appears near the top of the window containing that topic's messages (see **Figure 6**).
- In some instances, there will be two levels of folders before reaching messages: category folders and topic folders. Buttons within list windows will be labeled based on the type of folder.

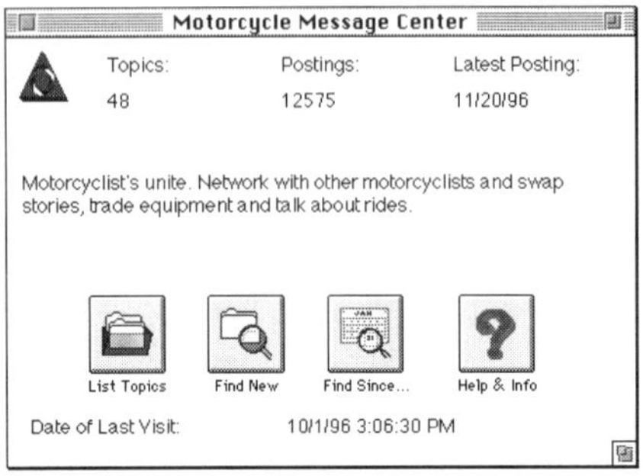


**Figure 4.** *A typical message board window displays the number of topics and messages, and the date of the last message posted.*

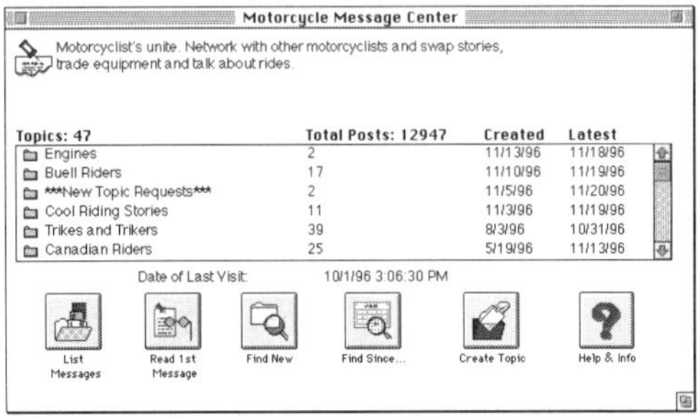


**Figure 5.** *Clicking the List Topics button in a message board window displays a list of topical folders in a window like this.*

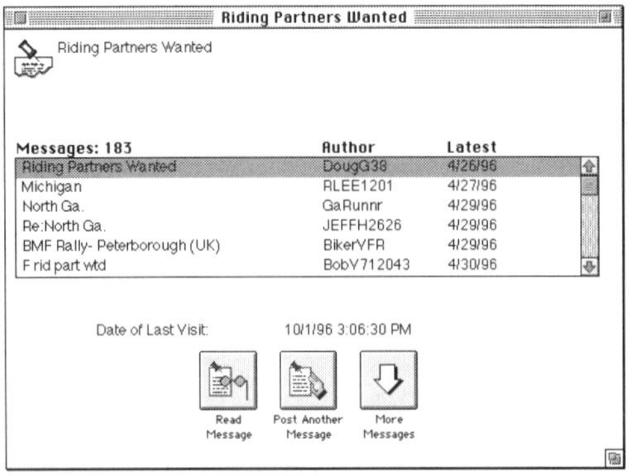


**Figure 6a.** *When you open a topic folder, a list of messages inside it appears. Here's an example of a standard message board's message list…*

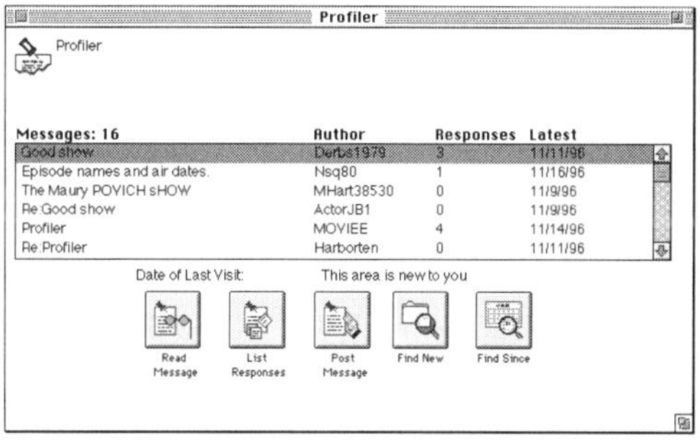


**Figure 6b.** *...and here's an example of a threaded message board's message list. Notice that the number of message responses is noted for each message.*

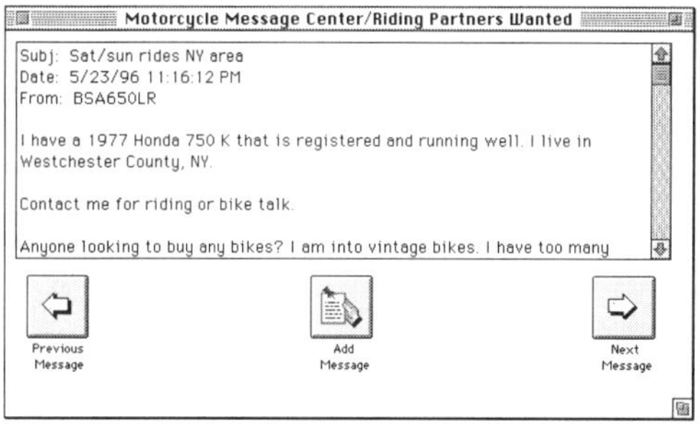


**Figure 7a.** *When you open a message, it appears in a window that contains the subject, date and time it was sent, and sender's screen name.*

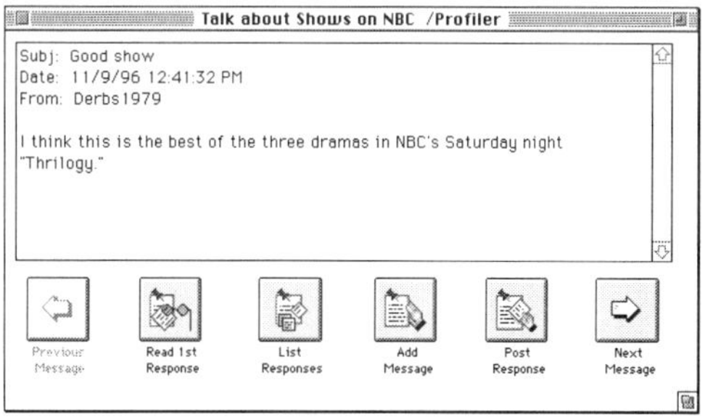


**Figure 7b.** *A threaded message board message, like this one, offers additional buttons for reading message responses.*

## To read a message

1. Follow the steps on the previous page to open a message window. **Figures 7a** and **7b** show examples.
2. Use the scroll bar to scroll through the entire message.

### ✔ Tip

- To read messages while you are not connected to AOL, use AOL's log feature to capture the text of each message you open. Consult **Chapter 10** for information about working offline.

## To read the next or previous message in a folder

To read the previous message in the folder, click the Previous Message button in a message window (see **Figures 7a** and **7b**) or press ←.

*or*

To read the next message in the folder, click the Next Message button in a message window (see **Figure 7a** and **7b**) or press →.

### ✔ Tip

- The Previous Message or Next Message button won't work if you're reading the first or last message in a folder.

## To read a response to a threaded message

To read the first response to a message, click the Read 1st Response button in a message window (see **Figure 7b**).

*or*

To display a list of responses to a message, click the List Responses button (see **Figure 7b**). You can then double-click a specific response in the list window that appears to read it.

## About Finding New & Recent Messages

AOL's software keeps track of your visits to areas and their message boards. You can see the date of your last visit in a message board's window:

- The first time you enter a message board, the message "This area is new to you" appears (see **Figure 8**).
- On subsequent visits to a message board, the date and time of your last visit appear in the window (see **Figures 4**, **5**, **6a**, and **6b**).

You can use one of two Find buttons to narrow down the display of topics or messages based on the date of your last visit or the number of days since a message was posted.

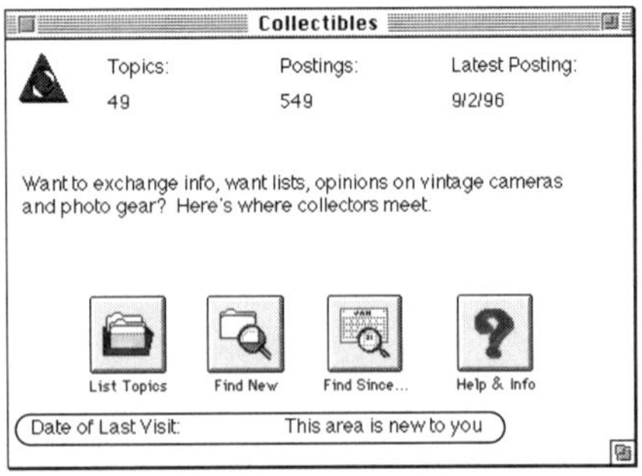


**Figure 8.** *AOL keeps track of your visits to a message board.*

### ✔ Tips

- Messages you've read when connected with one screen name will appear as new messages when connected with another screen name. Screen names are discussed in **Chapter 10**.
- To search an entire message board for recently posted messages, use the Find New or Find Since buttons in the main message board window (see **Figures 4** and **8**).
- To limit your search for recently posted messages to a single folder, click that folder in the list of folders (see **Figure 5**) to select it. Then use the Find New or Find Since button in that window to perform the search.
- When you use one of the Find buttons to find recently posted messages, AOL will display a window full of messages (see **Figure 9**) or topic folders (see **Figure 12**). If it displays folders, click the Show All button to display the messages inside all the folders in one list box.

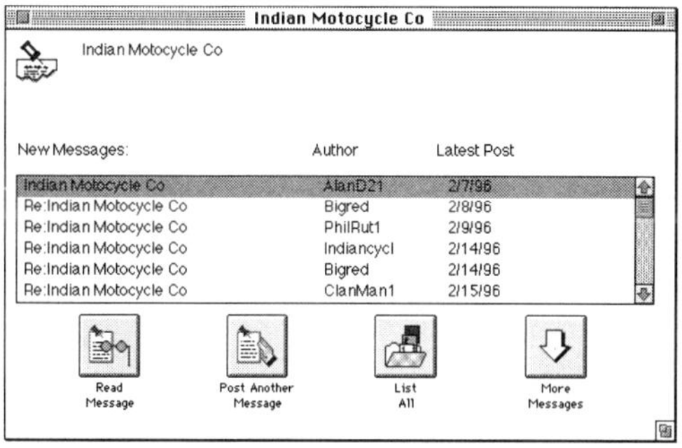


**Figure 9.** *Here's the result of a search for new messages in a specific folder.*

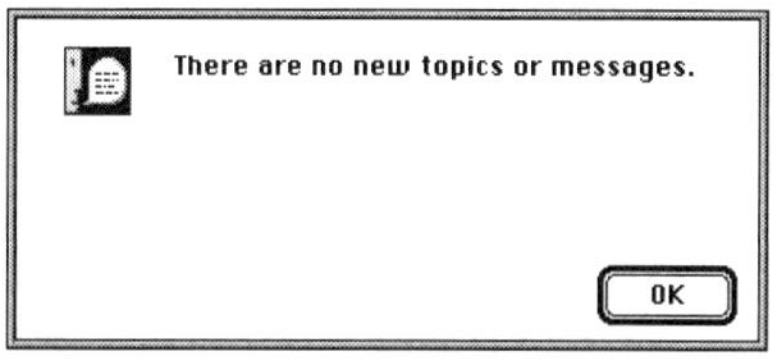


**Figure 10.** *If there are no new messages, AOL displays a dialog box like this.*

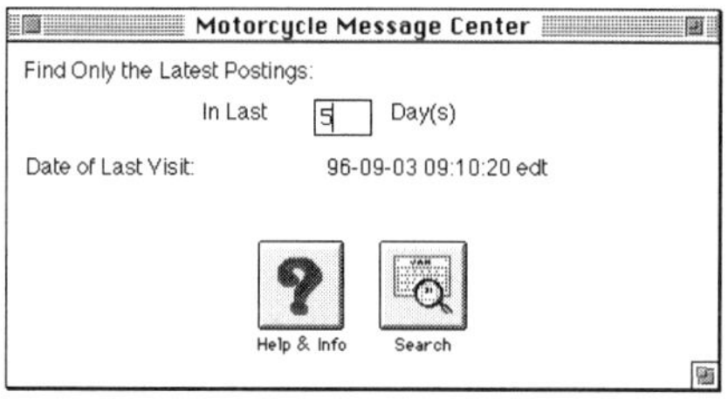


**Figure 11.** *Enter the age of the oldest message you want to see.*

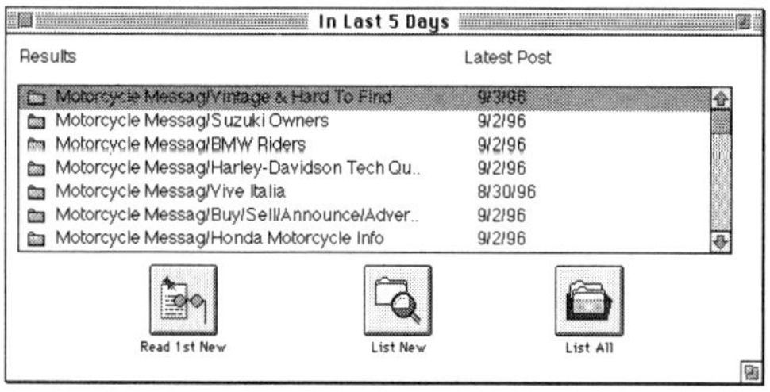


**Figure 12.** *Here's the result of a search for messages no more than 5 days old.*

## To find new messages

1. In the message board's main window (see **Figures 4** and **8**) or list of topic folders window (see **Figure 5**), click the Find New button.
2. If new messages have been posted since your last visit, a window containing a list of folders or messages (see **Figure 9**) appears. Browse and read them as discussed earlier in this chapter.

   *or*

   If no new messages have been posted since your last visit, a dialog box like the one in **Figure 10** appears. Click OK or press [Enter] to dismiss it.

## To find recent messages

1. In the message board's main window (see **Figures 4** and **8**) or list of topic folders window (see **Figure 5**), click the Find Since button.
2. In the dialog box that appears (see **Figure 11**), enter the age, in days, of the oldest message you want to see.
3. Click Search.
4. If new messages have been posted within the number of days you specified, a window containing a list of folders (see **Figure 12**) or messages appears. Browse and read them as discussed earlier in this chapter.

   *or*

   If no new messages have been posted since your last visit, a dialog box like the one in **Figure 10** appears. Click OK or press [Enter] to dismiss it.

## About Adding Messages

Reading messages is only half the message board story. You can also add your own messages to a message board topic folder or reply to messages in a threaded message board. The messages you add can be read by any other AOL member.

### ✔ Tips

- Adding messages to a message board is a great way to answer questions, ask others with similar interests for information, and make new friends online.
- Before adding a message to an AOL message board, be sure that you're familiar with AOL's Terms of Service, which warns against posting messages that could be offensive to some AOL members. You can read the Terms of Service while online for free by using a keyword of TOS.
- When adding messages to a message board, make sure your message is in line with the folder's topic. Adding an off-topic message is a surefire way to annoy regular message board participants. It will also make it difficult for people who would be interested in your message to find it.
- Many of AOL's message boards allow AOL members to create their own topic folders. If a message board doesn't already include a folder that's right for your message, you may be able to create a new one to put your message in.
- If the message list window is open when you post your message, the message will not immediately appear in the list. To see your message listed, close the message list window and then reopen it. The message will appear at the bottom of the list.
- You cannot delete or unsend messages you post to message boards.

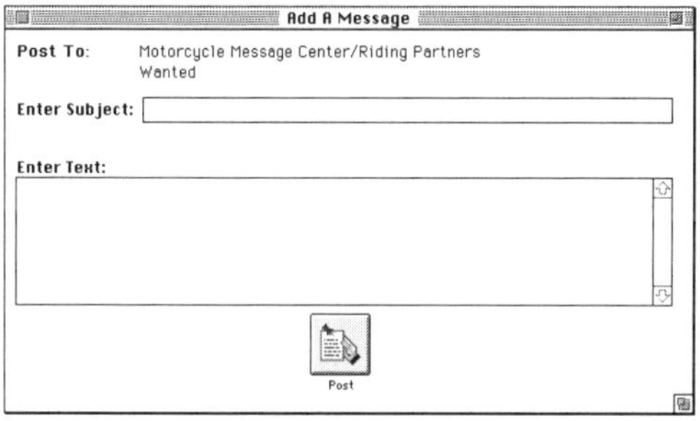


**Figure 13.** *Use the Add A Message window to compose your message.*

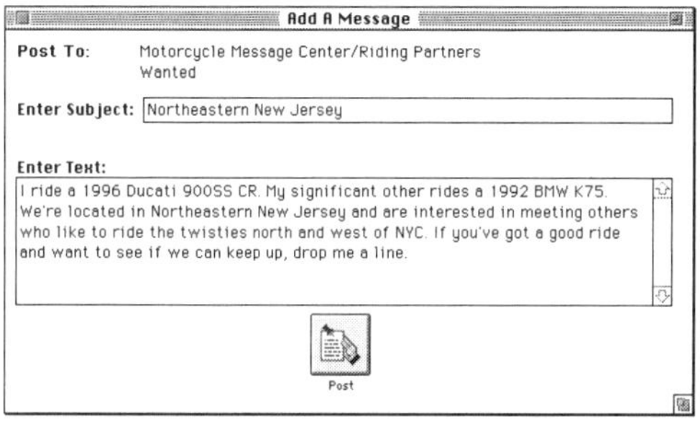


**Figure 14.** *Here's an example of a completed message.*

**Figure 15.** *A dialog box like this appears when your message has been added.*

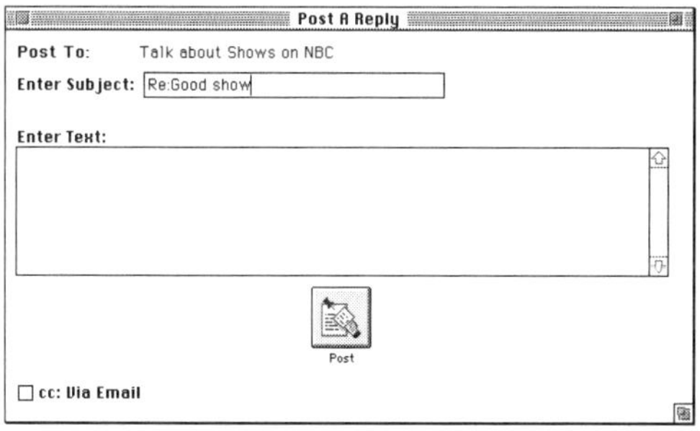


**Figure 16.** *Use the Post A Reply window to compose a reply to a message in a threaded message board.*

## To add a message

1. In the list of messages window, click the Post Another Message button (see **Figure 6a**) or the Post Message button (see **Figure 6b**).

   *or*

   Click the Add Message button in a message window (see **Figure 7a** and **7b**).
2. In the Add A Message window that appears (see **Figure 13**), enter the subject and text of your message in the appropriate boxes (see **Figure 14**).
3. Click the Post button.
4. A dialog box like the one in **Figure 15** appears, telling you that your message has been successfully sent. Click OK or press Enter to dismiss it.

## To reply to a message in a threaded message board

1. Click the Post Response button in the message window (see **Figure 7b**).
2. In the Post A Reply window that appears (see **Figure 16**), edit the subject (if desired) and enter the text of your reply in the appropriate boxes.
3. To send a copy of the reply as an e-mail message to the person who wrote the message to which you are replying, turn on the cc: Via Email check box.
4. Click the Post button.
5. A dialog box like the one in **Figure 15** appears, telling you that your message has been successfully sent. Click OK or press Enter to dismiss it.

## To add a folder

1. In the message topic list window (see **Figure 5**), click the Create Topic button.
2. In the Create folder window that appears, enter a title and description for the topic in the appropriate edit boxes (see **Figure 17**).
3. Click the Create button.
4. In the dialog box that appears (see **Figure 18**), click the Add Message button.
5. An Add A Message form appears. Follow steps 2 through 4 on the previous page to compose and add your message.

### ✔ Tips

- New folders do not immediately appear in the topic list. To see your folder, close the topic list window and reopen it. Your folder will appear at the bottom of the list (see **Figure 19**).
- Message boards can accept a limited number of topics. If the message board already has all the topics it can handle, you'll see a dialog box like the one in **Figure 20** if you try to add another.
- Not all message boards allow regular AOL members to create topic folders. If you try to create a folder and don't have the necessary privileges to do so, a dialog box like the one in **Figure 21** will appear.

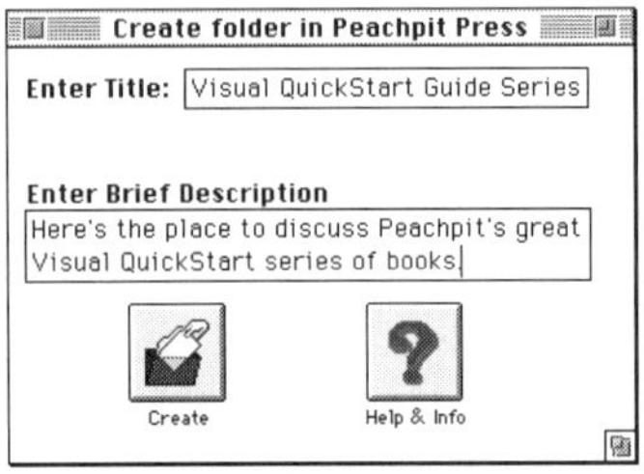


**Figure 17.** *Use the Create folder window to add a topic or category folder to a message board.*

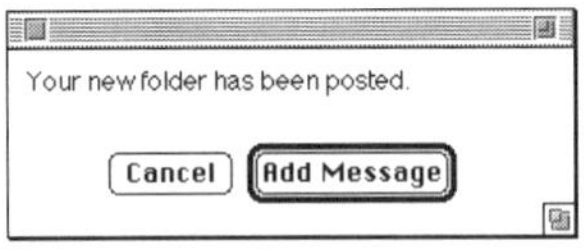


**Figure 18.** *AOL confirms that your folder has been created.*

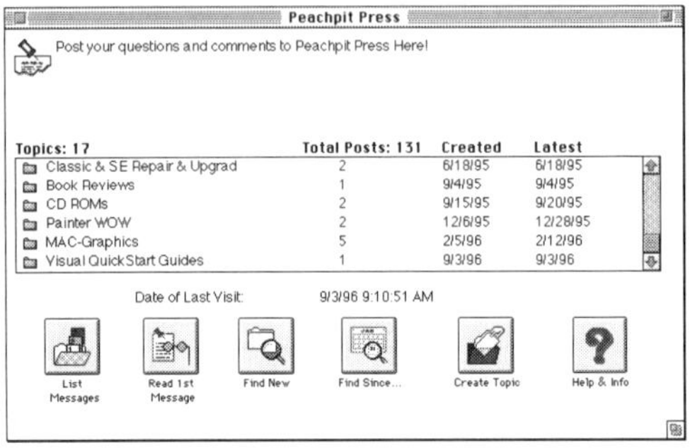


**Figure 19.** *The topic folder you create appears at the bottom of the topic list when you reopen the window.*

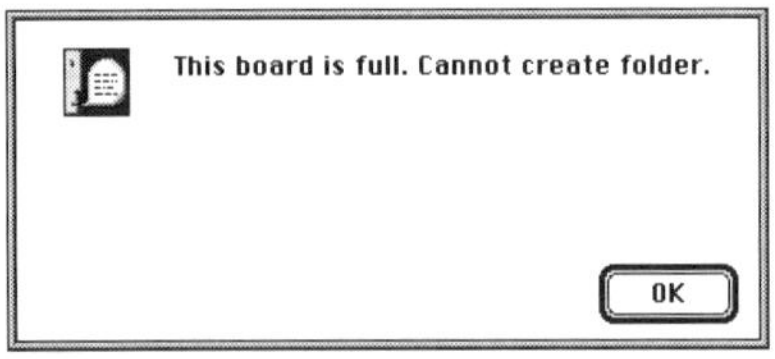


**Figure 20.** *A dialog box like this appears when a board already has all the topics allowed.*

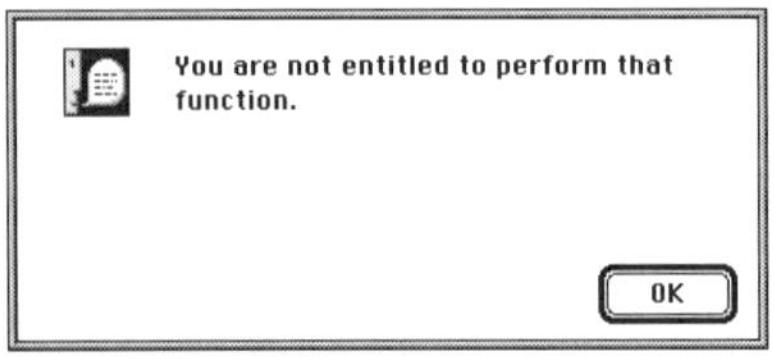


**Figure 21.** *When you're not allowed to add a topic, AOL tells you.*

**Figure 22.** *To save a message, choose Save from the File menu.*

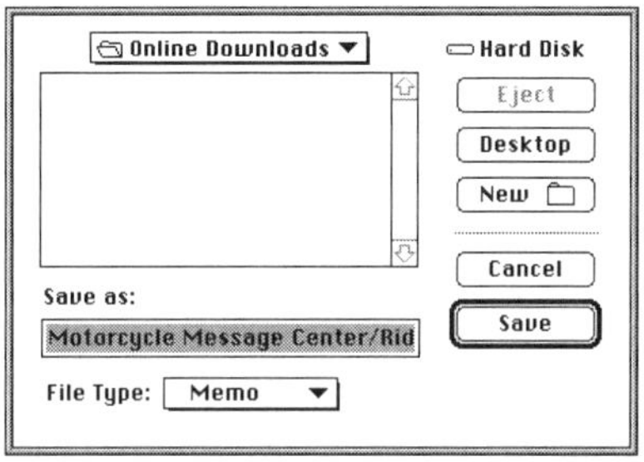


**Figure 23.** *Use the Save As dialog box to save a copy of the message.*

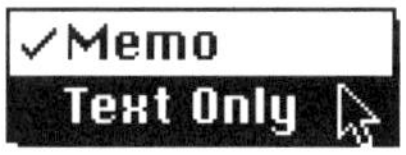


**Figure 24.** *To save the message as plain text, be sure to choose Text Only from the File Type pop-up menu.*

# About Saving & Printing Messages

You can save or print the message board messages you read or add on AOL. This makes it easy to keep copies of messages you find particularly interesting or useful.

## To save a message

1. Open the message you want to save.
2. Choose Save from the File menu (see **Figure 22**).

   *or*

   Press [⌘S].
3. In the standard Save As dialog box that appears (see **Figure 23**), specify a name and location for the file.
4. To save the file as a plain text document, choose Text Only from the File Type pop-up menu (see **Figure 24**).
5. Click Save or press [Enter].

## ✔ Tips

- Once you've saved a message as a text file on disk, you can choose Open from the File menu or press [⌘O] to open it within AOL or any other Macintosh program that supports plain text.
- If you prefer, you can use AOL's logging feature to automatically save every message you open. Consult **Chapter 10** for more information about AOL's logging feature and working offline.

## To print a message

1. Open the message you want to print.
2. Choose Print from the File menu (see **Figure 25**).

   *or*

   Press [⌘][P].

   *or*

   Click the Print button on the toolbar.

3. In the Print dialog box that appears (see **Figure 26**), specify print options and click Print or press [Enter].
4. While the document is being spooled to the printer, a small dialog box appears. When it disappears, you can continue working with AOL.

**Figure 25.** *To print a message, choose Print from the File menu.*

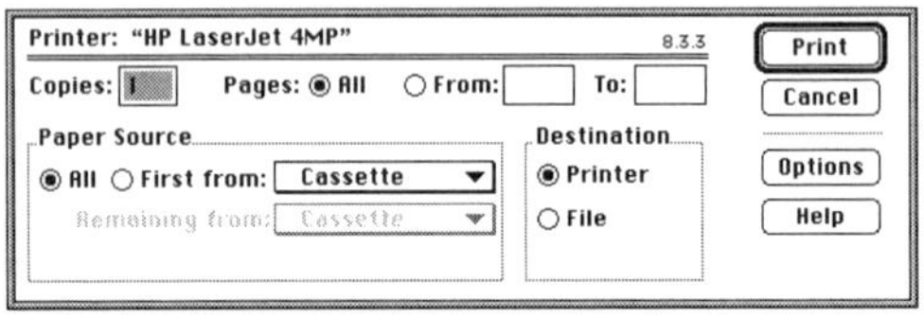


**Figure 26.** *Use a standard Print dialog box to set printing options.*

## ✔ Tips

- The appearance of the Print dialog box will vary depending on the printer you have selected in the Chooser. Consult the documentation that came with your Macintosh for more information about using the Chooser.
- A printed message includes the message header (Subj, Date, and From fields), followed by the message contents. A footer at the bottom of the page includes the date, screen name, and page number.

# EXCHANGING FILES 6

## About AOL's Files

AOL is an excellent source of computer files, including:

- Complete software programs that enable you to perform tasks on your computer.
- Software demos, which offer you an opportunity to try out some or all of the features in a software program.
- Software updates and add-ons, which provide bug fixes and feature enhancements for software you already own.
- Data or document files, like templates and information files, which work with software programs.

AOL's files can be found in a number of places online:

- The Software Center in the Computers & Software channel. This is the "mother lode" of software on AOL, with libraries for a wide range of topics.
- Hardware and software company support area libraries. This is where you'll get the latest updates and add-ons for your favorite commercial software.
- Other area software libraries. Many areas have their own libraries with files pertaining to the area topic. For example, you might find an outlining program in the Writer's Club.
- FTP sites on the Internet. The Internet offers a whole world of files—if you know where to look. FTP and the Internet are discussed in **Chapter 9**.
- File attachments from friends. As discussed in **Chapter 4**, you can attach files to e-mail messages. This is a great way to exchange files with friends.

## About Copyright Issues that Affect Exchanging Files

Generally speaking, all files are divided into two broad categories:

- *Distributable files* are those which can be legally exchanged between users. This includes:
  - *Shareware*, which is sometimes known as *try-before-you-buy software*, is distributed for free but requires compensation for the file's creator.
  - *Freeware*, which is completely free to use.
  - *Public domain software*, which is completely free to use, change, and redistribute in another form.
- *Commercial files* are those which *cannot* be legally exchanged between users. This includes most software you'd find in your local computer store.

All software, with the exception of public domain software, is copyrighted by its creator or owner.

### ✔ Tips

- Don't confuse *copyright* with *commercial*. Copyright refers to the rights of the creator/owner and user. Commercial refers to a distribution method which requires users to pay for the software before acquiring and using it.
- Distribution terms are normally spelled out in a document accompanying the software. Read this document carefully to understand whether the software can be shared and, in the case of shareware, whether you owe the program's author anything for using his product.
- If you're not sure whether a software product can be shared with others, *don't* share it. Exchanging commercial software is illegal.

## About Exchanging Files

When you exchange files with AOL, you do one of two things:

- When you *upload* a file, you send a copy of it from your computer to AOL's server.
- When you *download* a file, you retrieve a copy of it from AOL's server to your computer.

The AOL software makes uploading and downloading very easy to do. Just click a button, then specify which file should be uploaded or where you want to put the file that will be downloaded.

### ✔ Tips

- When you attach a file to an e-mail message you send, you are uploading the file. When you save a file that was attached to an e-mail message you received, you are downloading the file.
- The words upload and download are often abbreviated u/l and d/l.

## About File Compression

The larger a file is, the more time it takes to transfer from one computer to another. For this reason, AOL encourages the use of *file compression* software. This software encodes the file in a way that reduces the file's size. The file can then be transferred more quickly, saving both the uploader and downloader time and money.

### ✔ Tips

- The most commonly used compression schemes for Macintosh are StuffIt (.sit) and Compact Pro (.cpt). The AOL software will automatically decompress files compressed with either of these compression schemes.
- AOL can use StuffIt file compression to compress the files you upload.

## About File Libraries

The vast majority of AOL's files can be found in its file libraries. File libraries are normally organized by topic, making it easy to browse for files that interest you.

## To browse the Software Center's Mac Software Libraries

1. If necessary, activate the Channels window by choosing Channels from the Go To menu or clicking the Channels button on the toolbar.

2. In the Channels window, click the Computers & Software button (see **Figure 1**).
3. In the Computers & Software window (see **Figure 2**), click The Software Center button.
4. In the Macintosh Software Center window (see **Figure 3**), double-click the Browse the Software Libraries item in the scrolling list.
5. In the Browse the Software Libraries window (see **Figure 4**) double-click the name of the library you want to browse.
6. In the forum library window that appears (see **Figure 5**), double-click the topic that interests you.
7. In the file list window (see **Figure 6**), click the name of a file that interests you to select it and then click the View Description button or just double-click the name of the file.
8. Read the file's description in the file description window (see **Figure 7**).

**Figure 1.** *Click this…*

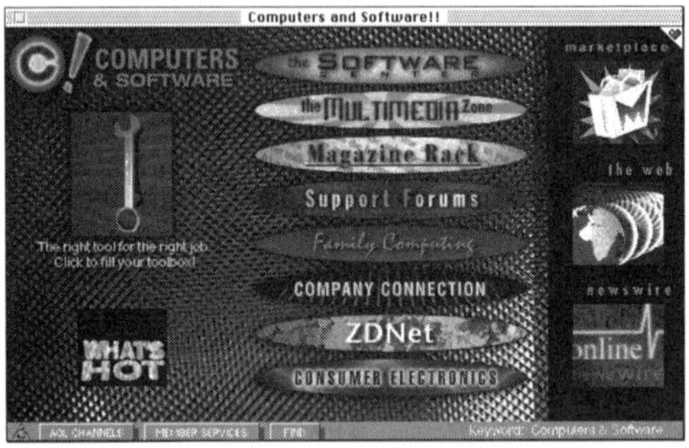


**Figure 2.** *…to go to the Computers & Software channel.*

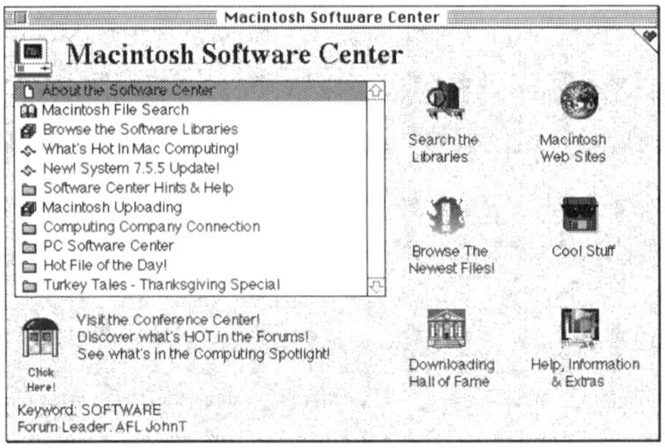


**Figure 3.** *The Software Center offers access to a variety of areas that contain software.*

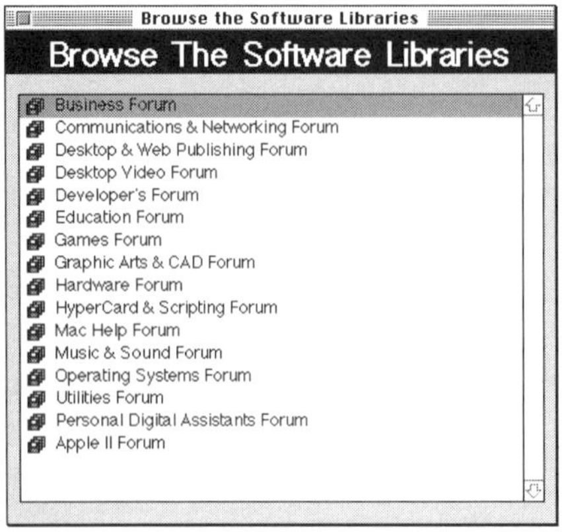


**Figure 4.** *Within the Browse the Software Libraries window are folders for separate libraries full of files.*

**Figure 5.** *The Business Forum (MBS) libraries window lists all the topics within the library.*

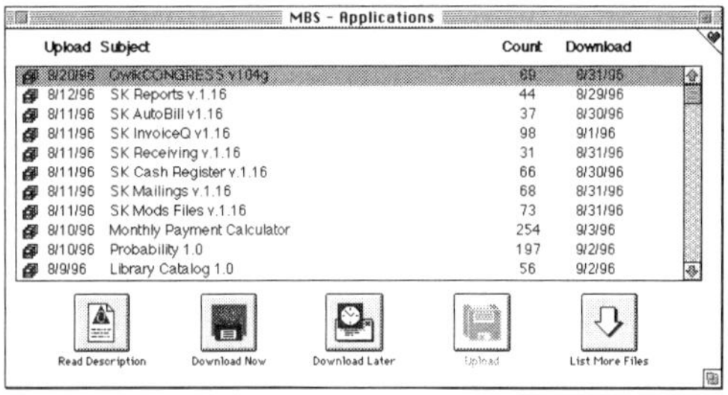


**Figure 6.** *The MBS Applications window lists business application files available for download.*

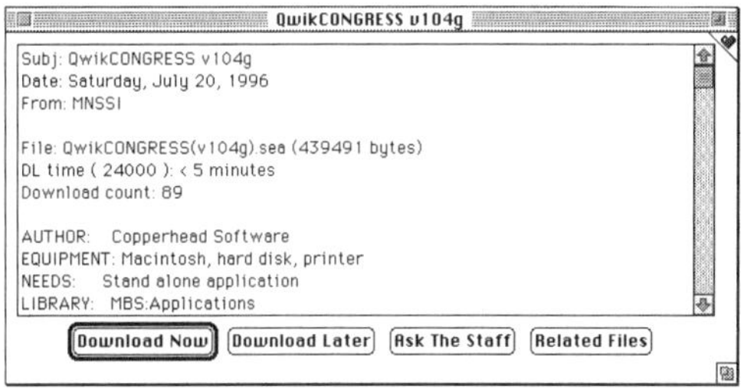


**Figure 7.** *A file's description window explains what the file is and what you need to use it.*

## ✔ Tips

- A quicker way to get to the Macintosh Software Center is to use the keyword SOFTWARE CENTER.
- AOL uses standard icons in its library window scrolling lists. These icons are illustrated and described in **Chapter 2**.
- In many instances, you'll have to open several library folders or disk icons to reach a file list. You'll know when you've reached a file list because the list usually includes an upload date, file name, download count, and last date downloaded (see **Figure 6**).
- You can download a file from a file list window (see **Figures 6** and **12**) or a file description window (see **Figure 7**). Downloading files is discussed later in this chapter.

## To browse other areas' libraries

1. Using any combination of menus, buttons, or keywords, navigate to an area that interests you. **Figures 8**, **9**, and **10** show three examples.
2. Locate and click the Libraries button (see **Figures 8**, **9**, and **10**) or list item within the area.
3. Double-click on list items in subsequent windows to zero in on the topics and files that interest you.

### ✔ Tips

- For more information about navigating throughout AOL, consult **Chapter 3**.
- As shown in **Figures 8**, **9**, and **10**, the name of the button or list item that takes you to an area's library varies by area. Look for the word *library*, *download*, *software*, or *file* in a button or item name when searching for an area's file libraries.
- For examples of library, file list, and file description windows, consult **Figures 4** through **7** on the previous two pages.

**Figure 8.** *The Mac Business and Home Office Forum offers another way to access the MBS Software Library.*

**Figure 9.** *The Writers Club includes file libraries of interest to writers.*

**Figure 10.** *The Dreyfus Online Investment Center offers files of interest to investors.*

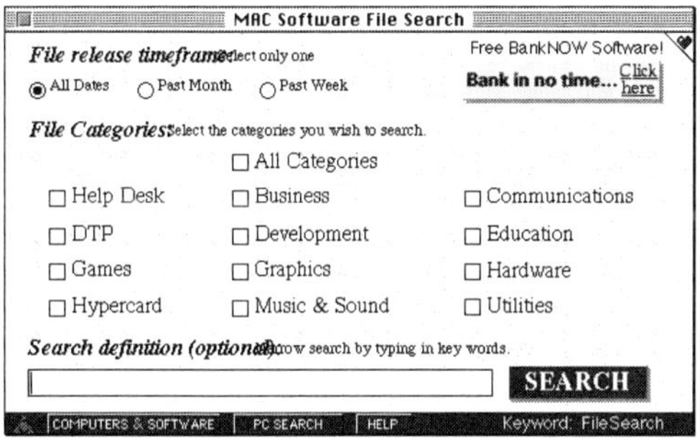


**Figure 11.** *Use the MAC Software File Search window to enter search criteria.*

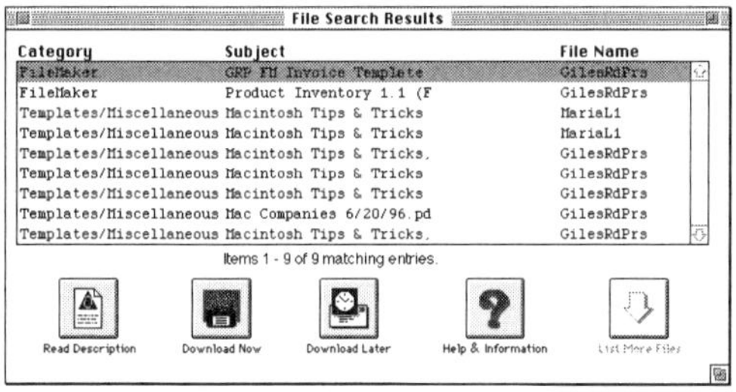


**Figure 12.** *Here's an example of the results of a search. The criteria entered in the MAC Software File Search window were* All Dates, Business *(for Category), and* Giles FileMaker *(for keywords).*

**Figure 13.** *When AOL can't find files that match your criteria, it displays a dialog box like this.*

## About File Searches

AOL's Software Search feature offers a quick and easy way to search the Macintosh Software Center or other areas for files. You enter a search word or phrase, narrow down the search by selecting categories and/or date ranges, and tell AOL to start looking. When it's finished, it displays a list of the files it found that match the criteria you specified. You can then browse through the list to get more information about files.

## To search the Macintosh Software Center for files

1. Click the File Search button on the toolbar or use the keyword FILESEARCH to display the Macintosh Software File Search window (see **Figure 11**).
2. Select a time period radio button at the top of the window.
3. Select one or more category check boxes in the middle of the window.
4. Enter a search word or phrase in the text box near the bottom of the window.
5. Click the List Matching Files button or press [Enter].
6. In the list window that displays the results of your search (see **Figure 12**), double-click an item to display a description window for it.

## ✔ Tips

- If AOL can't find files that match the criteria you entered, it displays a dialog box like the one in **Figure 13**. Click OK or press [Enter] to dismiss it.
- Not all files can be found by using the use of the MAC Software File search window (see **Figure 11**). To find files in a specific vendor or topical area, you must search that specific area.

## To search a specific area for files

1. Using any combination of menus, buttons, or keywords, navigate to a file library that includes access to the Software Search feature. **Figures 5** and **14** show examples.
2. Click the Software Search button or double-click a Software Search list item to display a search window like the one in **Figure 15** or **16**.
3. Follow steps 2 through 6 on the previous page to search for files within that area.

## ✔ Tips

- The name of the Software Search button or list item varies by area. Look for the word *search* in a button or list item name when trying to access a library's Software Search feature.
- Not all areas that have file libraries offer access to the Software Search feature. Generally speaking, this feature is only accessible from within the larger file libraries on AOL.

## To search the PC Software Center for files

1. Use the keyword PC Software.
2. In the PC Software Center Main Screen window that appears, double-click the PC Software Libraries list item.
3. In the PC Software Libraries window that appears, double-click the File Search list item.
4. Follow steps 2 through 6 on the previous page to search for and open descriptions for the files you want to find.

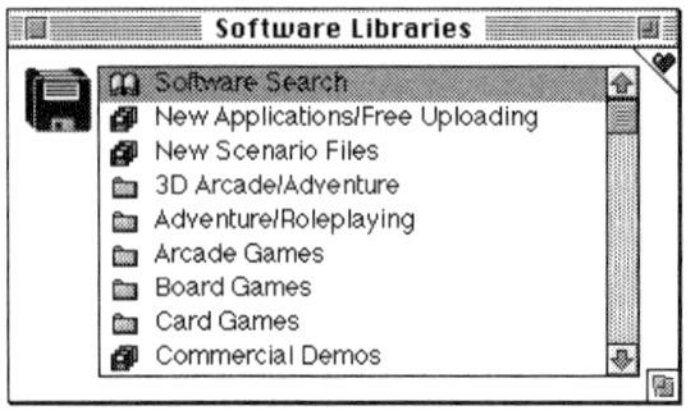


**Figure 14.** *The Games Software Libraries can be searched.*

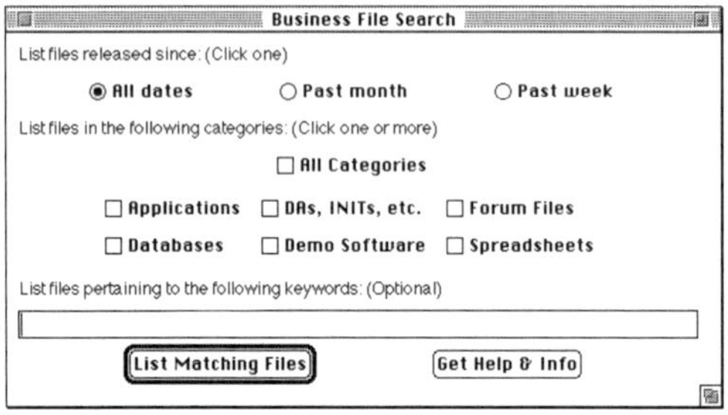


**Figure 15.** *Here's the search window for the Business (MBS) Software Library…*

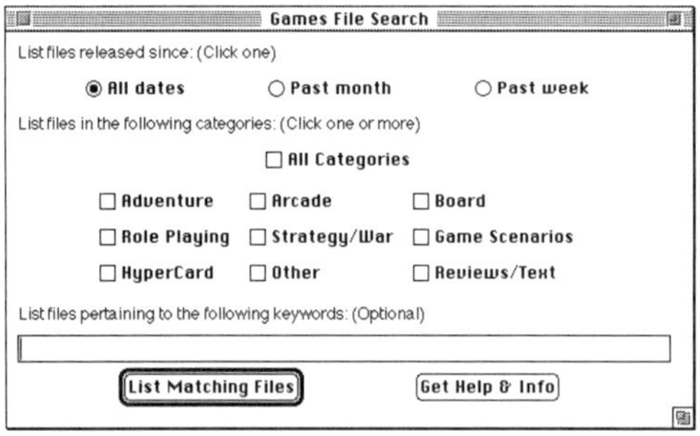


**Figure 16.** *…and here's the search window for the Games Software Library. As you can see, they're very similar.*

## About File Descriptions

A file's description window (see **Figure 7**) contains important information about a file, including:

- System requirements. Some program files have minimum RAM, hard disk, processor, or software requirements. If your system doesn't meet one or more of the requirements, the file won't work on your computer.
- Compatibility issues. Some programs conflict with others. If you use a conflicting program and aren't willing to give it up, the file won't work reliably on your computer.
- Changes since a previous version. Software updates are often for minor bug fixes that don't apply to you. You can save time by downloading only the updates that you really need.
- Shareware fees. If the program is beyond your budget, don't downloa it.
- Other information. This includes the creator's name, uploader's screen name, upload date, download count, technical support options, and a complete description of what the file does.

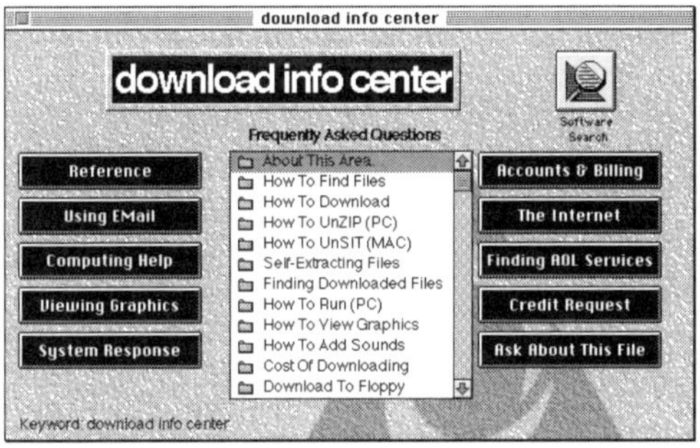


**Figure 17.** *The download info center window offers a wealth of information about downloading.*

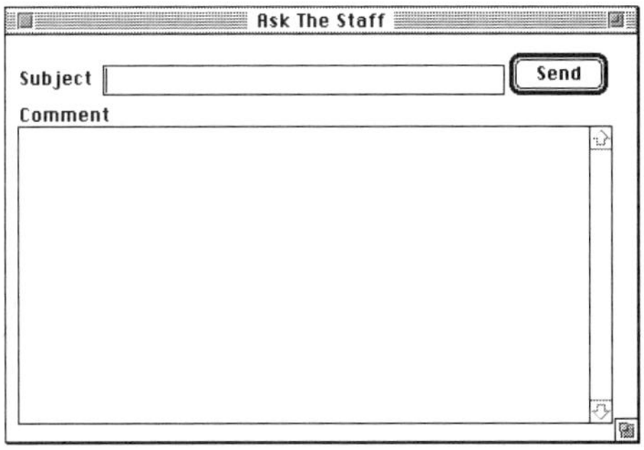


**Figure 18.** *Use the Ask The Staff window to compose and send a message about a file.*

## ✔ Tips

- To avoid wasting time and being disappointed, read the description for a file thoroughly before downloading the file.
- If you have questions or comments about a file, click the Ask The Staff button in the file's description window (see **Figure 7**) to open the download info center window (see **Figure 17**). Then click the Ask About This File button to display a message form like the one in **Figure 18**. Enter a subject and question or comment and click the Send button or press Enter to send your message to the AOL staff.

## About Downloading Files

When you find a file you like, you can download a copy of it to your computer so you can use it. You can download a file from one of two places:

- A file list window.
- A file description window.

## To download a file immediately

1. In a file list window, click the name of the file you want to download to select it and then click the Download Now button (see **Figures 6** and **12**).

   *or*

   In the file description window for the file you want to download, click the Download Now button (see **Figure 7**).
2. In the standard Save As dialog box that appears (see **Figure 19**), specify a file name and disk location for the file you want to download.
3. Click Save or press Enter.
4. A File Transfer window appears (see **Figure 20**) to show the progress of the download. You can wait until the file has been fully downloaded or continue working with AOL.

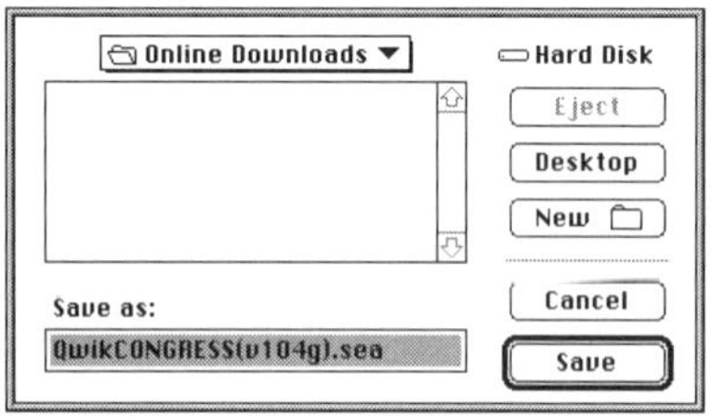


**Figure 19.** *Use a standard Save As dialog box to specify a name and a disk location for the file you want to download.*

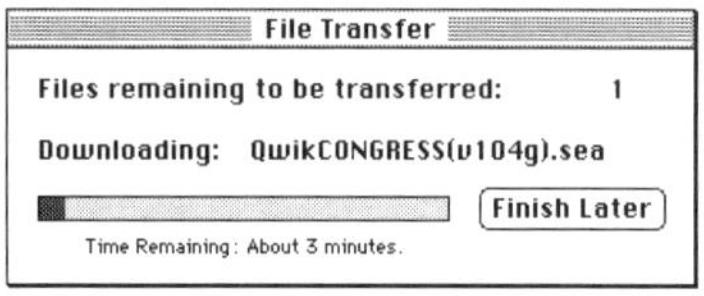


**Figure 20.** *The File Transfer window shows the progress of the transfer.*

### ✔ Tips

- By default, all files are downloaded into the Download folder inside the America Online 3.0 folder on your hard disk.
- If you click the Finish Later button in the File Transfer window (see **Figure 20**), the transfer is suspended until you use the Download Manager to complete it. The Download Manager is discussed later in this chapter.
- When the file transfer is finished the File Transfer window disappears and you'll hear a voice say, "File's Done!"

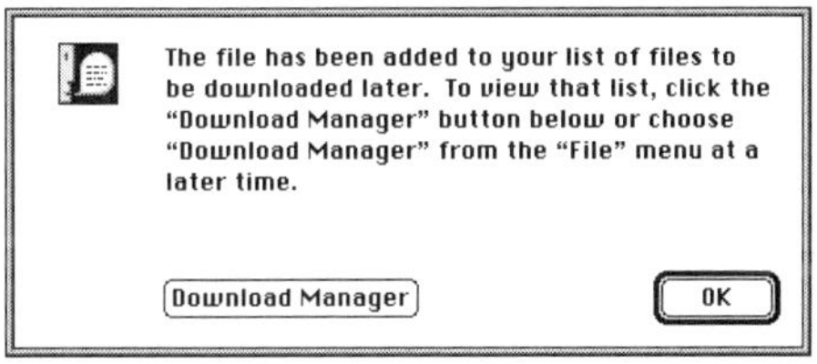


**Figure 21.** *When you click the Download Later button, the file is added to the list in the Download Manager.*

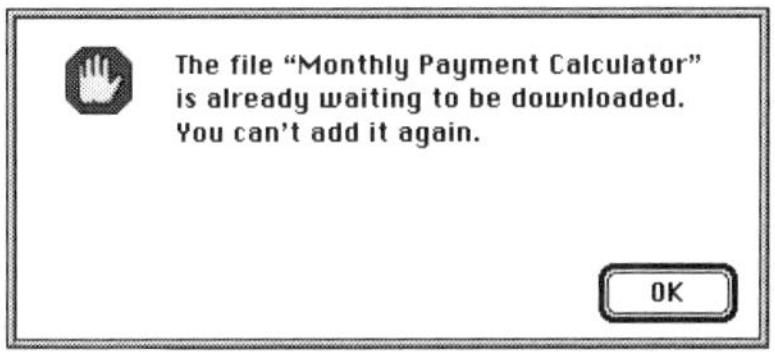


**Figure 22.** *This dialog box appears if you try to add a file to your download list a second time.*

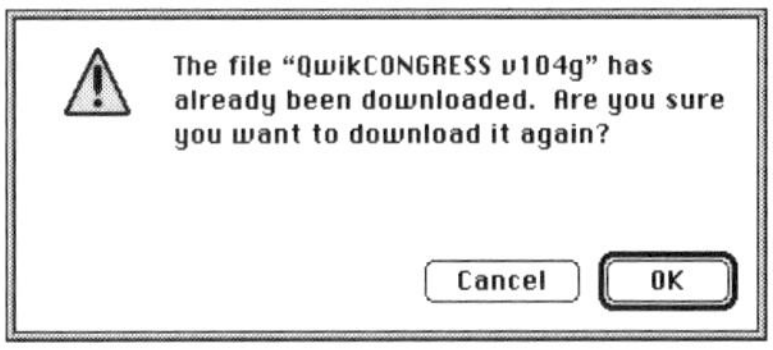


**Figure 23.** *This dialog box appears if you try to add a file to your download list that you've already downloaded.*

## To download a file later

1. In a file list window, click the name of the file you want to download to select it and then click the Download Later button (see **Figures 6** and **12**).

   *or*

   In a file description window for the file you want to download, click the Download Later button (see **Figure 7**).
2. A dialog box like the one in **Figure 21** appears, confirming that the file has been added to your download list. Click OK or press Enter to dismiss it.

## ✔ Tips

- You can add as many files as you like to the list of files to be downloaded later.
- If you have already added the file to the Download Manager list, a dialog box like the one in **Figure 22** appears. Click OK or press Enter to dismiss it.
- If you have already downloaded the file, a dialog box like the one in **Figure 23** appears. Click Cancel to continue without downloading the file again.

## About the Download Manager

The Download Manager (see **Figure 24**) keeps track of the files scheduled to be downloaded for a specific screen name. Each time you click a Download Later button, the selected file is added to the Download Manager's list for the screen name with which you are connected to AOL.

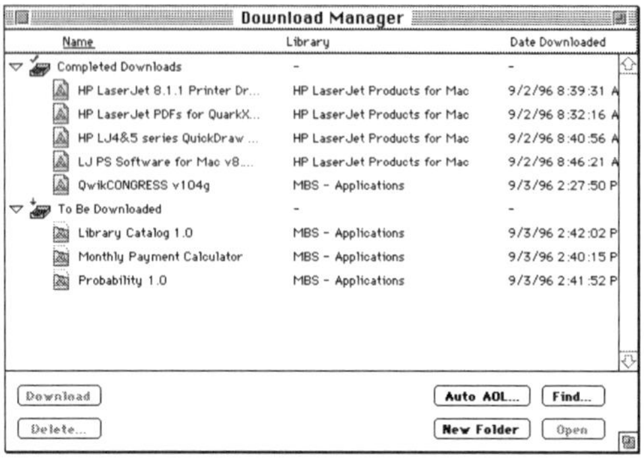


**Figure 24.** *The Download Manager keeps track of the files you've downloaded—and the ones scheduled to be downloaded.*

### ✔ Tips

- You can view, modify, or change options for the Download Manager any time you like—even while disconnected from AOL.
- Screen names are discussed in detail in **Chapter 10**.

## To open the Download Manager window

Choose Download Manager from the File menu (see **Figure 25**).

*or*

Click the Download Manager button in a dialog box like the one in **Figure 21**.

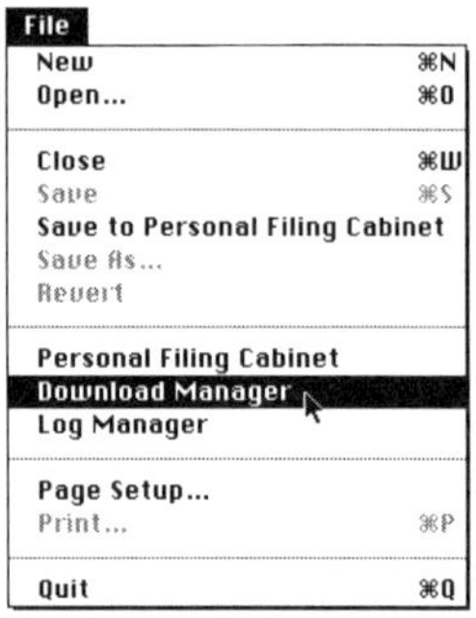


**Figure 25.** *One way to open the Download Manager window is to choose Download Manager from the File menu.*

### ✔ Tips

- Another way to view the files listed in the Download Manager is by opening the Personal Filing Cabinet (see **Figure 26**). To open it, click the Personal Filing Cabinet button  on the toolbar or choose Personal Filing Cabinet from the File menu. The Personal Filing Cabinet is discussed in detail in **Chapter 10**.
- The Download Manager's contents are displayed in an outline view. To collapse or expand the outline, click the small triangles to the left of the Completed Downloads or To Be Downloaded folders.

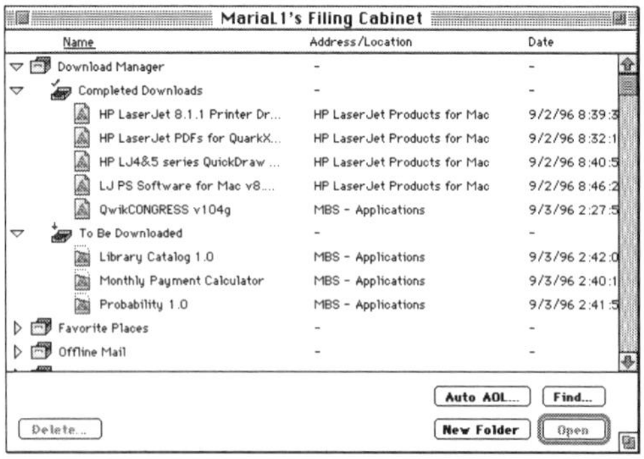


**Figure 26.** *Files listed in the Download Manager window also appear in the Personal Filing Cabinet window.*

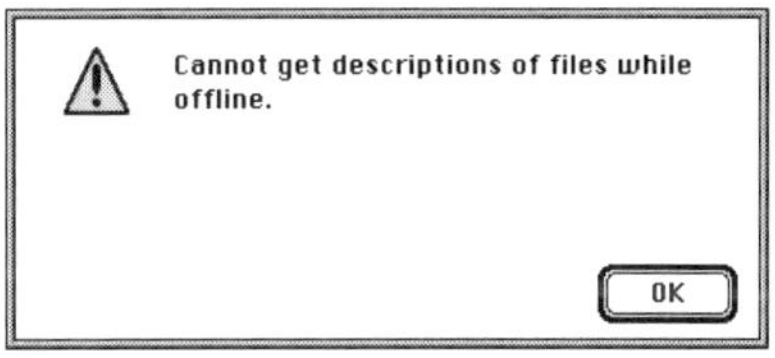


**Figure 27.** *If you're not signed on to AOL when you try to view a file description, a dialog box like this appears.*

## To view the description of a listed file

1. Open the Download Manager window (see **Figure 24**).
2. Click once on the file for which you want to view a description to select it and then click the Open button.
3. Read the description in the window that appears (see **Figure 7**).

### ✔ Tip

- You must be connected to AOL to view a description for a file listed in the Download Manager. If you are not, a dialog box like the one in **Figure 27** appears. Click OK or press Enter to dismiss it.

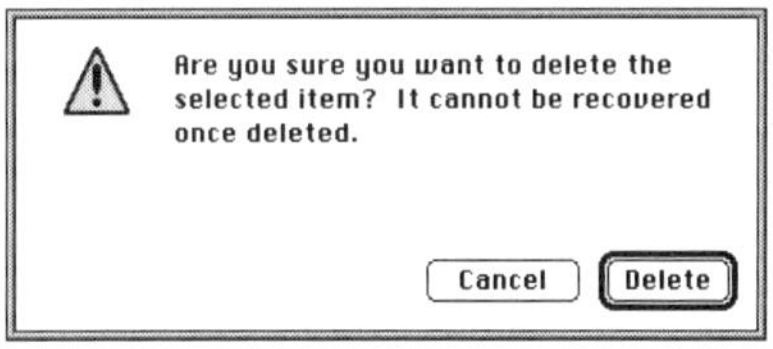


**Figure 28.** *Use this dialog box to confirm that you really do want to remove an item from the Download Manager list.*

## To remove a file from the Download Manager list

1. Open the Download Manager window (see **Figure 24**).
2. Click once on the file you want to remove to select it and then click the Delete button.
3. A confirmation dialog box (see **Figure 28**) appears. Click Delete to remove the item and dismiss the dialog box.

## To start downloading Download Manager files

1. Open the Download Manager window (see **Figure 24**).
2. Click on the name of the file you want to download to select it. You can select more than one file by holding down [Shift] while while clicking on each file's name.
3. Click the Download button.
4. A File Transfer window like the one in **Figure 29** appears. It shows the total number of files to be transferred and provides an estimate of the total download time. You can wait while the files are transferred or continue working with AOL.

**Figure 29.** *The File Transfer window shows the progress of the batch download.*

### ✔ Tips

- A quick way to select all the files in the To Be Downloaded folder is to select the folder. When you click the Download button, a dialog box like the one in **Figure 30** appears. Click Yes or press [Enter] to download all the files in the folder.
- The File Transfer window will disappear and you'll hear a male voice announce, "File's done!" when the single or batch file transfer is complete.
- Another way to download files listed in the Download Manager is to activate a FlashSession. Be sure the "Download files marked to be downloaded later" option is turned on in the Auto AOL Preferences window (see **Figure 31**) before activating the FlashSession. Auto AOL is discussed in detail in **Chapter 10**. Preferences are discussed in **Chapter 11**.
- If a file has been removed from AOL by AOL Staff before you have a chance to download it, the file will no longer be available and it won't be downloaded.

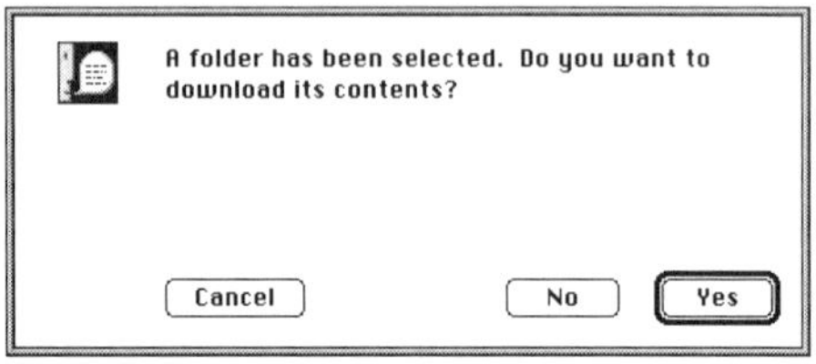


**Figure 30.** *You can select a Download Manager folder to download its contents.*

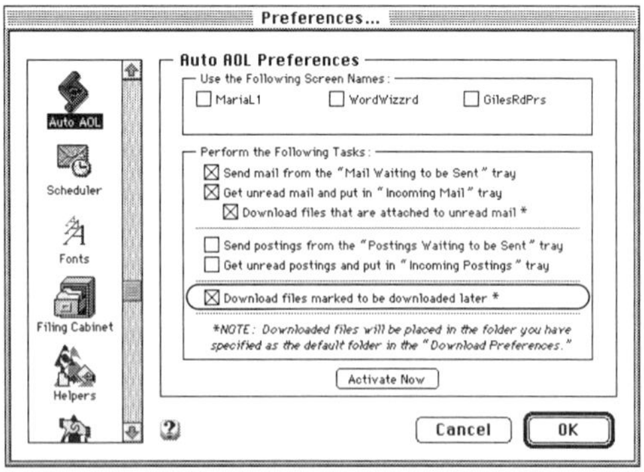


**Figure 31.** *Be sure the "Download files marked to be downloaded later" option is turned on in the Auto AOL Preferences window.*

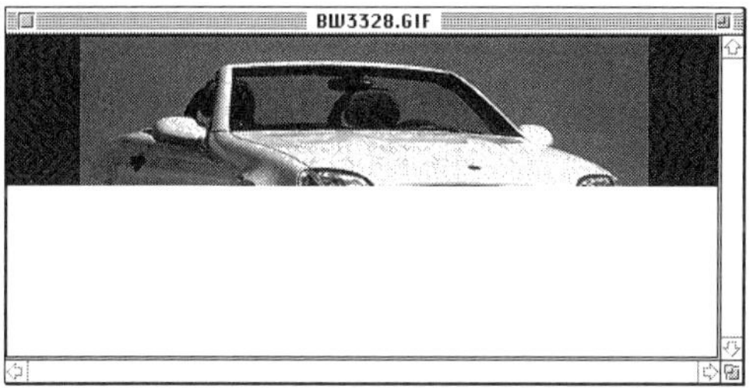


**Figure 32.** *Graphic images appear as they are downloaded.*

**Figure 33.** *When the download is complete, so is the image on your screen.*

## About Graphic Files

Throughout AOL's areas, you'll find graphic files that you can download. These files are automatically displayed in a window on your screen as you download them.

### To download and view a graphics file

1. Follow the instructions in the section titled "To download a file immediately" to begin the download.
2. In addition to the File Transfer window that appears for all downloads, an image window appears. As the file is downloaded, the image appears in this window, starting from the top (see **Figure 32**).
3. When the image has been completely downloaded, the entire image appears in the image window (see **Figure 33**).

### ✔ Tip

- AOL supports several different graphics file formats, including .GIF (Graphics Interchange Format), .BMP (Windows bitmaps), .JPG (JPEG or Joint Photographic Experts Group), and .PCX (Paintbrush format).

## About Uploading Files

If you've got a file you want to share with the rest of the world, uploading it to an appropriate file library on AOL is a good way to do it. Best of all, uploads are free!

Before you upload your file, however, make sure it meets the following requirements:

- Does the upload include all the files that are part of the program? This includes any program, documentation, or registration files.
- Is the software distributable? Make sure the licensing agreement or shareware notice with the file states that the file may be shared with others.
- Has the software been compressed into one archive file? Use file compression software like StuffIt or Compact Pro to create a *.sit* or *.sea* archive.

Your upload must meet these requirements to be released to AOL members.

### ✔ Tips

- Remember that AOL has members of all ages and all backgrounds. If you submit a file that is inappropriate or offensive, the AOL staff will not make it available to others.
- You are not billed for the time you spend uploading files to AOL's file libraries.
- Some libraries have a separate area called "New Files & Free Uploading" (see **Figure 34**) or something similar. Use the keyword UPLOAD to display a list of Mac Software Center upload libraries.
- StuffIt and Compact Pro are two shareware file compression programs that are available in AOL's file libraries. StuffIt is the preferred compression package.

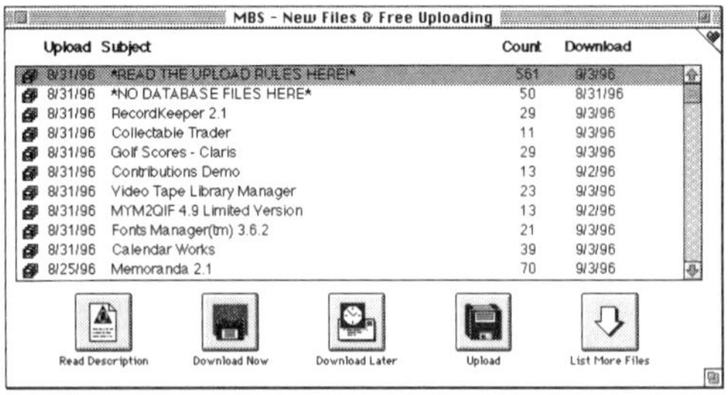


**Figure 34.** *Whenever appropriate, upload your files to an area's Upload library.*

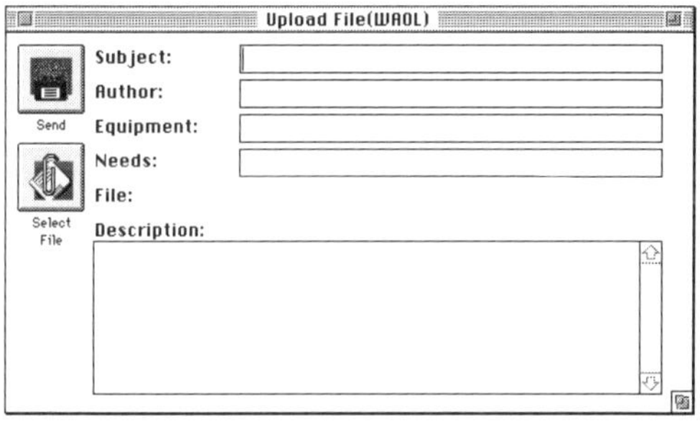


**Figure 35.** *The Upload File window has edit boxes you can use to enter information about your file.*

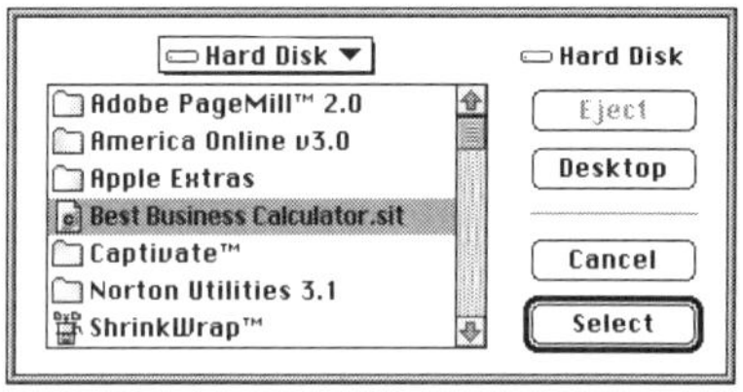


**Figure 36.** *Use a standard Open dialog box to select the file you want to upload.*

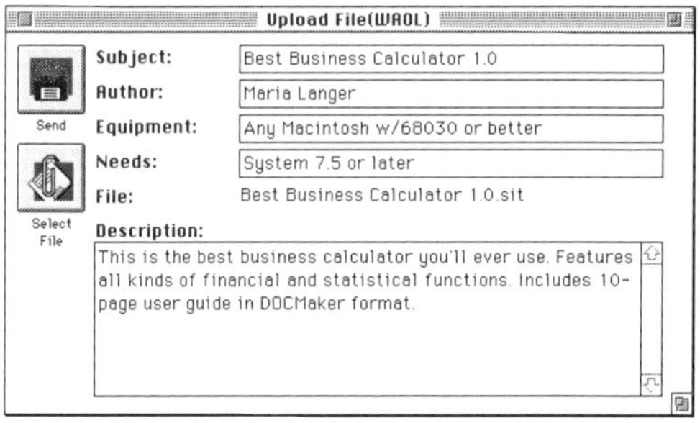


**Figure 37.** *Here's an example of a filled in Upload File window.*

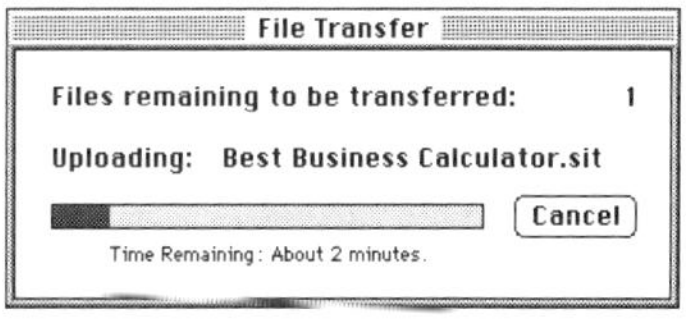


**Figure 38.** *A File Transfer window shows upload progress.*

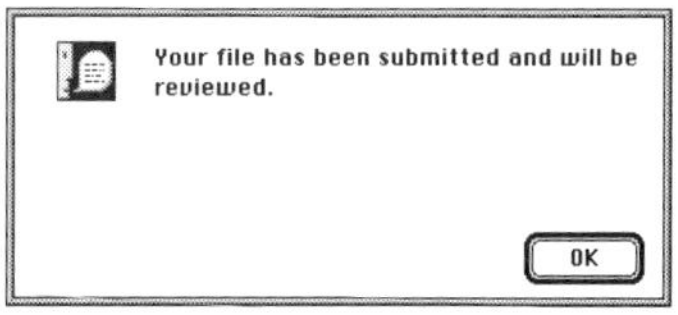


**Figure 39.** *A dialog box like this appears when your upload is complete.*

## To upload a file

1. Using any combination of menus, buttons, or keywords, navigate to an appropriate file library (see **Figure 34**).
2. Click the Upload button to display an Upload File window (see **Figure 35**).
3. Enter the full name of the file in the Subject edit box.
4. Enter the author's name in the Author edit box.
5. Enter any special computer equipment required to use the file in the Equipment edit box.
6. Enter any special software required to use the file in the Needs edit box.
7. Enter a complete description for the file in the Description edit box.
8. Click the Select File button.
9. Use the standard Open dialog box that appears (see **Figure 36**) to locate and select the file you want to upload. Then click Select or press Enter. The Upload File dialog box might look something like the one in **Figure 37** when you're finished.
10. Click the Send button.
11. A File Transfer window like the one in **Figure 38** appears as the file is transferred. When the transfer is finished, a dialog box like the one in **Figure 39** appears. Click OK or press Enter to dismiss it.

## ✔ Tip

- Files you upload are not made available to other AOL members until they are reviewed and approved by AOL staff.

# PARTICIPATING IN LIVE CHATS 7

## About Chatting

Online chatting—exchanging text messages live with a group of other members—is one of the most popular features of AOL. It's an excellent way to meet other AOL members and interactively learn about things that interest you.

AOL offers the following features to chat with other members:

- Public and private chat rooms and conference halls let you exchange live messages with many other members, as well as guest "speakers."
- Instant messages let you exchange live messages with another AOL member without moving to a chat room or conference hall.

### ✔ Tips

- Chatting with other members or attending conferences can be time consuming. If you're on a budget, be sure to keep track of the amount of time you spend in chat rooms and conference halls.
- The conduct of members in public chat areas is determined in part by AOL's Terms of Service, which warns against offensive or otherwise inappropriate behavior. You can read the Terms of Service while online for free by using the keyword TOS.
- If you are concerned about your children participating in chats that are inappropriate for their age group, you can use AOL's Parental Control feature to limit their access. Consult **Chapter 11** for more information about parental controls.

## About People Connection Chat Rooms

A *chat room* is a place on AOL where members participate in live chats. The People Connection offers three kinds of chat rooms:

- Public chat rooms are created by AOL for a variety of topics. They're accessible to any member, 24 hours a day.
- Member chat rooms are chat rooms created by AOL members like you. They're accessible to any member.
- Private chat rooms are also created by members, but they're only open to other members who know the exact chat room name.

When you enter a chat room, a chat window appears (see **Figures 1** and **14**):

- Comments from members in the chat room appear in the large scrolling list window, which scrolls to accommodate new, incoming messages.
- You enter brief comments in the edit box at the bottom of the window and send them to the chat room by clicking the Send button or pressing Enter.
- A small scrolling list at the top of the window displays the screen names of everyone in the room.
- Buttons at the top of the window let you access other rooms and features.

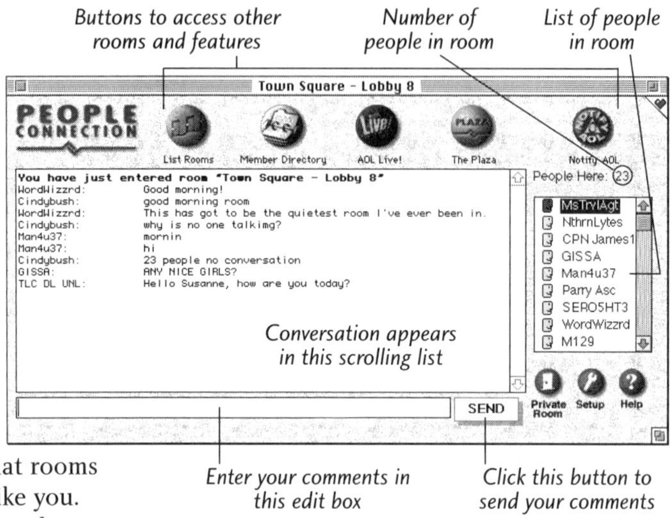


**Figure 1.** *A typical People Connection chat window.*

### ✔ Tips

- In addition to the chat rooms in the People Connection, you can also find chat or conference rooms in many AOL areas. Area chat and conference rooms are discussed later in this chapter.
- The Chat Preferences and Parental Control features are discussed in **Chapter 11**.

**Figures 2a & 2b.** *The People Connection buttons in the Channels window (top) and Welcome window (bottom) offer two ways to enter the People Connection.*

## To enter the People Connection

Click the People Connection button on the toolbar.

*or*

Click the People Connection button in the Channels window (see **Figure 2a**).

*or*

Click the People Connection button in the Welcome window (see **Figure 2b**).

*or*

Use the keyword PEOPLE CONNECTION.

A Lobby chat window like the one in **Figure 1** appears.

### ✔ Tips

- When you first enter the People Connection, a Lobby chat window appears. AOL automatically creates lobbies as needed to accommodate members coming into the People Connection. Lobby names consist of the word *Lobby* followed by a number.
- You do not need to go to a specific chat room to start chatting with other AOL members. You can chat with members in the Lobby chat window that opens when you first enter the People Connection.
- Each People Connection chat room (including lobbies) can accommodate 23 members plus AOL staff.

## To enter a public chat room

1. In any People Connection Lobby or chat room window (see **Figure 1**), click the List Rooms button.
2. Double-click a chat room category in the scrolling list on the left side of the Public Rooms window that appears (see **Figure 3**).
3. Scroll through the chat rooms in the scrolling list on the right side of the Public Rooms window. When you find one that interests you, click its name once to select it and then click the Go button or just double-click its name.

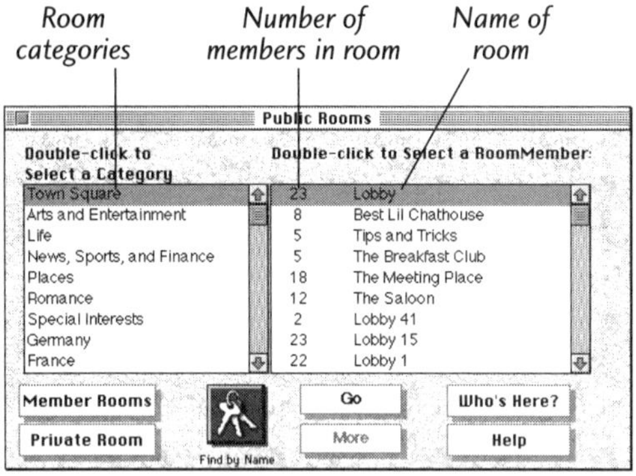


**Figure 3.** *The Public Rooms window offers access to all of the AOL-created public rooms.*

### ✔ Tips

- If the More button at the bottom of the Public Rooms window is not gray, you can use it to display more public rooms at the end of the list.
- You'll know you've successfully changed to a different room because the name of the room you've entered will be noted in the chat window (see **Figure 4**).
- If the public chat room you selected is full, a dialog box like the one in **Figure 5** will appear. Click Yes or press [Enter] to go to another room with the same topic. Click No to choose a different room.
- If the last time you used the List Rooms button in step 1 above was to view Member Rooms, the Member Rooms window may appear instead of the Public Rooms window. The Member Rooms window is discussed on the next page.

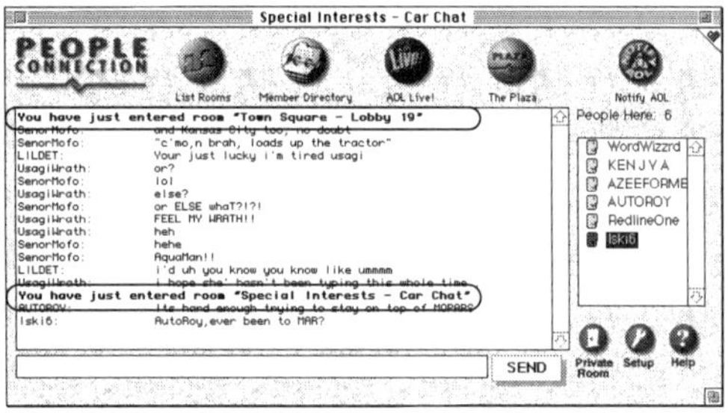


**Figure 4.** *When you move from one room to another, you're informed of the room change in the chat window.*

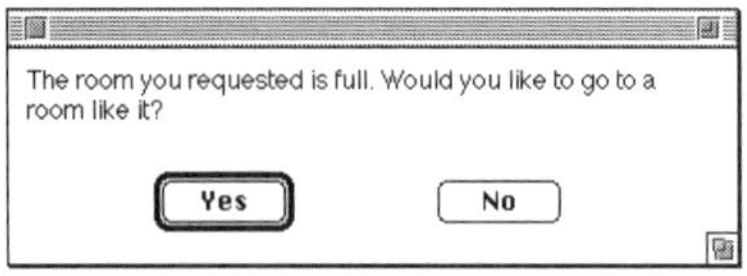


**Figure 5.** *If a public chat room is full, AOL offers to put you in a room like it.*

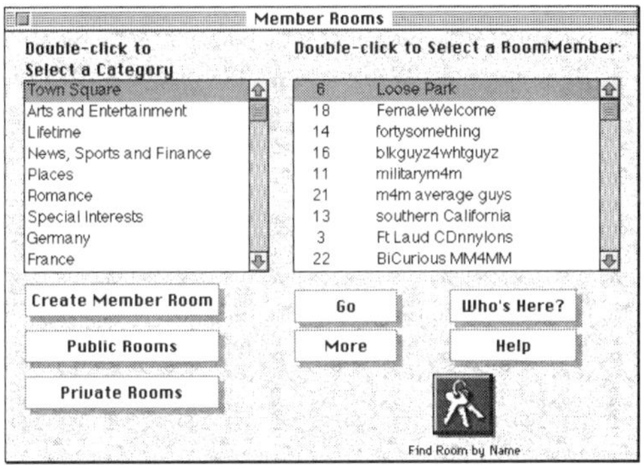


**Figure 6.** *The Member Rooms window looks and works very much like the Public Rooms window in* Figure 3.

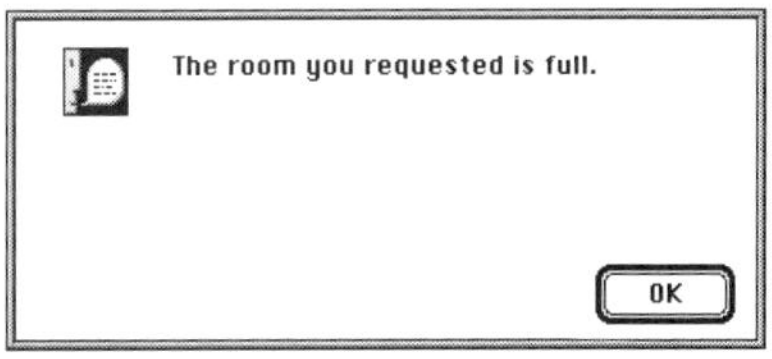


**Figure 7.** *If the member chat room you selected is full, a dialog box like this appears.*

## To enter a member chat room

1. In any People Connection Lobby or chat room window (see **Figures 1** and **4**), click the List Rooms button.
2. In the Public Rooms window that appears (see **Figure 3**), click the Member Rooms button.
3. Double-click a chat room category in the scrolling list on the left side of the Member Rooms window that appears (see **Figure 6**).
4. Scroll through the chat rooms in the list on the right side of the Member Rooms window. When you find one that interests you, click its name once to select it and then click the Go button or just double-click its name.

### ✔ Tips

- If the More button at the bottom of the Member Rooms window is not gray, you can use it to display more member rooms at the end of the list.
- You'll know you've successfully changed to a different room because the name of the room you've entered will be noted in the chat window (see **Figure 4**).
- If the member chat room you selected is full, a dialog box like the one in **Figure 7** will appear. Click OK or press Enter to dismiss the dialog box and choose a different room.
- Another way to go to a specific member chat room is to click the Create Member Room button in the Member Rooms window (see **Figure 6**). In the Create a Member Room dialog box that appears (see **Figure 11**), enter the name of an existing member chat room and click Create. Creating member chat rooms is discussed later in this chapter.

## To find a specific chat room by name

1. In any People Connection Lobby or chat room window (see **Figures 1** and **4**), click the List Rooms button.
2. To find a specific public room, make sure the Public Rooms window is displayed. If it is not, click the Public Rooms button in the Member Rooms window (see **Figure 6**).

   *or*

   To find a specific member room, make sure the Member Rooms window is displayed. If it is not, click the Member Rooms button in the Public Rooms window (see **Figure 3**).
3. Click the Find by Name (see **Figure 3**) or Find Room by Name (see **Figure 6**) button.
4. In the dialog box that appears, enter the name of the room you want to find (see **Figures 8a** and **8b**).
5. Click the Find button. Rooms with names that match the name you entered are displayed in a window like the ones in **Figures 9a** and **9b**.
6. To go to a room, click once on the room's name to select it and then click the Go button or just double-click the room's name.

### ✔ Tips

- You must enter the full, exact name of the room you want to find. If you enter only part of the name, AOL will not be able to find it.
- If no rooms have names that match the name you entered, a dialog box like the one in **Figure 10** will appear. Click OK or press Enter to dismiss it and try again.

**Figures 8a & 8b.** *Use dialog boxes like these to enter the name of a public room (above) or member room (below) that you want to find.*

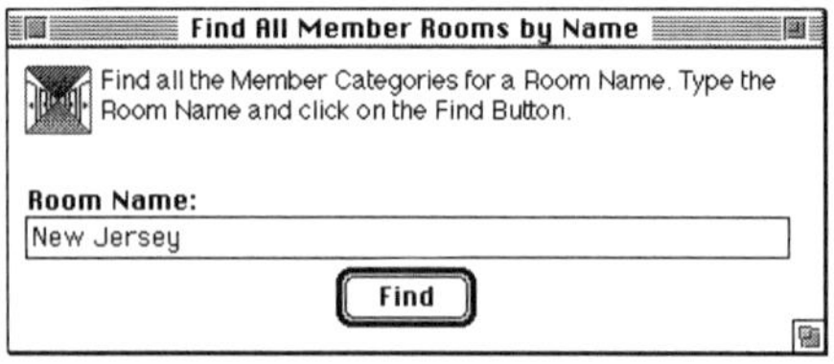


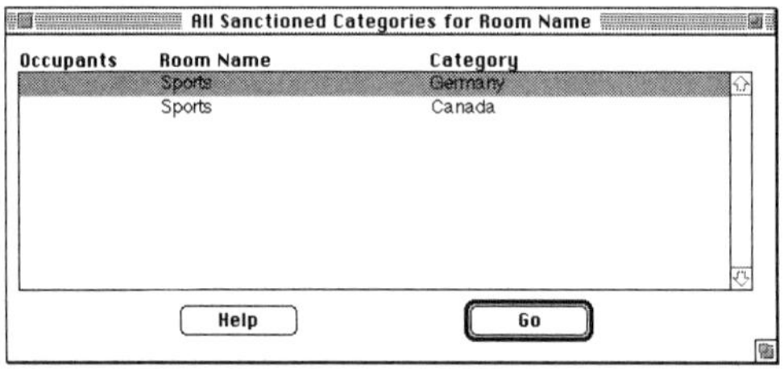


**Figures 9a & 9b.** *AOL displays a list of all the rooms with the name you specified, along with the room's category and number of occupants.*

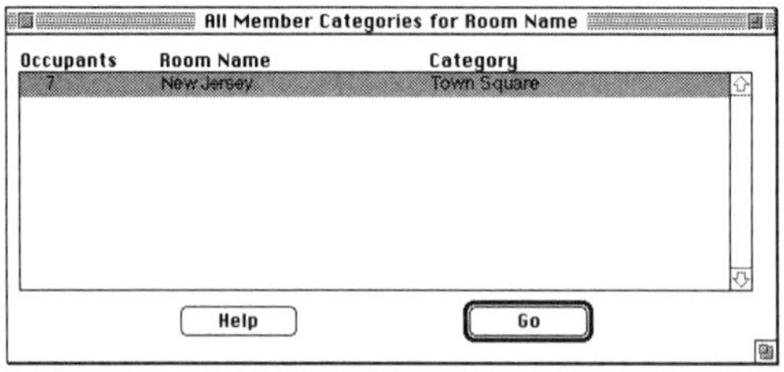


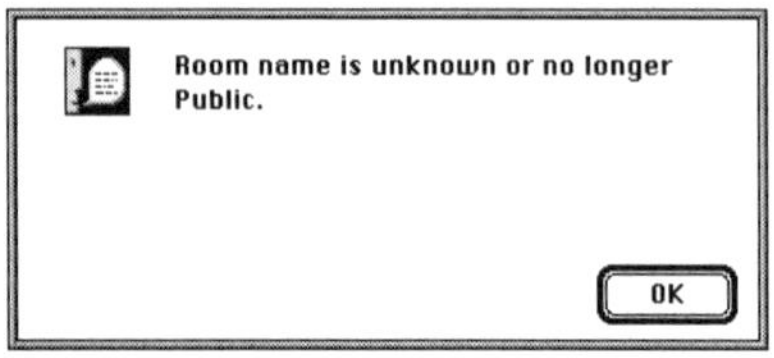


**Figure 10.** *If AOL can't find the room you're looking for, it displays a dialog box like this.*

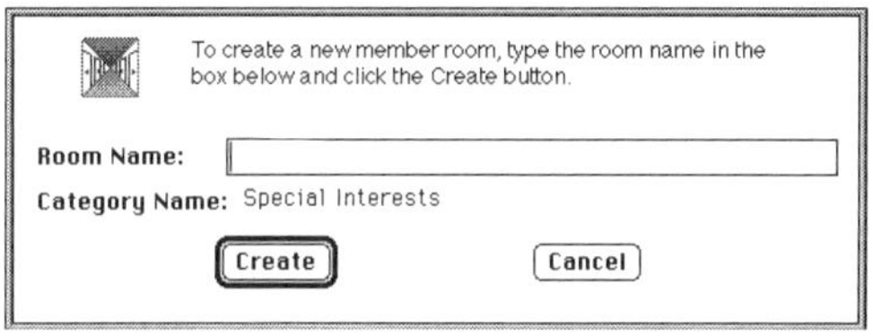


**Figure 11.** *Create a member room by entering a name for it in this dialog box.*

## To create a member chat room

1. In any People Connection Lobby or chat room window (see **Figures 1** and **4**), click the List Rooms button.
2. If the Public Rooms window appears (see **Figure 3**), click the Member Rooms button.
3. In the Member Rooms window (see **Figure 6**), double-click on the name of the category under which you want your room to be listed.
4. Click the Create Member Room button.
5. In the dialog box that appears (see **Figure 11**), enter a name for the room in the Room Name edit box.
6. Click Create or press Enter to create the room and enter it.

## ✔ Tips

- If you try to create a room with the same name as an existing room, you will enter that room rather than create a new one.
- Try to give your room a name that will give others an idea of the topics that will be discussed within it.

## To learn who is in your chat room

Use the scroll bar on the scrolling list in the upper right corner of the chat room window (see **Figures 1** and **4**) to view the screen names of all members currently in the room.

### ✔ Tip

- By default, newcomers to the room appear at the top of the scrolling list. Members who have been in the room for a while appear near the bottom of the list.

## To learn who is in another chat room

1. In the Public Rooms window (see **Figure 3**) or Member Rooms window (see **Figure 6**), click once on the name of the room in which you are interested to select it.
2. Click the Who's Here button to display a list of room occupants in the People window (see **Figure 12**).

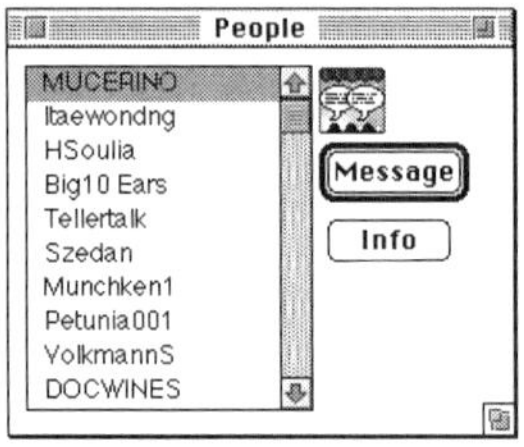


**Figure 12.** *The People window shows you who is in a selected chat room.*

### ✔ Tips

- You can double-click a screen name or use the Info button in the People window to display the Member Profile for a chat room occupant. Member Profiles are discussed in detail in **Chapter 8**.
- You can use the Message button in the People window to send an Instant Message to a selected chat room occupant. Instant Messages are discussed later in this chapter.

## To create and/or enter a private chat room

1. In any People Connection Lobby or chat room window (see **Figures 1** and **4**), click the Private Room button.

   *or*

   In the Public Rooms or Member Rooms window (see **Figures 3** and **6**), click the Private Room button.

2. In the Enter a Private Room dialog box that appears (see **Figure 13**), enter the exact name of the private room you want to create or enter.

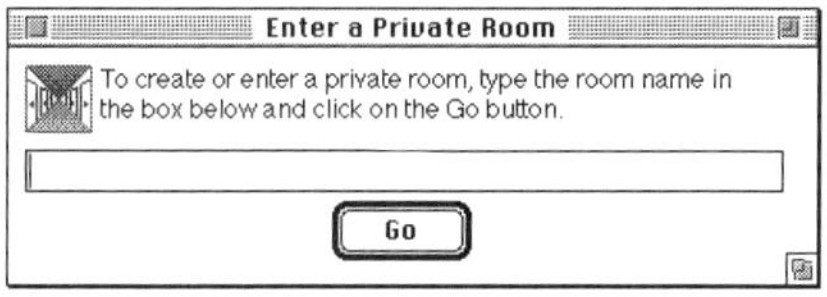


**Figure 13.** *Create or enter a private room by entering its name in the Enter a Private Room dialog box.*

3. Click Go or press Enter. If the room does not exist, you will create and enter it. If the room already exists, you will enter it.

### ✔ Tips

- The names of private chat rooms are not listed anywhere on AOL. That's what keeps them private.
- To enter an existing private chat room, you must know the exact name of the room. If you enter an incorrect name, you will create a new private chat room with the name you entered.
- If you'd like to have a private chat with one or more AOL members, use the Instant Message or Buddy List Invite feature to invite them to a private chat room that you create. Be sure to include the name of the room in your invitation. The Instant Message feature is discussed later in this chapter. The Buddy List Invite feature is discussed in **Chapter 8**.

## About Area Chat & Conference Rooms

Many AOL areas include one or more chat rooms. These rooms (see **Figure 14**) are similar in appearance and function to People Connection chat rooms.

### ✔ Tip

- Don't be surprised if you go to an area's chat or conference room and find that you're the only one there. Many area conference rooms attract visitors only when there's a scheduled event.

## To enter an area's chat or conference room

1. Use navigation techniques discussed in **Chapter 3** to go to an AOL area that interests you.
2. In the area's main window (see **Figure 15**), look for a Chat or Conference button and click it.
3. If the area has more than one chat or conference area, a window similar to the one in **Figure 16** may appear. Click the chat or conference area's button or double-click its name in the scrolling list to open a chat window like the one in **Figure 14**.

### ✔ Tip

- In step 2 above, if an area's main window does not include a Chat or Conference button, look for a chat or conference area name in a scrolling list (see **Figure 16**) and double-click it. You can identify chat or conference areas by the Chat icon to the left of the item name in a list.

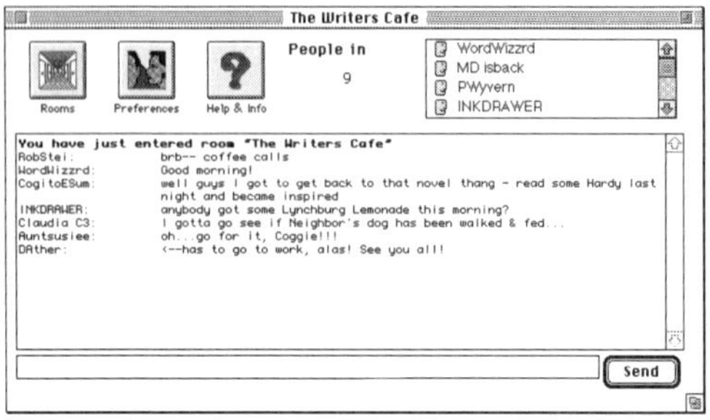


**Figure 14.** *The Writers Cafe is a conference room in AOL's Writers Club. Other areas have similar chat rooms.*

**Figure 15.** *In this example from The Writers Club, a Chat button offers access to all of the area's conference rooms.*

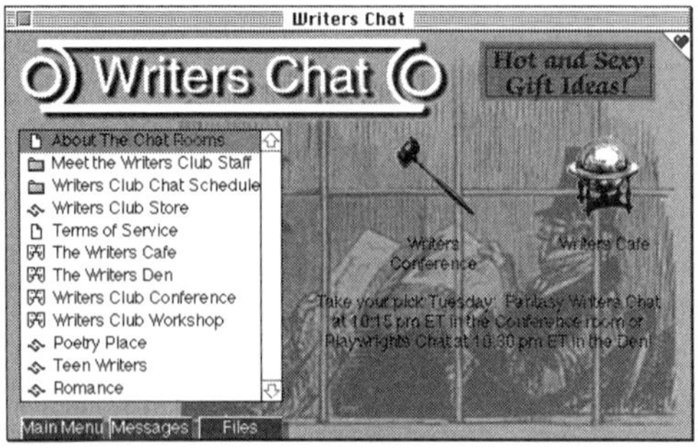


**Figure 16.** *Clicking the Chat button in the Writers Club window displays this window. You can double-click any of the conference names in the scrolling list.*

## About Participating in a Chat

Once you've opened a chat or conference window, you can participate in the chat.

- Read chat comments sent by others.
- Send chat comments that can be read by others.
- Send sounds that can be heard by others.
- Ignore comments sent by specific participants.

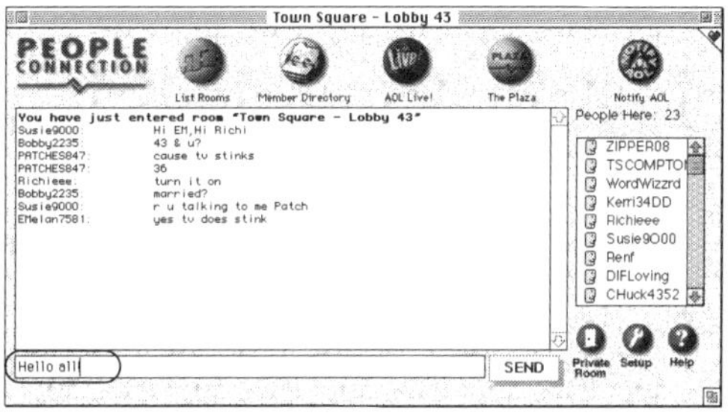


**Figure 17.** *Chat comments appear in the chat window. You contribute a comment by entering it in the edit box at the bottom of the window.*

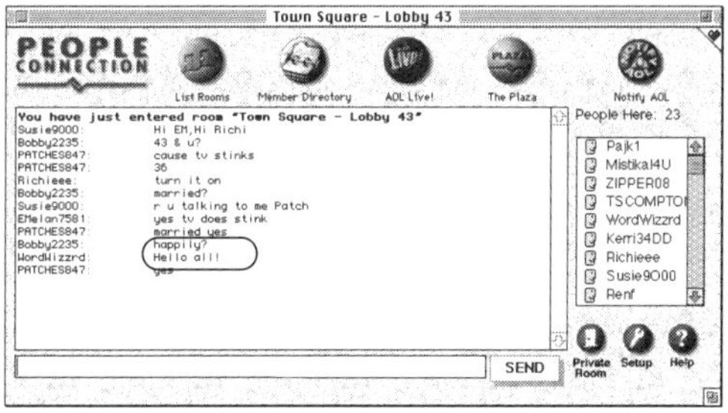


**Figure 18.** *When you click the Send button, the comment you entered is added to the chat window.*

## To read and send chat comments

1. Use techniques discussed on the previous pages to enter a chat room that interests you.
2. In the chat window (see **Figure 17**), read the messages sent by others.
3. To send a comment, enter it in the edit box at the bottom of the chat window (see **Figure 17**). Click the Send button or press Enter. Your comment appears with the others (see **Figure 18**).

### ✔ Tips

- Chat comments appear at the bottom of the window as they are received by the AOL server.
- Chat comments scroll up as they are received. The more frequently comments are received, the more quickly the window's contents scroll. Use the scroll bars to read comments you missed.
- Chat comments are limited to 92 characters. To send more, you must send multiple comments.
- People in chat rooms make extensive use of online shorthand and smileys. Commonly used online shorthand abbreviations and smiley character combinations are provided in **Appendix C**.

## To send a chat sound

1. In the edit box at the bottom of a chat room window (see **Figure 19**), enter {S followed by a space and the name of a sound within the AOL application or your System. For example, enter {S Welcome to send AOL's welcome sound.
2. Click Send or press Enter. The sound name appears in the chat room window (see **Figure 20**). The sound is also played on the computer of anyone in the chat room with the Enable Chat Room Sounds option turned on and the sound file installed on their computer.

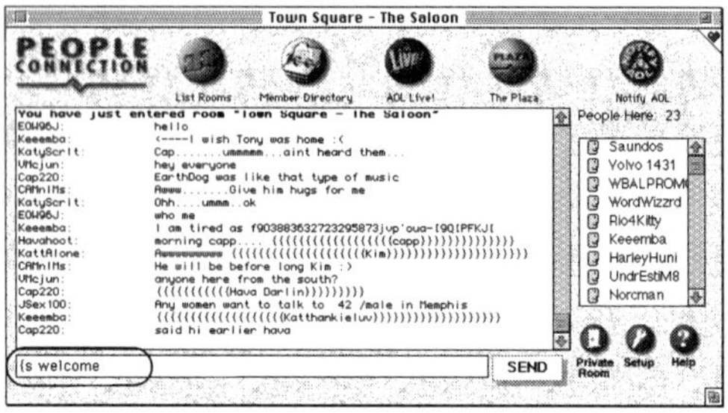

**Figure 19.** *Enter {S and the name of a sound within AOL or your System in the edit box at the bottom of the chat window.*

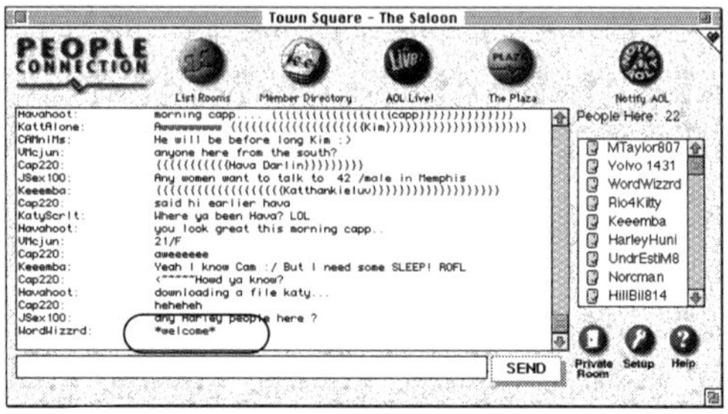

**Figure 20.** *Then click the Send button to send the sound to the chat room.*

## ✔ Tips

- The Enable Chat Room Sounds option is one of the Chat Preferences, which are discussed in **Chapter 11**.
- **Table 1** provides a list of the sound files within the AOL software.
- You can download additional sound files for use in chat rooms. Use the File Search feature to search for AOL Chat Mac Sounds. Downloading files and using the File Search feature are discussed in **Chapter 6**.

| Sound Name | Chat Room Entry |
|---|---|
| File's Done | {S File's Done |
| Goodbye | {S Goodbye |
| IM | {S IM |
| Turn Page | {S Turn Page |
| Welcome | {S Welcome |
| You've Got Mail | {S You've Got Mail |

**Table 1.** *List of sounds within the AOL application.*

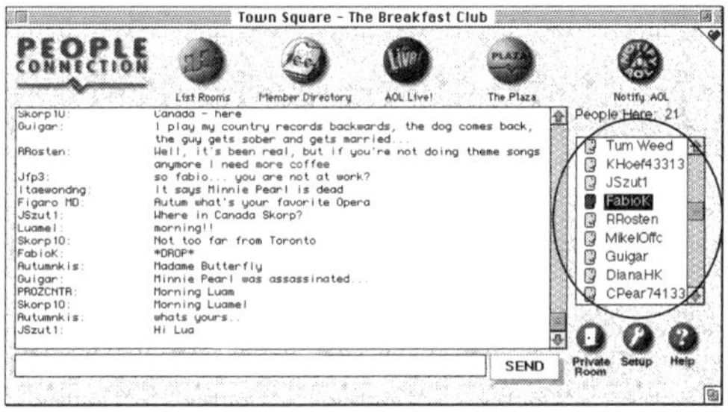


**Figure 21.** *To ignore comments sent by a specific chat participant, begin by double-clicking his name in the chat room window's list of chat participants.*

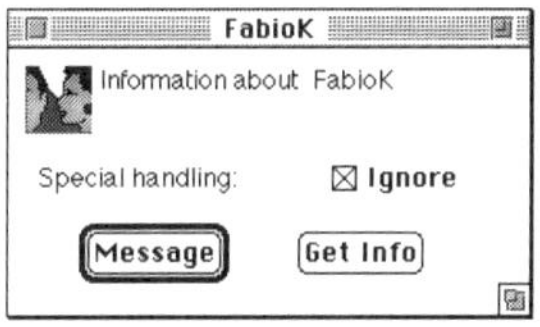


**Figure 22.** *The information window lets you ignore, send an Instant Message to, or view the Member Profile for a chat participant.*

## To ignore a chat participant

1. In the list of chat participants in the chat room window (see **Figure 21**), double-click the screen name of a person whose messages you do not want to see.
2. In the Information window that appears, turn on the Ignore check box (see **Figure 22**).
3. Click the Information window's close box to close it.

## ✔ Tips

- When you ignore a chat participant, his messages do not appear in the chat window. This is an excellent way to filter out conversation that does not interest you.
- You can click the Message button in the Information window (see **Figure 22**) to send an Instant Message to a chat room occupant. Instant Messages are discussed later in this chapter.
- You can click the Get Info button in the Information window (see **Figure 22**) to display the Member Profile for a chat room occupant. Member Profiles are discussed in detail in **Chapter 8**.

## To report a Terms of Service violation in a chat room

1. Use your mouse to select the chat comment(s) that caused the violation.
2. Choose Copy from the Edit menu (see **Figure 23**) or press ⌘C.
3. Click the Notify AOL button in the People Connection chat room window (see **Figure 21**).
4. In the Notify AOL window that appears (see **Figure 24**), enter the information about the violation in the appropriate edit boxes.
5. Click in the Paste Chat Text Here edit box and choose Paste from the Edit menu (see **Figure 25**) or press ⌘V to paste in the chat comment.
6. When your entries are complete, click the Send This Report button.
7. A dialog box like the one in **Figure 26** appears. Click OK or press Enter to dismiss it.
8. Click the Close box in the Notify AOL window to close it.

**Figure 23.** *You can copy offensive chat comments by selecting them and then choosing Copy from the Edit menu.*

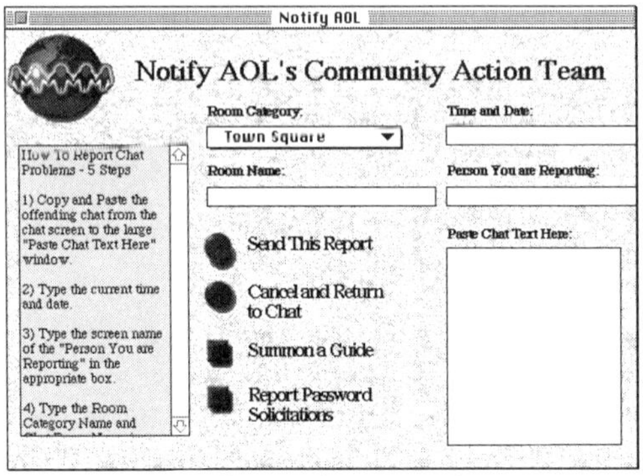


**Figure 24.** *Use the Notify AOL window to report Terms of Service violations in chat rooms.*

### ✔ Tips

- Violations you report with the Notify AOL window are submitted to AOL's Community Action Team for review. Action is taken within 48 hours of your report.
- If the problem is serious and needs immediate attention, you can click the Summon a Guide button in the Notify AOL window to contact an official AOL Guide. Please use this feature only in emergency situations.
- You can also use the Notify AOL window to report password solicitations. Remember, real AOL employees will *never* ask for your password online!

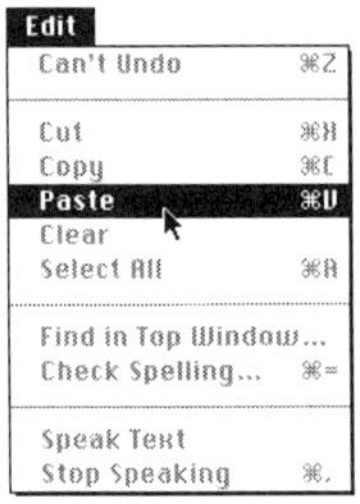


**Figure 25.** *Click in the Paste Chat Text Here box and choose Paste from the Edit menu.*

**Figure 26.** *A dialog box like this confirms that your message to AOL's Community Action Team has been sent.*

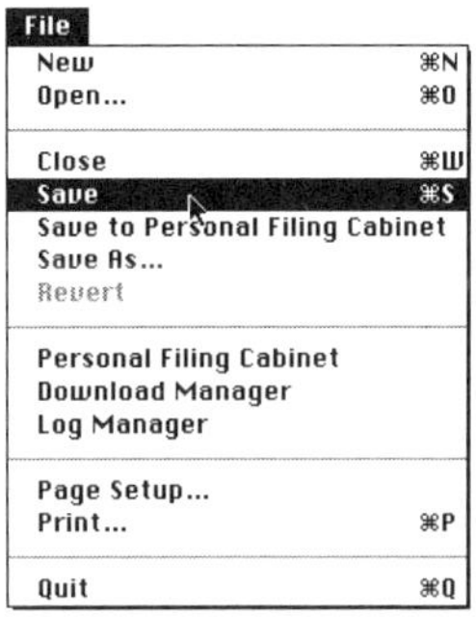


**Figure 27.** *To save a chat transcript, choose Save from the File menu.*

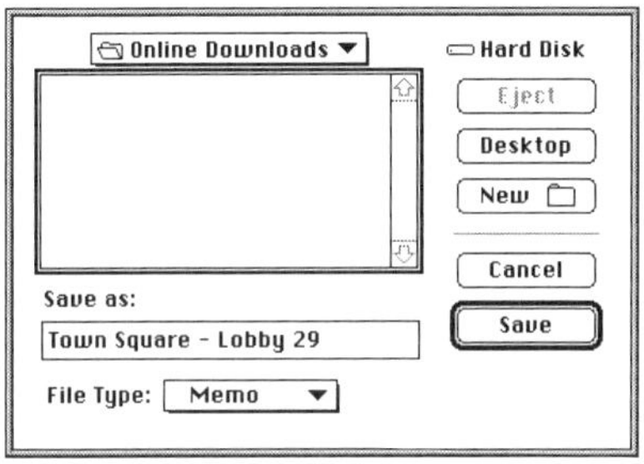


**Figure 28.** *Use the standard Save As dialog box to name and save the contents of the chat room window.*

**Figure 29.** *Choose Text Only from the File Type pop-up menu to save the chat transcript as a plain text file.*

**Figure 30.** *To leave a chat, close its window by choosing Close from the File menu.*

## To save a chat transcript

1. Before closing the chat room window at the end of a chat or conference, choose Save from the File menu (see **Figure 27**) or press ⌘S.
2. In the standard Save dialog box that appears (see **Figure 28**), specify a name and a disk location for the chat transcript file.
3. To save the transcript as a plain text file, choose Text only from the File Type pop-up menu (see **Figure 29**).
4. Click Save or press Enter.

## ✔ Tips

- If a chat transcript is 32K or less in size, you can open it from within AOL with the Open command under the File menu. Use another text editor or word processor to open larger files.
- Another way to create a chat transcript is to use the Chat Log feature. This prevents the loss of early comments that can scroll away during a lengthy chat. Logging is discussed in **Chapter 10**.

## About Leaving a Chat

Leaving a chat is as simple as closing the chat window or going to another chat room.

## To leave a chat

Choose Close from the File menu (see **Figure 30**).

*or*

Press ⌘W.

*or*

Click the chat window's Close button.

*or*

Follow instructions earlier in this chapter to go to a different chat room.

## About Live Events & Auditoriums

AOL frequently schedules live events with guest "speakers." If a live event is expected to draw over 100 members, it is held in an *auditorium*. An auditorium is similar to a chat or conference room in that it enables you to exchange live messages with other AOL members. Auditoriums, however, have the following additional features:

- *Rows*, which are like chat rooms within the auditorium. You can chat with other people in your row without disturbing event attendees with your comments.
- *Interact button*, which enables you to submit questions or comments to the host or speaker.
- *Polling* feature, which enables you to vote on topics under discussion when appropriate.

### ✔ Tip

- Auditoriums are very similar in appearance to chat rooms. **Figure 31** shows an example of a live event in one of AOL's auditoriums.

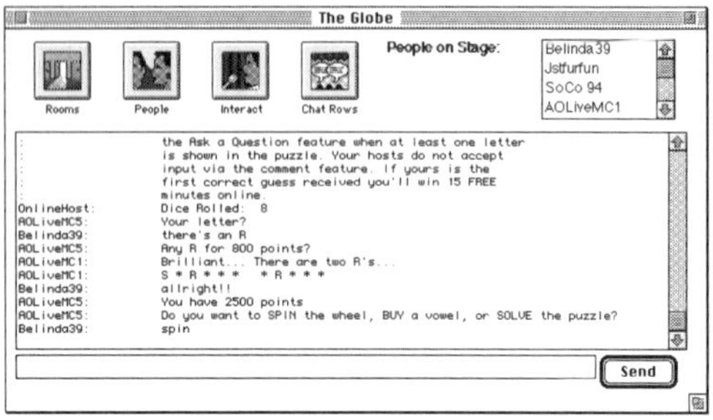


**Figure 31.** *The Globe is one of AOL's many auditoriums, where live events are held.*

**Figure 32.** *The AOL Live Main Screen is your starting point for getting information about live events.*

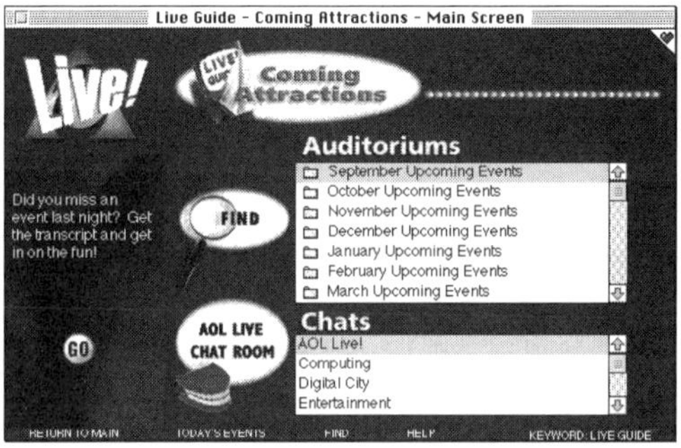


**Figure 33.** *The Live Guide window offers folders full of information about upcoming events and chats.*

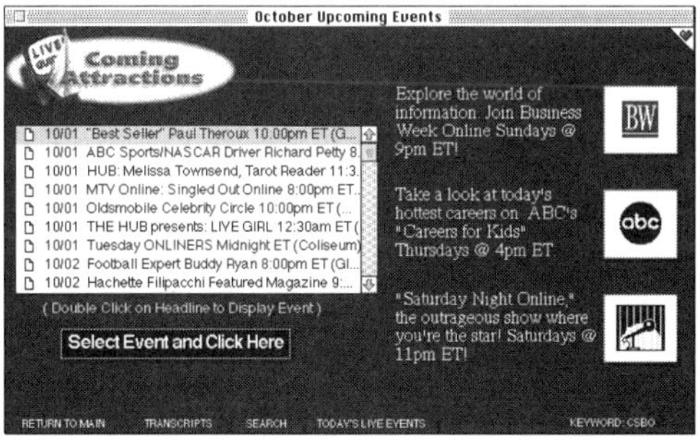


**Figure 34.** *The Upcoming Events window displays all the scheduled events for a specific month.*

## To learn about live events

1. Click the AOL Live button on the Channels window.

   *or*

   Choose Center Stage from the Go To menu or press ⌘6.

   *or*

   Use the keyword LIVE.
2. In the AOL Live Main Screen window that appears (see **Figure 32**), click the Coming Attractions button.
3. In the Live Guide window that appears (see **Figure 33**), double-click the list item for a month.
4. In the Upcoming Events window that appears (see **Figure 34**), double-click a list item that interests you to display a window with information about the event (see **Figure 35**).

## ✔ Tips

- For events scheduled for the current date, click the Today's Live Events button in the AOL Live Main Screen (see **Figure 32**) and browse the window that appears.
- The steps outlined above detail just one way to learn about upcoming events. As you browse AOL, you'll see announcements for other events. In many cases, you can click on an announcement button or list item to display a window with details about the event.
- Many AOL areas also have their own live events. Check your favorite areas for upcoming events that may interest you.
- The host for a live event often saves a transcript of the chat and makes it available for download in related areas on AOL. Downloading files is discussed in **Chapter 6**.

## To enter an auditorium

In the window describing an event, click the Go to auditorium button (see **Figure 35**).

**Figure 35.** *For each event, there's a description window like this one.*

### ✔ Tip

- When you enter an auditorium, a window like the one in **Figure 31** appears. The comments that appear in the window include:
  - ▲ Questions or comments submitted to the host or guest.
  - ▲ Answers or comments composed and sent by the host or guest.
  - ▲ Conversations among AOL members in your chat row.

## To chat in your row

1. In the auditorium window (see **Figure 36**), read the messages sent by others.
2. To send a comment, enter it in the edit box at the bottom of the auditorium window and click the Send button or press Enter. Your comment appears with the others with the number of your row before it (see **Figure 36**).

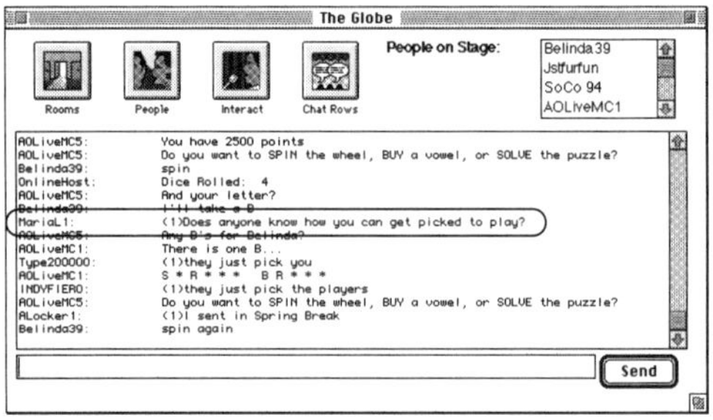


**Figure 36.** *When you send a comment, it appears in the auditorium window for everyone else in your chat row.*

### ✔ Tip

- Chat comments you send in an auditorium are visible only to the people in your chat row. To make your comments visible to everyone in the auditorium, you must interact with the host. Interacting with the host is discussed later in this chapter.

Entering an Auditorium, Chatting in a Row

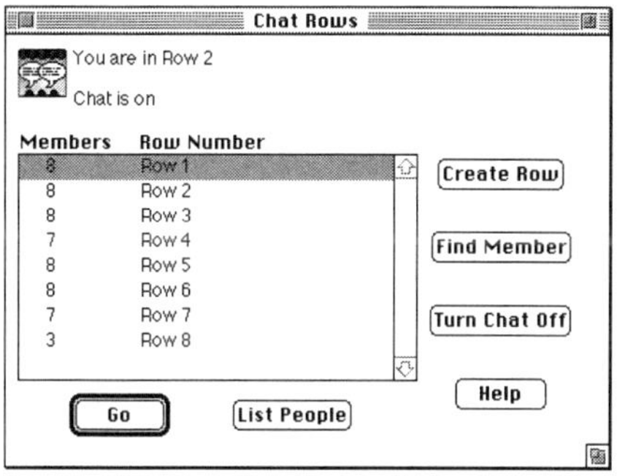


**Figure 37.** *The Chat Rows window lists all the active chat rows.*

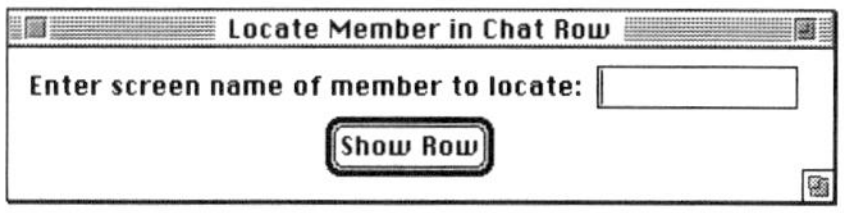


**Figure 38.** *Use this dialog box to locate a member in the auditorium.*

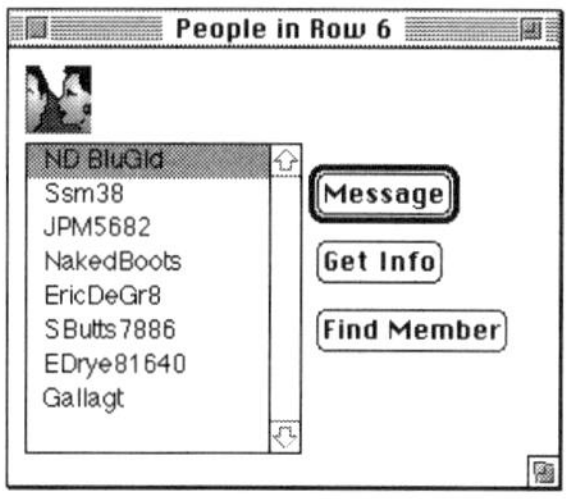


**Figure 39.** *A successful search for a member yields a window like this one for the member's row.*

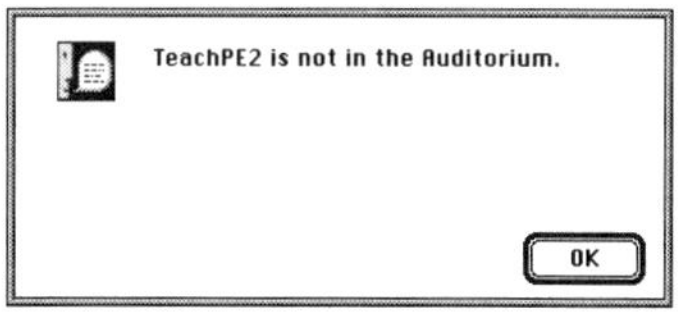


**Figure 40.** *An unsuccessful search for a member yields this dialog box.*

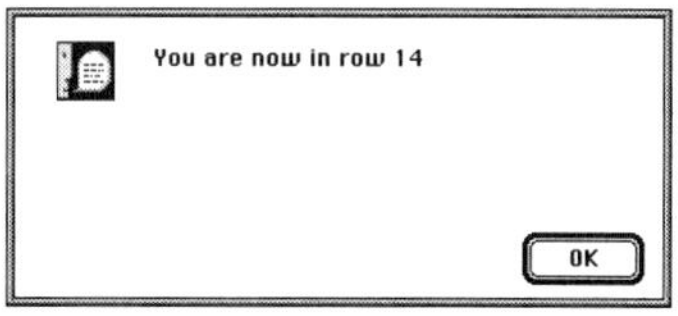


**Figure 41.** *AOL displays this dialog box when you move from row to row.*

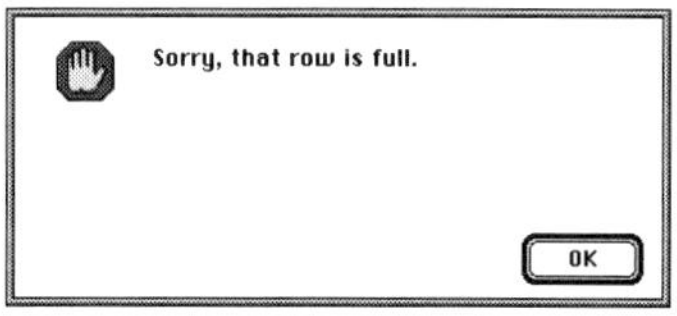


**Figure 42.** *If the row you select is full, a dialog box like this appears.*

## To find someone's chat row

1. Click the Chat Rows button in the auditorium window (see **Figures 31** and **36**).
2. In the Chat Rows window that appears (see **Figure 37**), click the Find Member button.
3. In the Locate Member in Chat Row dialog box that appears (see **Figure 38**), enter the screen name of the member you want to find in the auditorium.
4. Click the Show Row button or press Enter. A People in Row window for the person's row appears (see **Figure 39**).

### ✔ Tip

- If the member you are looking for is not in the auditorium, a dialog box like the one in **Figure 40** appears. Click OK or press Enter to dismiss it.

## To move from one row to another

1. Click the Chat Rows button in the auditorium window (see **Figures 31** and **36**).
2. In the Chat Rows window that appears (see **Figure 37**), click the row to which you want to move to select it and click the Go button.
3. If you successfully change rows, a dialog box like the one in **Figure 41** will appear. Click OK or press Enter to dismiss it.

### ✔ Tip

- If the row you select is full, a dialog box like the one in **Figure 42** will appear. Click OK or press Enter to dismiss it and choose another row.

## To turn off chatting

1. Click the Chat Rows button in the auditorium window (see **Figures 31** and **36**).
2. In the Chat Rows window that appears (see **Figure 37**), click the Turn Chat Off button.

### ✔ Tips

- You can tell whether chat is turned on or off by looking at the indicator in the Chat Rows window (see **Figure 43**).
- Turning off the chat feature is a good way to eliminate distractions so you can enjoy the event.
- To turn chat back on, click the Turn Chat On button in the Chat Rows window (see **Figure 43**).

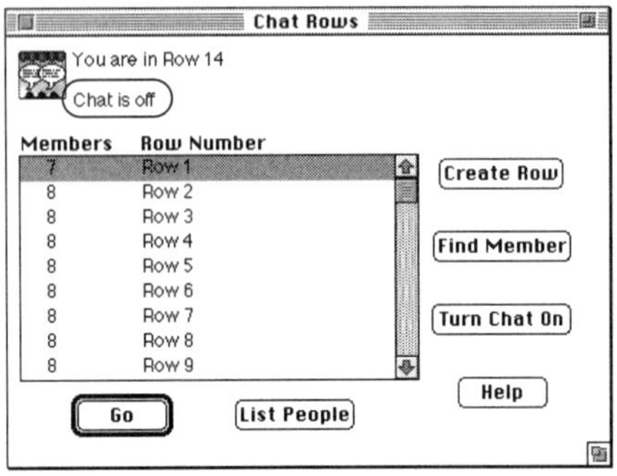


**Figure 43.** *The Chat Rows window indicates whether chat is turned on or off.*

## To interact with the host

1. Click the Interact button in the auditorium window (see **Figures 31** and **36**).
2. In the Interact with Host dialog box that appears (see **Figure 44**), enter your question or comment in the scrolling edit box.
3. To send your entry as a question, click the Ask a Question button. To send your entry as a comment, click the Send a Comment button.
4. A dialog box like one in **Figure 45a** or **45b** appears to confirm that your question or comment has been received by the host. Click OK or press Enter to dismiss it.

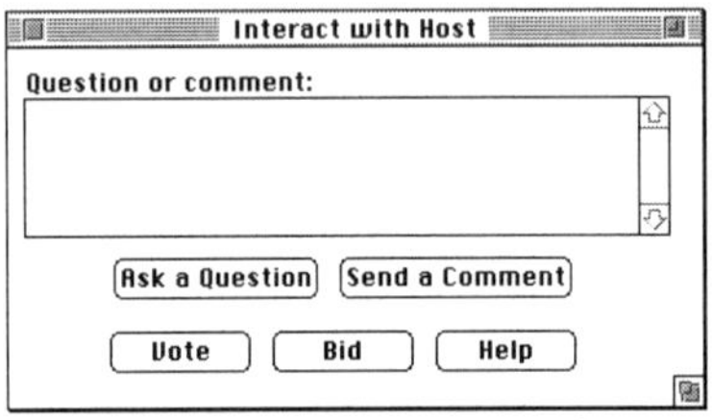


**Figure 44.** *Use the Interact with Host dialog box to enter and send questions, comments, votes, and bids.*

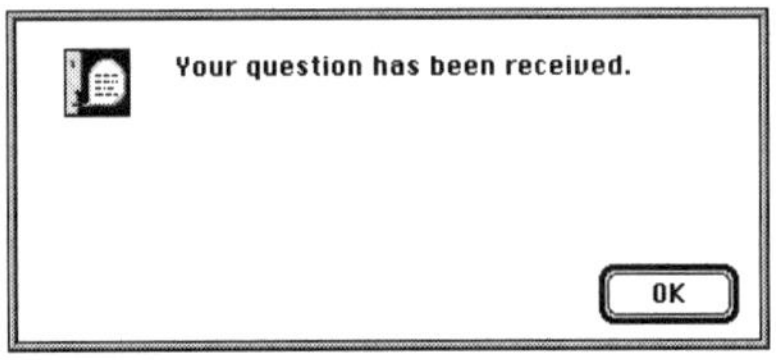


**Figures 45a & 45b.** *A dialog box like one of these appears when your question (above) or comment (below) is received by the host.*

### ✔ Tips

- If you have a question for the guest, get to the auditorium early. Questions are saved and asked by the host in the order in which they arrived. If there are many questions, those at the end of the list may not be used at all.
- Interacting with the host is the *only* way to send your question or comment to the guest and the rest of the people in the auditorium.

**Figure 46.** *One way to send an Instant Message is to choose Send an Instant Message from the Members menu.*

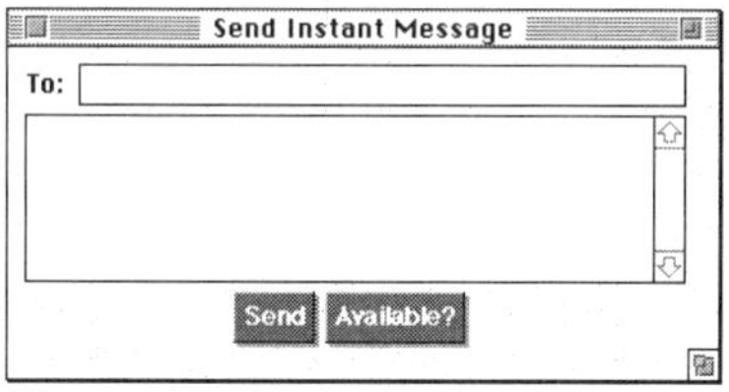


**Figure 47.** *Use the Send Instant Message window to send an Instant Message.*

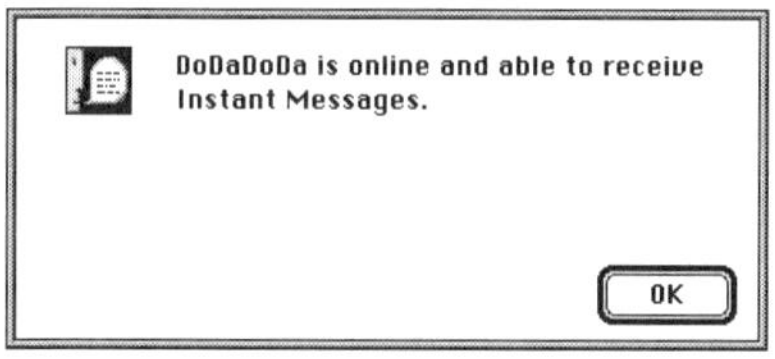


**Figure 48.** *This dialog box confirms that the recipient is available to receive Instant Messages.*

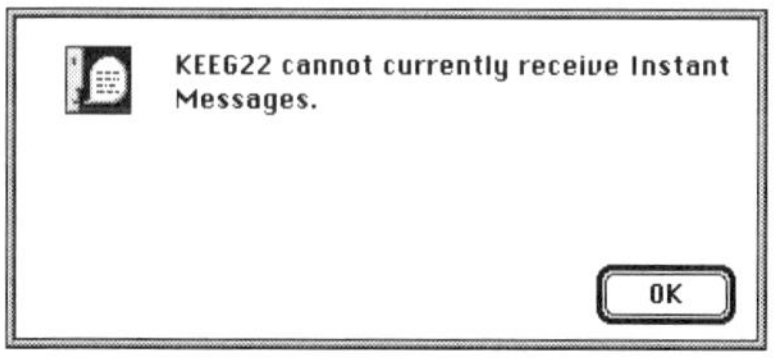


**Figure 49.** *This dialog box confirms that the recipient is signed on, but cannot receive Instant Messages.*

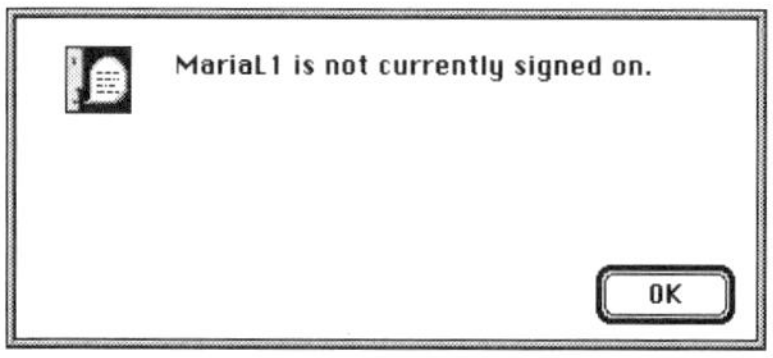


**Figure 50.** *This dialog box informs you that the recipient is not signed on.*

## About Instant Messages

AOL's *Instant Message* (or *IM*) feature lets you exchange live, private messages with another connected member—no matter where you are on AOL.

### ✔ Tips

- Using the Instant Message feature is like having a private chat room you can open and use any time you like.
- You cannot send Instant Messages while you are in a free area. Free areas are discussed in **Chapters 3** and **11**.

## To send an Instant Message

1. Choose Send Instant Message from the Members menu (see **Figure 46**) or press ⌘ I.

   *or*

   Click a screen name in the People window (see **Figure 12** or **39**) and then click the Message button.

   *or*

   Click the Message button in the Information window (see **Figure 22**).
2. In the Send Instant Message window that appears (see **Figure 47**), enter the screen name of the intended recipient in the To edit box. Then enter the text of the message in the box beneath it.
3. Click the Send button or press Enter.

### ✔ Tip

- In the Send Instant Message window (see **Figure 47**), enter the recipient's name in the To edit box and then click the Available? button to determine whether the recipient can receive Instant Messages. **Figures 48**, **49**, and **50** illustrate the kinds of responses you'll get.

## To format an Instant Message

1. Follow the instructions on the previous page to address and compose an Instant Message.
2. Select text you want to format within the message box (see **Figure 51**).
3. Choose a formatting command from the appropriate submenu under the Format menu (see **Figure 52**). **Figure 53** shows an example of text with Bold and Italic formatting applied.
4. When you are finished applying formats, click the Send button or press Enter to send the message.

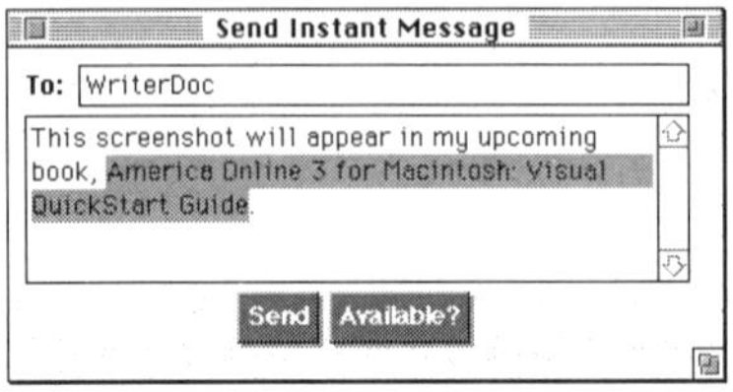


**Figure 51.** *Select the text you want to format.*

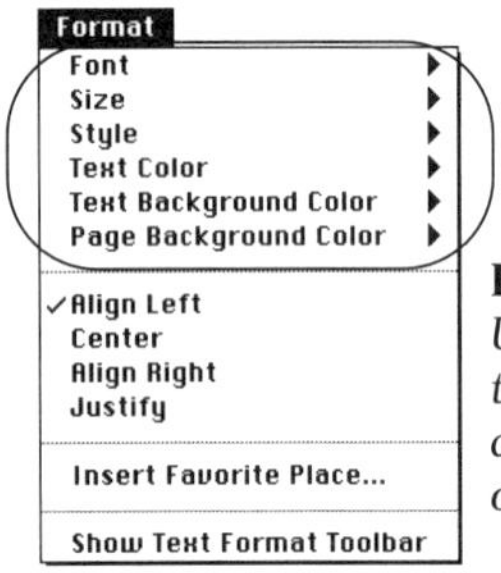


**Figure 52.** *Use commands under the Format menu to change the appearance of selected text.*

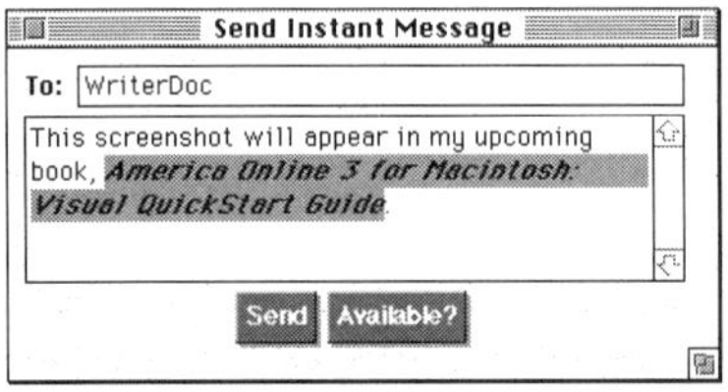


**Figure 53.** *In this example, two Style commands were used to change the appearance of selected text: Bold and Italic.*

### ✔ Tips

- Text formatting and commands under the Format menu are discussed in greater detail in **Chapter 4**.
- You can apply almost any combination of text formatting to selected characters in the Instant Message window.
- Avoid using colors to highlight text unless you're sure that the person receiving the Instant Message has a color monitor.
- Text formatting of Instant Messages are not seen at all by anyone using a version of the AOL software prior to version 3.

Formatting Instant Messages

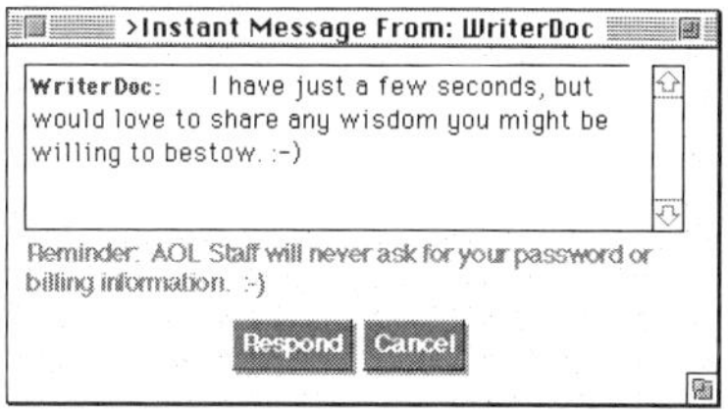


**Figure 54.** *An incoming Instant Message appears in a window like this.*

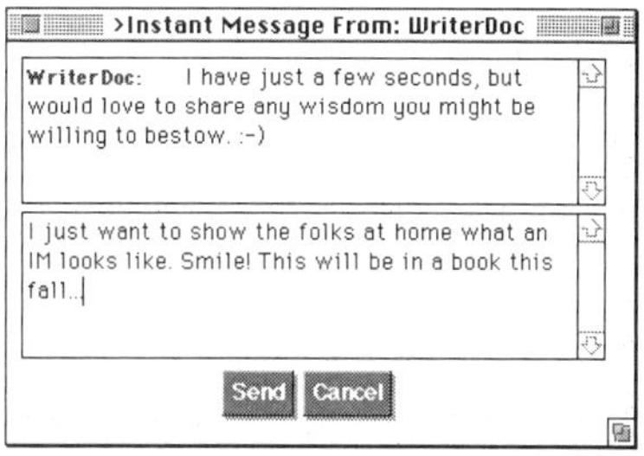


**Figure 55.** *When you click Respond, the window expands to give you a place to type in and format your response.*

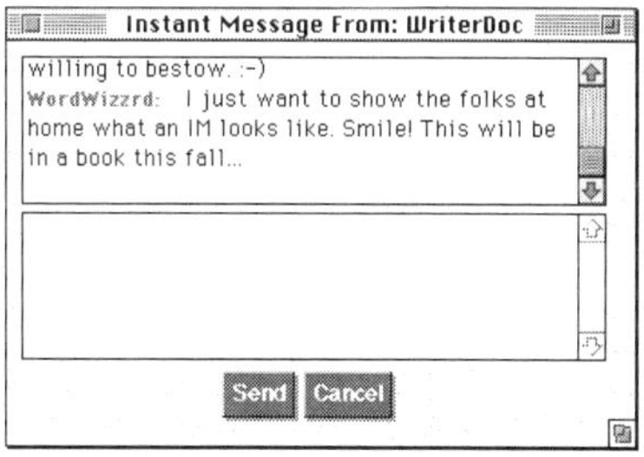


**Figure 56.** *Sending the response puts it into the scrolling list at the top of the Instant Message window, creating a mini chat window.*

## To receive an Instant Message

When you receive an Instant Message, your computer will play the IM sound and a window like the one in **Figure 54** will appear. You don't have to do a thing.

## To close an Instant Message without replying

Click the Cancel button.

*or*

Close the Instant Message window.

## To reply to an Instant Message

1. In the Instant Message window (see **Figure 54**), click the Respond button.
2. Enter your reply in the bottom of the Instant Message window (see **Figure 55**). You may format it as discussed on the previous page if desired.
3. Click Send. The message appears in the top of the Instant Message window on your computer (see **Figure 56**) as well as in the Instant Message window on the recipient's computer.

## ✔ Tips

- By leaving the Instant Message window open, you create a mini chat window where you can have a one-on-one conversation with another member.
- You can have as many Instant Message windows open as you like.

## To block incoming Instant Messages

1. Choose Send Instant Message from the Members menu (see **Figure 46**).

   *or*

   Press ⌘ I.
2. In the To edit box of the Send Instant Message window that appears, enter $im_off (see **Figure 57**).
3. In the message scrolling edit box of the Send Instant Message window, enter at least one character.
4. Click Send.
5. A confirmation dialog box like the one in **Figure 58** appears. Click OK or press Enter to dismiss it.

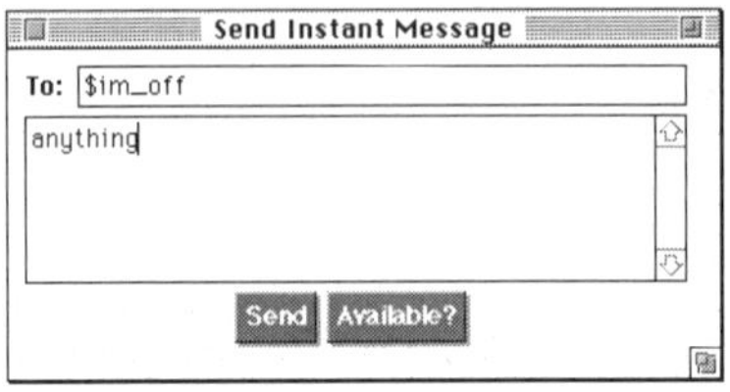


**Figure 57.** *To block incoming Instant Messages, send an Instant Message like this.*

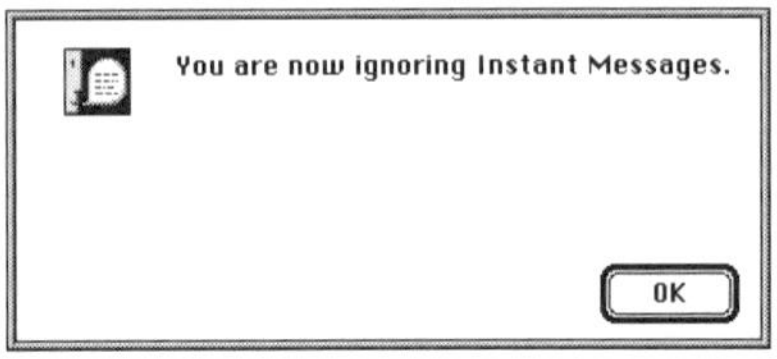


**Figure 58.** *AOL confirms that you've disabled incoming Instant Messages.*

### ✔ Tips

- Blocking incoming Instant Messages remains in effect for the current AOL session only.
- To unblock incoming Instant Messages, follow the above steps but enter $im_on in the To edit box in step 2 above. A confirmation dialog box like the one in **Figure 59** should appear after sending the message.

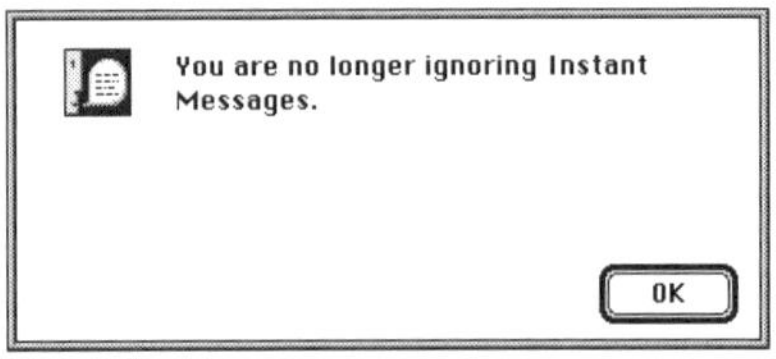


**Figure 59.** *AOL also confirms that you've enabled incoming Instant Messages.*

# KEEPING TRACK OF ONLINE FRIENDS 8

## About Online Friends

The more you use AOL's features, the more likely you are to make friends with other AOL members. Here are some examples:

- While attending a chat session in your favorite forum, you may meet another AOL member who shares your views about the topics discussed.
- After posting a request for information in a message board, you may get a message from another member who has just the information you need.
- After sending feedback to a shareware program's author, you may find yourself on the beta team for the next release of the product.

This chapter provides information about AOL features designed to help you keep track of your online friends:

- The Member Directory feature helps you find other members based on name, location, interests, or other information.
- The Member Profile feature helps you learn more about other AOL members.
- The Address Book feature lets you store e-mail addresses for the people with whom you exchange e-mail messages.
- The Buddy List feature lets you store screen names for online friends so they're easy to find and contact when they connect while you're online.

## About the Member Directory

AOL's Member Directory feature offers an easy way to locate AOL members based on their names (see **Figure 1**), screen names, locations, interests, or other information entered into their Member Profiles. You enter search information and AOL displays a list of members who match it.

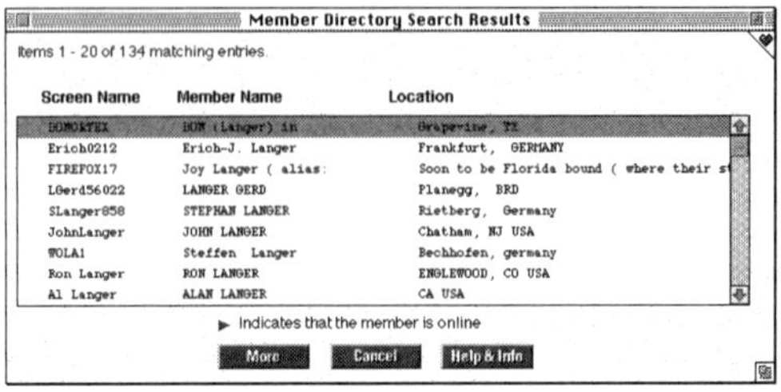


**Figure 1.** *The Member Directory lets you find members based on a variety of search criteria. This example shows the result of a search by member name.*

### ✔ Tips

- The Member Directory is useful for finding the exact screen name of an online friend to whom you want to send e-mail, since sending e-mail to an incorrect screen name will result in an error. Consult **Chapter 4** for more information about e-mail.
- The Member Directory works by searching for members based on information provided in their Member Profiles. If a member did not provide a member profile, you will not find him in the Member Directory.
- The Member Directory search feature will only retrieve the first 250 matches to the criteria you enter.
- Once you locate a member in the Member Directory, you can use the Member Profile feature to learn more about him. Member Profiles are discussed in detail later in this chapter.

**Figure 2.** *To search the Member Directory, begin by choosing Member Directory from the Members menu.*

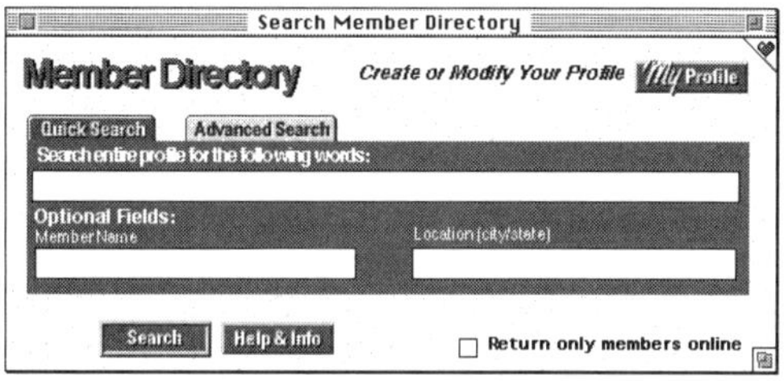


**Figure 3.** *The Quick Search tab of the Search Member Directory window lets you search by anything in a Member Profile, member name, or location.*

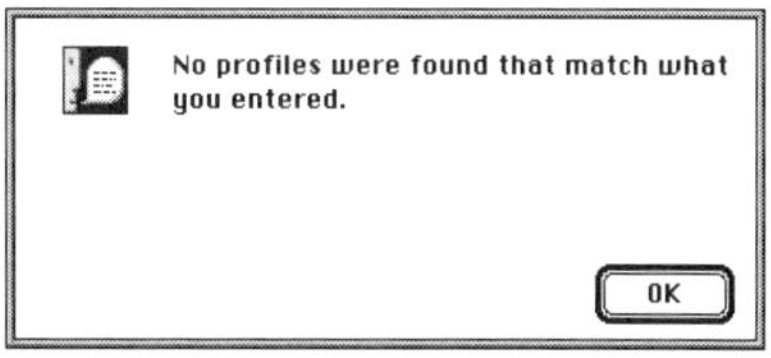


**Figure 4.** *If there are no profiles that match the criteria you entered, AOL tells you with a dialog box like this.*

## To perform a quick search of the Member Directory

1. Choose Member Directory from the Members menu (see **Figure 2**).

   *or*

   Use the keyword MEMBER DIRECTORY.
2. In the Search Member Directory window that appears, make sure the Quick Search tab is selected (see **Figure 3**).
3. Enter search criteria as follows:
   - ▲ To search for a person based on any word or phrase in the person's Member Profile, enter the word or phrase in the top edit box.
   - ▲ To search for a person by name, enter the name in the Member Name edit box.
   - ▲ To search for a person by location, enter the city and/or state of the location in the Location edit box.
4. Click the Search button or press Enter.

## ✔ Tips

- If your search is successful, a list of matches should appear in the Member Directory Search Results window (see **Figure 1**). If there are more than 20 matches, click the More button as necessary to display them all.
- If there are no Member Profiles that match the search criteria you entered, a dialog box like the one in **Figure 4** appears. Click OK or press Enter to dismiss it.
- You can use any combination of criteria in the Search Member Directory window to narrow down your search and reduce the number of matches.

## To perform an advanced search of the Member Directory

1. Choose Member Directory from the Members menu (see **Figure 2**).

   *or*

   Use the keyword MEMBER DIRECTORY.
2. Click the Advanced Search tab in the Search Member Directory window. The window expands to offer additional fields for search criteria (see **Figure 5**).
3. Enter search criteria as instructed in step 3 on the previous page. You can also enter appropriate search criteria in the following fields:
   - ▲ Birth date
   - ▲ Sex
   - ▲ Marital Status
   - ▲ Hobbies/Interests
   - ▲ Occupation
   - ▲ Computers
   - ▲ Quote
4. To limit your search so that only those members who are online appear in the Member Directory Search Results window, turn on the "Return only members online" check box.
5. Click the Search button or press [Enter].

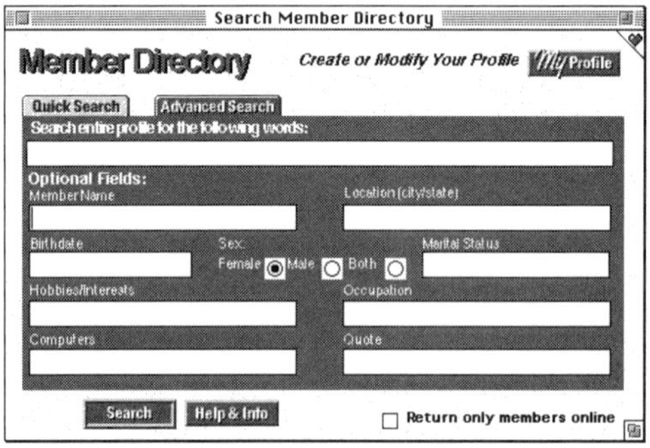


**Figure 5.** *Clicking the Advanced Search tab expands the window to offer additional fields for search criteria.*

## ✔ Tips

- ■ If your search is successful, a list of matches should appear in the Member Directory Search Results window (see **Figure 1**). If there are more than 20 matches, click the More button as necessary to display them all.
- ■ If there are no Member Profiles that match the search criteria you entered, a dialog box like the one in **Figure 4** appears. Click OK or press [Enter] to dismiss it.
- ■ You can use any combination of criteria in the Search Member Directory window to narrow down your search and reduce the number of matches.

### To use advanced search criteria

You can include additional characters or expressions in your Member Directory search criteria to help narrow down your searches.

- *Wildcard characters* take the place of single or multiple specific characters:
  - ▲ ? (question mark) can represent any single character. For example, *gr?y* will find profiles containing the words *gray* or *grey*.
  - ▲ * (asterisk) can represent any number of characters. For example, *writ** will find profiles containing the words *write, writer, writing,* or *writers.*
- *Boolean expressions* are search phrases that include one of the following words:
  - ▲ *AND* matches both words in the search phrase. For example, *motorcycle AND racing* will find profiles that contain both the word *motorcycle* and the word *racing*. Putting a space between search words is the same as using the word *AND.*
  - ▲ *OR* matches either word in the search phrase. For example, *motorcycle OR racing* will find profiles that contain either the word *motorcycle* or the word *racing.*
  - ▲ *NOT* matches the first word in the search phrase but omits the second. For example, *motorcycle NOT racing* will find profiles that contain the word *motorcycle* if the word *racing* is not included.
- *Parentheses* can group parts of a search phrase. For example *(Maria OR Norbert) AND Langer* will find profiles that contain the words *Maria* and *Langer* or the words *Norbert* and *Langer.*

## About Member Profiles

An AOL member can create a Member Profile for each screen name on his account. A Member Profile can include any combination of the following information:

- Name
- City, State, and Country
- Birthday
- Sex
- Marital Status
- Hobbies
- Computers Used
- Occupation
- Personal Quote

**Figure 6** shows an example of a Member Profile with some of the possible information provided.

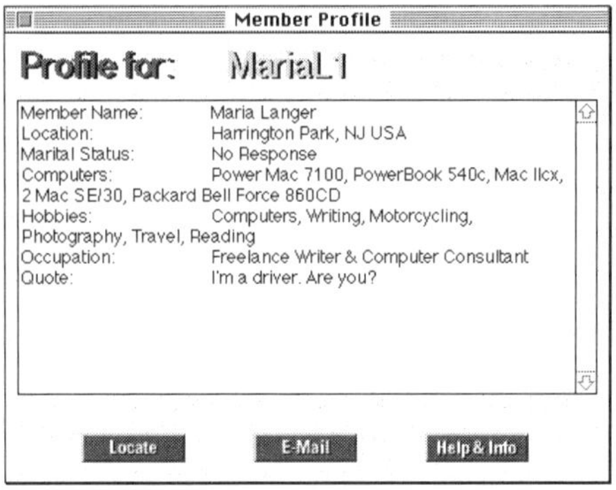


**Figure 6.** *Here's an example of a Member Profile that includes only some of the possible information.*

### ✔ Tips

- If you do not create a Member Profile for a screen name, that screen name will never be found in a search of the Member Directory.
- Member Profiles are a great way to provide more information about yourself and learn more about other members.
- You can create, change, or delete a member profile for one of your screen names any time you're connected to AOL using that screen name.

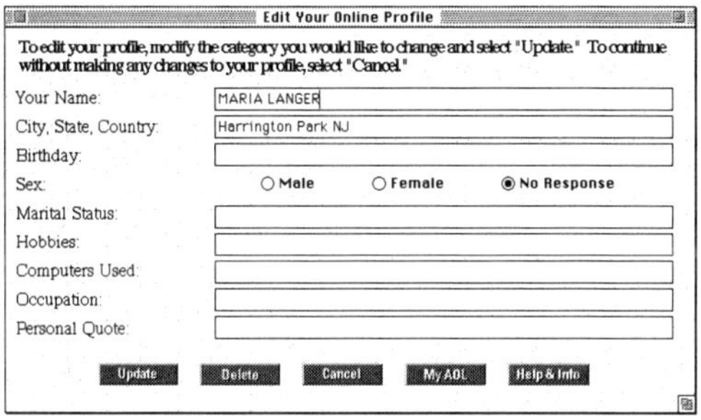


**Figure 7.** *Enter information about yourself in a simple form.*

**Figures 8a & 8b.** *AOL confirms that your profile is being created (above) or updated (below) when you c:eate or modify it.*

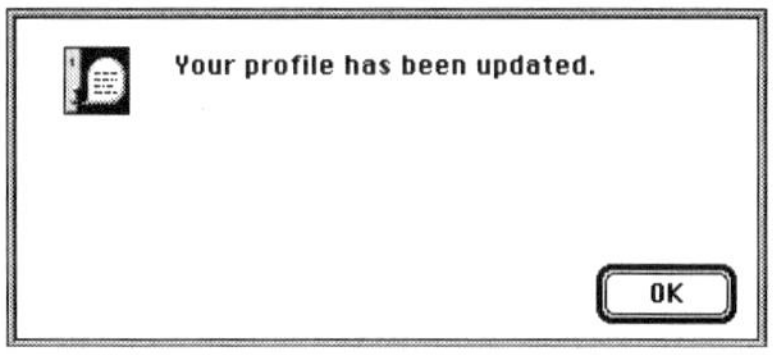


## To create or modify your Member Profile

1. Choose Member Directory from the Members menu (see **Figure 2**) and then click the My Profile button in the Search Member Directory window (see **Figure 3**).

   *or*

   Use the keyword PROFILE.
2. In the Edit Your Online Profile window that appears (see **Figure 7**), enter or edit information about yourself as desired.
3. Click Update.
4. A dialog box like the one in **Figure 8a** or **8b** appears, letting you know that your profile is being created or updated. Click OK or press Enter to dismiss it.

## ✔ Tips

- When the Edit Your Online Profile dialog box first appears, it includes the name, city, state, and country of the AOL account holder (see **Figure 7**). You can edit this information if it does not apply to you—for example, if the name that appears is your parent's or spouse's.
- If you leave a field empty in the Edit Your Online Profile dialog box (see **Figure 7**), that field will be omitted from the profile.
- Think twice about entering personal information about yourself in your Member Profile. Remember, any AOL member can access the information you enter. You may be surprised by the way this information is used by other members.

## To delete your Member Profile

1. Choose Member Directory from the Members menu (see **Figure 2**) and then click the My Profile button in the Search Member Directory window (see **Figure 3**).

   *or*

   Use the keyword PROFILE.
2. In the Edit Your Online Profile window that appears (see **Figure 7**), click the Delete button.
3. In the confirmation dialog box that appears (see **Figure 9**), click Yes.
4. Another dialog box appears, confirming that your profile has been deleted (see **Figure 10**). Click OK or press Enter to dismiss it.

**Figure 9.** *AOL checks to make sure you really do want to delete your Member Profile before deleting it.*

**Figure 10.** *AOL also confirms that your profile has been deleted once the job is done.*

### ✔ Tips

- If you delete your Member Profile, other users will not be able to look you up in the Member Directory. The Member Directory is discussed earlier in this chapter.
- Deleting a Member Profile is not the same as deleting a screen name. Consult **Chapter 11** for information about deleting screen names.

**Figure 11.** *Choose Get a Member's Profile from the Members menu.*

**Figure 12.** *Use this dialog box to enter the screen name for the member whose profile you want to see.*

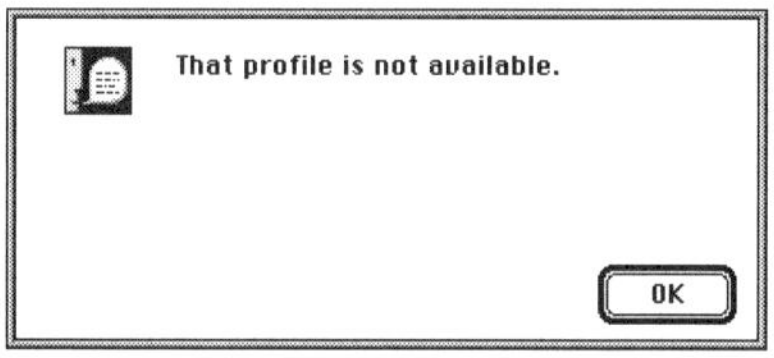


**Figure 13.** *If there is no Member Profile for the screen name you enter, a dialog box like this appears.*

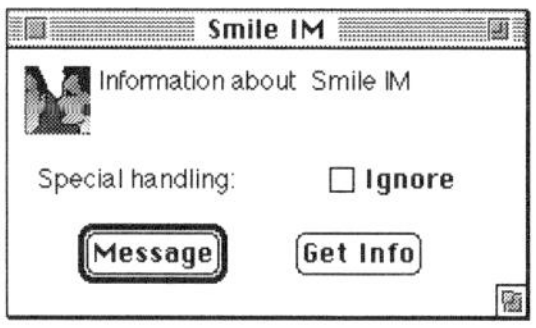


**Figure 14.** *You can also view a member's profile by clicking the Get Info button in an Information window.*

## To view a member's profile

1. Choose Get a Member's Profile from the Members menu (see **Figure 11**).

   *or*

   Press [⌘G].
2. In the Get a Member's Profile dialog box that appears (see **Figure 12**), enter the exact screen name for the member whose profile you want to view.
3. Click OK or press [Enter].

## ✔ Tips

- The member's profile appears in a window like the one in **Figure 6**.
- You can use the Copy and Paste commands under the Edit menu to copy a selected screen name from an e-mail message, message board message, or chat window and paste it into the Get a Member's Profile dialog box (see **Figure 12**) rather than type it.
- If there is no Member Profile for the screen name you entered, a dialog box like the one in **Figure 13** appears. Click OK or press [Enter] to dismiss it. Then check the screen name and try again. If a Member Profile still does not appear, that member probably does not have a profile on file.
- Another way to view a member's profile is to double-click his screen name in the Member Directory Search Results window (see **Figure 1**). The Member Directory is discussed earlier in this chapter.
- Yet another way to view a member's profile is to double-click his screen name in the list on the right side of a chat window. Then click the Get Info button in the Information window that appears (see **Figure 14**). AOL's chat feature is discussed in detail in **Chapter 7**.

Viewing Member Profiles

## About the Address Book

AOL's built-in address book lets you keep track of the e-mail addresses of people with whom you exchange e-mail.

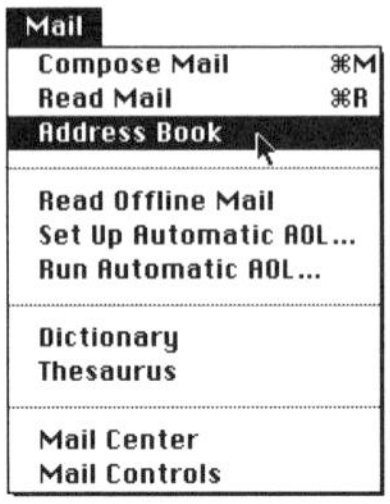


**Figure 15.** *Choose Address Book from the Mail menu to open the Address Book.*

### ✔ Tips

- The Address Book is available whenever you address an e-mail message, making it a handy tool for entering lengthy or hard-to-remember e-mail addresses.
- An Address Book entry can include e-mail addresses for more than one person. This makes it easy to send an e-mail message to a group of people.
- The E-Mail Address field for an address book entry should contain the person's screen name if he is an AOL member or the person's complete e-mail address if he has an e-mail account on another online service or the Internet. E-mail addresses are discussed in detail in **Chapter 4**.
- You do not have to be connected to AOL to create, edit, delete, or use an Address Book entry.

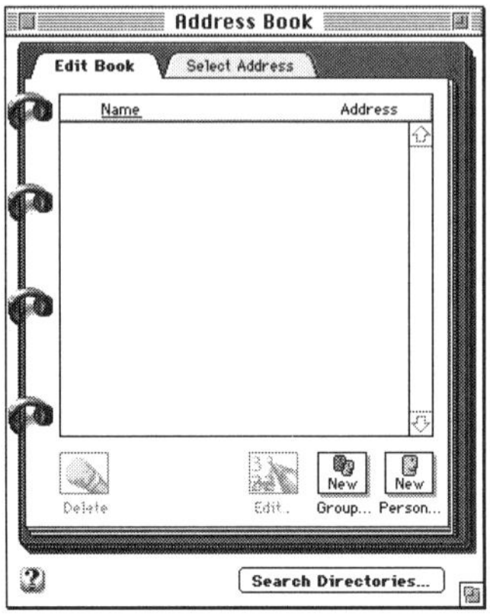


**Figure 16.** *The Address Book window offers tabs to create/edit or select stored e-mail addresses.*

## To create an address book entry for a person

1. Choose Address Book from the Mail menu (see **Figure 15**).
2. In the Address Book window that appears (see **Figure 16**), click the New Person button.
3. Fill in the edit boxes in the New Person window (see **Figure 17**) with the person's first name, last name, and e-mail address. You can include comments in the scrolling window at the bottom of the form if you like.
4. Click OK or press Enter. The entry appears in the Address Book window (see **Figure 24**).

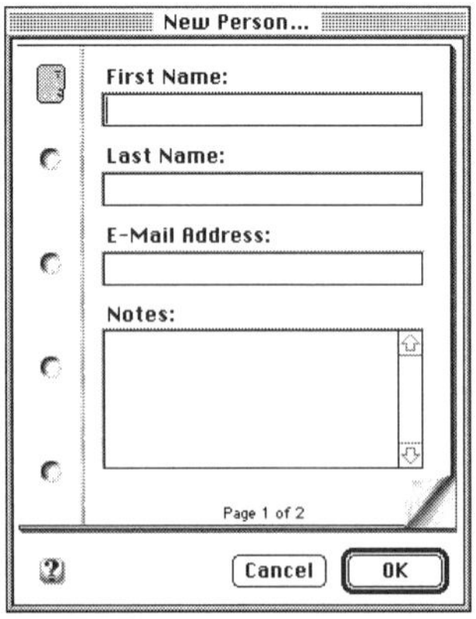


**Figure 17.** *Use the New Person window to enter name, e-mail address, and comments for each person with whom you correspond.*

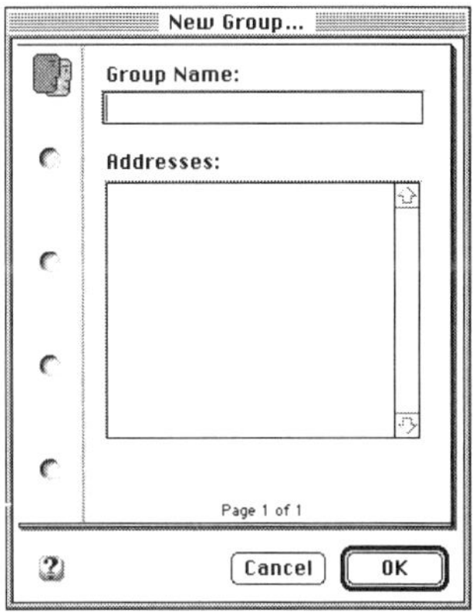


**Figure 18.** *Use the New Group window to create e-mail mailing lists that contain more than one e-mail address.*

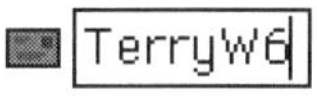


**Figure 19.** *For each entry in the Addresses scrolling list, an envelope icon and expandable edit box appears.*

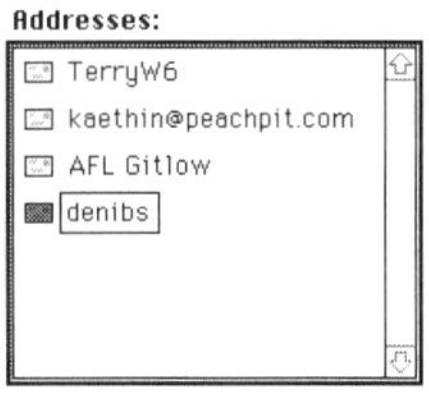


**Figure 20.** *As your list of address entries grows, it might look something like this.*

## To create an address book entry for a group of people

1. Choose Address Book from the Mail menu (see **Figure 15**).
2. In the Address Book window that appears (see **Figure 16**), click the New Group button.
3. In the New Group window that appears (see **Figure 18**), enter a name for the group in the Group Name edit box.
4. Press [Tab].

   *or*

   Click in the Addresses field.
5. Enter a screen name (for AOL members) or complete e-mail address (for non-AOL members) in the box beside the envelope icon that appears (see **Figure 19**). To complete the entry and enter another address, press [Return].
6. Repeat step 5 for each person in the group. As your list grows, it might look something like the one in **Figure 20**.
7. When you're finished adding addresses, click OK or press [Enter] to accept the entries and dismiss the New Group window. The entry appears in the Address Book window (see **Figure 24**).

### ✔ Tip

- Group address book entries are a great way to create mailing lists of people with similar interests.

## To create an address book entry from incoming e-mail

1. Open an incoming containing the e-mail address you want to add.
2. In the From/To field of the message window, click once on the e-mail address you want to add (see **Figure 21**).
3. Click the Add button to the right of the From/To field.
4. An entry window with the name of the person appears (see **Figure 22**). Edit the entry as necessary to include the correct first and last name.
5. Click OK or press Enter to add the entry to the address book.

### ✔ Tips

- If more than one e-mail address is selected in the e-mail message window (see **Figure 21**), all selected addresses will be added to the Address Book. The entry window in step 4 above, however, will not appear. To select more than one address, hold down Shift while clicking each address.
- If you prefer, you can drag the icon beside the address in an e-mail message window (see **Figure 21**) to the window of the Edit Book tab of the Address Book window (see **Figure 16**).
- Another way to create an address book entry is to drag the icon beside the namc in a chat window (see **Figure 23**) to the window of the Edit Book tab of the Address Book window (see **Figure 16**). AOL's chat feature is discussed in detail in **Chapter 7**.

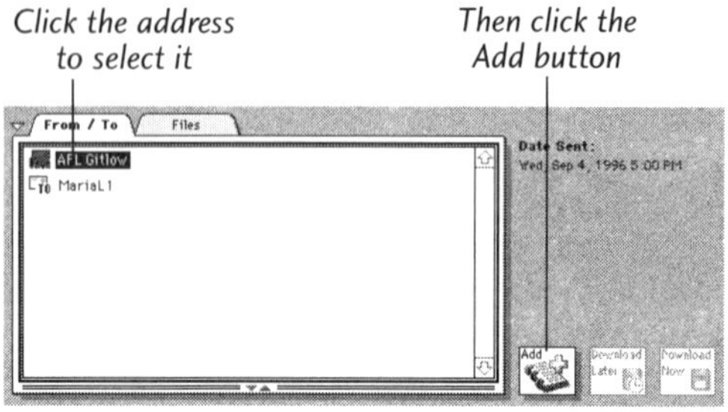


**Figure 21.** *In the message window, select the e-mail address you want to add and then click the Add button.*

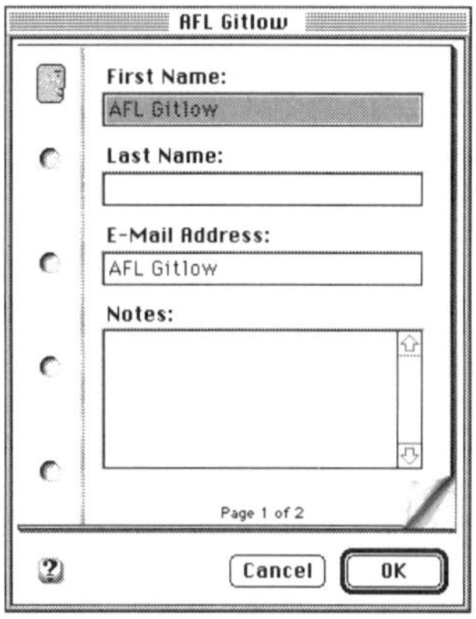


**Figure 22.** *Use this entry window to enter the correct first and last name of the person you're adding.*

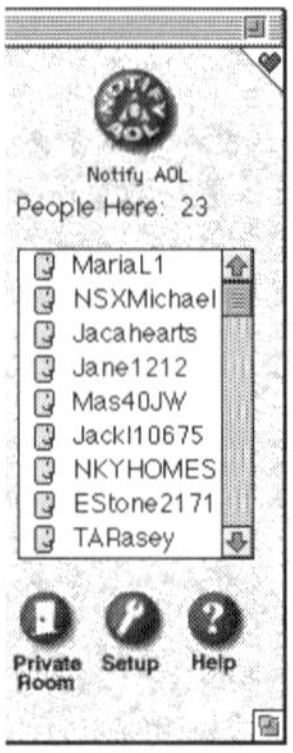


**Figure 23.** *You can also add an entry to your address book by dragging the icon beside a name in a chat window to your address book window.*

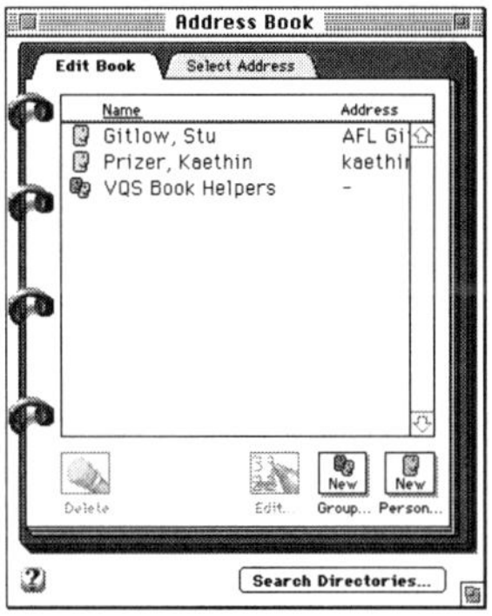


**Figure 24.** *Address book entries are automatically alphabetized. You can tell the difference between person and group entries by the icon to the left of the entry name.*

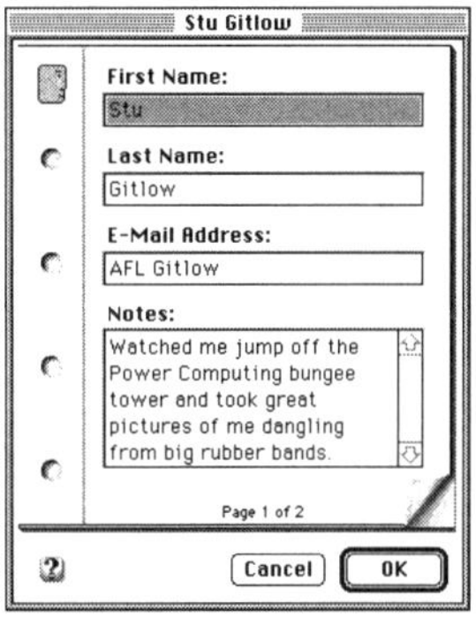


**Figure 25.** *Modify a person entry by changing the contents of the edit boxes in the entry form.*

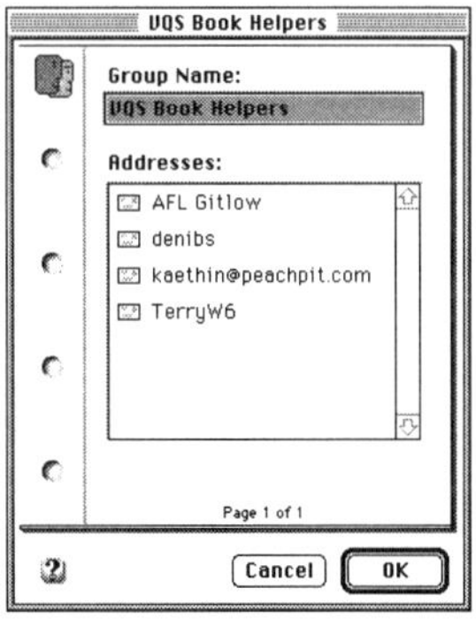


**Figure 26.** *Modify a group entry by changing contents of the Group Name field or changing, adding, or removing e-mail addresses.*

## To modify an address book entry

1. Choose Address Book from the Mail menu (see **Figure 15**).
2. In the Address Book window that appears (see **Figure 24**), click the name of the entry you want to modify to select it. Then click the Edit button.
3. An entry window like the one in **Figure 25** or **26** appears.
   - ▲ To change any part of a person entry, edit the contents of the appropriate edit box.
   - ▲ To change the name of a group entry, edit the contents of the Group Name.
   - ▲ To change an address in a group entry, click the address to select it. A black edit box appears around it. Edit the contents of the edit box and press Return.
   - ▲ To add an address to a group entry, click in the area beneath the last entry, type in the new entry, and press Return.
   - ▲ To remove an address from a group entry, click the icon beside the address to select it and press Delete.
4. When you're finished making changes in the entry window, click OK or press Enter to accept them.

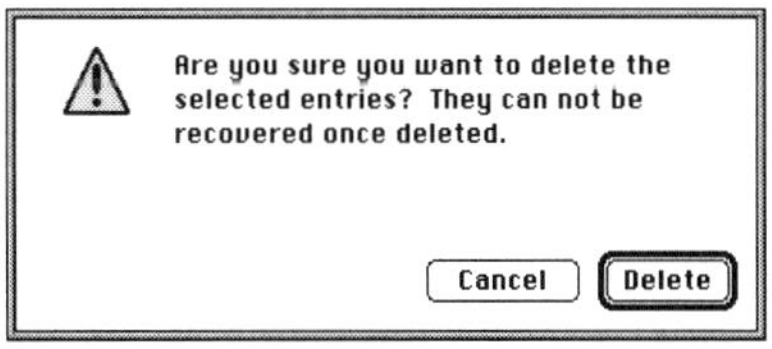


**Figure 27.** *AOL confirms that you want to delete an entry.*

## To delete an address book entry

1. Choose Address Book from the Mail menu (see **Figure 15**).
2. In the Address Book window that appears (see **Figure 24**), click the name of the entry you want to delete to select it.
3. Click the Delete button.
4. In the confirmation dialog box that appears (see **Figure 27**), click Delete.

## To use an Address Book entry

1. Choose Compose Mail from the Mail menu (see **Figure 28**).

   *or*

   Press [⌘][M].

   *or*

   Click the Compose Mail button on the toolbar. 
2. Click the Address Book button in the Compose Mail window that appears (see **Figure 29**).
3. In the Address Book window that appears (see **Figure 30**), click an entry you want to use and then click the TO, CC, or BCC button to add the address to the Compose Mail window as a To, CC, or Blind CC address.

   *or*

   Drag an entry from the Address Book window to the Address To field of the Compose Mail window.
4. Repeat step 3 for each entry you want to use in the Address To field of the Compose Mail window.
5. When you are finished using Address Book entries, click the Address Book window's close box to close it.
6. Complete and send the message as instructed in **Chapter 4**.

## ✔ Tips

- Composing e-mail messages is discussed in detail in **Chapter 4**.
- You can enter one or more addresses manually and use the Address Book to enter others.
- You can also add Address Book entries by dragging them from the Select Address tab of the Address Book window (see **Figure 30**) to the Address To field of the Compose Mail window (see **Figure 29**).

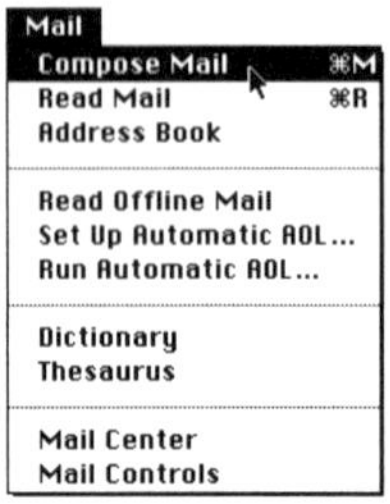


**Figure 28.** *Choose Compose Mail from the Mail menu.*

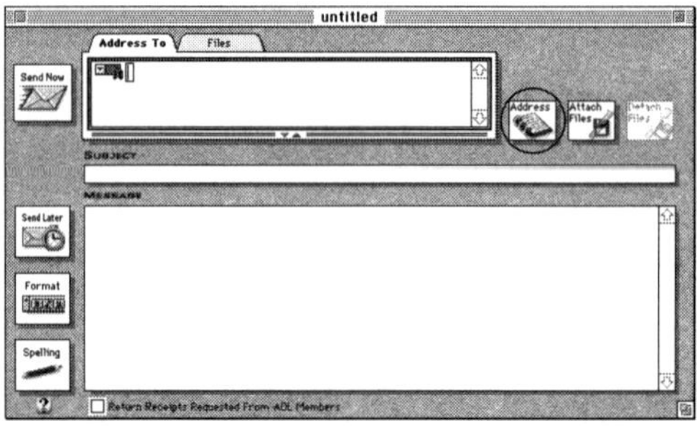


**Figure 29.** *To use an Address Book entry, click the Address Book button in a Compose Mail window.*

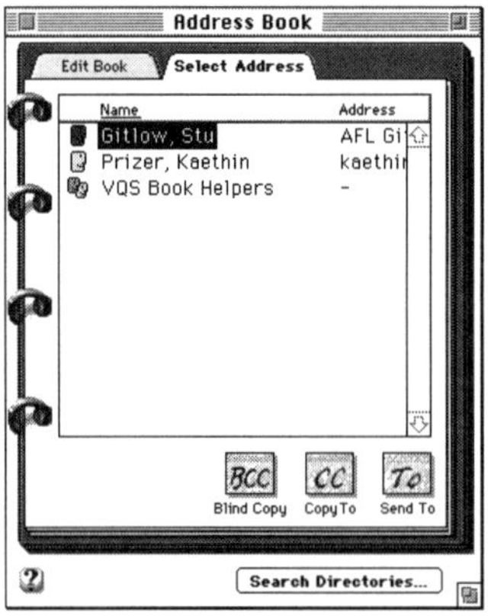


**Figure 30.** *Select the entry you want to use, then click the TO, CC, or BCC button to add the address to the Address To field of the Compose Mail window.*

**Figure 31.** *To see if a member is online, begin by choosing Locate a Member Online from the Members menu.*

## About Locating Members Online

Hundreds of thousands of AOL's six million members can be online at the same time—including your online friends. While you're online, you can easily find out whether a specific person is connected and, if so, whether he is in a chat area.

### ✔ Tips

- If a friend is online, you can send him an Instant Message to let him know that you're online, too. Then rendezvous in a chat room for a live conversation. Instant Messages and chat rooms are covered in **Chapter 7**.
- If you frequently check to see if friends are online, try the Buddy List feature (discussed on the next page) which makes it easy to track online friends.

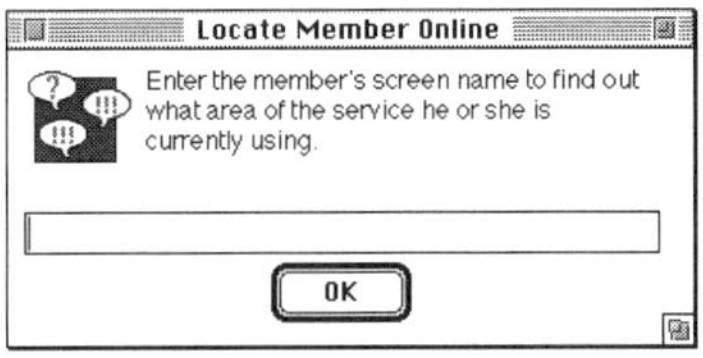


**Figure 32.** *Use the Locate Member Online dialog box to enter the screen name of the person you want to find.*

## To locate a member online

1. Choose Locate a Member Online from the Members menu (see **Figure 31**).

   *or*

   Press [⌘L].
2. In the Locate Member Online dialog box that appears (see **Figure 32**), enter the exact screen name for the member you want to find.
3. Click OK or press [Enter].
4. A dialog box like the one in **Figure 33a**, **33b**, or **33c** appears.
   - ▲ If your friend is not online click OK or press [Enter] to dismiss the dialog box (see **Figure 33a**).
   - ▲ If your friend is online, click the Send IM button (see **Figures 33b** and **33c**) to send him an Instant Message.
   - ▲ If your friend is online and in a chat area (see **Figure 33c**), click the Go button to join him.

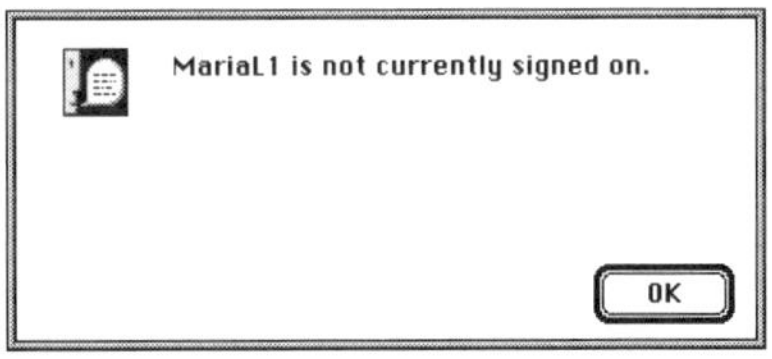


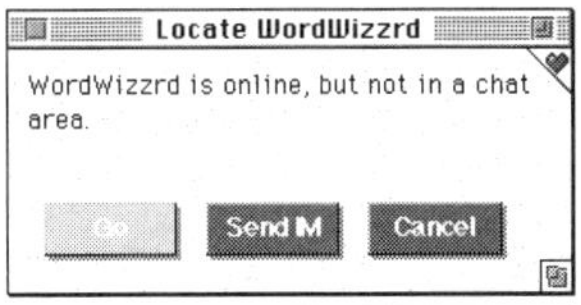


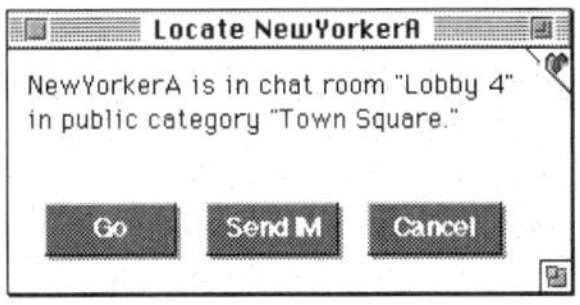


**Figures 33a, 33b, & 33c.** *Dialog boxes like these tell you whether a member is online and, if so, where he is.*

## About Buddy Lists

AOL's Buddy List feature lets you create lists of online friends called *Buddy Lists.* Then, when one of your buddies connects or disconnects, AOL automatically notifies you by playing a sound.

### ✔ Tip

- You can have up to 10 Buddy Lists per screen name.

## To create a Buddy List

1. Choose Buddy Lists from the Members menu (see **Figure 34**).

   *or*

   Use the keyword BUDDY.
2. In the Buddy Lists window that appears (see **Figure 35**), click the Create button.
3. In the Create a Buddy List window (see **Figure 36**), enter a name for the list in the Buddy List Name edit box.
4. Enter the screen name for the first friend you want to include on the list in the Enter a Screen Name edit box.
5. Click the Add Buddy button. The name you entered is added to the Buddies on List scrolling list window.
6. Repeat steps 4 and 5 for each friend you want to include on the list.
7. When you're finished adding names, the Create a Buddy List window might look something like the one in **Figure 37**. Click the Save button.
8. A dialog box like the one in **Figure 38** appears, confirming that your Buddy List has been saved. Click OK or press [Enter] to dismiss it.

**Figure 34.** *To create a Buddy List, begin by choosing Buddy Lists from the Members menu.*

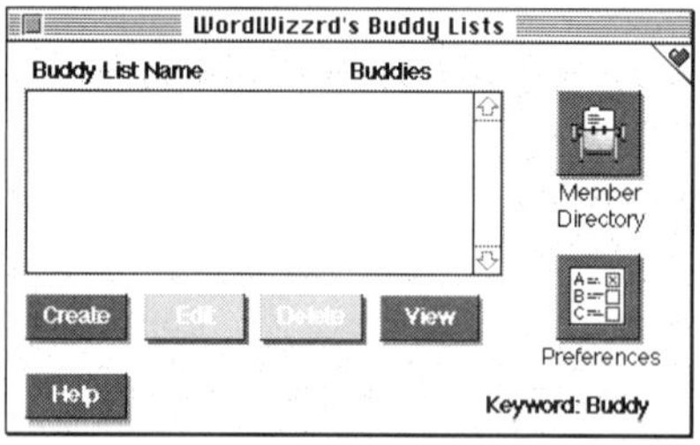


**Figure 35.** *The Buddy Lists window lets you create, edit, delete, or view Buddy Lists.*

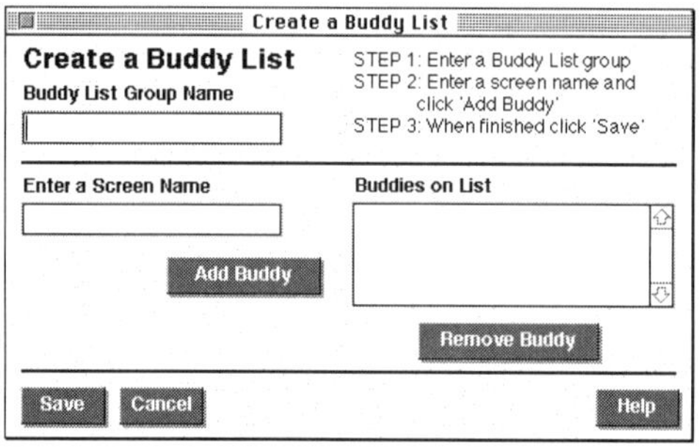


**Figure 36.** *Use this dialog box to create a Buddy List and add online friends to it.*

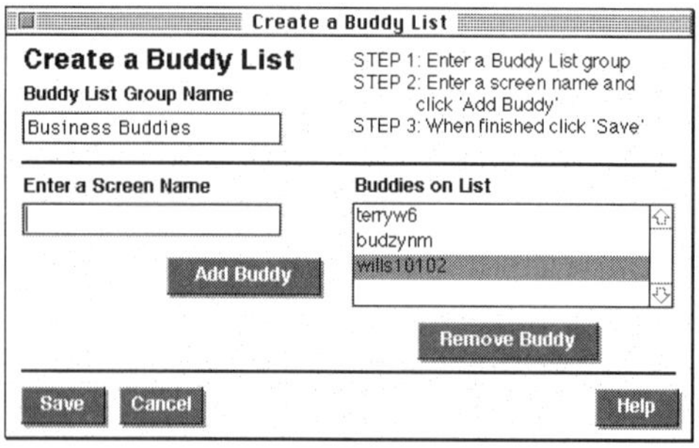


**Figure 37.** *Here's what a completed Buddy List might look like.*

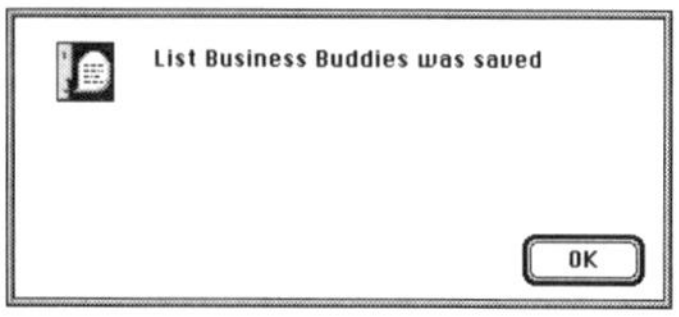


**Figure 38.** *When you save a Buddy List, a dialog box like this appears.*

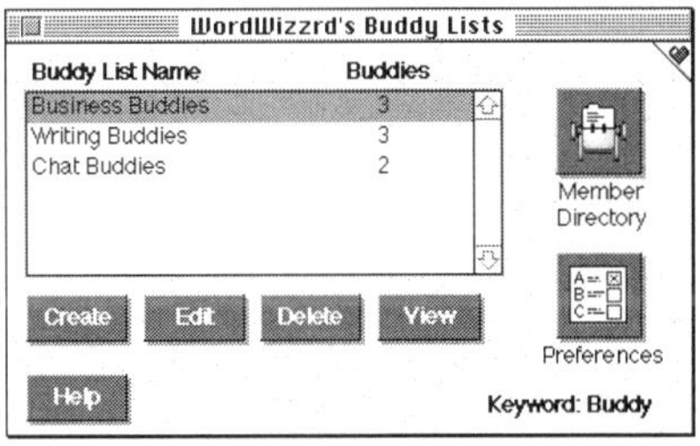


**Figure 39.** *To change or delete a Buddy List, begin by selecting it.*

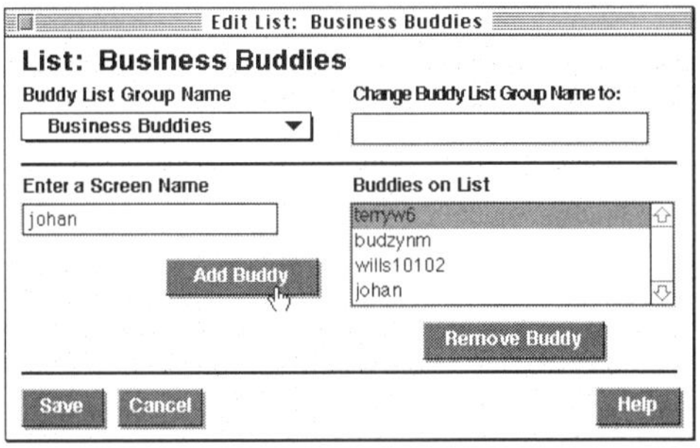


**Figure 40.** *The Edit List window lets you add or remove friends from a Buddy List.*

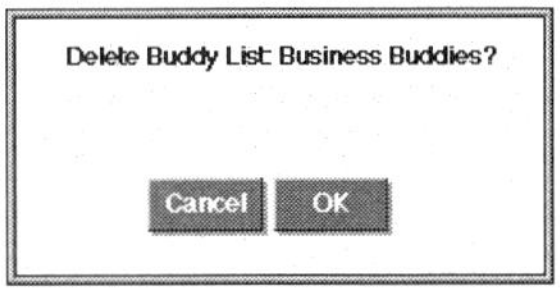


**Figure 41.** *Before deleting a Buddy List, AOL confirms that you really do want to delete it.*

## To edit a Buddy List

1. Choose Buddy Lists from the Members menu (see **Figure 34**).

   *or*

   Use the keyword BUDDY.
2. In the Buddy List window that appears (see **Figure 39**), click the Buddy List you want to modify to select it and then click the Edit button to display the Edit List window (see **Figure 40**).
3. To add a screen name to the list, enter the name in the Enter a Screen Name edit box and click the Add Buddy button (see **Figure 40**).

   *or*

   To remove a screen name from the list, click the name in the Buddies on List scrolling list window to select it and then click the Remove Buddy button.
4. Repeat step 3 for each change you want to make to the list.
5. When you're finished changing the list, click the Save button. (Do *not* simply close the window!)
6. A dialog box like the one in **Figure 38** appears, confirming that your Buddy List has been saved. Click OK or press Enter to dismiss it.
7. Click the Close box or press ⌘W to close the Edit List window.

## To delete a Buddy List

1. Choose Buddy Lists from the Members menu (see **Figure 34**).

   *or*

   Use the keyword BUDDY.
2. In the Buddy List window that appears (see **Figure 39**), click the Buddy List you want to delete to select it and then click the Delete.
3. In the confirmation dialog box that appears (see **Figure 41**), click OK.

## To set Buddy List preferences

1. In the Buddy Lists window (see **Figure 39**), click the Preferences button.
2. Select any combination of check boxes in the top half of the Buddy List Preferences window (see **Figure 42**) to:
   - ▲ Display your Buddy List when you connect to AOL.
   - ▲ Play a sound when a buddy connects.
   - ▲ Play a sound when a buddy disconnects.
3. Select one of the four options in the bottom half of the Buddy List Preferences dialog box (see **Figure 42**) to:
   - ▲ Allow any AOL member to add you to a Buddy List.
   - ▲ Prevent any AOL member from adding you to a Buddy List.
   - ▲ Allow only specific AOL members to add you to a Buddy List.
   - ▲ Prevent only specific AOL members from adding you to a Buddy List.
4. If you choose one of the bottom two options, enter the screen names for the members in the edit box near the bottom of the window. Separate one screen name from the next with a comma. **Figure 43** shows an example.
5. Click the Save button.
6. Click OK or press [Enter] to dismiss the confirmation dialog box that appears (see **Figure 44**).

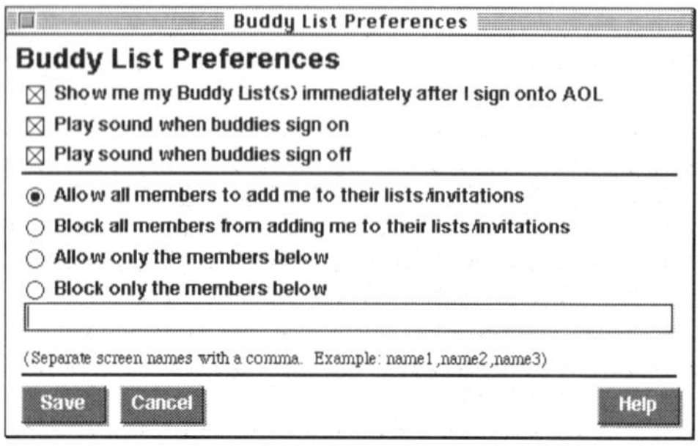


**Figure 42.** *The Buddy List Preferences window is where you customize the way Buddy Lists work.*

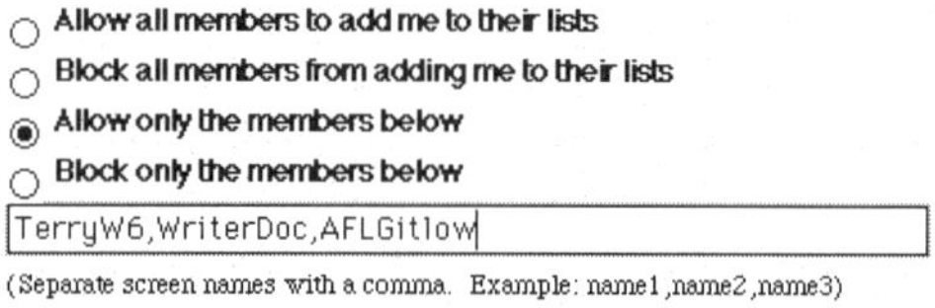


**Figure 43.** *In this example, only three people can add me to their Buddy Lists.*

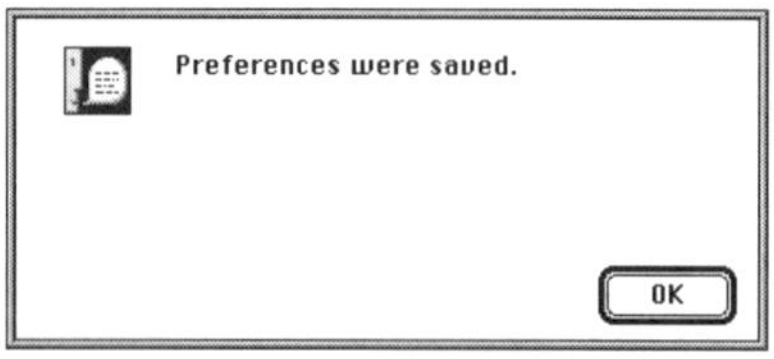


**Figure 44.** *AOL confirms that Buddy List preference changes are saved.*

**Figure 45.** *The Buddy Lists View window displays your Buddy Lists and the screen names of connected buddies.*

**Figure 46.** *Double-clicking a Buddy List name collapses the outline view of the list, hiding the screen names of buddies who are connected.*

## To open the Buddy Lists View window

Choose Buddy Lists from the Members menu (see **Figure 34**). In the Buddy Lists window that appears (see **Figure 39**), click the View button.

*or*

Use the keyword BUDDYVIEW.

## ✔ Tips

- The Buddy Lists View window opens automatically when you connect if you turned on the first option in the Buddy List Preferences dialog box (see **Figure 42**).
- The Buddy Lists View window (see **Figure 45**) lists all your Buddy Lists, along with the number of members in each list and the number of list members currently connected.
- If a member of a Buddy List is connected, his screen name appears beneath the list he's in (see **Figure 45**).
- To hide the names of connected buddies, double-click the name of the Buddy List in the Buddy Lists View window. The list collapses to hide the names (see **Figure 46**).
- Use buttons at the bottom of the Buddy Lists View window (see **Figures 45** and **46**) to access to other options:
  - ▲ *Locate* displays the Locate a Member Online dialog box, which was discussed earlier in this chapter.
  - ▲ *IM* displays the Send Instant Message dialog box, which is discussed in **Chapter 7**.
  - ▲ *Setup* displays the Buddy Lists dialog box, which was discussed earlier in this chapter.
  - ▲ *Invite* displays the Group Invite window, which is discussed on the next page.

## To use the Group Invite feature

1. Follow the instructions on the previous page to display the Buddy List View window (see **Figures 45** and **46**).
2. Click the Invite button to display the Group Invite window (see **Figure 47**).
3. In the Screen Names to Invite edit box, enter the screen names for the members to whom you want to send the invitation.
4. If desired, enter an invitation message in the Message to Send edit box.
5. Choose one of the location radio buttons and, if necessary, enter a location in the edit box beneath it:
   - ▲ Select Private Chat Room to meet your buddies for a private chat. You can then enter a name for the private chat room in the edit box. You can leave the edit box blank to have AOL automatically create a private chat room for you.
   - ▲ Select Keyword/Favorite Place to meet your buddies in a specific AOL area. You must then enter a keyword or favorite place location in the edit box.
6. Click the Send button or press Enter.

## ✔ Tips

- To enter the location for a favorite place in step 5 above, you can drag the heart icon from the location's window or your Favorite Places window to the edit box.
- When you send the invitation, a window like the one in **Figure 48** will appear on the screens of each person you invited. Invitation recipients can click buttons to go right to the location, send you an Instant Message reply, or ignore the invitation.

**Figure 47.** *Use the Group Invite window to invite your buddies to a private chat room or other location on AOL.*

**Figure 48.** *The people you invite to a chat room or AOL area see a window like this.*

# ACCESSING THE INTERNET 9



## About the Internet

The Internet is a global network of mainframe, mini, and personal computers. Originally, when the Internet was first conceived, only governmental and educational institutions had access. Today, with the help of Internet Service Providers like AOL, anyone with a personal computer can access the information available on the Internet.

AOL offers access to the following Internet resources:

- E-mail, which is direct, text-based messaging between individuals with Internet access. E-mail is discussed in detail in **Chapter 4**.
- Usenet newsgroups, which are topical message areas with many participants.
- The World Wide Web, which offers a graphical interface for accessing information, complete with hypertext links.
- FTP (or File Transfer Protocol), which offers access to file libraries all over the world.
- Gopher and WAIS, which can be used to search libraries of text articles for virtually any topic.

This chapter will tell you how to get started accessing the Internet with AOL.

### ✔ Tips

- The Internet is not part of AOL. It is a separate network, much larger than AOL, to which AOL is linked.
- The Internet is not governed by AOL's Terms of Service (TOS). Because of this, there's an "anything goes" mentality that may offend (or at least surprise) some AOL members.

## About Accessing the Internet

You can access the full range of Internet features through two different AOL windows:

- The Welcome to the Internet! window (see **Figure 1**) offers Best of and Search options for each Internet area.
- The Internet Connection window (see **Figure 2**) offers buttons for each Internet area, as well as access to *FAQs (Frequently Asked Questions)*.

## To open the Welcome to the Internet! window

Click the Internet button (see **Figure 3**) on the Welcome window.

*or*

Use the keyword NET HIGHLIGHTS.

## To open the Internet Connection window

Click the Internet Connection button (see **Figure 4**) on the Channels window.

*or*

Use the keyword NET or INTERNET.

*or*

Click the Internet Connection button on the Welcome to the Internet! window (see **Figure 1**).

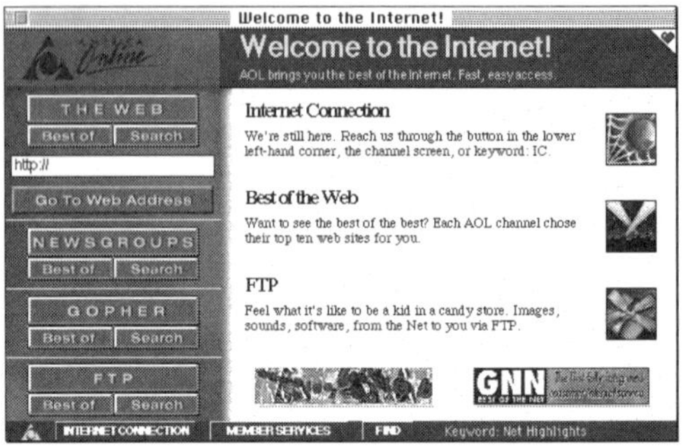


**Figure 1.** *The Welcome to the Internet! window offers access to Best of and Search features for each Internet area.*

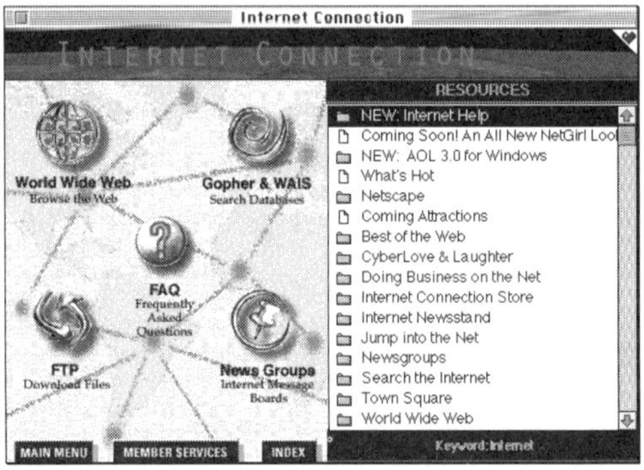


**Figure 2.** *The Internet Connection window offers direct access to each Internet area.*

**Figure 3.** *Click the Internet button on the Welcome window to open the Welcome to the Internet! window.*

**Figure 4.** *Click the Internet Connection button on the Channels window to open the Internet Connection window.*

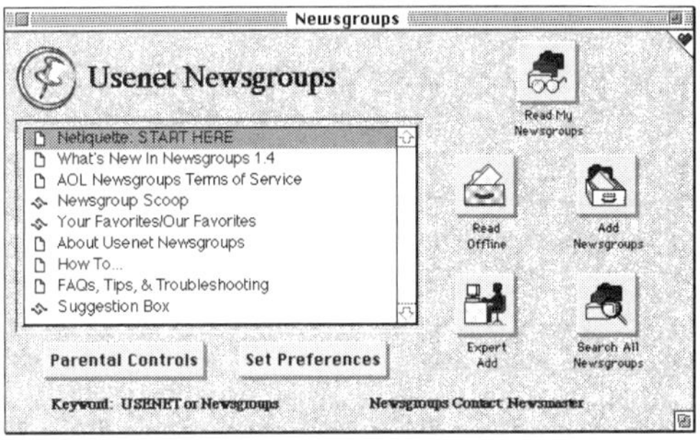


**Figure 5.** *The Newsgroups window is your starting place for setting up and reading newsgroups.*

## About Usenet Newsgroups

Usenet newsgroups are topical message areas. They are similar in purpose to the message boards you'll find throughout AOL. Rather than being limited to AOL areas and members, however, Usenet newsgroups cover over 20,000 topics and are open to everyone on the Internet.

You access newsgroups through the Newsgroups window (see **Figure 5**). You begin by adding specific newsgroups to a list of those you want to read. Then you open a newsgroup on the list and read and reply to messages.

### ✔ Tips

- Since many newsgroups can get literally hundreds of messages a day, you may find it more cost effective to read them offline. Reading newsgroups offline is discussed in **Chapter 10**.
- Newsgroups are not protected by AOL's Terms of Service. If you have young children who may be accessing the Internet through AOL, you can use Parental Controls to limit their access. The Parental Controls feature is discussed in **Chapter 11**.

### To open the Newsgroups window

1. Click the Internet Connection button (see **Figure 4**) in the Channels window.
2. Click the News Groups button in the Internet Connection window (see **Figure 2**).

*or*

Use the keyword USENET or NEWSGROUPS.

## To search for newsgroups by name

1. Click the Search All Newsgroups button in the Newsgroups window (see **Figure 5**).
2. In the Search Newsgroups window that appears (see **Figure 6**), enter a word or phrase that you want to find in a newsgroup name.
3. Click the Search button or press Enter. After a moment, a Search Results window (see **Figure 7**) will appear, listing the matches.

**Figure 6.** *Use the Search Newsgroups window to find newsgroups by name.*

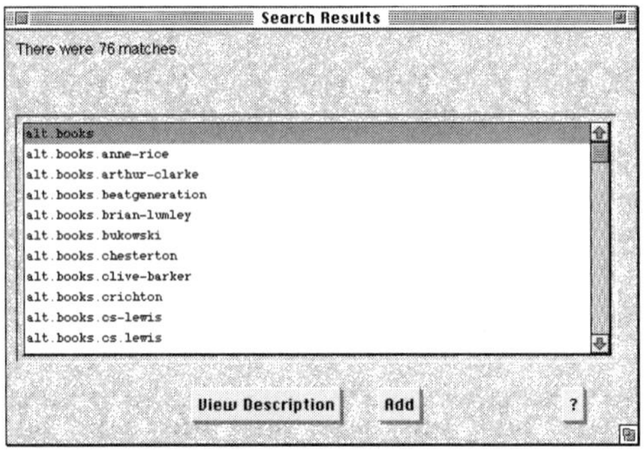


**Figure 7.** *Here are the search results using the word* books *as a search phrase.*

### ✔ Tips

- You may find the Search Newsgroups window helpful when you know only part of a newsgroup name and need to find the full name.
- To see a description of a newsgroup, click the name of the newsgroup in the Search Results window (see **Figure 7**) and click the View Description button. A Newsgroup Description window like the one in **Figure 8** appears for the newsgroup.
- To subscribe to a newsgroup you want to read regularly, click the name of the newsgroup in the Search Results window (see **Figure 7**) and click the Add button. A dialog box like the one in **Figure 9** confirms that you have been subscribed to the newsgroup.

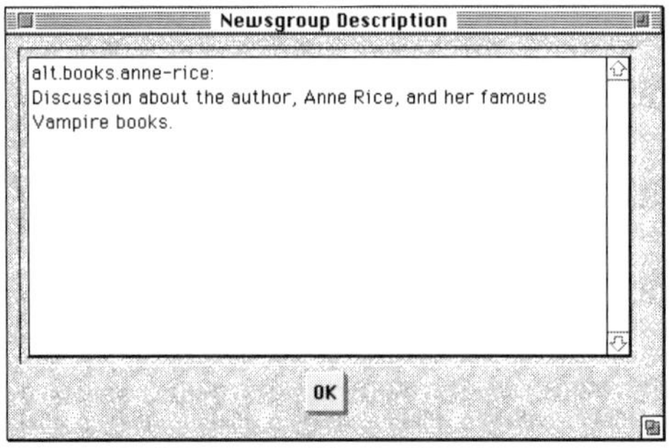


**Figure 8.** *When you click the View Description button, a description window for the selected newsgroup appears.*

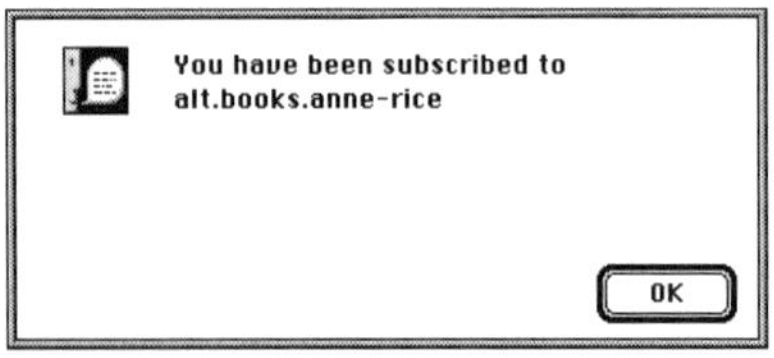


**Figure 9.** *This dialog box appears when you click the Add button.*

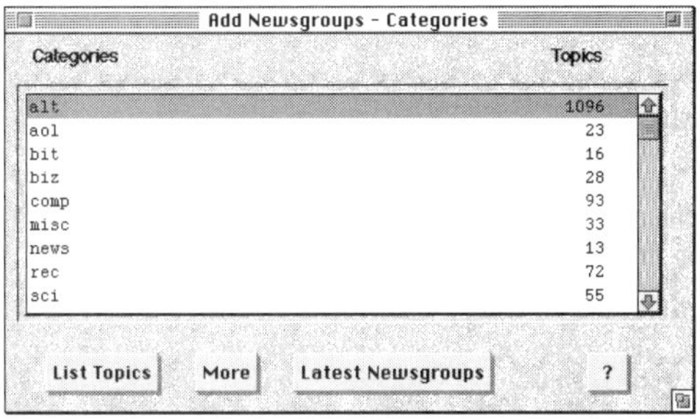


**Figure 10.** *Start with a list of categories...*

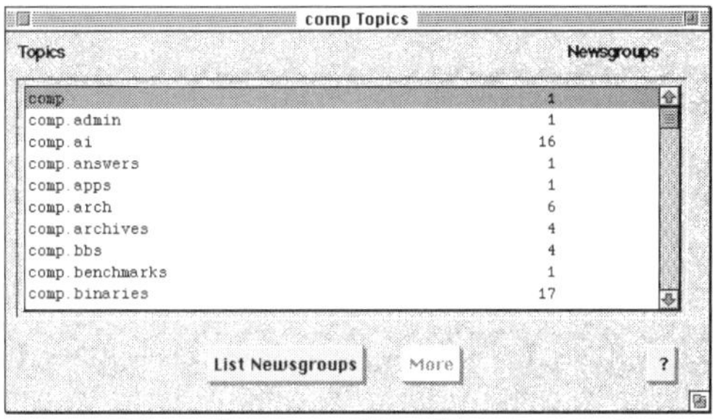


**Figure 11.** *...then view a list of category topics...*

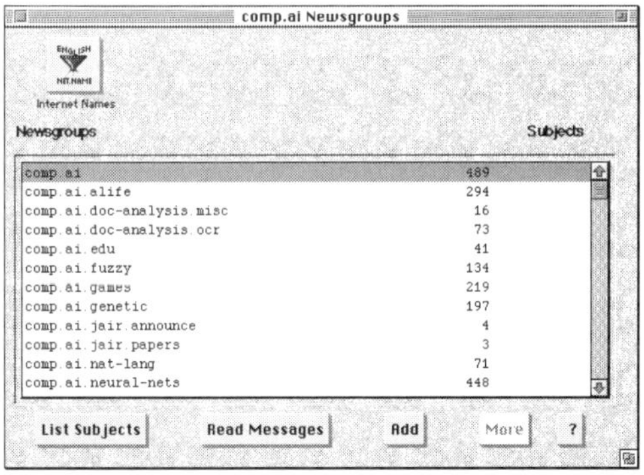


**Figure 12.** *...and finally, a list of topic newsgroups.*

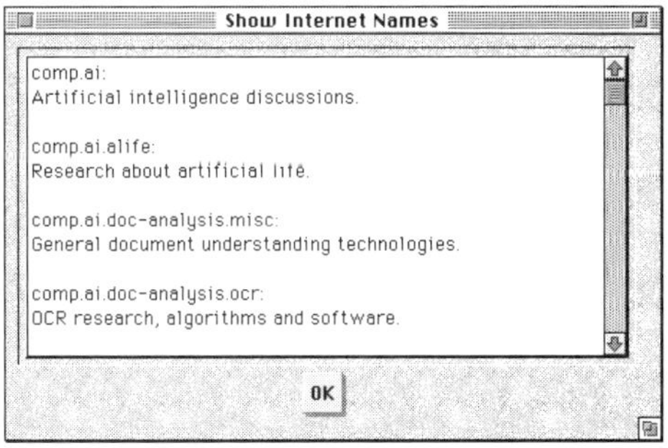


**Figure 13.** *Click the Internet Names button for brief descriptions of each newsgroup.*

## To browse newsgroups by topic

1. Click the Add Newsgroups button in the Newsgroups window (see **Figure 5**).
2. In the Add Newsgroups - Categories window (see **Figure 10**), double-click the category whose topics you want to view.
3. In the Topics window that appears (see **Figure 11**), double-click the topic whose newsgroups you want to view.
4. The Newsgroups window that appears (see **Figure 12**) lists all newsgroups in a topic.

## ✔ Tips

- To subscribe to a newsgroup you want to read regularly, click the name of the newsgroup in the Newsgroups window (see **Figure 12**) and click the Add button. A dialog box like the one in **Figure 9** confirms that you have been subscribed to the newsgroup.
- To get a better idea of what is discussed in a newsgroup, you can select a newsgroup in the Newsgroup window (see **Figure 12**) and click the List Subjects or Read Messages button to view a list of subjects or read individual messages in the newsgroup.
- To see the "English" names for newsgroups listed in the Newsgroup window (see **Figure 12**), click the Internet Names button. A window like the one in **Figure 13** lists the Internet Names followed by a brief description in plain English.

## To use the Expert Add feature

1. Click the Expert Add button in the Newsgroups window (see **Figure 5**).
2. In the Expert Add window that appears (see **Figure 14**), enter the exact name of the newsgroup you want to add.
3. Click the Add button.

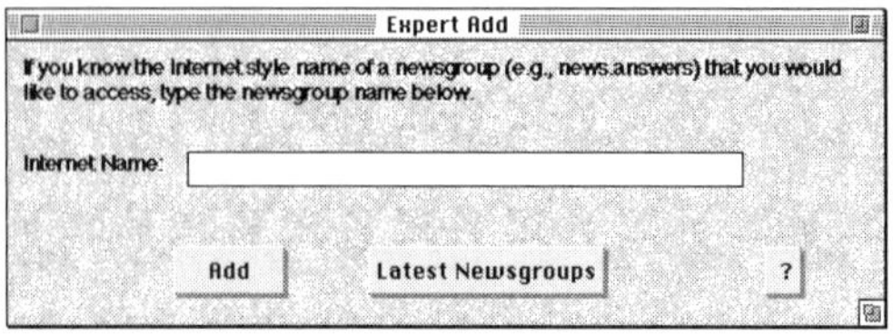


**Figure 14.** *Enter the exact name of a newsgroup you want to add in the Expert Add window.*

### ✔ Tips

- If you've successfully entered the name of the newsgroup, a confirmation dialog box like the one in **Figure 9** will appear.
- If you entered the name of a newsgroup that does not exist, a dialog box like the one in **Figure 15** appears. Click OK to dismiss it. Then try again.
- You must know the exact name of a newsgroup to add it with the Expert Add feature.

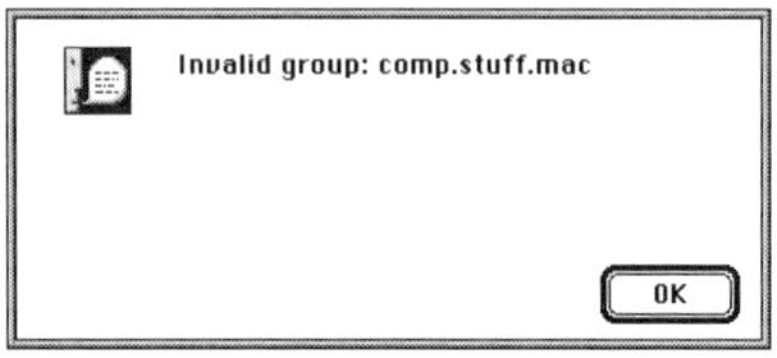


**Figure 15.** *If you try to add a newsgroup that does not exist, you'll see this dialog box.*

## To browse a list of recently added newsgroups

1. Click the Latest Newsgroups button in the Add Newsgroups - Categories window (see **Figure 10**) or the Expert Add window (see **Figure 14**).
2. A dialog box like the one in **Figure 16** appears, listing the newsgroups that have been added to AOL recently.

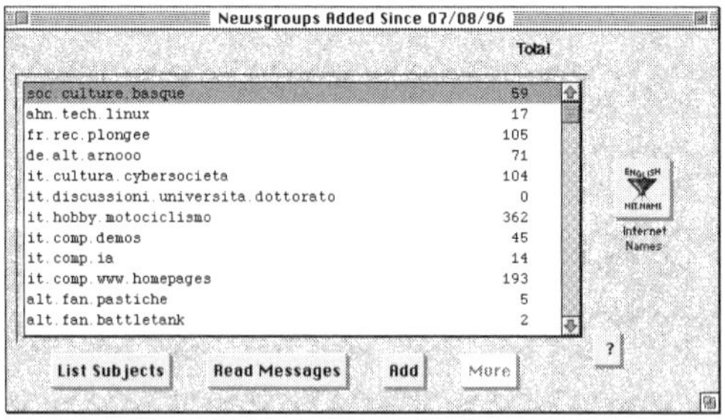


**Figure 16.** *A dialog box like this lists recently added newsgroups.*

### ✔ Tips

- You can click the List Subjects or Read Messages button (see **Figure 16**) to see content and get a better idea of what a selected newsgroup is all about.
- You can click the Add button (see **Figure 16**) to subscribe to a selected newsgroup.

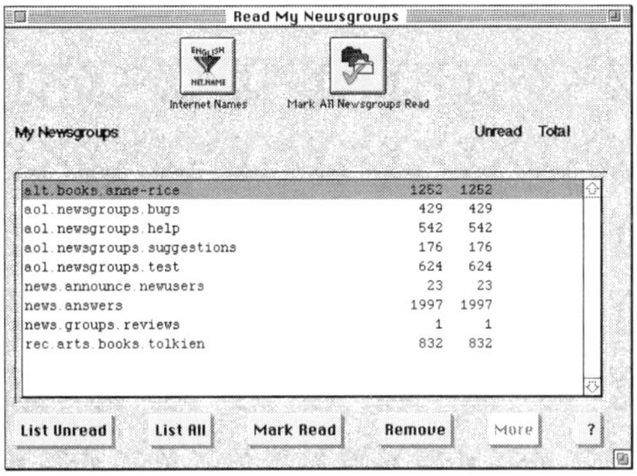


**Figure 17.** *Use the Read My Newsgroups window to work with the newsgroups to which you subscribe.*

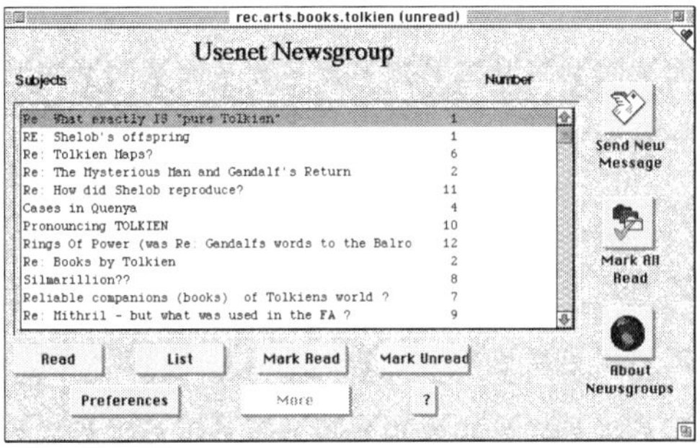


**Figure 18.** *Use this window to work with the subjects and messages within a specific newsgroup.*

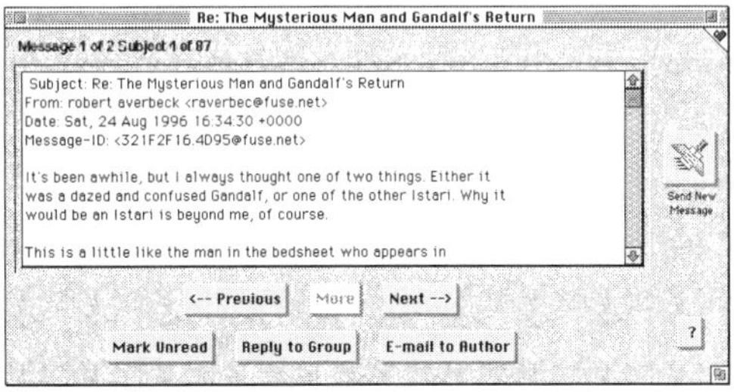


**Figure 19.** *Newsgroup messages appear in a window like this.*

## To read newsgroup messages

1. Click the Read My Newsgroups button in the Newsgroups window (see **Figure 5**).
2. In the Read My Newsgroups window that appears (see **Figure 17**), double-click the name of a newsgroup you want to read.
3. In the list of subjects that appears (see **Figure 18**), click the name of a subject you want to read.
4. Click the Read button.
5. Read the message in a window like the one in **Figure 19**.

## ✔ Tips

- Each newsgroup subject (see Figure 18) consists of a message and the replies to it. Together, the messages and replies form what's called a *thread*. By reading the messages a thread, you can follow a message-based conversation between several newsgroup participants.
- You can click the Previous or Next buttons in the message window (see **Figure 19**) to move backward and forward through the messages in a newsgroup, one at a time.
- You can mark a subject or message as unread (so it will continue to appear in lists of unread messages) by clicking the Mark Unread button in the subject window (see **Figure 18**) or the message window (see **Figure 19**).
- You may find it more convenient or cost effective to read newsgroup messages offline. You can learn how in **Chapter 10**.

## To reply to a newsgroup message

1. Follow the instructions on the previous page to open a message window (see **Figure 19**) for a message to which you want to reply.
2. To send your reply to the newsgroup, click the Reply to Group button to display the Post Response window (see **Figure 20**).

   *or*

   To reply only to the person who sent the original message, click the E-mail to Author button to display the Reply to Author window (see **Figure 21**).
3. If desired, change the contents of the Subject text box.
4. Enter your reply in the Reply or Response area.
5. Click the Send button.

### ✔ Tips

- To reply to both the newsgroup and the author of the message, turn on the "Copy author of original message via e-mail" check box (see **Figure 20**) or the "Copy to newsgroup" check box (see **Figure 21**).
- To automatically append your Internet signature to the message, turn on the "Use signature (set in global preferences)" check box (see **Figures 20** and **21**). Internet signature files are discussed in **Chapter 11**.
- If you give your message a different subject in step 3 above, you will break the thread of messages about that subject and create a new subject.

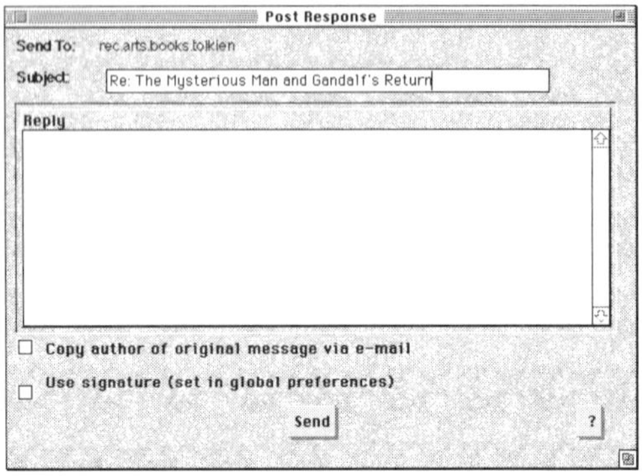


**Figure 20.** *Use the Post Response window to send a reply to the newsgroup.*

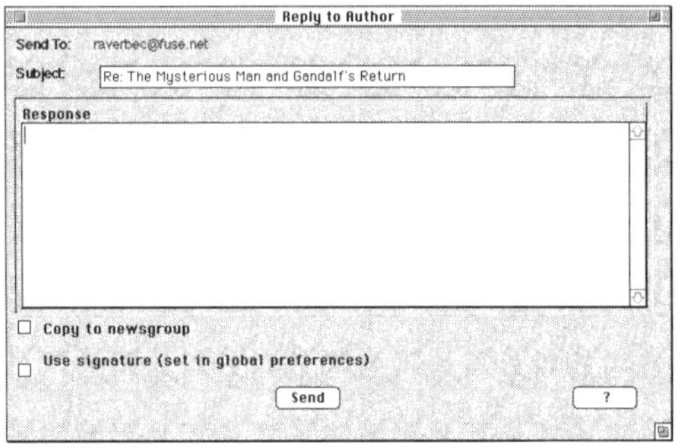


**Figure 21.** *Use the Reply to Author window to reply only to the person who wrote the message.*

Replying to Newsgroup Messages

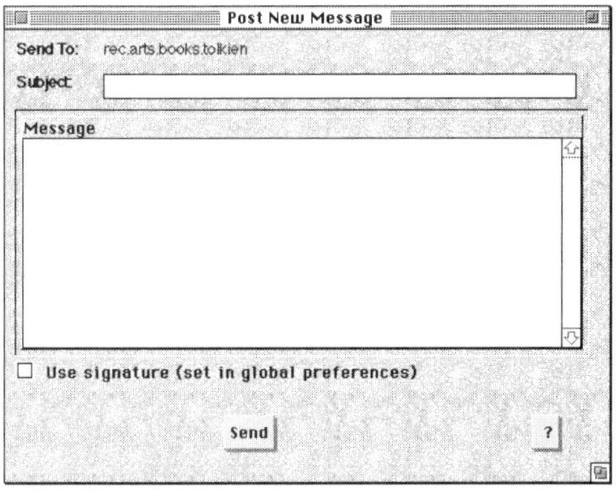


**Figure 22.** *Use the Post New Message window to add a message to a newsgroup.*

## To send a new message to a newsgroup

1. In the Read My Newsgroups window (see **Figure 17**), double-click the name of a newsgroup to which you want to add a message.
2. In the Usenet Newsgroup window (see **Figure 18**), click the Add Message button to display the Post New Message window (see **Figure 22**).
3. Enter a subject for the message in the Subject text box.
4. Enter the text of your message in the Message text box.
5. Click the Send button.

## ✔ Tips

- To automatically append your Internet signature to the message, turn on the "Use signature (set in global preferences)" check box in the Post New Message window (see **Figure 22**). Internet signature files are discussed in **Chapter 11**.
- Another way to open the Post New Message window is to click the Send New Message button in the subjects window (see **Figure 18**) or message window (see **Figure 19**).

## To unsubscribe from a newsgroup

1. In the Read My Newsgroups window (see **Figure 17**), click on the name of a newsgroup from which you want to unsubscribe to select it.
2. Click the Remove button.
3. A confirmation dialog box like the one in **Figure 23** appears. Click OK or press [Enter] to dismiss it.

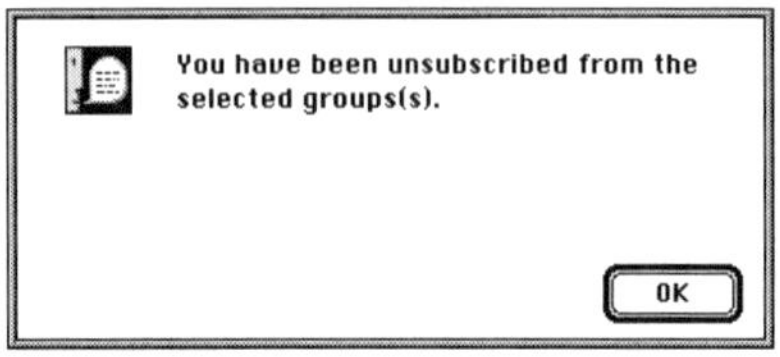


**Figure 23.** *This dialog box appears when you unsubscribe from a newsgroup.*

### ✔ Tip

- AOL automatically subscribes you to several *aol.* and *.news* newsgroups (see **Figure 17**). If these newsgroups don't interest you, unsubscribe from them.

## To mark a newsgroup as read

1. In the Read My Newsgroups window (see **Figure 17**), click on the name of a newsgroup you want to mark as read.
2. Click the Mark Read button.
3. A confirmation dialog box like the one in **Figure 24** appears. Click OK or press [Enter] to dismiss it.

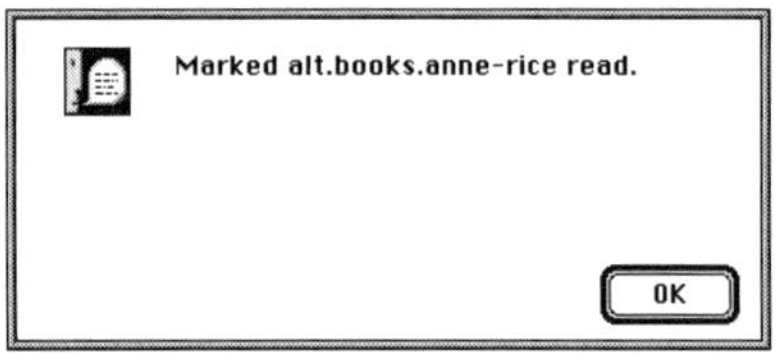


**Figure 24.** *AOL confirms when you mark a newsgroup as read.*

### ✔ Tips

- When you mark a newsgroup as read, the number of unread messages does not change in the Read My Newsgroups window until you close and then reopen the window (see **Figure 25**).
- You can mark specific subjects as read. Select the subject in the Usenet Newsgroup window (see **Figure 18**) and click the Mark Read button.
- You can also mark all newsgroups as read. Click the Mark All Newsgroups Read button in the Read My Newsgroups window (see **Figure 17**).

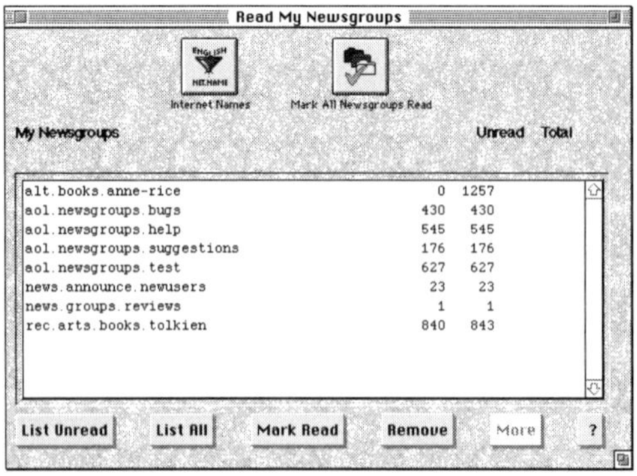


**Figure 25.** *The number of unread messages changes to 0 when you reopen the Read My Newsgroups window.*

## About the World Wide Web

The World Wide Web offers information, graphics, and files with an easy-to-use, graphic user interface. Although a relatively new part of the Internet, it is one of the fastest growing—probably because it's so easy to publish information on the World Wide Web.

To access the World Wide Web, you use a special kind of software program called a *browser* to view Web *pages*. Web pages are specially coded text documents that the browser displays as formatted text and graphics. Each page has a specific location or *URL* (Uniform Resource Locator) on a Web server that can be anywhere in the world. By clicking text or graphic *links*, you can access related pages quickly and easily.

**Figure 26.** *The Microsoft Internet Explorer lets you access the World Wide Web from within AOL.*

### ✔ Tip

- Although the Microsoft Internet Explorer browser (see **Figure 26**) is fully integrated into AOL 3, you can use any browser you like to access the Web through AOL. Simply connect to AOL, then launch your own browser. It will connect right through your connection with AOL. The information in this book applies to AOL's browser.

### To open the Web browser

1. Click the Internet Connection button (see **Figure 4**) in the Channels window.
2. Click the World Wide Web button in the Internet Connection window (see **Figure 2**).

*or*

Click the World Wide Web button on the toolbar.

*or*

Use the keyword WEB or WWW.

## To browse the Web

1. Open AOL's browser as discussed on the previous page.
2. Click on hypertext or graphic links to other pages:
   ▲ Hypertext links are underlined text, usually blue or purple.
   ▲ Graphic links are images that often have blue borders around them.

   The page for the link you clicked appears (see **Figure 27**).

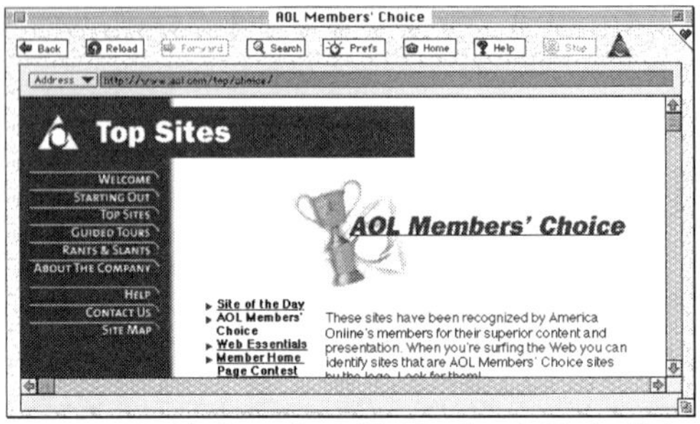


**Figure 27.** *Clicking the AOL Members' Choice link in* **Figure 26** *displays this page.*

## ✔ Tips

- Unless otherwise set in browser preferences or in the Web page itself, blue links are for pages you have not yet viewed and purple links are for pages you have already viewed.
- You can identify a graphic link without a colored border by positioning the mouse pointer over it. If the mouse pointer turns into a finger pointing up (see **Figure 28**), the graphic is a link.
- The URL for the page you will access when clicking a link appears in the bottom left corner of the browser window when your mouse pointer is positioned over the link (see **Figure 28**). URLs are discussed on the next page.
- To move backward and forward through the pages you've already viewed, click the Back or Forward button near the top of the Web browser window (see **Figures 26** and **27**).
- To view any page you've already seen during the current session, click on the arrow to the far right of the text box displaying the current page's URL to display a menu of URLs (see **Figure 29**) and choose the one you want.

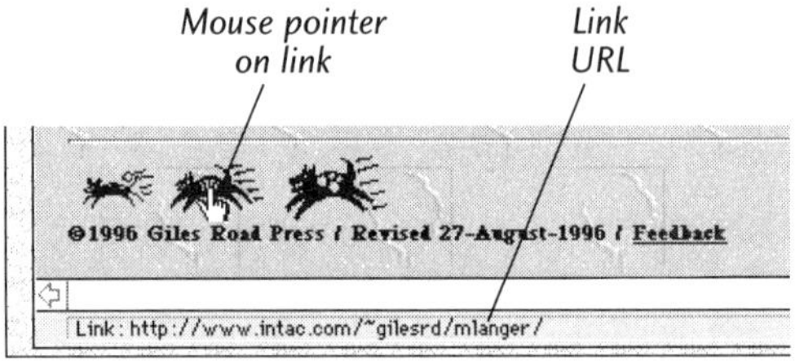


**Figure 28.** *The mouse pointer turns into a pointing finger when positioned over a link. The URL for the link appears at the bottom of the window.*

**Figure 29.** *The browser keeps track of the pages you've visited. Select one from this pop-up menu near the top of the window to visit it again.*

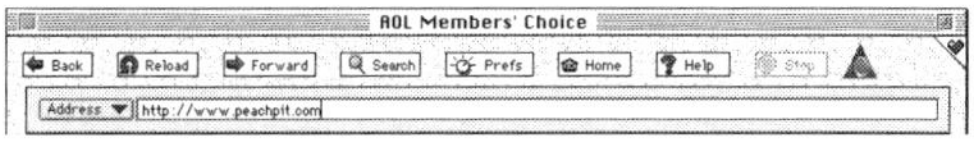


**Figure 30.** *Enter the URL for the page you want to view in the address box at the top of the browser window.*

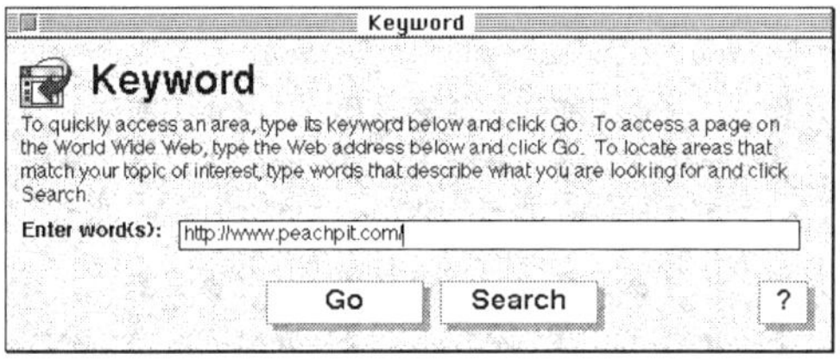


**Figure 31.** *If you prefer, you can enter the URL for the page you want to view in the Keyword dialog box.*

**Figure 32.** *If you correctly enter a URL, its page appears when you press* [Enter].

## To view a specific URL

1. Type in the complete URL for the page you want to view in the Address edit box at the top of the Web browser window (see **Figure 30**).
2. Press [Enter].

*or*

1. Choose Keyword from the Go To menu.

   *or*

   Press [⌘][K].
2. Enter the complete URL for the page you want to view in the edit box in the Keyword dialog box (see **Figure 31**).
3. Click the Go button or press [Enter].

## ✔ Tips

- *URL* stands for *Universal Resource Locator*. Think of it as an address for Web pages. You must have a complete and accurate URL for a page in order to view it as instructed above.
- Using the Keyword dialog box and keywords is discussed in **Chapter 3**.
- If you entered the URL correctly in either step 2 above, its page will appear (see **Figure 32**) when you press [Enter].
- If you entered the URL incorrectly in step 2 above or the URL points to a page that no longer exists, you'll see a Web page with a message telling you that the URL cannot be retrieved. Repeat the steps above to try again.
- To return to AOL's Home page (see **Figure 26**), click the Home button at the top of the Web browser window (see **Figures 30** and **32**).
- Remember, you can store URLs for Web pages as Favorite Places. Consult Chapter 3 for more information about AOL's Favorite Places feature.

## To search for a page

1. If necessary, return to AOL's Home Page (see **Figure 26**) by clicking the Home button at the top of the browser window or following the instructions on the previous page to view the URL *http://www.aol.com*.
2. Enter a search word or phrase in the edit box at the top of the page (see **Figure 33**).
3. Click the Search button.
4. Wait while AOL's search program or *engine* compiles a list of matches. When it's finished, it appears in a window like the one in **Figure 34**.

## ✔ Tips

- To go to a page that appears in a list of search results, simply click its link.
- AOL uses a search engine called *WebCrawler* for searching the Web. Other popular search engines include:
  - ▲ *Alta Vista* - www.alta-vista.com (see **Figure 35**)
  - ▲ *Excite* - www.excite.com
  - ▲ *Yahoo!* - www.yahoo.com

  Each of these search engines may produce different results.
- Click the Search button at the top of the browser window to access AOL's Search the Internet page (see **Figure 36**), which offers a variety of search features and options.
- You can use links on any of the search pages (see **Figures 34**, **35**, and **36**) to get more information about searching, including detailed searching instructions and tips.

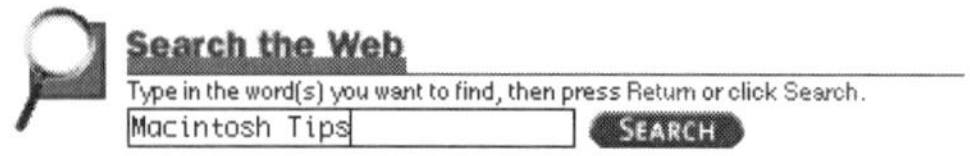


**Figure 33.** *Enter a search word or phrase in the Search edit box on AOL's Home Page.*

**Figure 34.** *The results of the search appear in a window like this one.*

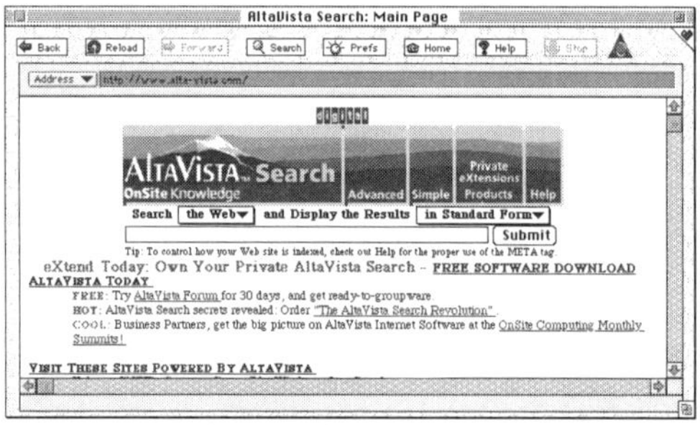


**Figure 35.** *Other popular search engines include this one, Alta Vista.*

**Figure 36.** *AOL's Search the Internet page offers other searching options.*

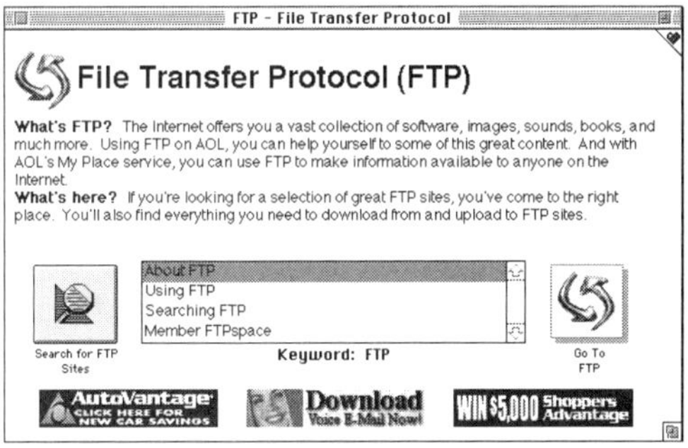


**Figure 37.** *The FTP - File Transfer Protocol window is your starting point for obtaining files via FTP.*

## About FTP

*FTP* (*File Transfer Protocol*) enables you to download files stored in computers all over the world. With FTP, you're not limited to the file libraries on AOL—there are thousands of other libraries you can access.

AOL's FTP - File Transfer Protocol window (see **Figure 37**) offers two different ways to use the FTP feature from AOL:

- Search for FTP sites based on a topic, then browse the site and download files that interest you.
- Go directly to an FTP site that contains a file you want and download the file.

### ✔ Tips

- Many commercial software developers have their own FTP sites, where product updates are posted as soon as they're available.
- FTP is often referred to as *anonymous FTP* because an account on the system on which the files are located is not required to access the files. AOL, following standard FTP procedure, automatically connects you to the FTP site with the user name *anonymous*, using your e-mail address as your password.
- AOL's file libraries are discussed in **Chapter 6**.

### To open the FTP - File Transfer Protocol window

1. Click the Internet Connection button (see **Figure 4**) in the Channels window.
2. Click the FTP button in the Internet Connection window (see **Figure 2**).

*or*

Use the keyword FTP.

## To search for FTP sites

1. In the FTP - File Transfer Protocol window (see **Figure 37**), click the Search for FTP Sites button.
2. Enter a search word or phrase in the edit box near the top of the Ftp Search window that appears (see **Figure 38**).
3. Click the Search button.

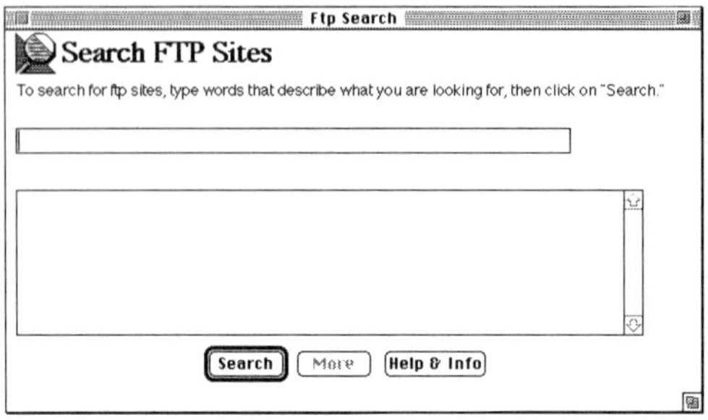


**Figure 38.** *Enter a search word or phrase in the Ftp Search window's edit box.*

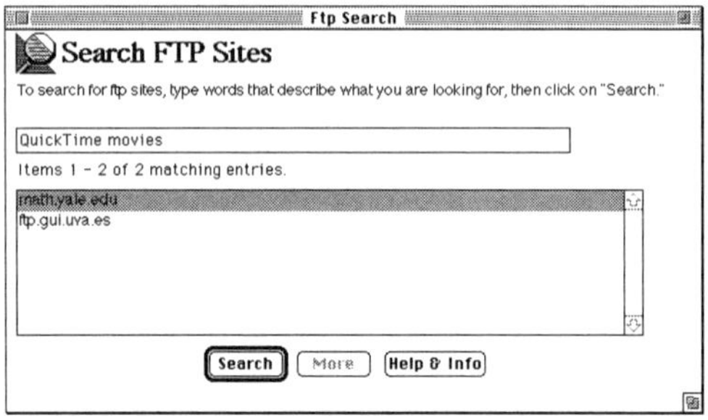


**Figure 39.** *Here's an example of the sites found with a search phrase of* QuickTime movies.

**Figure 40.** *If there are no matches for the search criteria, a dialog box like this appears.*

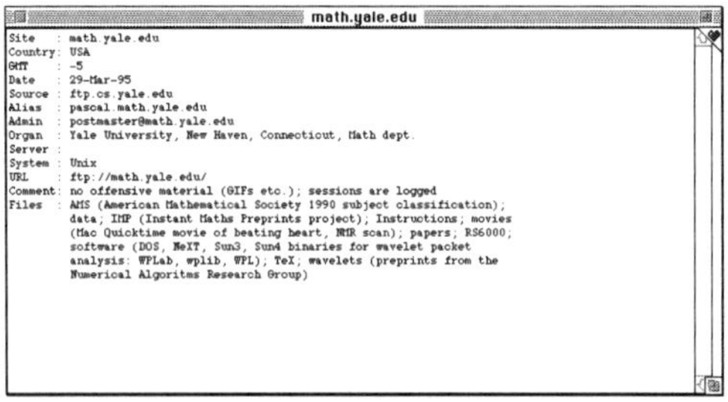


**Figure 41.** *Double-clicking a site name in the Ftp Search window displays a description of the site.*

## ✔ Tips

- If your search was successful, a list of sites whose descriptions contain the search word or phrase appears in the Ftp Search window (see **Figure 39**).
- If your search was unsuccessful, a dialog box like the one in **Figure 40** appears. Click OK or press Enter to dismiss it and try again.
- To get a description of a site in the Ftp Search window's results list box, double-click the site's name. A window like the one in **Figure 41** appears, providing more information about the site.

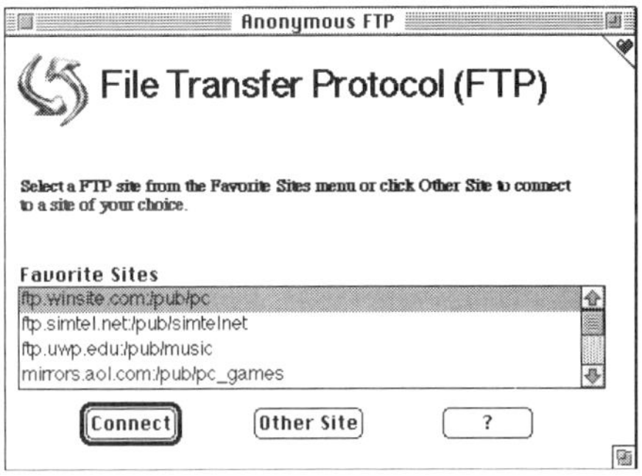


**Figure 42.** *When you're ready to connect to a site, open this window.*

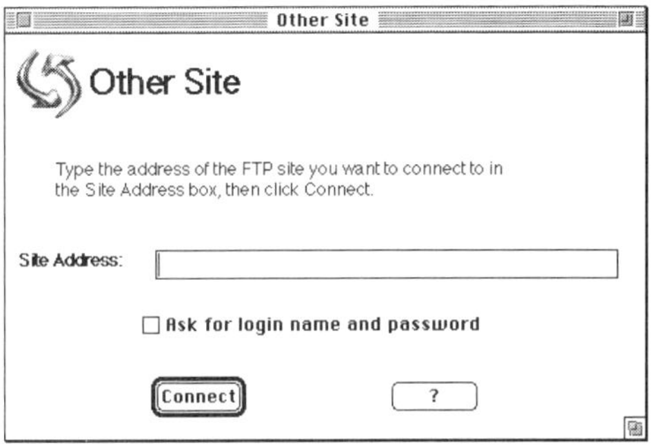


**Figure 43.** *Use the Other Site window to connect to a site other than one of AOL's favorites.*

**Figure 44.** *If you have an account on the system you want to connect to, you can enter your login name and password in this window.*

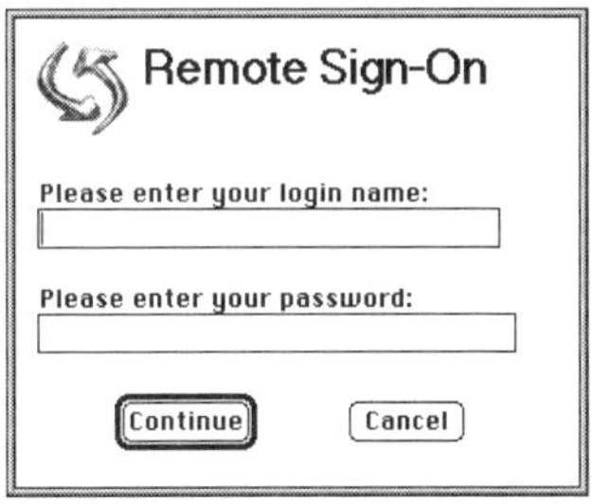


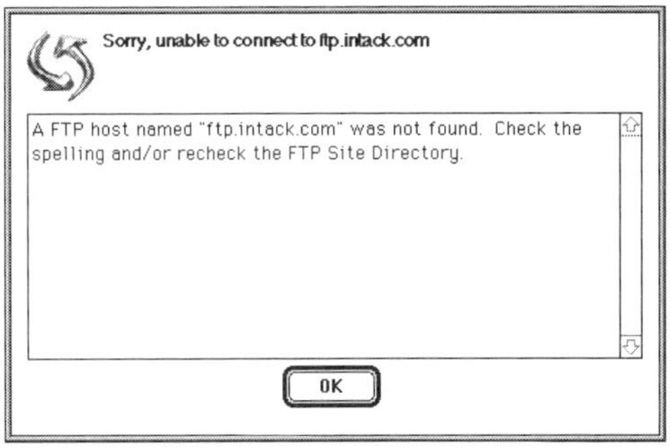


**Figure 45.** *If you enter an incorrect address, AOL tells you.*

## To connect to one of AOL's favorite sites

1. In the FTP - File Transfer Protocol window (see **Figure 37**), click the Go to FTP button.
2. In the Anonymous FTP window that appears (see **Figure 42**), select one of the sites listed in the Favorite Sites scrolling list.
3. Click the Connect button.

## To connect to another site

1. In the FTP - File Transfer Protocol window (see **Figure 37**), click the Go to FTP button.
2. In the Anonymous FTP window that appears (see **Figure 42**), click the Other Site button.
3. In the Other Site window that appears (see **Figure 43**), enter the complete address for the site in the Site Address text box.
4. Click the Connect button.

## ✔ Tips

- If you have an account on the system whose site you want to access, you can turn on the "Ask for login name and password" check box in the Other Site window (see **Figure 43**). When you click the Connect button, you'll be prompted to enter your login name and password with a dialog box like the one in **Figure 44**. This will give you privileges not available to anonymous users.
- If you enter an incorrect address for a site in step 3 above, a dialog box like the one in **Figure 45** appears. Click OK or press Enter to dismiss the window and try again.

## To browse an FTP site

1. Follow the instructions on the previous page to connect to an FTP site.
2. Read the information in the window that appears when you first connect (see **Figure 46**). Then click OK or press [Enter] to dismiss the window.
3. In the main FTP directory window that appears (see **Figure 47**), scroll through the list of folders and files to locate items that interest you.
4. To open a folder, double-click it. This opens another window displaying the contents of the folder (see **Figure 48**).

   *or*

   To close a folder window, click the window's close box or, press [⌘W].

## ✔ Tips

- Each time you open a folder, a new window is opened. You can navigate from one folder to another by selecting the name of the folder you want from the list at the bottom of the Window menu.
- When you close all of the windows for an FTP site, you'll be returned to the Anonymous FTP (see **Figure 42**) or Other Site (see **Figure 43**) window.

**Figure 46.** *When you first connect to a site, an information window like this one may appear.*

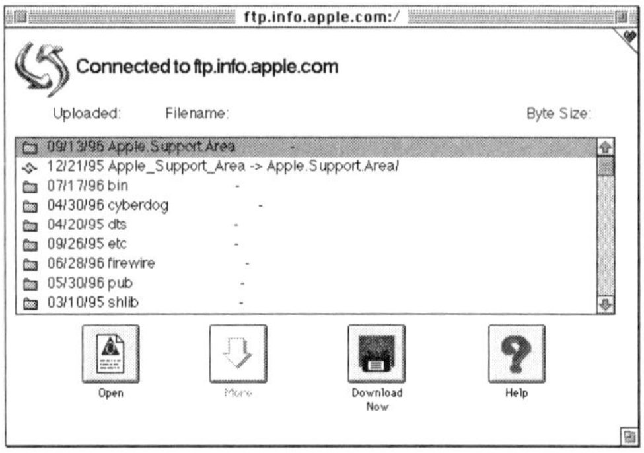


**Figure 47.** *The main FTP directory window displays files and folders or subdirectories.*

**Figure 48.** *Opening a folder displays a window that lists the contents of the folder.*

**Figure 49.** *A dialog box like this appears briefly when you click the Download Now button.*

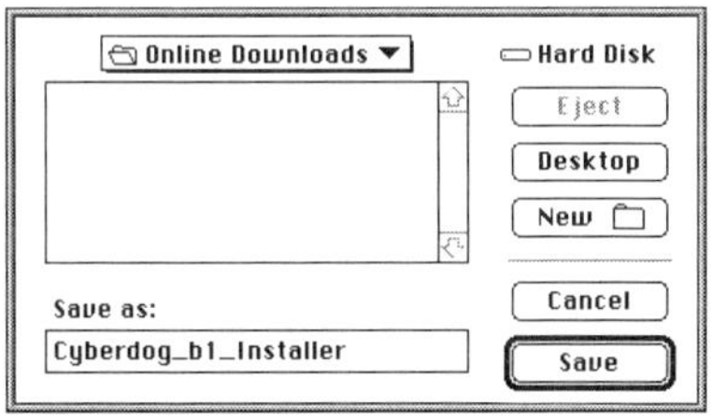


**Figure 50.** *Use a standard Save As dialog box to specify a name and disk location for the file.*

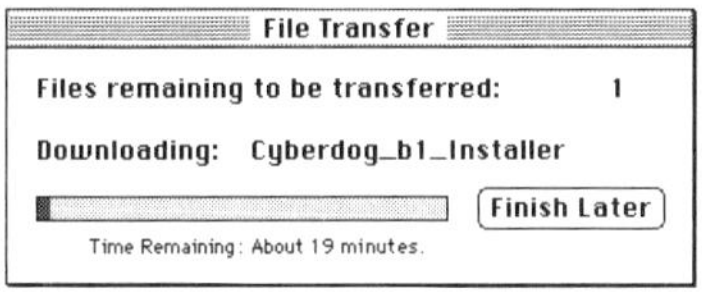


**Figure 51.** *A dialog box like this appears as the file is transferred.*

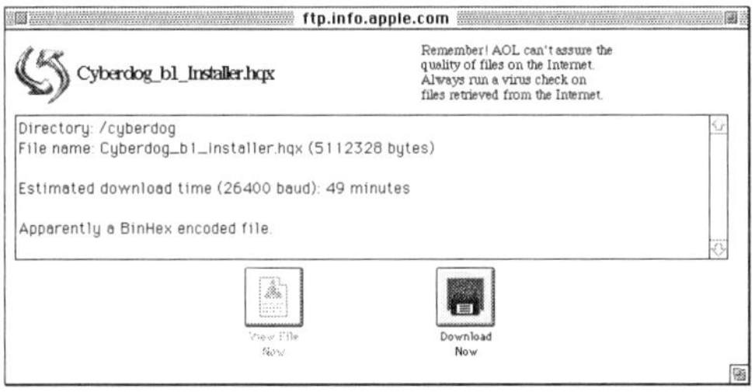


**Figure 52.** *Double-clicking a file in a directory window displays a description of the file.*

**Figure 53.** *If the file you downloaded is compressed, AOL offers to decompress it for you.*

## To download a file from an FTP site

1. Follow the instructions on the previous page to browse a site until you find a file you want to download.
2. In the directory window (see **Figures 47** and **48**), click the name of the file once to select it.
3. Click the Download Now button.
4. A dialog box like the one in **Figure 49** appears as AOL obtains the file. When it disappears, a standard Save As dialog box takes its place (see **Figure 50**). Use it to specify a name and disk location for the file. Then click OK.
5. A File Transfer window appears (see **Figure 58**) as the file is downloaded. You can wait until the file is completely downloaded or continue working with AOL.

## ✔ Tips

- To learn more about a file, double-click it. A description window like the one in **Figure 52** appears.
- You can also click the Download Now button within a file's description window (see **Figure 52**) to begin downloading the file.
- When the download is complete, you'll hear a male voice say, "File's done!"
- Text files you download are automatically displayed in a window when the download is complete.
- If the file you download is compressed, a dialog box like the one in **Figure 53** will appear. Click Decompress or press Enter to decompress the file. File compression is discussed in **Chapter 6**.

## To access your member FTP space

1. Use the keyword MY PLACE.
2. In the My Place window that appears (see **Figure 54**), click the Go to My Place button.
3. The directory window that appears (see **Figure 55**) displays the contents of your FTP space on AOL's server. Use the buttons at the bottom of the window to add, remove, and organize files in this space.

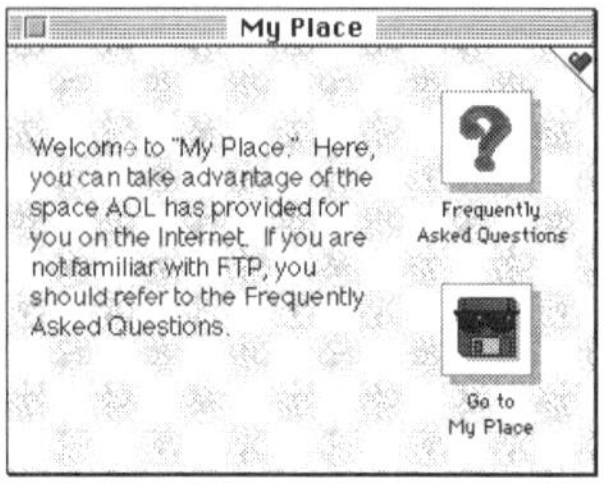


**Figure 54.** *Use the My Place window to learn more about My Place and to access your member FTP space on AOL's server.*

## ✔ Tips

- AOL often refers to your member FTP space as *My Place.*
- The files you place in your member FTP space are available to anyone with FTP access—even people who are not members of AOL.
- You are limited to 2 MB of disk space in your FTP space for each screen name on your account. Adding screen names is discussed in **Chapter 11**.
- You can use your member FTP space to create and maintain your own web site. Simply create a home page and upload it as a plain text file to your main directory with the name *index.htm*. To see this file, use AOL's Web browser to view the URL *http://members.aol.com/screenname/* where *screenname* is your screen name on AOL. You can create Web pages with any Web publishing tool, including AOLpress, Adobe PageMill, and Claris Home Page. Uploading files to your member FTP space is discussed later in this section.

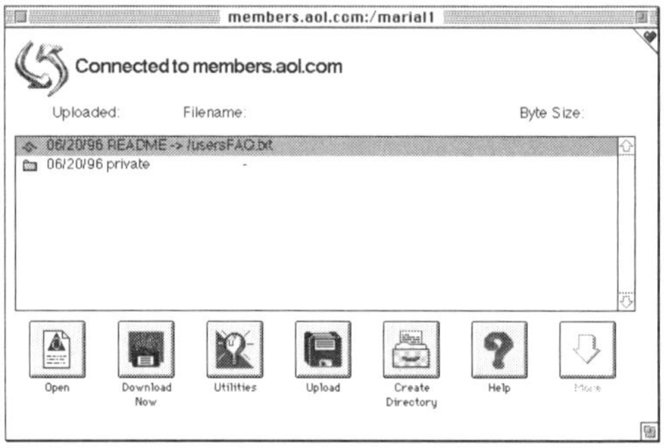


**Figure 55.** *Here's what your member FTP space might look like before you add files or directories.*

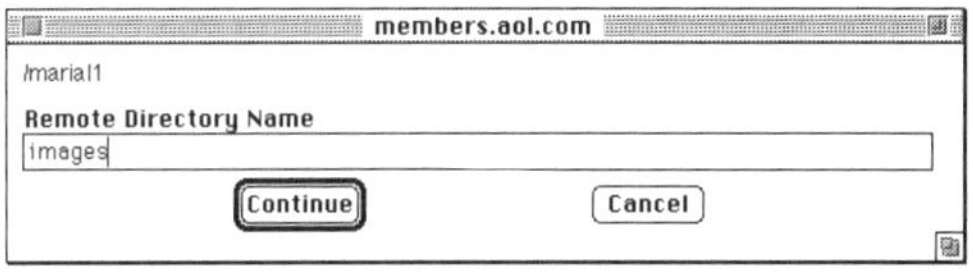


**Figure 56.** *Use a dialog box like this to create new directories in your member FTP space.*

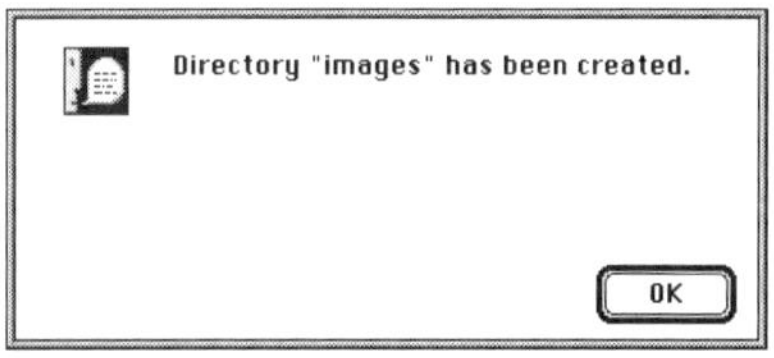


**Figure 57.** *AOL confirms that your directory has been created.*

## To create a directory in your member FTP space

1. Follow the instructions on the previous page to connect to your member FTP space.
2. If necessary, open the directory folder in which you want to create the new directory.
3. Click the Create Directory button at the bottom of the directory window (see **Figure 55**).
4. In the dialog box that appears (see **Figure 56**), enter the name for your new directory.
5. Click the Continue button or press Enter.
6. A dialog box like the one in **Figure 57** confirms that the directory has been created. Click OK or press Enter to dismiss it.
7. Repeat steps 4 through 6 for each directory you want to create.

   *or*

   Click cancel in the dialog box (see **Figure 56**) to dismiss it.

## ✔ Tips

- Anyone can read files in the directories you create. You are the only person, however, who can write to the directories you create.
- To create a directory that anyone in the world can upload to, name it *incoming*.
- Directory names cannot include spaces or special characters.
- You can use the instructions above to create a directory in any FTP space for which you have write permission.

## To upload a file to your member FTP space

1. Follow the instructions on the previous page to connect to your member FTP space.
2. If necessary, open the directory folder to which you want to upload the file.
3. Click the Upload button at the bottom of the directory window (see **Figure 55**).
4. In the dialog box that appears (see **Figure 58**), type in the name of the file as you want it to appear in the FTP directory window.
5. Choose one of the transfer mode radio buttons:
   - ▲ ASCII is for plain text documents, like "Read Me" files and Web pages.
   - ▲ Binary is for applications and graphic files.
6. Click the Continue button.
7. In the Upload File window that appears (see **Figure 59**), click the Select File button.
8. Use the Standard Open dialog box that appears (see **Figure 60**) to locate the file you want to upload. Click the file name once to select it and then click the Select button or press Enter.
9. Back in the Upload File window (see **Figure 59**), click the Send button.
10. A File Transfer window appears briefly as the file is sent to AOL's server. When it's finished, a dialog box like the one in **Figure 61** appears. Click OK or press Enter to dismiss it.
11. Repeat steps 4 through 10 for each file you want to upload.

    *or*

    Click cancel in the dialog box (see **Figure 58**) to dismiss it.

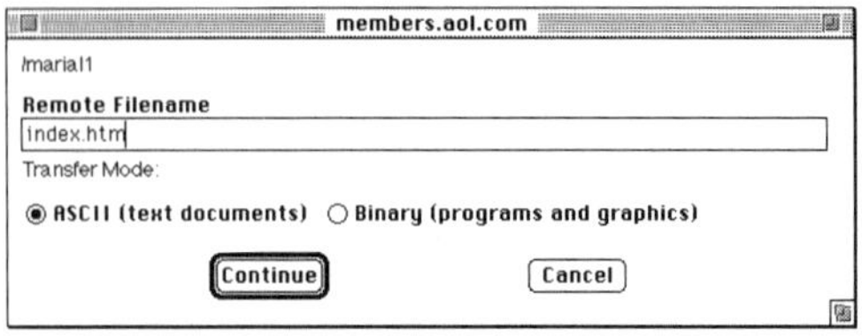


**Figure 58.** *Enter the name of the file as you want it to appear in the FTP directory window.*

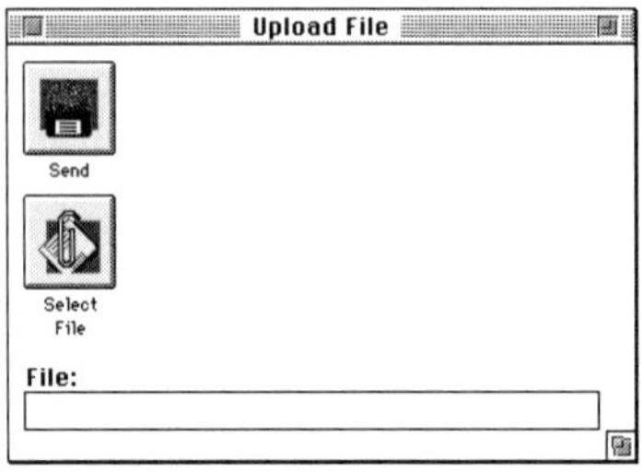


**Figure 59.** *Use the Upload File window to select and then send a file.*

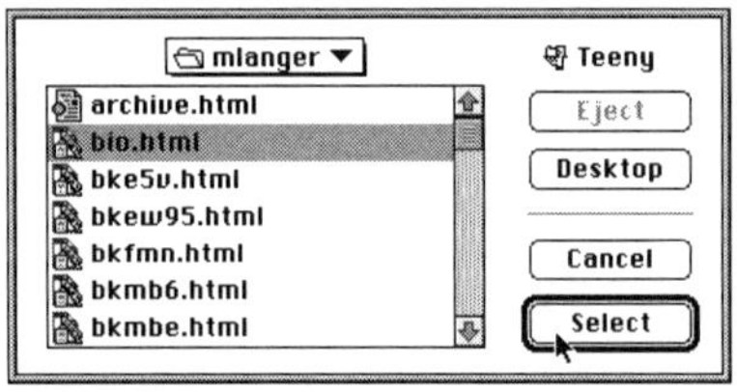


**Figure 60.** *Use a standard Open dialog box to locate and select a file to upload.*

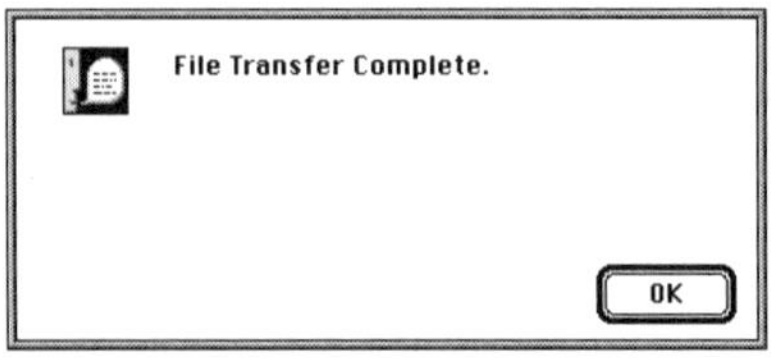


**Figure 61.** *A dialog box like this tells you when the transfer is complete.*

**Figure 62.** *Use AOL's Gopher window to access Gopher and WAIS servers worldwide.*

## About Gopher

*Gopher* and *WAIS* (*Wide Area Information Server*) offer two additional methods that organizations use to make information available on the Internet. By storing text articles on Gopher and WAIS servers, individuals with access to the Internet can search for articles covering specific topics and retrieve them quickly and easily.

AOL's Gopher window (see **Figure 62**) gives you access to Gopher and WAIS servers worldwide:

- Consult a list of featured Gopher articles for topics that interest you.
- Browse lists of Gopher sites to find those that are likely to contain the information you need.
- Search Gopher sites to find articles containing words you specify.

### ✔ Tip

- AOL presents Gopher lists and articles in a Web browser window. AOL's Web browser is discussed earlier in this chapter.

## To open the Gopher window

1. Click the Internet Connection button (see **Figure 4**) in the Channels window.
2. Click the Gopher & WAIS button in the Internet Connection window (see **Figure 2**).

*or*

Use the keyword GOPHER.

## To read a featured Gopher article

1. In the Gopher window (see **Figure 62**), click the Gopher Treasures button.
2. In the Gopher Treasures window that appears (see **Figure 63**), double-click an article topic that interests you.
3. A window containing a review or description of the article and a number of buttons appears (see **Figure 64**). Read the review.
4. If you want to see the article, click the large browser window button on the left side of the window. The article appears in a Web browser window (see **Figure 65**).

### ✔ Tips

- The articles listed in the Gopher Treasures window represent only a small portion of what is available on Gopher servers.
- For more information on using a Web browser window, consult the World Wide Web section earlier in this chapter.

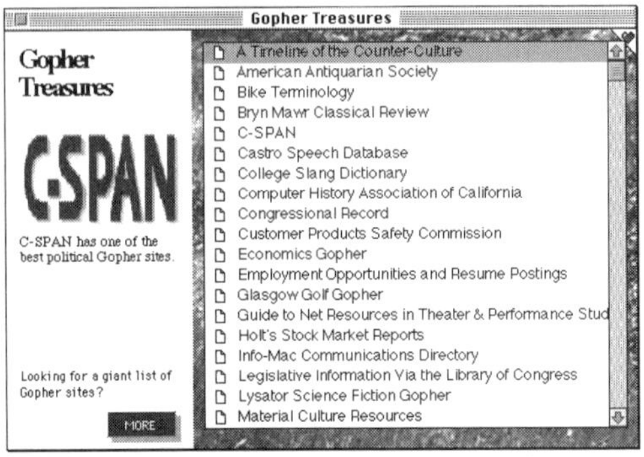


**Figure 63.** *The Gopher Treasures window lists reviewed Gopher sites and articles.*

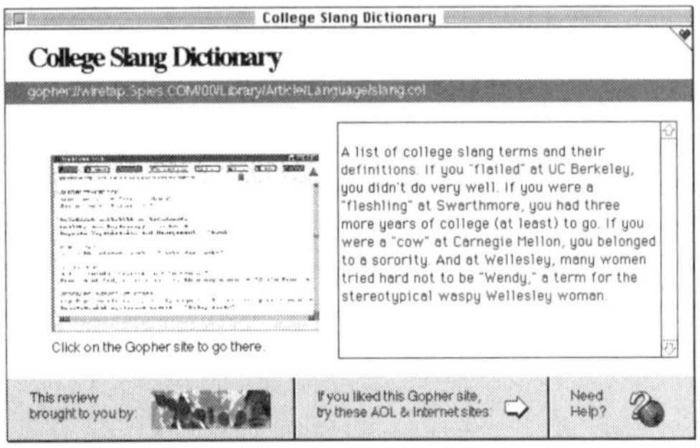


**Figure 64.** *Read the site or article review in this window. To see the actual site or article, click the browser window button.*

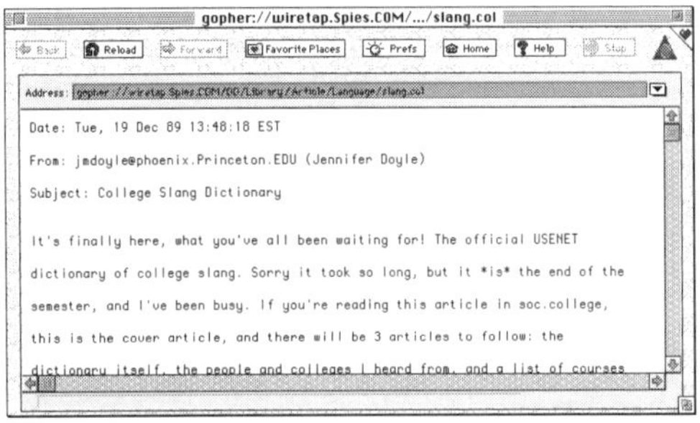


**Figure 65.** *Gopher articles appear in Web browser windows like this one.*

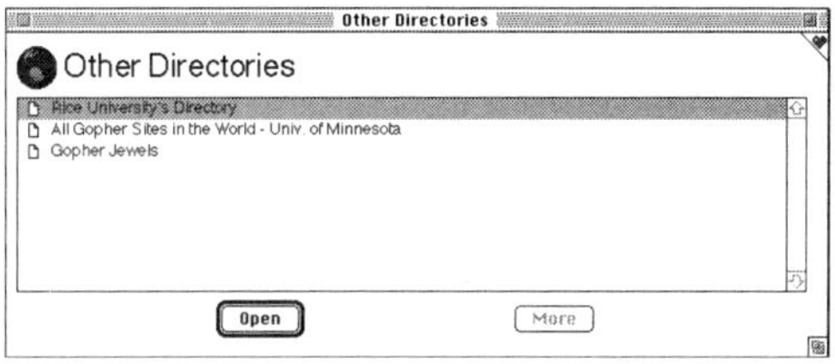


**Figure 66.** *The Other Directories window lists Gopher directories.*

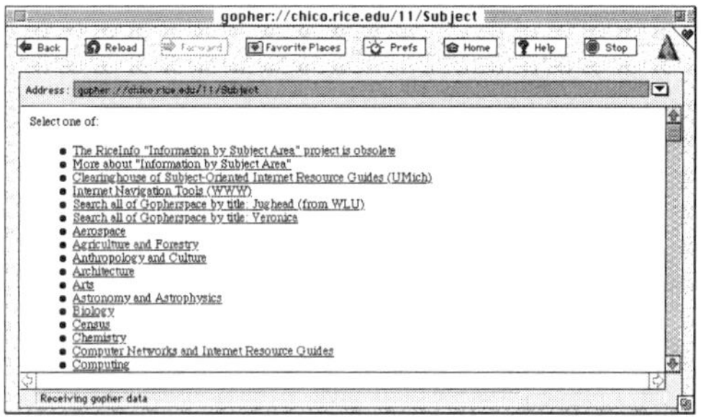


**Figure 67.** *The directory you chose appears in a Web browser window.*

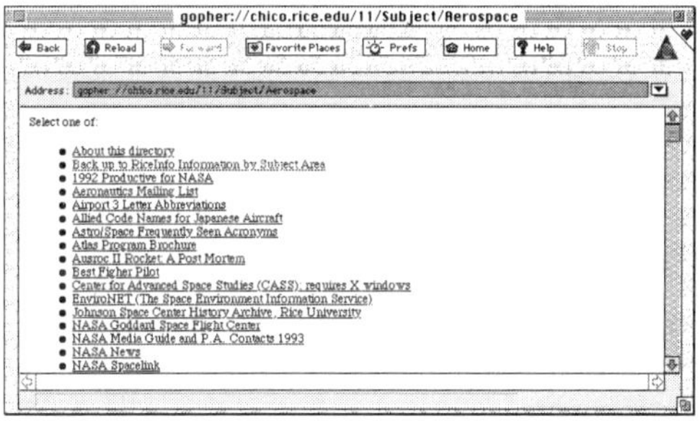


**Figure 68.** *Clicking the name of a topic in* **Figure** *67 displays a list of articles for that topic.*

## To browse Gopher sites

1. In the Gopher window (see **Figure 62**), click the Gopher Directory button.
2. In the Other Directories window that appears (see **Figure 66**), double-click the name of a directory that interests you.
3. AOL's Web browser window opens with the contents of the directory you specified within it (see **Figure 67**). Click blue or purple underlined hypertext links to open topic lists (see **Figure 68**) and articles (see **Figure 65**).

## ✔ Tip

- For more information on using a Web browser window, consult the World Wide Web section earlier in this chapter.

## To search for Gopher articles

1. In the Gopher window (see **Figure 62**), click the Search button to display a web browser window named Searching the TradeWave Galaxy (see **Figure 69**).
2. Enter a search word or phrase in the edit box near the top of the page.
3. If necessary, turn off the Search the Web check box and turn on the Gopher Titles check box. When you're finished the search page might look something like the one in **Figure 70**.
4. Click the Search button.
5. A list of the articles that match the search word or phrase appears in a Web browser window (see **Figure 71**). Click the blue or purple hypertext link for the article you want to read.

## ✔ Tips

- AOL utilizes the TradeWave Internet search engine to search for Gopher documents. As you explore the Internet, you may find other search engines that can perform Gopher searches. Use the one that you like best.
- For more information on using a Web browser window, consult the World Wide Web section earlier in this chapter.

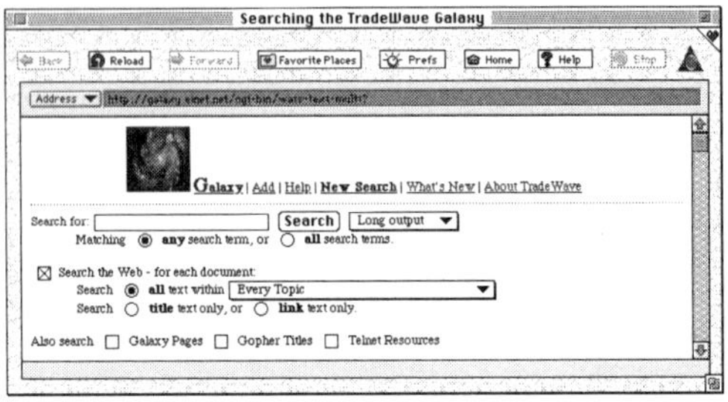


**Figure 69.** *Clicking the Search button displays a Web page with a search engine capable of searching for Gopher documents.*

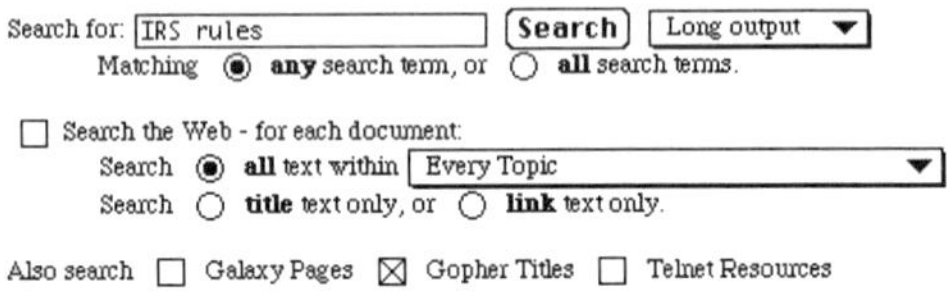


**Figure 70.** *Enter a search word or phrase, then toggle check boxes to indicate that you want to search Gopher titles instead of Web pages.*

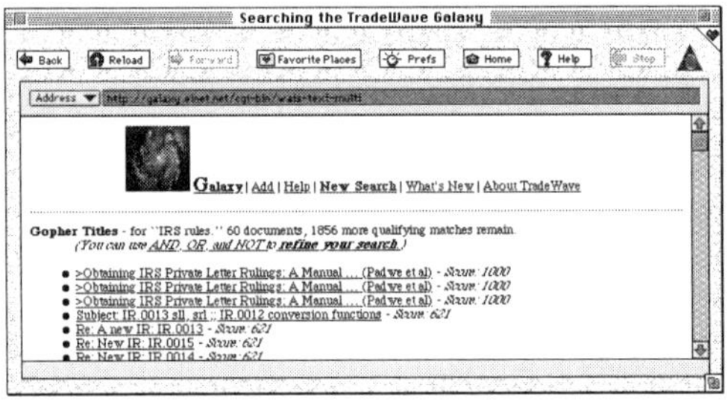


**Figure 71.** *The results of a search appear in a Web browser window.*

# WORKING OFFLINE 10

## About Working Offline

Some of AOL's features can be very time consuming to use, keeping you and your phone line tied up for hours. Fortunately, several time-consuming tasks can be performed at your convenience *offline*, while not connected to AOL:

- Read and compose e-mail messages.
- Review old messages you've received or sent.
- Read and compose Internet newsgroup messages.
- Review lists of files you've downloaded or plan to download.
- Review transcripts of online chats in which you've participated, instant messages you've sent or received, and message boards you've browsed.

This chapter tells you how you can work offline. It also tells you about some convenient automation features AOL offers.

### ✔ Tips

- If your billing plan is based on the amount of time spent online, the more time you spend online in excess of included time, the more you'll pay AOL at the end of the billing period. Working offline can save you money!
- Many of the specific AOL features covered in this chapter are discussed in detail elsewhere throughout this book. This chapter is devoted to using AOL features offline.

## About Automatic AOL Sessions

The *Automatic AOL* (or *Auto AOL*) feature offers a quick and easy way to:

- Retrieve incoming e-mail messages and file attachments.
- Send outgoing e-mail messages and file attachments.
- Download files you've added to the Download Manager list.
- Retrieve incoming Internet newsgroup messages.
- Send outgoing Internet newsgroup messages.

The Auto AOL routines automatically retrieve and send messages and files without having to manually navigate AOL's features. This makes Auto AOL Sessions fast.

### ✓ Tips

- You can set up and/or activate an Auto AOL session while online or offline.
- You can set up an Auto AOL session for any combination of screen names on your AOL account.
- You can use the Auto AOL Scheduler to automatically activate Auto AOL sessions, even when you are away from your computer.
- Auto AOL sessions are also sometimes referred to as FlashSessions.

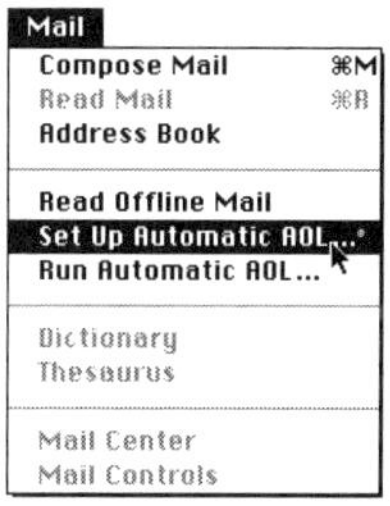


**Figure 1.** *To set up an Auto AOL session, begin by choosing Set Up Automatic AOL from the Mail menu.*

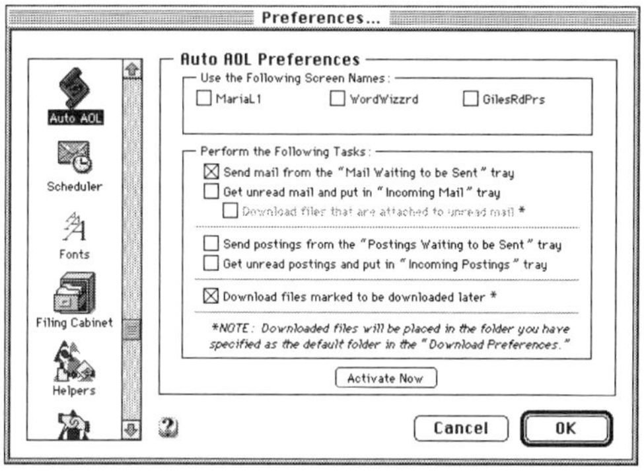


**Figure 2.** *Use the Auto AOL section of the Preferences dialog box to set Auto AOL options.*

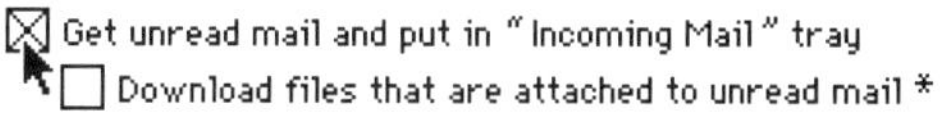


**Figure 3.** *To turn on the "Download files that are attached" option, you must first turn on the "Get unread mail" option.*

## ✔ Tips

- If the password for a screen name you selected in step 2 is not stored in AOL's Password preferences, the Auto AOL session for that name will fail. Storing passwords is discussed in **Chapter 11**.
- When you activate Auto AOL sessions while offline, a session for each screen name you selected in step 2 is conducted. Your selections are not consid ered, however, when you activate an Auto AOL session while online.
- For more information about e-mail, downloading files, and Internet newsgroups, consult **Chapters 4**, **6**, and **9**.

## To set up an Auto AOL session

1. Choose Set Up Automatic AOL from the Mail menu (see **Figure 1**)
2. Set options in the Auto AOL Preferences window (see **Figure 2**) as desired:
   - ▲ *Use the Following Screen Names* lets you turn on check boxes for the screen name(s) for which you want to run Auto AOL sessions.
   - ▲ *Send mail from the "Mail Waiting to be Sent" tray* sends any outgoing mail in your Filing Cabinet.
   - ▲ *Get unread mail and put in "Incoming Mail" tray* retrieves any unread mail and puts it in your Filing Cabinet.
   - ▲ *Download files that are attached to unread mail* downloads any files that are attached to retreived mail. You must turn on the *Get unread mail and put in "Incoming Mail" tray* option to use this option (see **Figure 3**).
   - ▲ *Send postings from the "Postings Waiting to be Sent" tray* sends any outgoing newsgroup messages in your Filing Cabinet.
   - ▲ *Get unread postings and put in "Incoming Postings" tray* retrieves any newsgroup messages for newsgroups you've marked to read offline and puts them in your Filing Cabinet.
   - ▲ *Download files marked to be downloaded later* downloads any files to be downloaded that are listed in the Download Manager.
   - ▲ *Activate Now* immediately activates an Auto AOL session.
3. When you are finished making changes, click OK or press Enter to save them.

## To activate an Auto AOL session

1. Choose Run Automatic AOL from the Mail menu (see **Figure 4**).

   *or*

   Click the Activate Now button in the Auto AOL section of the Preferences dialog box (see **Figure 2**).

2. In the dialog box that appears (see **Figures 5a** and **5b**), click the Begin button.

**Figure 4.** *To activate an Auto AOL session immediately, choose Run Automatic AOL from the Mail menu.*

### ✔ Tips

- You can activate an Auto AOL session whether or not you are connected to AOL. If you are not connected when you activate the session, the AOL software will connect automatically.
- The appearance of the dialog box that appears when you choose Run Automatic AOL from the Mail menu varies depending on whether you are connected (see **Figure 5a**) or not connected (see **Figure 5b**).
- In step 2, you can use the Signoff When Done check box (see **Figures 5a** and **5b**) to determine whether you want to remain connected when the Auto AOL session finishes.
- To check your Auto AOL settings, click the Preferences button inside the dialog box that appears when you the choose Run Automatic AOL command. Setting Auto AOL options is discussed on the previous page.
- An Automatic AOL Status window like the one in **Figure 6** appears when you activate an Auto AOL session You can see the progress of the session by reading the messages that scroll by inside it. It's a good idea to review the contents of this window at the end of a session to be sure no errors were encountered during the session.

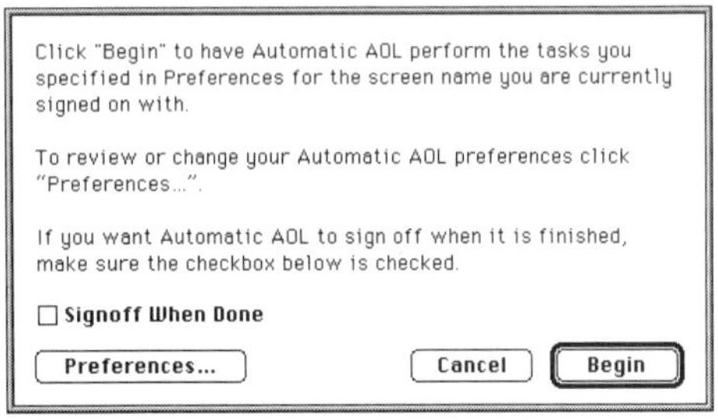


**Figures 5a & 5b.** *The dialog box that appears when you choose the Run Automatic AOL command varies depending on whether you are connected (above) or not connected (below).*

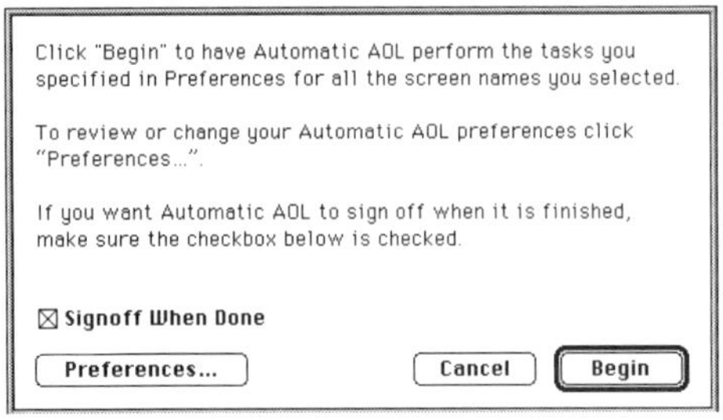


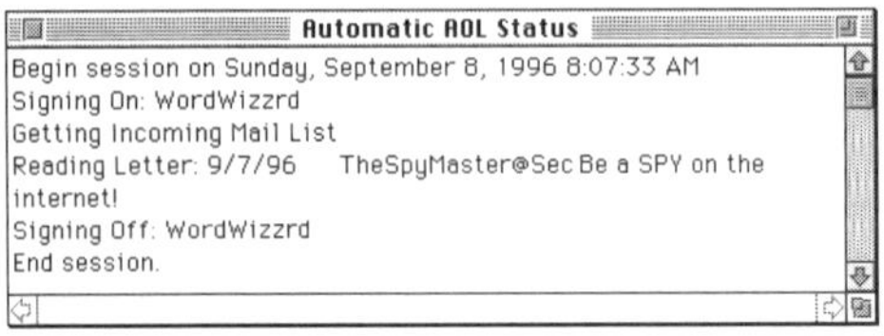


**Figure 6.** *The Automatic AOL Status window tells you exactly what's going on when you activate an Auto AOL session.*

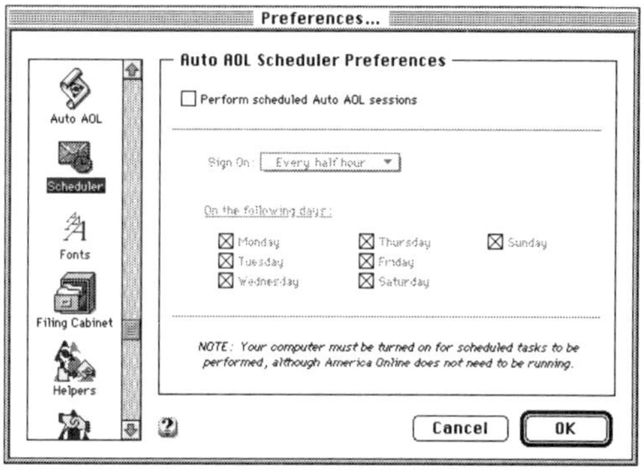


**Figure 7.** *Use the Auto AOL Scheduler Preferences window to schedule Auto AOL sessions.*

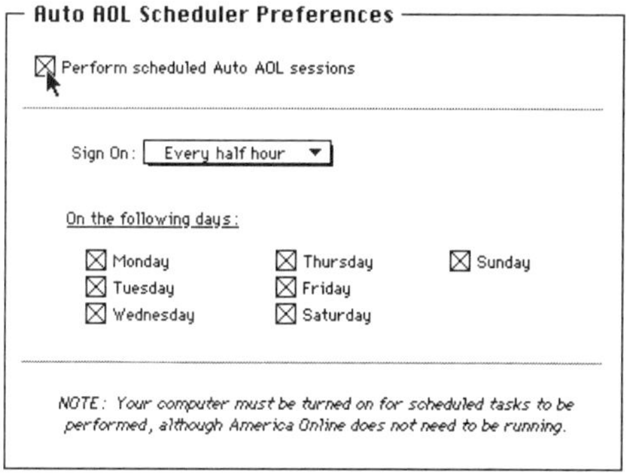


**Figure 8.** *Turn on the "Perform scheduled Auto AOL sessions" check box to enable the other options.*

**Figure 9.** *You can schedule an Auto AOL session as often as once a half-hour and as seldom as once a day—or once a week if you select only one day in* **Figure 8**.

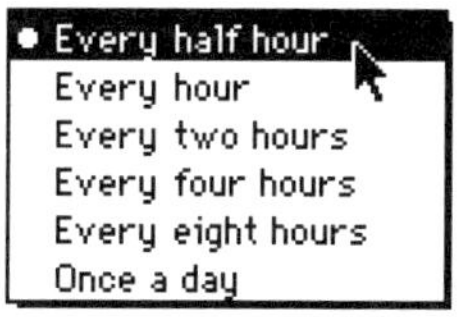


## To schedule Auto AOL sessions

1. Choose Set Up Automatic AOL from the Mail menu (see **Figure 1**).
2. In the Preferences dialog box that appears (see **Figure 2**), click the Scheduler icon to display the Auto AOL Scheduler Preferences (see **Figure 7**).
3. Turn on the "Perform scheduled Auto AOL sessions" check box to enable the other options in the dialog box (see **Figure 8**).
4. Set the check boxes for the days of the week to schedule Auto AOL sessions.
5. Use the Sign On pop-up menu (see **Figure 9**) to set the Auto AOL session frequency to one of the predefined intervals.
6. Click OK or press Enter to accept your settings.

### ✔ Tips

- In order for scheduled Auto AOL sessions to occur, your computer must be turned on. Since Auto AOL sessions utilize a program called AOL Scheduler, which is installed in your Startup Items folder and runs automatically each time you start your Macintosh, you do not have to keep the AOL software running to use the Auto AOL Scheduler.
- At the scheduled time(s), Auto AOL sessions will be conducted for each screen name you specified when setting up Auto AOL. Setting Auto AOL options was discussed earlier in this chapter.

## About Offline Mail

Offline mail is the mail stored on your hard disk. You can access offline mail with the Offline Mail window (see **Figure 10**), which includes three *trays*:

- The *Incoming Mail* tray includes the messages retrieved during an Auto AOL session.
- The *Mail Waiting To Be Sent* tray includes the messages you compose and save with the Send Later button in the Compose Mail window.
- The *Mail You've Sent* tray includes messages you sent during Auto AOL sessions.

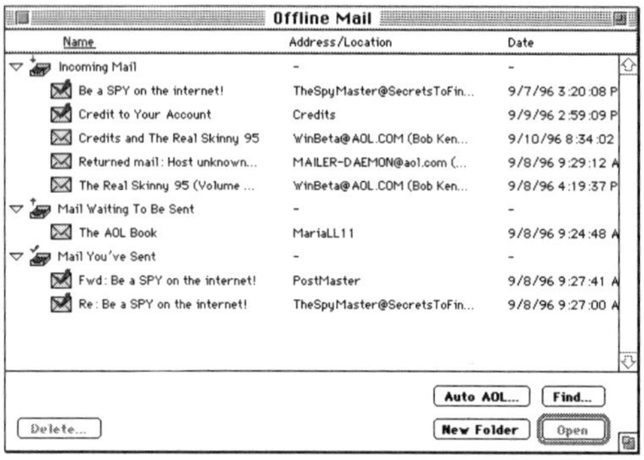


**Figure 10.** *Use the Offline Mail window to read the mail stored on your hard disk.*

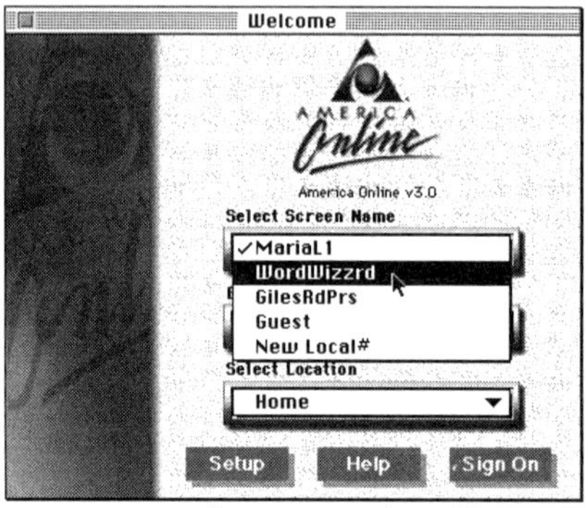


**Figure 11.** *Before opening the Offline Mail window, choose the screen name whose mail you want to read from the Select Screen Name pop-up menu.*

## ✔ Tips

- Because offline mail is saved on your hard disk, you do not need to be connected to AOL to read it.
- If you have more than one screen name, you must select the screen name for which you want to read, edit, or compose offline mail *before* you open the Offline Mail window. Choose the screen name from the Screen Name pop-up menu in the Welcome window (see **Figure 11**). Consult **Chapter 1** for more information about screen names and the Welcome window.
- If you have your Mail preferences set up to retain copies of mail you read and send while online, these messages will automatically be copied to your hard disk. You can find them in your Incoming Mail and Mail You've Sent trays respectively. Mail preferences are discussed in **Chapter 11**.
- Mail remains in the offline mail window until you delete it unless you set Personal Filing Cabinet preferences to delete it automatically. Personal Filing Cabinet preferences are discussed in **Chapter 11**.
- Offline mail is sometimes referred to as *FlashMail* since that is what the Automatic AOL feature was originally called.

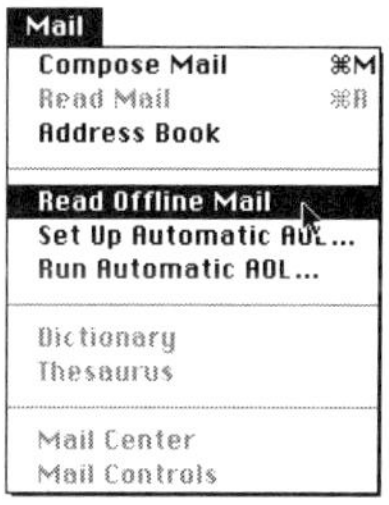


**Figure 12.** *Choose Read Offline Mail from the Mail menu.*

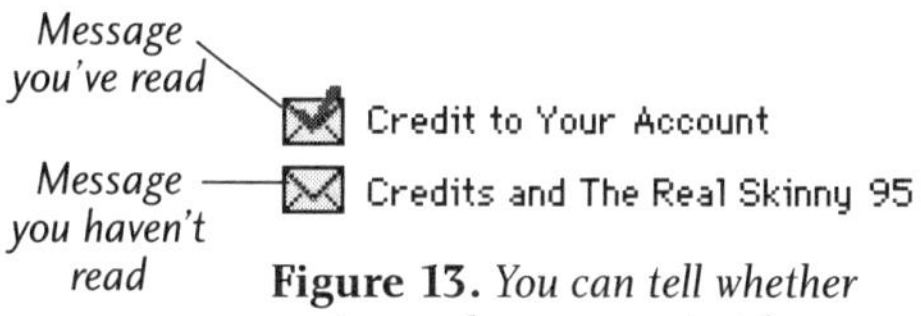


**Figure 13.** *You can tell whether you've read a message just by looking at its icon.*

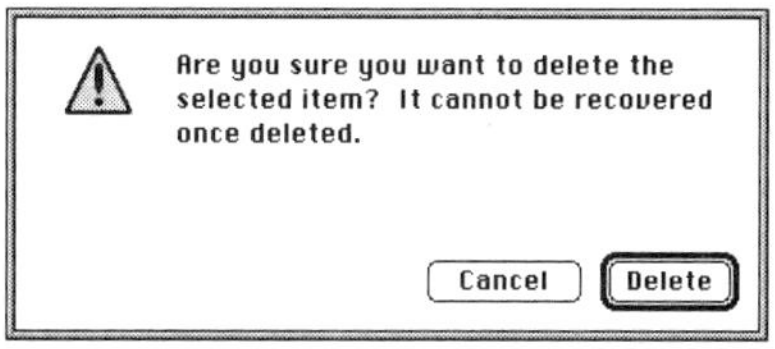


**Figure 14.** *AOL checks to make sure you really do want to delete a message before it deletes it.*

## To open the Offline Mail window

Choose Read Offline Mail from the Mail menu (see **Figure 12**).

### ✔ Tip

- The Offline Mail window displays only the mail for the screen name selected in the Welcome window.

## To read offline mail

1. Open the Offline Mail window (see **Figure 10**).
2. Click the message you want to read to select it and then click the Open button.

   *or*

   Double-click the message you want to read.
3. Read, reply to, forward, save, or print the message using techniques covered in detail in **Chapter 4**.

### ✔ Tip

- Messages you have already read appear in the Offline Mail window with a check mark over their icons (see **Figure 13**).

## To delete offline mail

1. In the Offline Mail window (see **Figure 10**) click the message you want to delete to select it and then click the Delete button.
2. In the confirmation dialog box that appears (see **Figure 14**), click Delete or press Enter.

## To compose an offline mail message

1. Choose Compose Mail from the Mail menu (see **Figure 15**).

   *or*

   Press [⌘][M].

   *or*

   Click the Compose Mail button on the toolbar.

2. Follow the instructions in **Chapter 4** to address, compose, and format your e-mail message.
3. Click the Send Later button (see **Figure 16**) in the Compose Mail window.
4. A dialog box like the one in **Figure 17** appears, telling you that your message has been saved for later delivery. Click OK or press [Enter] to dismiss it.

**Figure 15.** *Choose Compose Mail from the Mail menu.*

**Figure 16.** *Click the Send Later button to save a message for Auto AOL session delivery.*

### ✔ Tip

■ If you do not activate an Auto AOL session for the screen name under which a message was composed, the message will not be sent.

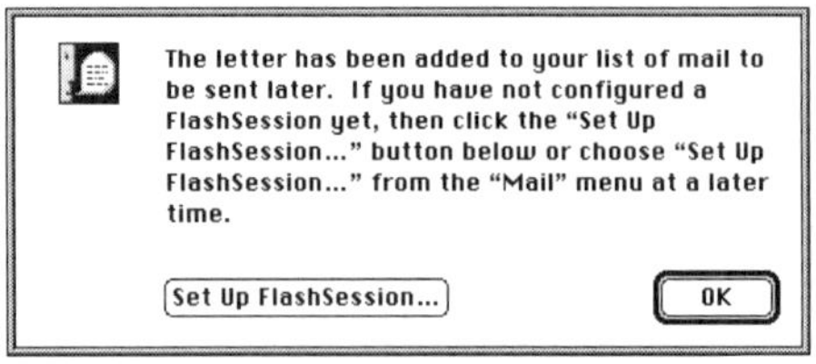


**Figure 17.** *Clicking Send Later displays a dialog box like this one.*

## To edit an offline mail message

1. Open the Offline Mail window (see **Figure 10**).
2. In the Mail Waiting To Be Sent tray, double-click the message you want to edit.
3. In the Compose Mail window that appears, make changes as desired.
4. Click the Send Later button (see **Figure 16**) in the Compose Mail window.
5. A dialog box like the one in **Figure 17** appears, telling you that your message has been saved for later delivery. Click OK or press [Enter] to dismiss it.

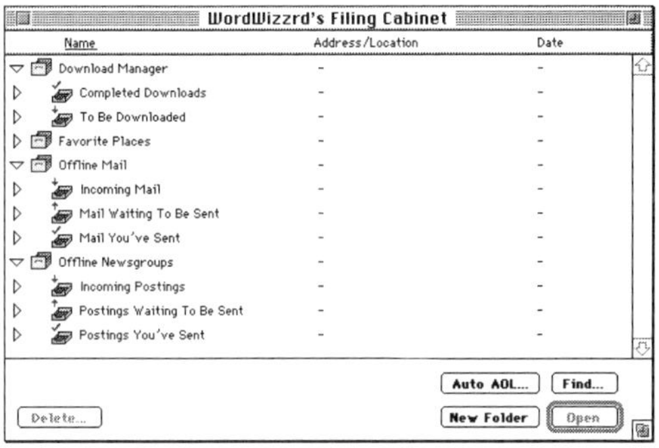


**Figure 18.** *You can store e-mail, newsgroup messages, and other files in the Personal Filing Cabinet.*

## About the Personal Filing Cabinet

The *Personal Filing Cabinet* (see **Figure 18**) is a central storage place for information you gather on AOL:

- *Download Manager* items, including completed downloads and files to be downloaded. (The Download Manager is discussed in detail in **Chapter 6**.)
- *Favorite Places* links. (The Favorite Places feature is discussed in detail in **Chapter 3**.)
- *Offline Mail*, including incoming mail, mail waiting to be sent, and mail you've sent. (E-mail is discussed in detail in **Chapter 4** and Offline Mail is discussed earlier in this chapter.)
- *Offline Newsgroups*, including incoming postings, postings waiting to be sent, and postings you've sent. (Newsgroups are discussed in detail in **Chapter 9** and again later in this chapter.)

Since you don't need to be connected to AOL to view the contents of the Personal Filing Cabinet, you can work with the files inside it while offline.

## ✔ Tips

- The contents of the Personal Filing Cabinet are different for each screen name on an AOL account. Choose a screen name from the Screen Name pop-up menu in the Welcome window (see **Figure 11**) *before* you open the Personal Filing Cabinet. **Chapter 1** provides more information about screen names and the Welcome window.
- The Personal Filing Cabinet uses drawer, tray, and folder icons to organize items in an outline-like view (see **Figure 18**). You can click the triangle to the left of an icon to expand or collapse the view.
- Consult **Chapter 11** for information about setting Personal Filing Cabinet and e-mail preferences.

## To open the Personal Filing Cabinet

Choose Personal Filing Cabinet from the File menu (see **Figure 19**).

*or*

Click the Personal Filing Cabinet button on the toolbar.

## To open a Filing Cabinet item

Click once on the item to select it and then click the Open button.

*or*

Double-click the item you want to open.

## ✔ Tips

- If the item you open is a drawer, tray, or folder, a list of items within it appears in a new window (see **Figure 20**).
- If the item you open is a Download Manager item and you are connected to AOL, a description of the item appears. If you are not connected, a dialog box like the one in **Figure 21** appears, reminding you that you must be connected to view a file description.
- If the item you open is a Favorite Place and you are connected to AOL, you will go to that place. If you are not connected, you'll hear an error sound.
- If the item you open is an e-mail or newsgroup message, the message appears in a message window.

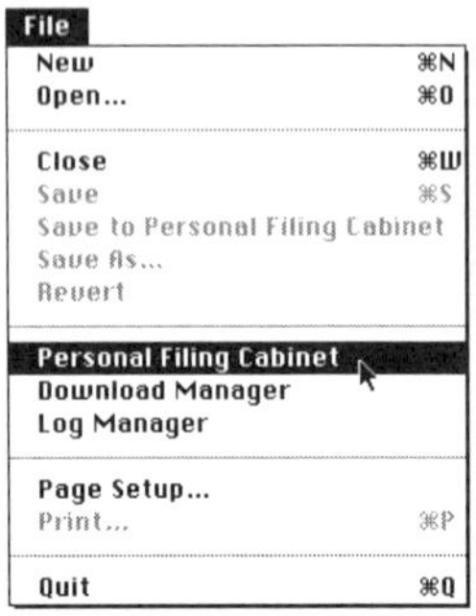


**Figure 19.** *Choose Personal Filing Cabinet from the File menu.*

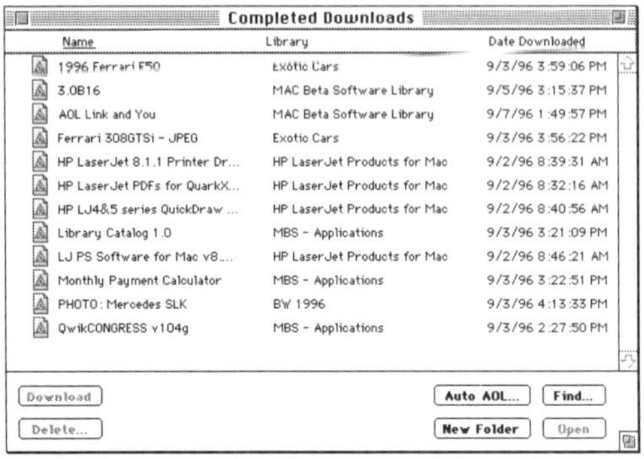


**Figure 20.** *Double-clicking a drawer, tray, or folder icon opens a window with a list of its contents.*

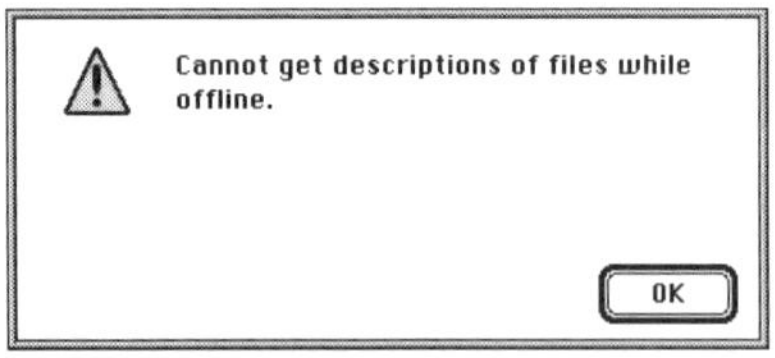


**Figure 21.** *If you try to open a Download Manager item when you aren't connected to AOL, a dialog box like this appears.*

**Figure 22.** *Clicking the New Folder button adds an untitled folder with an edit box around its name.*

**Figure 23.** *To move an item, simply drag it onto the drawer, tray, or folder in which you want to place it.*

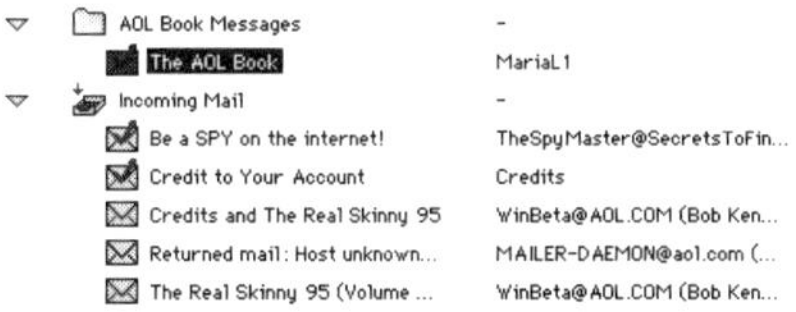


**Figure 24.** *When you release the mouse button, the item moves.*

## To add folders to the Personal Filing Cabinet

1. In the Filing Cabinet window, click on the drawer, tray, or folder in which you want to add a folder to select it.
2. Click the Add Folder button. An untitled folder, with an edit box around its name, appears (see **Figure 22**).
3. Enter a name for the folder and press Enter to accept it.

## ✔ Tip

■ A new folder is added to the drawer, tray, or folder that was selected when you clicked the New Folder button (see **Figure 22**). If a file was selected when you clicked the New Folder button, the new folder is added to the same location as the file.

## To move Personal Filing Cabinet items

1. In the Filing Cabinet window, position your mouse pointer on the icon for an item you want to move.
2. Press the mouse button down and drag the icon on top of the drawer, tray, or folder icon into which you want to move the item (see **Figure 23**).
3. Release the mouse button to complete the move (see **Figure 24**).

## To delete a Personal Filing Cabinet item

1. In the Filing Cabinet window, click once on the item you want to delete to select it.
2. Click the Delete button.
3. In the confirmation dialog box that appears (see **Figure 14**), click Delete or press [Enter].

## To change Personal Filing Cabinet sort order

In the Filing Cabinet window, click the heading for which you want the items sorted: Name, Address/Location, or Date.

### ✔ Tip

- The sort order affects the order of items within drawers, trays, or folders—not the drawers, trays, or folders themselves (see **Figure 25**).

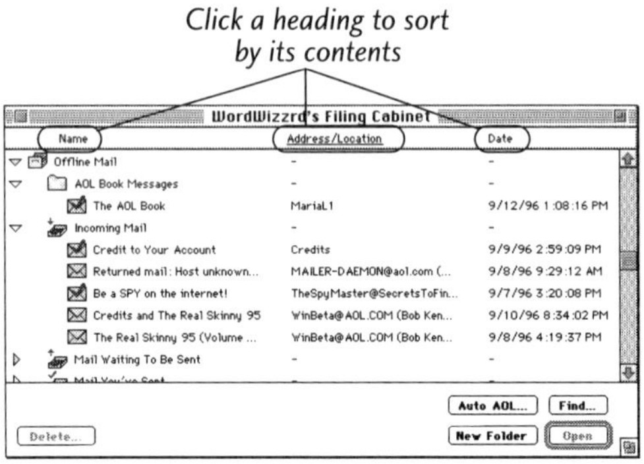


**Figure 25.** *Click the window heading for the order in which you want Filing Cabinet items to appear. In this example, items are sorted by Address/Location.*

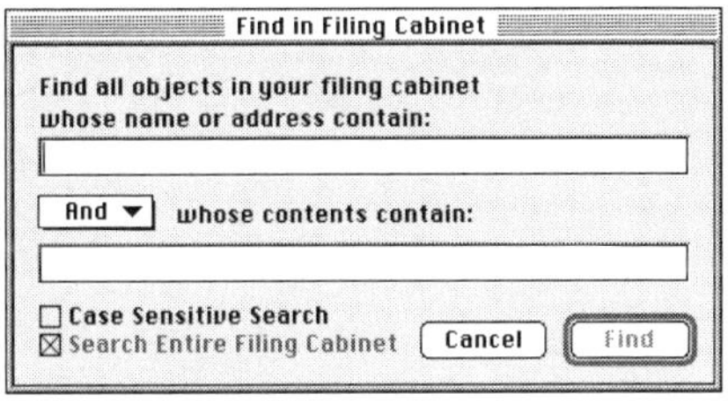


**Figure 26.** *Use the Find in Filing Cabinet dialog box to enter search criteria.*

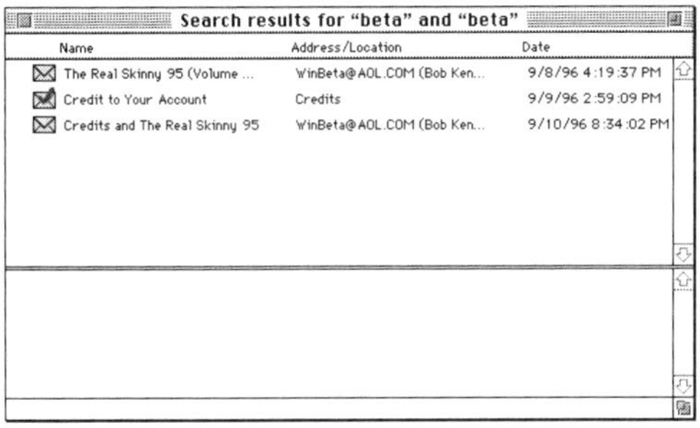


**Figure 27.** *The Search Results window lists all Filing Cabinet items that match the search criteria.*

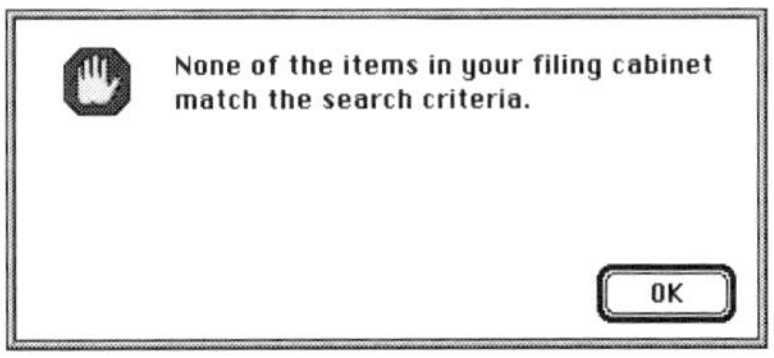


**Figure 28.** *If no items match the search criteria, you'll see a dialog box like this.*

## To search the Personal Filing Cabinet

1. In the Filing Cabinet window, click the Find button.
2. In the top edit box of the Find in Filing Cabinet dialog box (see **Figure 26**), enter all or part of a name or address you want to find in the Name or Address/Location field of a Personal Filing Cabinet item.
3. In the bottom edit box, enter a word or phrase you want to find in the contents of a Personal Filing Cabinet item.
4. To find criteria that match the contents of both edit boxes, choose And from the pop-up menu between them.

   *or*

   To find criteria that match the contents of either edit box, choose Or from the pop-up menu between them.
5. Click the Find button. The results of the search appear in a window like the one in **Figure 27**.
6. When you're finished with the Search Results window, click its close box or press ⌘W to dismiss it.

## ✔ Tips

- If you enter search criteria in only one of the edit boxes, be sure to choose And from the pop-up menu. Otherwise, the Search Results window will include all items in the Personal Filing Cabinet.
- To exactly match the capitalization of search criteria, turn on the Case Sensitive Search check box (see **Figure 26**).
- If none of the items match the criteria you specified in the Find in Filing Cabinet dialog box, a dialog box like the one in **Figure 28** appears.
- You can open an item in the Search Results window (see **Figure 27**) by double-clicking it.

# About Reading Newsgroups Offline

Internet newsgroups can generate dozens (or even hundreds) of new messages a day. Because of this, participating in newsgroups can be very time consuming.

Fortunately, you can select newsgroups to be saved to your Filing Cabinet. You can then read new newsgroup messages offline at your convenience.

## ✔ Tips

- Newsgroup messages are stored in the Personal Filing Cabinet, which organizes them by newsgroup name and message thread (see **Figure 29**).
- Reading, replying to, and composing newsgroup messages offline reduces the amount of time spent online, thus reducing online costs.
- Although the billing clock isn't running when you read newsgroup messages offline, it is running when you download the messages to your computer. If your billing plan bills based on time spent online, think twice before participating in high-volume newsgroups.
- To participate in newsgroups offline, you must specify which newsgroups you want to read offline and then properly use Auto AOL sessions to exchange newsgroup messages. Specifying newsgroups to download is discussed on the next page. Auto AOL sessions are discussed near the beginning of this chapter.
- Consult **Chapter 9** for more information about Internet newsgroups.

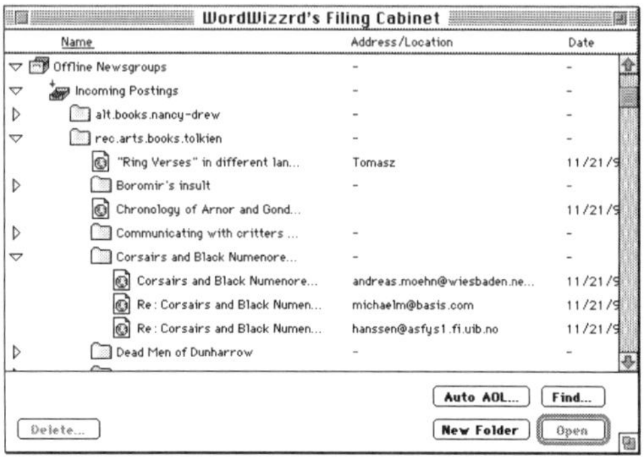


**Figure 29.** *Newsgroup messages are neatly organized in the Personal Filing Cabinet.*

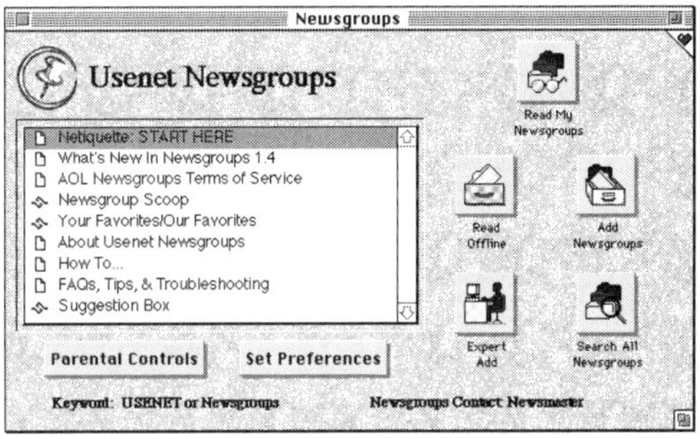


**Figure 30.** *Use the Newsgroups window to manage the newsgroups you read.*

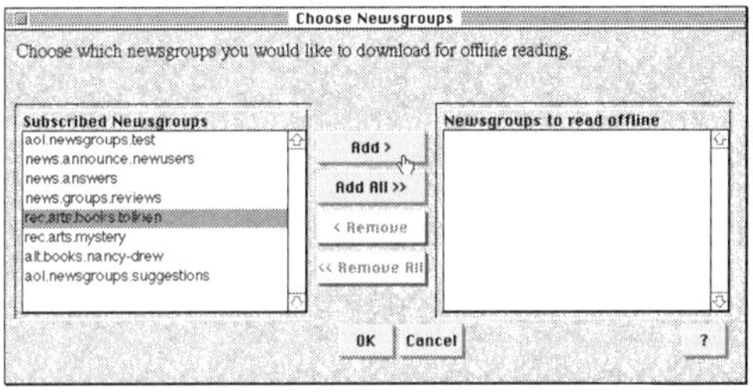


**Figure 31.** *Use the Choose Newsgroups window to select newsgroups you want to read offline.*

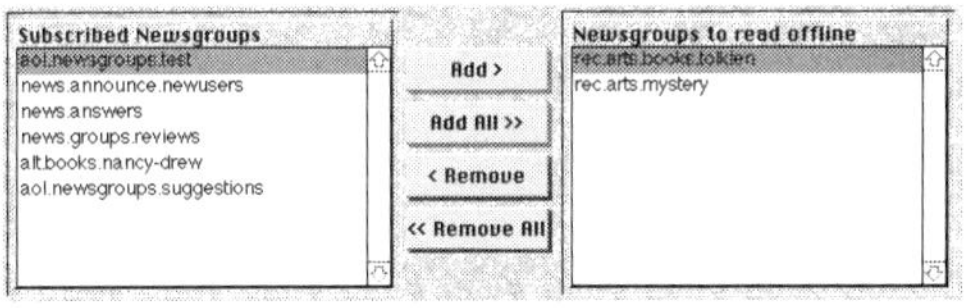


**Figure 32.** *When you click the Add button, the newsgroup is removed from one list and added to the other.*

## To specify newsgroups to read offline

1. If you are not already connected to AOL, sign on.
2. Use a keyword of NEWSGROUP to open the Newsgroups window (see **Figure 30**).
3. Click the Read Offline button to open the Choose Newsgroups window (see **Figure 31**).
4. In the Subscribed Newsgroups list, click the name of a newsgroup you want to read offline to select it.
5. Click the Add button to add it to the Newsgroups to Read Offline list.
6. Repeat steps 4 and 5 for each newsgroup you want to read offline. **Figure 32** shows an example with two newsgroups selected.
7. Click the OK button to accept your changes and dismiss the Choose Newsgroups window.

## ✔ Tips

- Before you can use the Choose Newsgroups window as instructed here, you must select the newsgroups in which you want to participate. Consult **Chapter 9** for more information about subscribing to newsgroups.
- To add all newsgroups, click the Add All button.
- To remove a newsgroup from the Newsgroups to Read Offline list, click it once to select it and then click the Remove button.

## To read newsgroup messages offline

1. Choose Personal Filing Cabinet from the File menu (see **Figure 19**).

   *or*

   Click the Personal Filing Cabinet button on the toolbar. 
2. In the Filing Cabinet window (see **Figure 29**), double-click the Incoming Postings tray to open it (see **Figure 33**).
3. Double-click the message you want to read to open it. **Figure 34** shows an example of an incoming newsgroup message.
4. Follow the instructions in **Chapter 9** to reply to the newsgroup or a message's author.

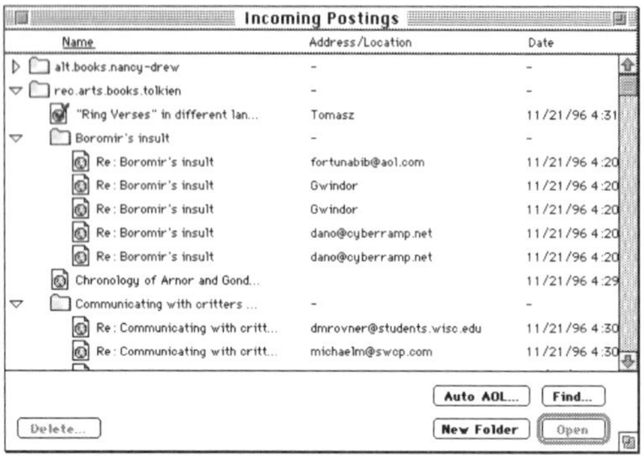


**Figure 33.** *Double-clicking the Incoming Postings tray displays all incoming newsgroup messages in a window like this.*

**Figure 34.** *Here's an example of an incoming newsgroup message read offline.*

## ✔ Tips

- To display the messages within a specific message thread, click the triangle to the left of the folder for a subject. An outline view of the folder's contents appears (see **Figures 29** and **33**).
- Newsgroup messages you have already read appear in your Filing Cabinet with a check mark over their icons (see **Figure 33**).

## To compose newsgroup messages offline

1. In a newsgroup message window (see **Figure 34**), click the New Message button.
2. Enter a subject and message text in the appropriate fields of the Post New Message window that appears (see **Figure 35**).
3. Click the Send Later button. The message is added to the Postings Waiting To Be Sent Tray in the Personal Filing Cabinet.

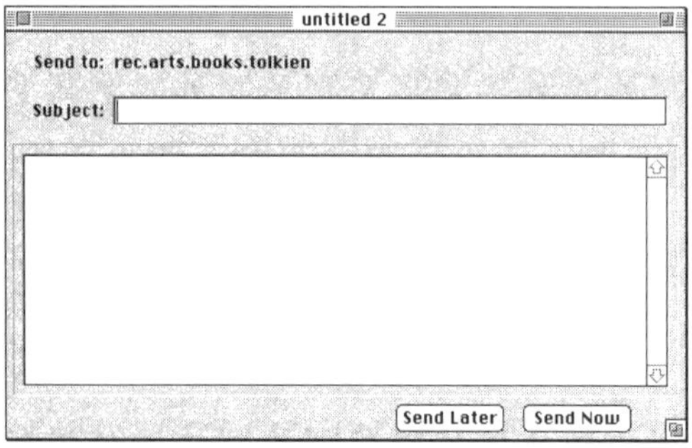


**Figure 35.** *You compose newsgroup messages offline in a window like this.*

Working with Newsgroups Offline

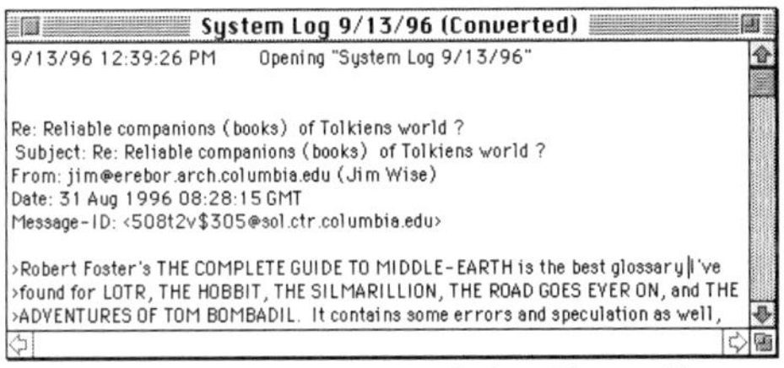


**Figure 36.** *A System log includes all text files opened while online.*

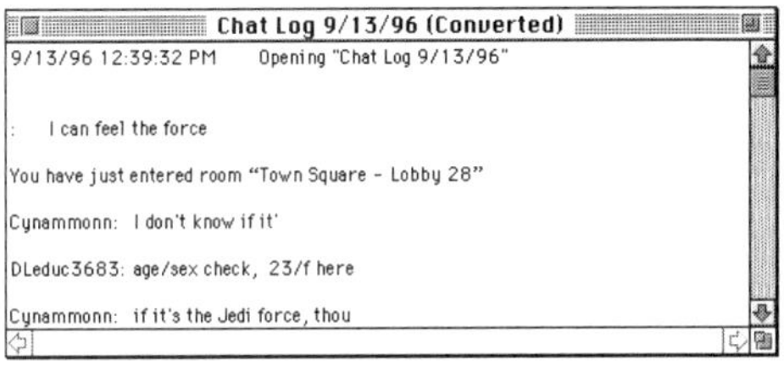


**Figure 37.** *A Chat log includes all messages exchanged in a chat or conference window.*

## About Logging

AOL's logging feature lets you save information you view online to a text file. You can open the file with any text editor to review an AOL session.

AOL's Log Manager lets you create three different kinds of logs:

- A *System log* (see **Figure 36**) keeps track of all text files that you open while online—like message board messages, news articles, and e-mail. It does not save menus, lists, or forms.
- A *Chat log* (see **Figure 37**) keeps track of all messages that appear in chat windows—like People Connection rooms, conference rooms, and forum chat rooms.
- An *Instant Message log* keeps track of all messages that appear in Instant Message windows.

### ✔ Tips

- Use a system log to speed through AOL features like message boards without stopping to read anything. Then, when you're offline, you can take your time reading messages saved to the log.
- Use a chat log to create and store transcripts of conferences you attend online.
- You can open all three kinds of logs at the same time.
- A log stays open until you close it or quit the AOL software.
- Consult **Chapter 5** about message boards. Consult **Chapter 7** for more information about chatting, conferences, and Instant Messages.

## To create a new log

1. Choose Log Manager from the File menu (see **Figure 38**).
2. In the Log Manager window that appears (see **Figure 39**), click the New Log button for the type of log you want to create.
3. Use the standard Save As dialog box that appears (see **Figure 40**) to specify a name and a disk location for the log file. Then click OK or press [Enter].
4. The name of the log appears in the Log Manager dialog box (see **Figure 41**). Click the window's close box or press [⌘W] to close the Log Manager window.

## To append to an existing log

1. Choose Log Manager from the File menu (see **Figure 38**).
2. In the Log Manager window that appears (see **Figure 39**), click the Append Log button for the type of log to which you want to append.
3. Use the standard Open dialog box that appears to locate and open an existing log file to which you want to append information.
4. The name of the log appears in the Log Manager dialog box (see **Figure 41**). Click the window's close box or press [⌘W] to close the Log Manager window.

**Figure 38.** *Choose Log Manager from the File menu.*

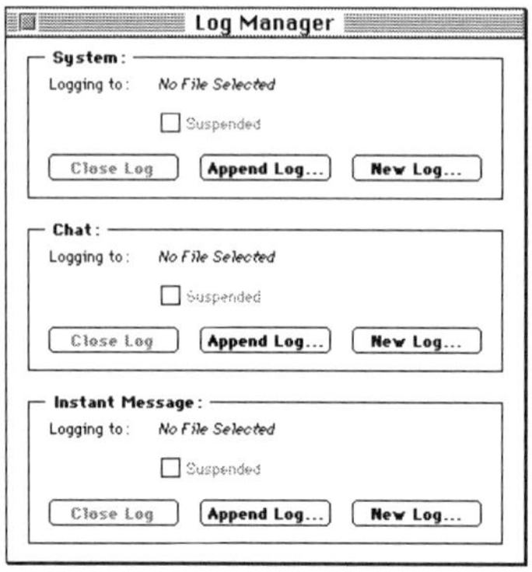


**Figure 39.** *The Log Manager window lets you create or append to three different kinds of logs.*

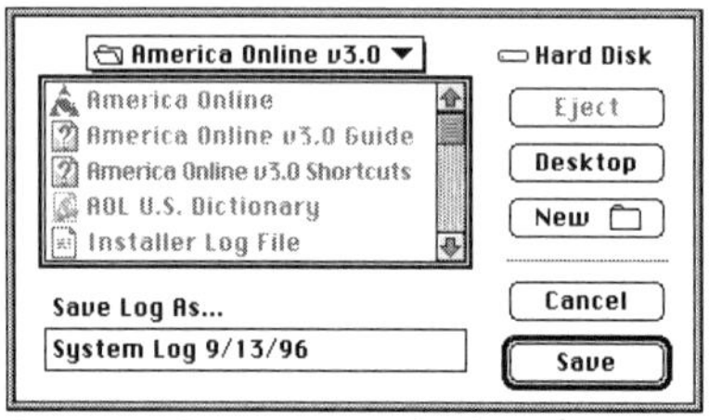


**Figure 40.** *Use a standard Save As dialog box like this to name and save a log file.*

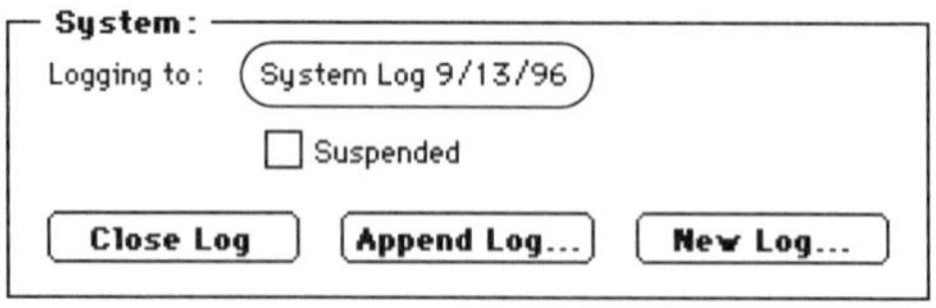


**Figure 41.** *The name of the log you create or append to appears in the Log Manager window.*

## To close or suspend a log

1. Choose Log Manager from the File menu (see **Figure 38**) to open the Log Manager window (see **Figure 39**).
2. Click the Close Log button for the type of log you want to close.

   *or*

   Turn on the Suspended check box for the log you want to suspend.
3. Click the Log Manager window's close box or press ⌘W to close it.

**Figure 42.** *Choose Open from the File menu.*

### ✔ Tip

- When you close a log, the name of the log file disappears from the Log Manager window and you must use the Append Log button to add more information to it. When you suspend a log, however, the log file remains open but no information is written to it. Simply turn off the Suspended check box to continue writing information to it.

## To read a log

1. Choose Open from the File menu (see **Figure 42**).

   *or*

   Press ⌘O.
2. Use the Open a File dialog box that appears (see **Figure 43**) to locate and open the log file you want to read. The log appears in a text editor window within AOL (see **Figures 36** and **37**).

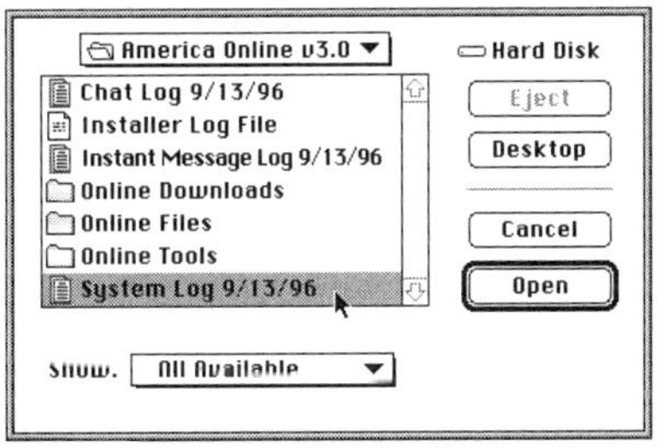


**Figure 43.** *Use a standard Open dialog box like this to locate and open the log file you want to read.*

### ✔ Tip

- If the log file is greater than 32K in size, you will not be able to open it with AOL's Open command. Instead, use your favorite word processor or text editor.

# CUSTOMIZING AOL 11

## About Customizing AOL

AOL's software offers a number of features you can use to customize it so it works just the way you want it to:

- Set preferences for features and options in a variety of categories, including General, Mail, Download, Chat, Passwords, Auto AOL, Scheduler, Fonts, Filing Cabinet, Helpers, AOL Link, Web, and Spelling.
- Create screen names that enable you and your family members to access AOL with separate, private log ons.
- Use Parental Controls to control what your children see while online.
- Change billing options to select a different billing plan or payment option.

This chapter explains all of these customization options and tells you how to use them to get the most out of AOL.

### ✔ Tips

- Many customization options can be set while offline.
- Auto AOL and Scheduler preferences are discussed in detail in **Chapter 10**.

## About Preferences

AOL lets you set preferences for a wide range of features, most of which are discussed throughout this book.

AOL offers two ways to set preferences:

- Use options in the My AOL window (see **Figure 1**) to have AOL walk you through the setup of important customizable features or to access other preference settings (see **Figure 2**).
- Use options in the Preferences window (see **Figure 3**) to select and customize specific categories of preferences.

This section discusses each of the preferences categories and tells you how you can change options so AOL works the way you want it to.

### ✔ Tips

- Many of the preferences options affect only the screen name which is set in the Welcome window or used to connect when the preference options are changed.
- If your billing plan charges based on the amount of time spent online, you may want to stop the billing clock while you adjust preferences while online. To do this, click the Member Service button on the toolbar to open the Member Services window to enter an unlimited use area and stop the billing clock. Then choose Preferences from the Members menu (see **Figure 4**). When you finish changing preference options and return to a regular area of AOL, the billing clock will start up again.
- Auto AOL and Scheduler preferences are discussed in detail in **Chapter 10**.

**Figure 1.** *The My AOL window offers many configuration options.*

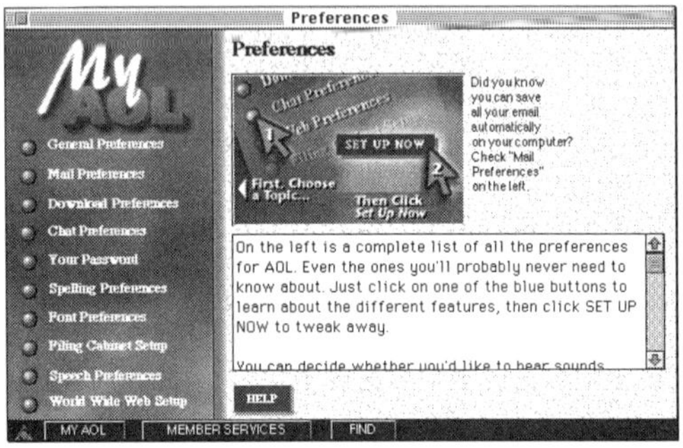


**Figure 2.** *The Preferences window in the My AOL area is slick-looking, but you must be connected to open it.*

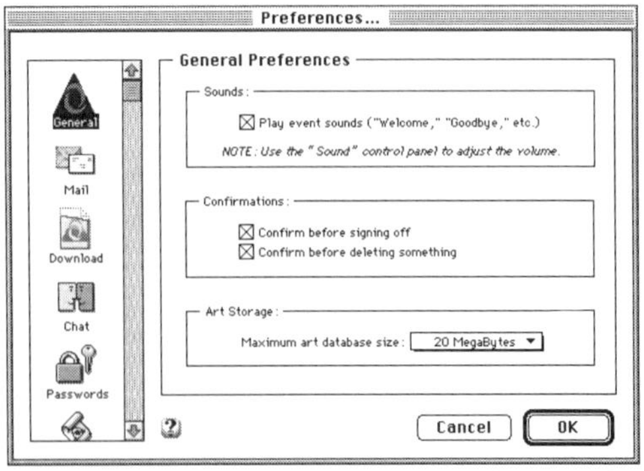


**Figure 3.** *This Preferences window can be opened even if you aren't connected to AOL.*

**Figure 4.** *Choose My AOL or Preferences from the Members menu to set your preferences.*

## To open the Preferences window in the My AOL area

1. Choose My AOL from the Members menu (see **Figure 4**).

   *or*

   Click the My AOL button on the toolbar. 

   *or*

   Use the keyword MY AOL.

2. Click the Preferences button in the My AOL window that appears (see **Figure 1**).

### ✔ Tip

- You must be connected to AOL to open the My AOL window (see **Figure 1**) and access its options.

## To open the Preferences window

Choose Preferences from the Members menu (see **Figure 4**).

*or*

Use the keyword PREFERENCES.

### ✔ Tip

- You do not need to be connected to AOL to open the Preferences window (see **Figure 3**).

## To set General preferences

1. In the Preferences window within My AOL (see **Figure 2**), click the General Preferences button. When the Set Up Now button appears in the lower right corner of the window (see **Figure 5**), click it.

   *or*

   Click the General icon in the scrolling list on the left side of the Preferences window (see **Figure 3**).

2. Set options in the General Preferences window (see **Figure 3**) as desired:

   ▲ *Play event sounds ("Welcome," "Goodbye," etc.)* plays preset sounds for specific AOL events. You can adjust the sound volume with the Sound control panel that's part of your System software.

   ▲ *Confirm before signing off* displays the Sign Off? window when you choose Sign Off from the Go To menu or the Quit? window when you choose Quit from the File menu while connected.

   ▲ *Confirm before deleting something* displays a confirmation dialog box each time you try to delete something.

   ▲ *Maximum art database size* lets you choose a maximum size from a pop-up menu (see **Figure 6**) for AOL's art files stored on your hard disk. This is especially useful if you have limited disk space and don't want AOL to take up more space than necessary.

3. When you are finished making changes, click OK or press Enter to save them.

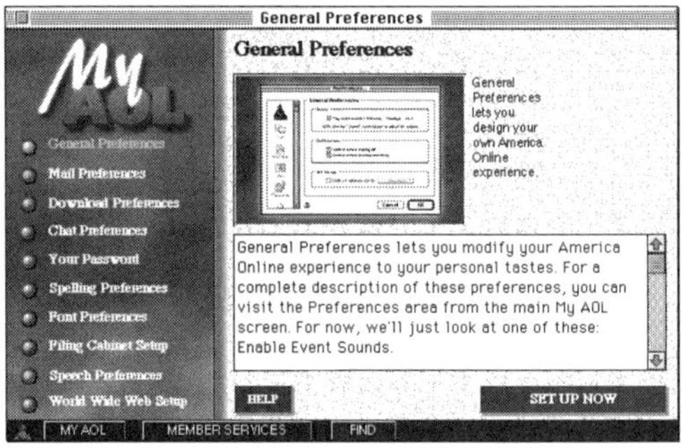


**Figure 5.** *Choose the preference category you want to change and then click the Set Up Now button.*

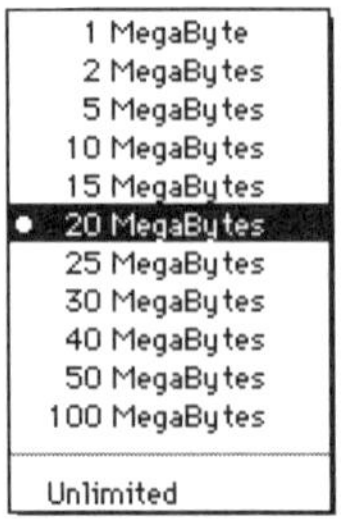


**Figure 6.** *Use this pop-up menu to specify how much disk space AOL should use for its art databases.*

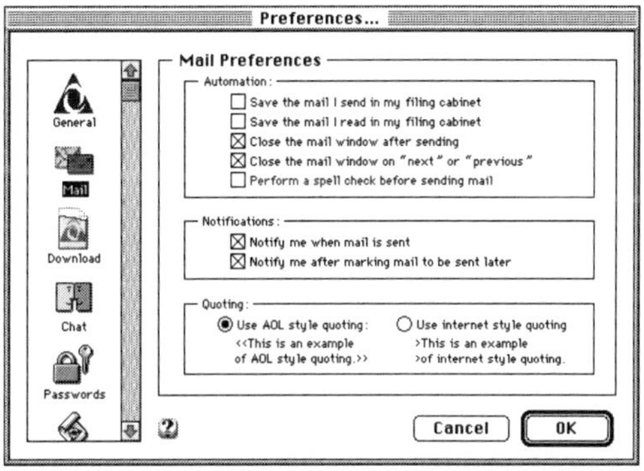


**Figure 7.** *Mail preferences change the way e-mail works. These are the default settings.*

- *Save the mail I send in my filing cabinet* saves a copy of every e-mail message you write in the Mail You've Sent folder in your Personal Filing Cabinet.
- *Save the mail I read in my filing cabinet* saves a copy of every e-mail message you read in the Mail You've Read folder in your Personal Filing Cabinet.
- *Close the mail window after sending* closes the mail window when you click the Send or Send Later button.
- *Close the mail window on "next" or "previous"* closes the message window for the current message when you click the Next or Previous button to read the next or previous message.

## To set Mail preferences

1. In the Preferences window within My AOL (see **Figure 2**), click the Mail Preferences button. When the Set Up Now button appears in the lower right corner of the window (see **Figure 5**), click it.

   *or*

   Click the Mail icon in the scrolling list on the left side of the Preferences window (see **Figure 7**).
2. Toggle check boxes and select a radio button in the Mail Preferences window (see **Figure 7**) as desired:
   - *Perform a spell check before sending mail* automatically performs a spelling check of an e-mail message when you click the Send or Send Later button in the mail window.
   - *Notify me when mail is sent* displays a confirmation dialog box each time you click the Send button in a mail window.
   - *Notify me after marking mail to be sent later* displays a confirmation dialog box each time you click the Send Later button in a mail window.
   - *Quoting* options lets you select one of two radio buttons for different quoting styles.
3. When you are finished making changes, click OK or press Enter to save them.

### ✔ Tip

- E-mail is discussed in detail in **Chapter 4**. The Personal Filing Cabinet is discussed in **Chapter 10**.

## To set Download preferences

1. In the Preferences window within My AOL (see **Figure 2**), click the Download Preferences button. When the Set Up Now button appears in the lower right corner of the window (see **Figure 5**), click it.

   *or*

   Click the Download icon in the scrolling list on the left side of the Preferences window (see **Figure 8**).

2. Set options in the Download Preferences window (see **Figure 8**) as desired:

   ▲ *Display image files as they download* displays the image files you download as you download them.

   ▲ *Automatically uncompress files at sign-off* uncompresses files you downloaded during a session when you disconnect from AOL.

   ▲ *Delete compressed files after expanding* deletes the compressed files you downloaded during a session when those files are uncompressed. The *Automatically uncompress files at sign-off* option must be turned on to turn on this option.

   ▲ *Notify me after marking files to be downloaded later* displays a confirmation dialog box when you click the Download Later button in a file list or file description window.

   ▲ *Notify me at signoff files to be downloaded* displays a reminder dialog box when you sign off if there are any files to be downloaded.

   ▲ *Default Folder* lets you choose the default folder for downloading files with the Download Manager. Click the Select Folder button and use the Save As dialog box that appears (see **Figure 9**) to choose a new disk location for downloaded files.

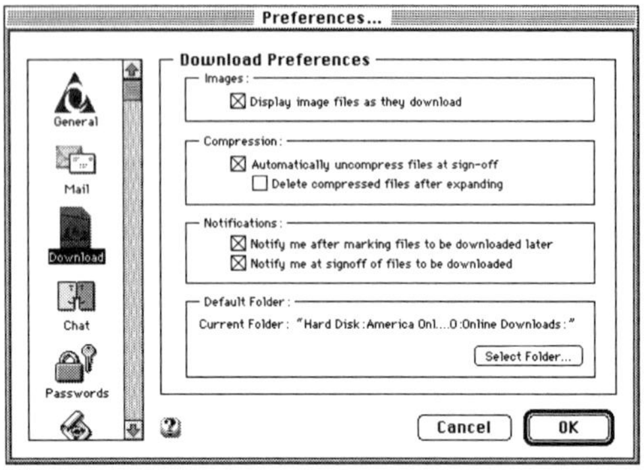


**Figure 8.** *Download preferences set options related to downloading files. These are the default settings.*

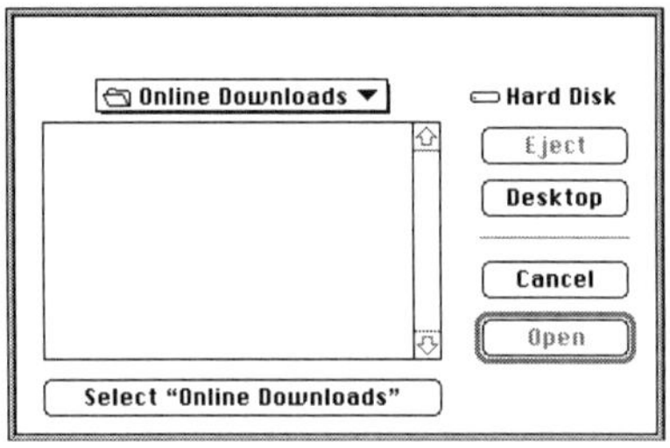


**Figure 9.** *Use this dialog box to navigate to and select a folder in which to save files you download with the Download Manager.*

3. When you are finished making changes, click OK or press Enter to save them.

## ✔ Tip

■ Downloading files and images and using the Download Manager are discussed in **Chapter 6**.

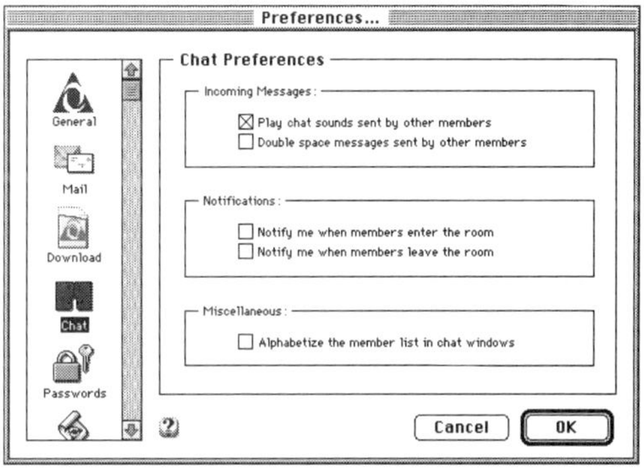


**Figure 10.** *Chat preferences determine how chat window features work. These are the default settings.*

## To set Chat preferences

1. In the Preferences window within My AOL (see **Figure 2**), click the Chat Preferences button. When the Set Up Now button appears in the lower right corner of the window (see **Figure 5**), click it.

   *or*

   Click the Chat icon in the scrolling list on the left side of the Preferences window (see **Figure 10**).

   *or*

   Click the Setup or Prefs button in a chat window.

2. Set options in the Chat Preferences window (see **Figure 10**) as desired:
   - ▲ *Play chat sounds sent by other members* plays the sounds that are sent by chat room participants if you have the appropriate sound installed.
   - ▲ *Double space messages sent by other members* puts additional space between each chat room participant's comment.
   - ▲ *Notify me when members enter the room* displays a message in the chat window when a new participant enters the chat room.
   - ▲ *Notify me when members leave the room* displays a message in the chat window when a participant leaves the chat room.
   - ▲ *Alphabetize the member list in chat windows* puts screen names in the list of chat participants in alphabetical order.

3. When you are finished making changes, click OK or press Enter to save them.

## ✔ Tip

- ■ AOL's chat feature is discussed in **Chapter 7**.

## To change your password

1. In the Preferences window within My AOL (see **Figure 2**), click the Your Password button. When the Set Up Now button appears in the lower right corner of the window (see **Figure 5**), click it. Then click the Change Your Password button in the Your Password window that appears (see **Figure 11**).

   *or*

   Use the keyword PASSWORD.
2. A dialog box like the one in **Figure 12** appears. Read the information inside it. Then click the Change Password button.
3. In the next window that appears (see **Figure 13**), enter your current password in the Old Password edit box. Then enter the new password you want to use in the other two edit boxes.
4. Click the Change Password button or press [Enter].
5. A confirmation dialog box like the one in **Figure 14** appears. Click OK or press [Enter] to dismiss it.

## ✔ Tips

- You can only change the password for the screen name with which you are connected to AOL.
- Don't give your password to anyone for any reason! There are no exceptions to this rule!
- If you have stored your old password in the Stored Passwords Preferences window (see **Figure 15**), be sure to change the stored password to match the new one.

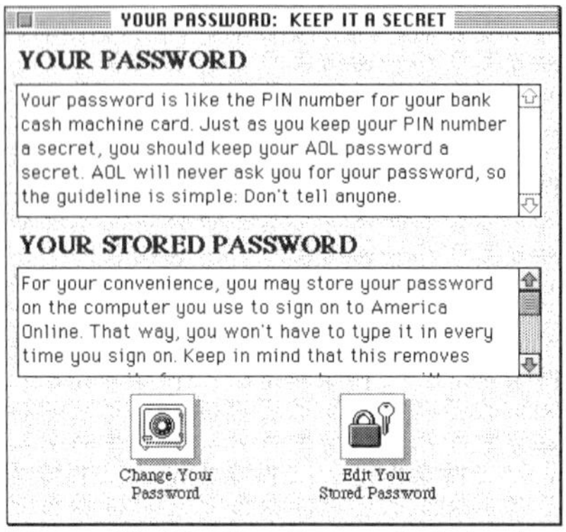


**Figure 11.** *The Your Password window lets you change your password or edit your stored passwords.*

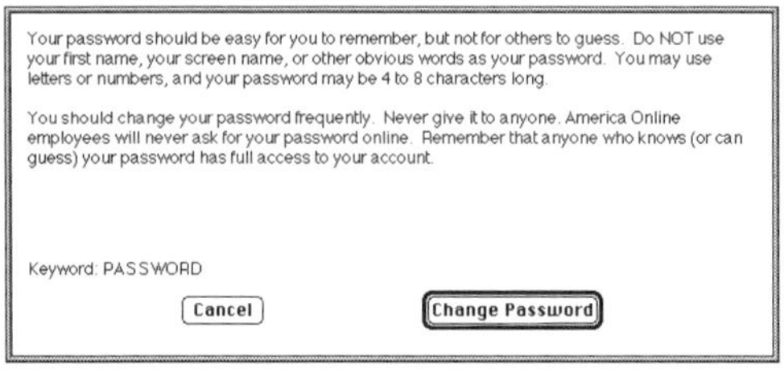


**Figure 12.** *This window offers some password tips.*

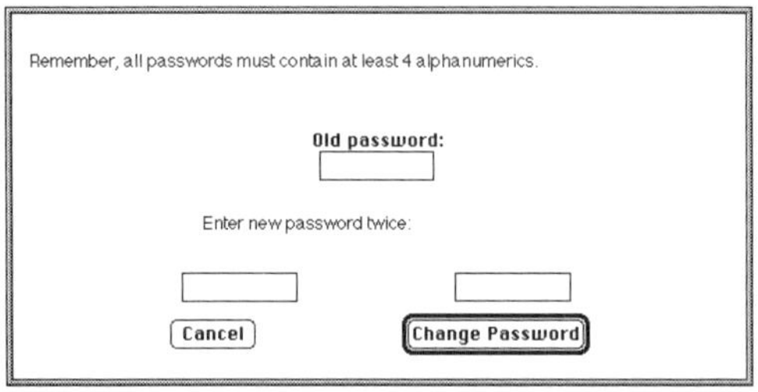


**Figure 13.** *To change your password, type the old one once and the new one twice.*

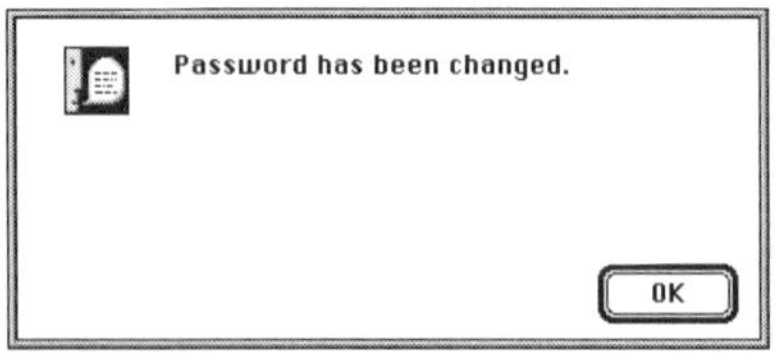


**Figure 14.** *AOL confirms that your password has been changed.*

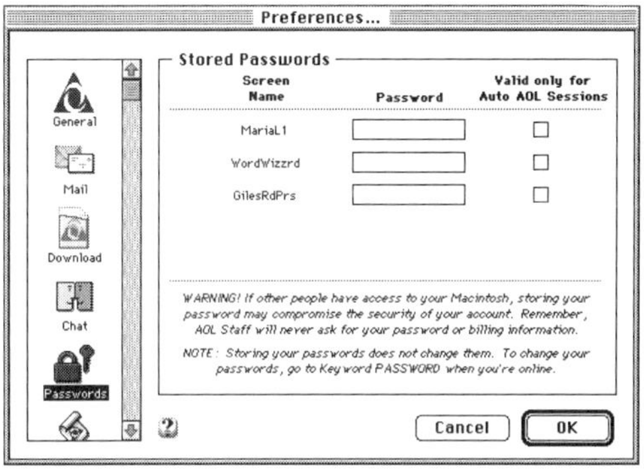


**Figure 15.** *Use the Stored Password Preferences window to store the passwords for any combination of screen names.*

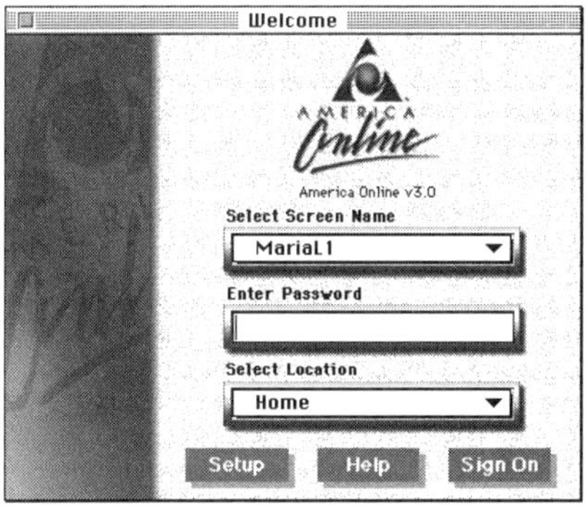


**Figures 16a & 16b.** *Before storing a password, you must enter it each time you connect (above). Once a password is stored, you never have to enter it to connect (below).*

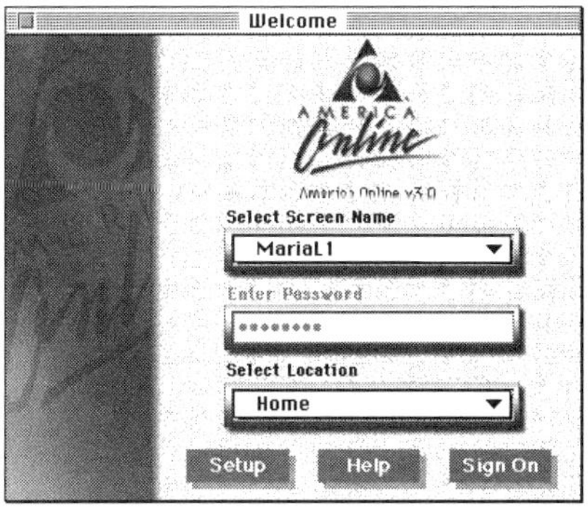


## To store passwords

1. In the Preferences window within My AOL (see **Figure 2**), click the Your Password button. When the Set Up Now button appears in the lower right corner of the window (see **Figure 5**), click it. Then click the Edit Your Stored Passwords button in the Your Password window that appears (see **Figure 11**).

   *or*

   Click the Password icon in the scrolling list on the left side of the Preferences window (see **Figure 15**).
2. In the Stored Passwords Preferences window (see **Figure 15**), enter the password for each screen name for which you want to store the password.
3. Turn on the check box beside any password you want to work for Auto AOL sessions only.
4. When you are finished making changes, click OK or press Enter to save them.

## ✔ Tips

- When you enter passwords in the Stored Passwords Preferences window (see **Figure 15**), the characters you enter are displayed as bullets, so type carefully!
- You can also follow the above steps to edit stored passwords.
- When you store your password in AOL, the password edit box is grayed out in the Welcome window (see **Figures 16a** and **16b**). The Welcome window is discussed in **Chapter 1**.
- If your computer is accessible by others, do not store your password. Doing so will make it possible for others to use your account.
- Auto AOL sessions are discussed in **Chapter 10**.

## To set Spelling preferences

1. In the Preferences window within My AOL (see **Figure 2**), click the Spelling Preferences button. When the Set Up Now button appears in the lower right corner of the window (see **Figure 5**), click it.

   *or*

   Click the Spelling icon in the scrolling list on the left side of the Preferences window (see **Figure 17**).

2. Set options in the Spelling Preferences window (see **Figure 17**) as desired:
   - ▲ *First word of sentences should be capitalized* checks to be sure that the first letter of the first word in a sentence is capitalized.
   - ▲ *Proper nouns should be capitalized* checks to be sure that proper nouns are capitalized.
   - ▲ *Warn if adjacent words are identical* informs you if you use the same word twice in a row.
   - ▲ *Allow numbers in words* stops the spelling checker from flagging words that contain numbers.
   - ▲ *Treat hyphenated words as two words* checks each part of a hyphenated word as a separate word.
   - ▲ *Don't allow spaces before punctuation marks* prevents you from typing spaces before periods, question marks, and exclamation points.
   - ▲ *Require two spaces after punctuation marks* places two spaces after periods, question marks, and exclamation points.
   - ▲ *Select Dictionary* displays a standard Open dialog box that you can use to locate and open another AOL-compatible dictionary file.

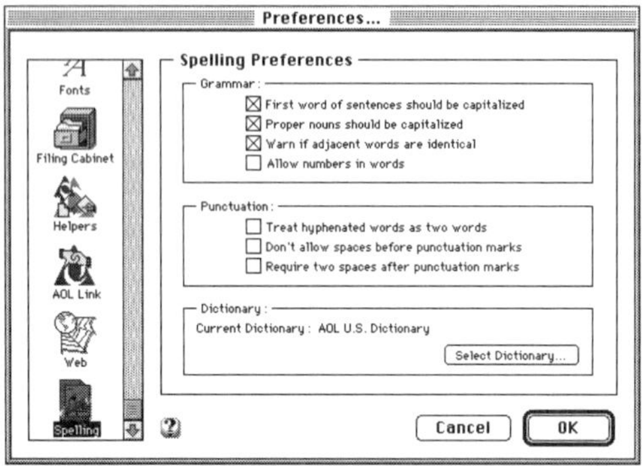


**Figure 17.** *The Spelling Preferences window lets you customize the way the spelling checker works.*

3. When you are finished making changes, click OK or press Enter to save them.

## ✔ Tip

- ■ AOL's spelling checker is discussed in **Chapter 4**.

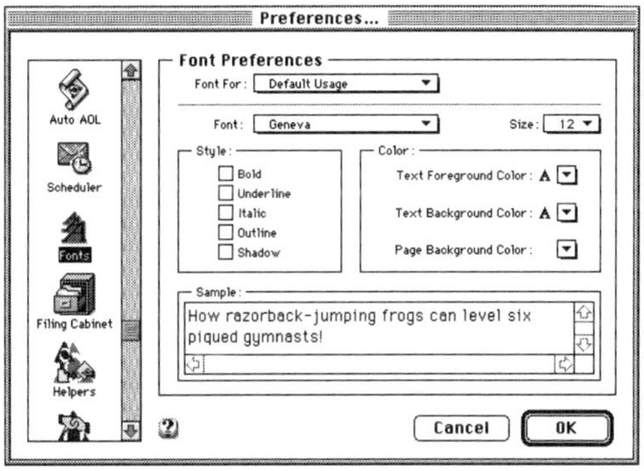


**Figure 18.** *Set the appearance of text in text windows, e-mail messages, and chat windows with options in the Font Preferences window.*

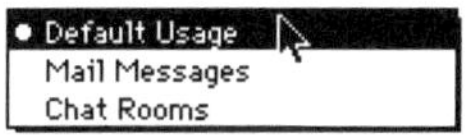


**Figure 19.** *Use the Font For pop-up menu to choose the font usage you want to change.*

**Figure 20.** *Choose one of the fonts installed on your system from the Font pop-up menu.*

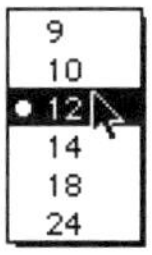


**Figure 21.** *Choose a font size from the Size pop-up menu.*

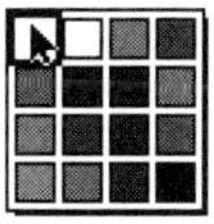

**Figure 22.** *Use the Text Foreground Color, Text Background Color, and Page Background Color pop-up menus to change color options. All of them look like this.*

## To set Font preferences

1. In the Preferences window within My AOL (see **Figure 2**), click the Font Preferences button. When the Set Up Now button appears in the lower right corner of the window (see **Figure 5**), click it.

   *or*

   Click the Fonts icon in the scrolling list on the left side of the Preferences window (see **Figure 18**).
2. Choose a font usage from the Font For pop-up menu (see **Figure 19**).
3. Choose a font from the Font pop-up menu (see **Figure 20**).
4. Choose a size from the Size pop-up menu (see **Figure 21**).
5. Toggle check boxes for various style options in the Style area of the Font Preferences window (see **Figure 18**).
6. Use the Text Foreground Color, Text Background Color, and Page Background Color pop-up menus (see **Figure 22**) to change text and background color options.
7. Repeat steps 2 through 6 for each font usage you want to change.
8. When you are finished making changes, click OK or press Enter to save them.

## ✔ Tips

- Only the fonts properly installed in your System will appear in the Font pop-up menu.
- The sample area near the bottom of the Font Preferences window (see **Figure 18**) shows exactly what the text will look like as you make changes.
- E-mail is discussed in **Chapter 4**. Chat is discussed in **Chapter 7**.

## To set Filing Cabinet preferences

1. In the Preferences window within My AOL (see **Figure 2**), click the Filing Cabinet Setup button. When the Set Up Now button appears in the lower right corner of the window (see **Figure 5**), click it.

   *or*

   Click the Filing Cabinet icon in the scrolling list on the left side of the Preferences window (see **Figure 23**).
2. To automatically delete Filing Cabinet items in one or more folders, turn on the "Automatically delete items in my filing cabinet" option. This enables the rest of the options in the window (see **Figure 24**).
3. For each Filing Cabinet folder whose items you want to automatically delete, choose an option from the Delete after pop-up menu (see **Figure 25**).
4. When you are finished making changes, click OK or press Enter to save them.

### ✔ Tip

- AOL's Filing Cabinet feature is discussed in **Chapter 10**.

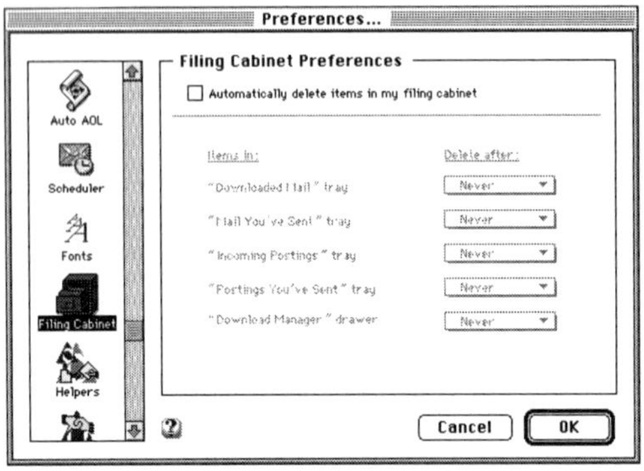


**Figure 23.** *Use the Filing Cabinet Preferences window to control whether items are automatically deleted from the Personal Filing Cabinet. By default, this feature is turned off, as shown here.*

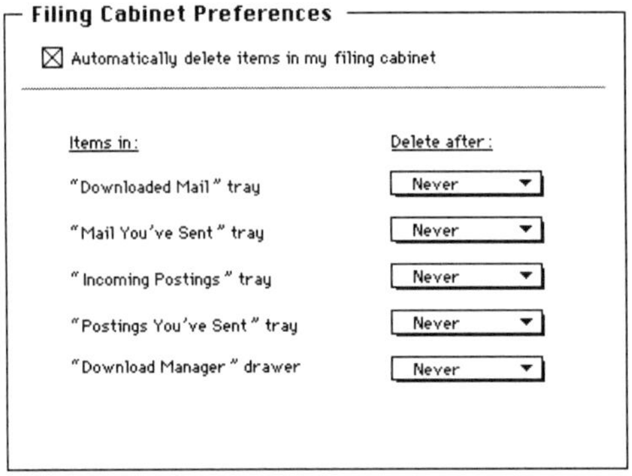


**Figure 24.** *Once you turn on the "Automatically delete items in my filing cabinet" option, you can configure the automatic deletion feature.*

**Figure 25.** *Use the Delete After pop-up menu to specify when Filing Cabinet items should be deleted.*

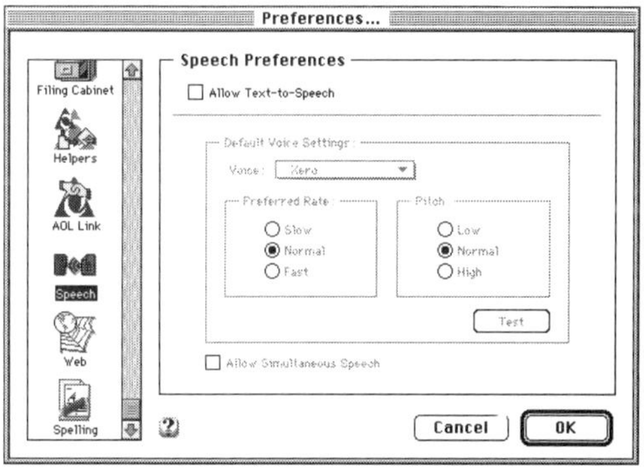


**Figure 26.** *Use the Speech Preferences window to set up the way e-mail and chat is read back to you. These are the default settings.*

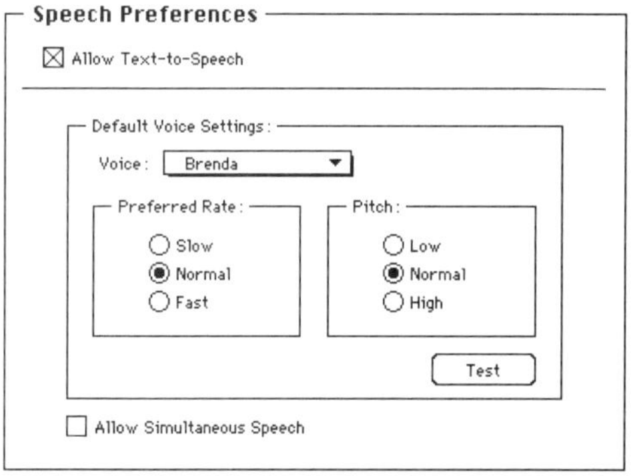


**Figure 27.** *Once you turn on the "Allow Text-to-Speech" check box, you can configure the speech feature.*

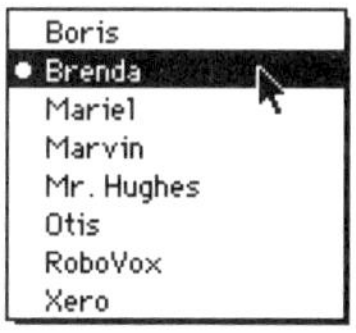


**Figure 28.** *Choose a default voice from the Voice pop-up menu. Only the voices that are properly installed in your System will appear on this menu.*

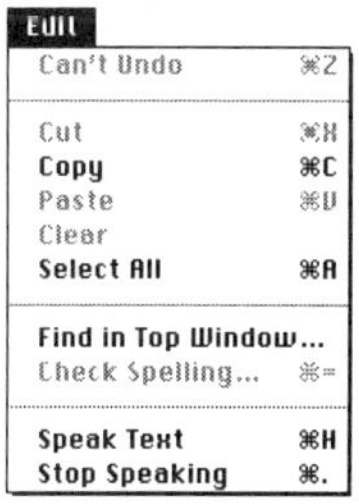


**Figure 29.** *Use the Speak Text and Stop Speaking commands under the Edit menu to control the way your Mac reads AOL text to you.*

## To set Speech preferences

1. In the Preferences window within the My AOL area (see **Figure 2**), click the Speech Preferences button. When the Set Up Now button appears in the lower right corner of the window (see **Figure 5**), click it.

   *or*

   Click the Speech icon in the scrolling list on the left side of the Preferences window (see **Figure 26**).
2. To enable the Speech feature, turn on the Allow Text-to-Speech check box (see **Figure 27**).
3. Choose a default voice from the Voice pop-up menu (see **Figure 28**).
4. Select radio buttons to set a Preferred Rate and Pitch for the voice.
5. If desired, click the Test button to listen to the voice and its settings.
6. To allow speech and sounds to play simultaneously, turn on the Allow Simultaneous Speech check box.
7. When you are finished making changes, click OK or press Enter to save them.

## ✔ Tips

- When you enable the Speech feature, all chat room comments are automatically played back as spoken text.
- You can use the Speak Text command under the Edit menu (see **Figure 29**) to read any text in a scrolling window—like e-mail message, chat comments, and text files.
- Use the Sound or Monitors & Sound Control panel to change the volume of all sounds on your System, including speech.

## To set Web preferences

1. In the Preferences window within My AOL (see **Figure 2**), click the World Wide Web Setup button. When the Set Up Now button appears in the lower right corner of the window (see **Figure 5**), click it.

   *or*

   Click the Web icon in the scrolling list on the left side of the Preferences window (see **Figure 30**).

2. Set options in the Web Preferences window (see **Figure 30**) as desired:

   ▲ *Show address bar* displays the URL of the current page near the top of the browser window.

   ▲ *Show images* displays all images on a page. Turning off this option will speed browsing, but you won't see any graphics.

   ▲ *Show status bar* displays the loading progress indicator in the bottom right corner of the browser window.

   ▲ *Show hyperlink destinations* displays a link's URL when you point to it.

   ▲ *Use compressed images* speeds up the loading of images on web pages.

   ▲ *Draw images once the entire page has been received* does not draw images until all page information has been downloaded.

   ▲ *Notify me when I first enter a secure web site* displays a dialog box when you enter a secure site.

   ▲ *Notify me when I first enter an unsecure web site* displays a dialog box when you enter an unsecure site.

   ▲ *Confirm my action before submitting an unsecure form* displays a confirmation dialog box when you submit information on an unsecure form.

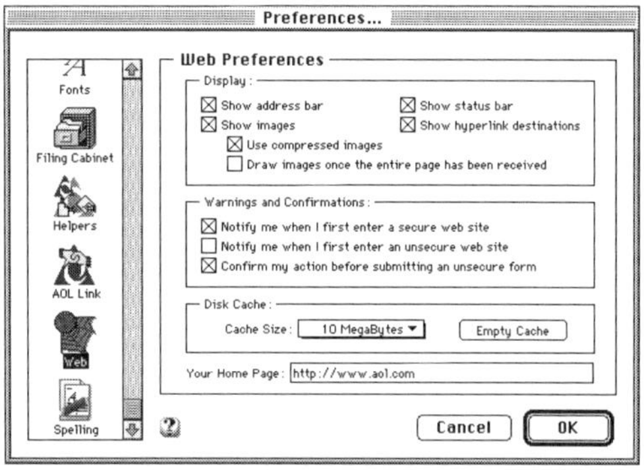


**Figure 30.** *Set preferences for the Web browser in the Web Preferences window. These are the default settings.*

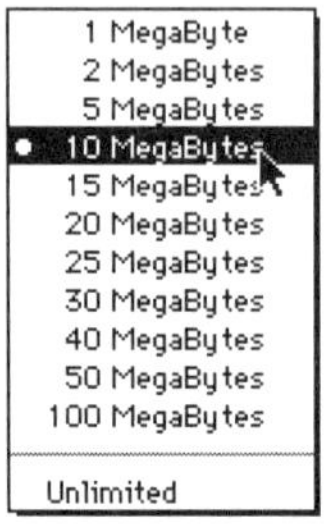


**Figure 31.** *Use the Cache Size pop-up menu to choose how much disk space the cache will occupy.*

   ▲ *Cache Size* lets you use a pop-up menu (see **Figure 31**) to select the total amount of disk space occupied by cached pages and images. *Cached files* are those saved on disk to speed subsequent loading during the same session.

   ▲ *Empty Cache* deletes all cache files.

   ▲ *Your Home Page* is the URL for the default Web page when you click the World Wide Web button on the toolbar or use the keyword WEB.

3. When you are finished making changes, click OK or press Enter to save them.

### ✔ Tip

■ The World Wide Web is discussed in **Chapter 9**.

## About AOL Link

AOL Link is a component of the AOL software that is added to your MacTCP or TCP/IP control panel when you install the AOL software. It's important for three reasons:

- It must be activated in order to connect to AOL with a modem.
- It enables you to use other Internet software, like Netscape Navigator or Fetch, while you're connected to AOL.
- When activated, it overwrites any MacTCP or TCP/IP control panel settings you may have for an Internet Service Provider (ISP) or Local Area Network (LAN).

If you access the Internet via an ISP or LAN, you'll use the AOL Link preferences for two things:

- To turn AOL Link on in order to access AOL after a TCP/IP connection to an ISP or LAN.
- To restore your MacTCP or TCP/IP control panel settings in order to make a TCP/IP connection to an ISP or LAN after connecting by modem to AOL.

### ✔ Tips

- If you always access AOL via modem and you don't have an ISP or LAN connection to the Internet, you don't have to worry about AOL Link—it's already set just the way it should be for you.
- If AOL Link is not properly set, a dialog box telling you to activate it will appear when you try to connect.

## To activate AOL Link after a TCP/IP connection to an ISP or LAN

1. Click the AOL Link icon in the scrolling list on the left side of the Preferences window (see **Figure 32**).
2. Click the Configure button in the AOL Link Preferences window (see **Figure 32**).
3. After a moment, a dialog box like the one in **Figure 33** appears. Click Restart or press Enter to restart your Macintosh and activate AOL Link.

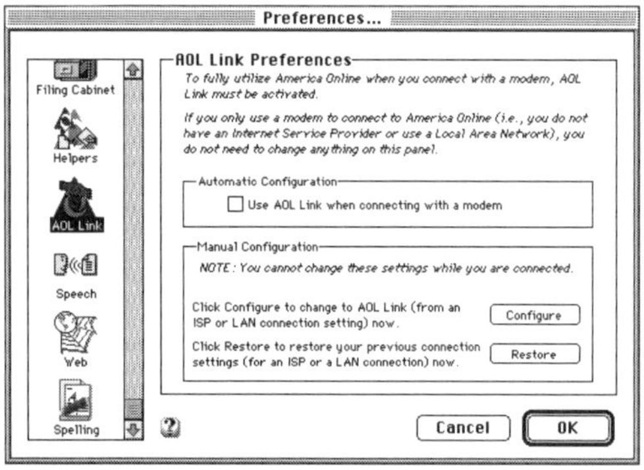


**Figure 32.** *Use AOL Link preferences to work with AOL Link if you also connect to an ISP or LAN.*

## To restore TCP/IP settings after a modem connection to AOL

1. Click the AOL Link icon in the scrolling list on the left side of the Preferences window (see **Figure 32**).
2. Click the Restore button in the AOL Link Preferences window (see **Figure 32**).
3. After a moment, a dialog box like the one in **Figure 33** appears. Click Restart to restart your Macintosh.

**Figure 33.** *A dialog box like this appears when you use the Configure button to activate AOL Link.*

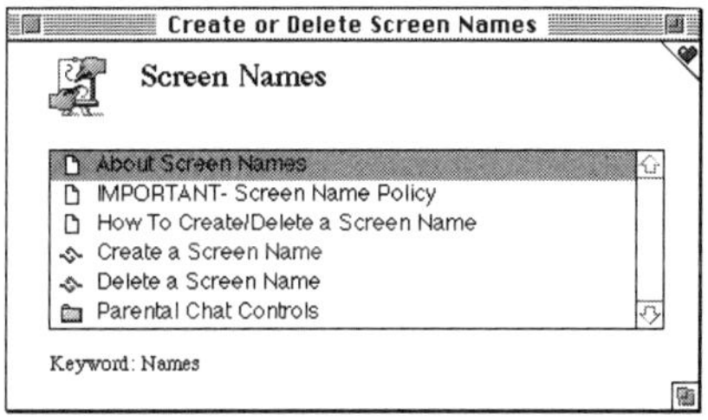


**Figure 34.** *Use this window to manage screen names.*

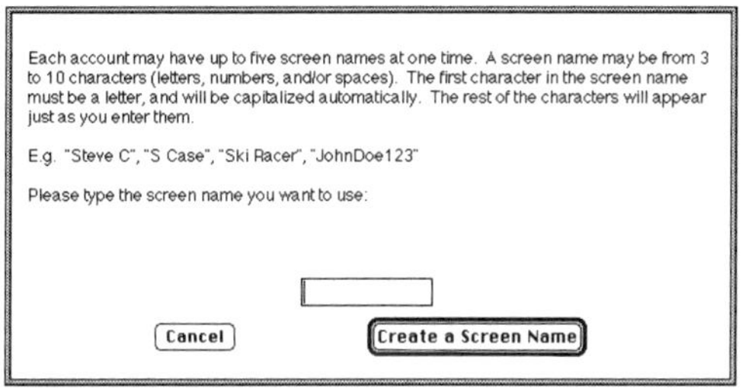


**Figure 35.** *Enter the screen name you'd like to add in the edit box here.*

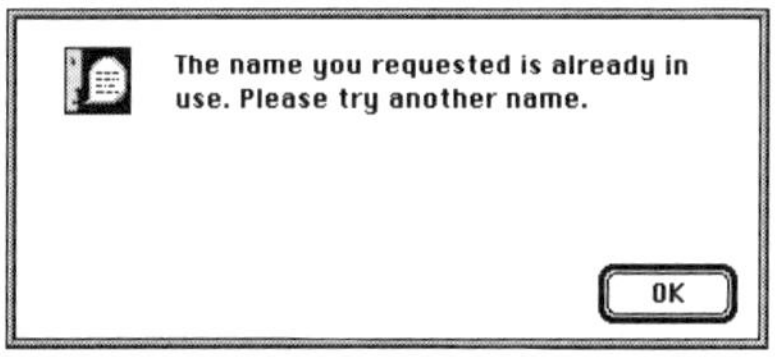


**Figure 36.** *If you enter a screen name already in use, this dialog box appears.*

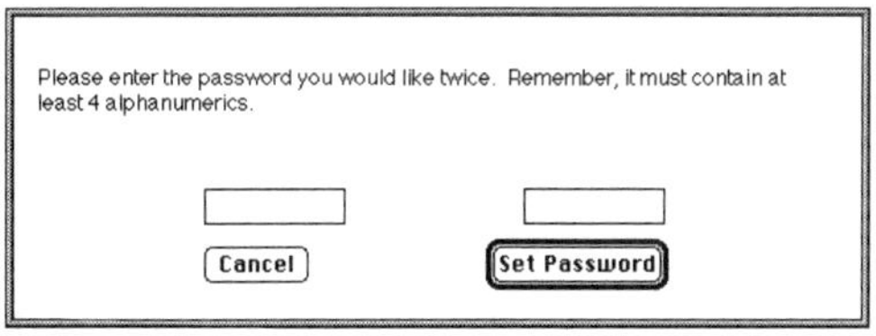


**Figure 37.** *After you've entered an original screen name, you'll be prompted to enter a password for it.*

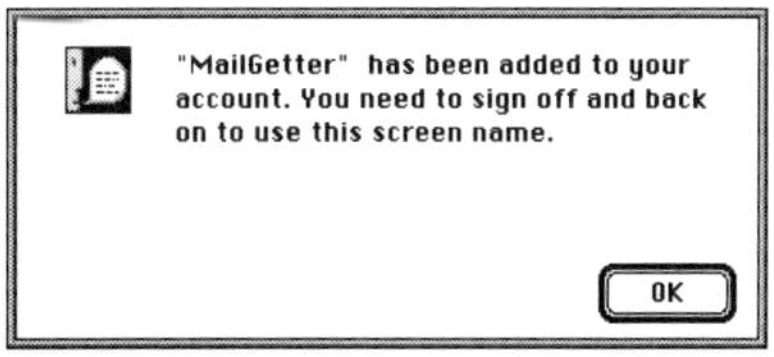


**Figure 38.** *A dialog box like this confirms that your new screen name has been added.*

## About Screen Names

Each AOL account can have up to five screen names. Each screen name has its own separate e-mail account and preference settings.

### ✔ Tips

- Use multiple screen names to put individual members of your family or company on one AOL account.
- The master screen name (the one you created when you first connected) cannot be changed.

## To create a screen name

1. Connect to AOL with the master screen name.
2. Use the keyword NAMES to open the Create or Delete a Screen Name window (see **Figure 34**).
3. Double-click the Create a Screen Name option.
4. Enter the screen name you want to add in the text box of the dialog box that appears (see **Figure 35**). Then click the Create a Screen Name button.
5. If the name you enter in step 4 above is already in use, a dialog box like the one in **Figure 36** will appear. Click OK to dismiss it and repeat step 4.
6. When a dialog box like the one in **Figure 37** appears, enter a password for the screen name in both edit boxes and click the Set Password button.
7. A confirmation dialog box like the one in **Figure 38** appears. Click OK or press Enter to dismiss it.

### ✔ Tip

- If you already have five screen names on your account, a dialog box like the one in **Figure 39** (on the next page) will appear if you try to add another.

## To delete a screen name

1. Connect to AOL with the master screen name.
2. Use the keyword NAMES to open the Create or Delete a Screen Name window (see **Figure 34**).
3. Double-click the Delete a Screen Name option.
4. In the confirmation dialog box that appears (see **Figure 40**) click the Continue button.
5. In the dialog box that appears (see **Figure 41**), click once on the screen name you want to delete to select it. Then click the Delete button.
6. A dialog box like the one in **Figure 42** appears to confirm that the screen name has been deleted. Click OK or press [Enter] to dismiss it.

## ✔ Tips

- When you delete a screen name, all incoming e-mail and other information for that name is deleted.
- Deleted screen names remain unavailable for six months. After that time, they can be used by any AOL member.

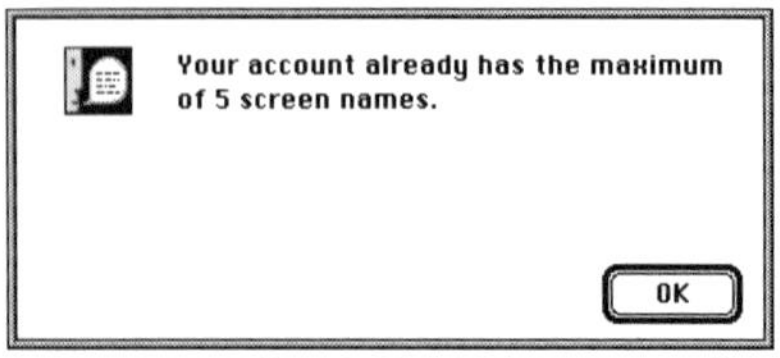


**Figure 39.** *This dialog box appears if you try to add a screen name when you already have five.*

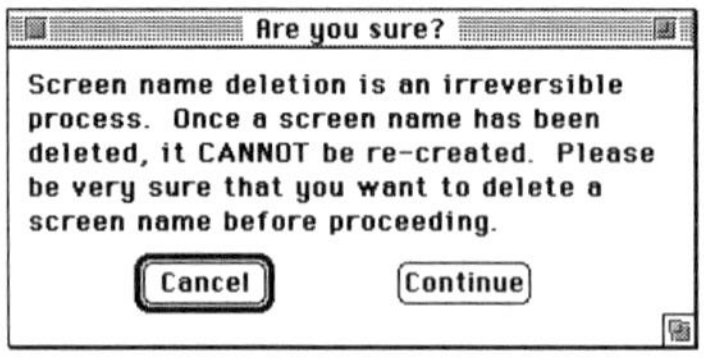


**Figure 40.** *Screen name deletion cannot be reversed, as this dialog box warns.*

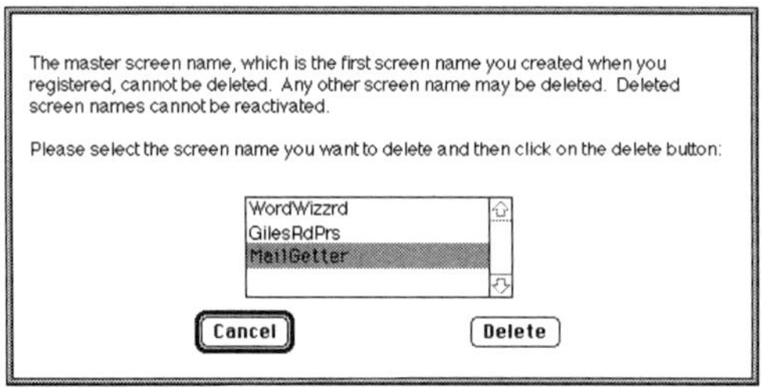


**Figure 41.** *Use this dialog box to delete one of your screen names.*

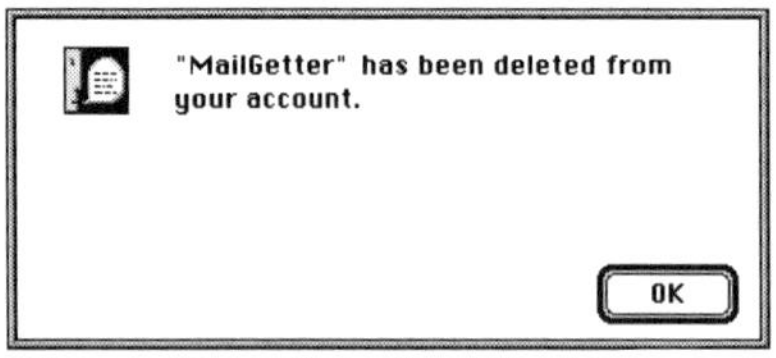


**Figure 42.** *A dialog box like this confirms that the screen name has been deleted.*

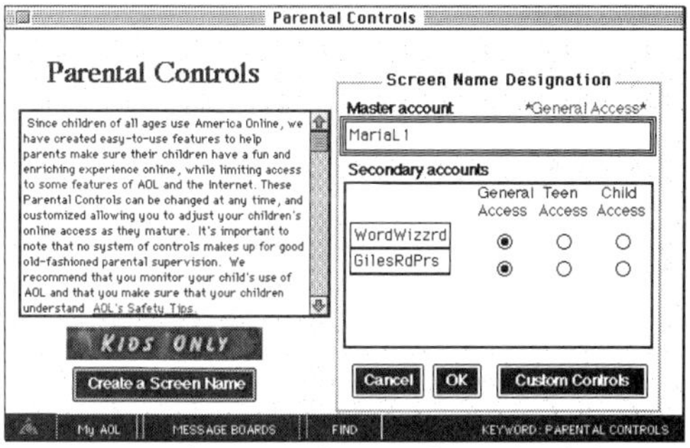


**Figure 43.** *The Parental Controls window helps you control what your kids see online.*

**Figure 44.** *Choose Parental Control from the Members menu.*

## About Parental Controls

AOL's Parental Controls feature helps parents control what their children see while online. This makes it possible for a child of any age to explore appropriate areas of AOL.

## ✔ Tips

- Parental Controls can be set and/or changed from the master account only.
- You must set up a screen name for each child whose access you want to restrict. Creating screen names is discussed earlier in this chapter.
- Although AOL's Terms of Service (TOS) sets down reasonable rules of conduct for all AOL members, not all members conduct themselves in accordance with the TOS. To learn more about the TOS, use the keyword TOS.
- To better understand how Parental Controls work, read the contents of the scrolling window in the Parental Controls window (see **Figure 43**).

## To open the Parental Controls window

1. Connect to AOL with the master screen name.
2. Choose Parental Control from the Members menu (see **Figure 44**).

   *or*

   Use the keyword PARENTAL CONTROL.

## To set Teen or Child access

1. In the Parental Controls window (see **Figure 43**), select the appropriate radio button for the screen name(s) you want to restrict.
2. Click OK.
3. A confirmation dialog box like the one in **Figure 45** appears. Click OK or press Enter to dismiss it.

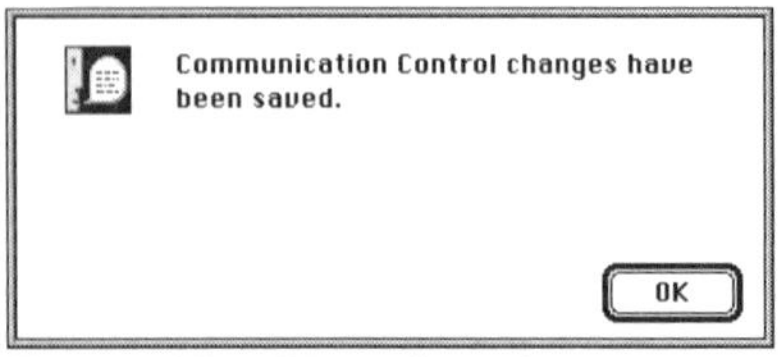


**Figure 45.** *AOL confirms that your changes have been saved.*

## ✔ Tips

- You must click OK to save the changes you make in the Parental Controls window.
- Teen Access, which is designed for children aged 13 to 16, allows full access to AOL, but restricts access to Internet Web sites and newsgroups that allow file attachments.
- Child Access, which is designed for children up to age 12, restricts access to Kid's Only areas on AOL and specific Web sites.
- The Welcome screen for a screen name with Child Access looks like the one in **Figure 46**. This window, as well as AOL's menus, toolbar, and keywords, allow access only to Kids Only areas.
- A dialog box like the one in **Figure 47** appears when you try to access a feature that is blocked.

**Figure 46.** *When a child signs on with a protected screen name, he sees a special Welcome window.*

**Figure 47.** *Your kids will see a dialog box like this one if they try to access an area that you've blocked from them.*

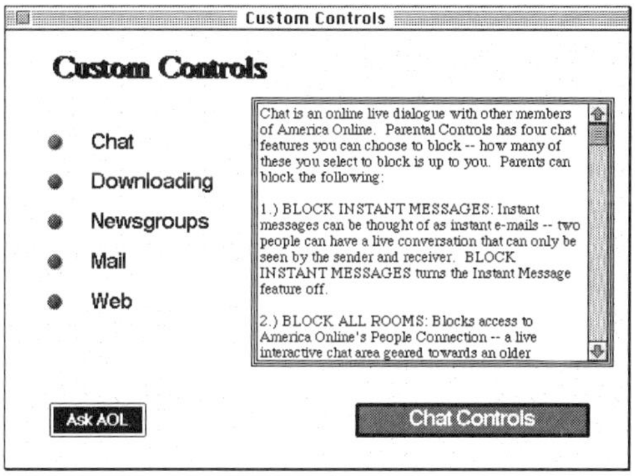


**Figure 48.** *Use options in this window to learn about and access custom controls for what your kids see while online.*

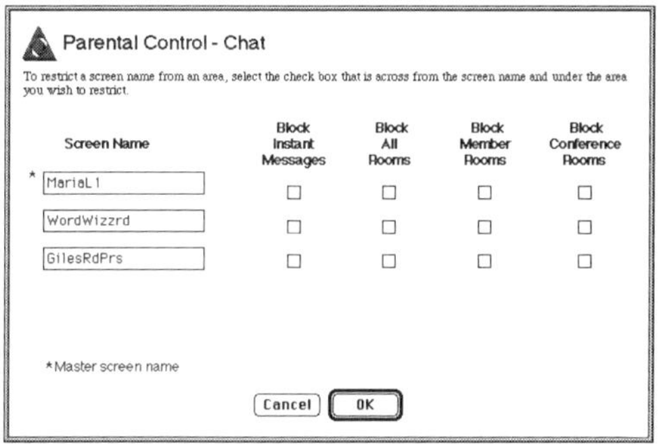


**Figure 49.** *Chat controls let you block chat-related features.*

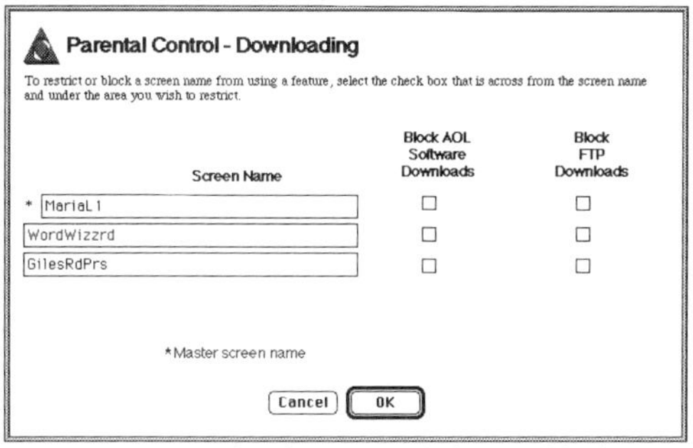


**Figure 50** *Downloading controls let you block AOL or FTP downloads.*

## To set custom controls

1. In the Parental Controls window (see **Figure 60**), click the Custom Controls button.
2. In the Custom Controls window that appears, click the button for the type of control you want to set. The scrolling window inside the window changes to display information about the kind of control you selected (see **Figure 48**).
3. Click the button that appears below the scrolling window to open a dialog box to set specific controls (see **Figures 49** through **53**).
   - ▲ *Chat* (see **Figure 49**) controls access to Instant Messages and specific kinds of chat rooms. Chatting is discussed in **Chapter 7**.
   - ▲ *Downloading* (see **Figure 50**) controls access to AOL or FTP downloads. Downloading files on AOL is discussed in **Chapter 6**; FTP is discussed in **Chapter 9**.
   - ▲ *Newsgroups* (see **Figure 51**) controls access to Internet newsgroups. Newsgroups are discussed in **Chapter 9**.
   - ▲ *Mail* (see **Figure 52**) controls access to e-mail. E-mail is discussed in **Chapter 4**.
   - ▲ *Web* (see **Figure 53**) controls access to World Wide Web sites. The Web is discussed in **Chapter 9**.
4. When you're finished, click the OK button to save your changes.
5. A confirmation dialog box like the one in **Figure 45** appears. Click OK or press Enter to dismiss it.
6. Repeat steps 2 through 5 for each type of control you want to change.

## ✔ Tips

- In step 3 you may have to select a screen name before you can specify settings for newsgroup and mail controls.
- Parental Controls buttons within certain area windows also offer access to custom control windows.
- Another way to access mail controls is to choose Mail Controls from the Mail menu.

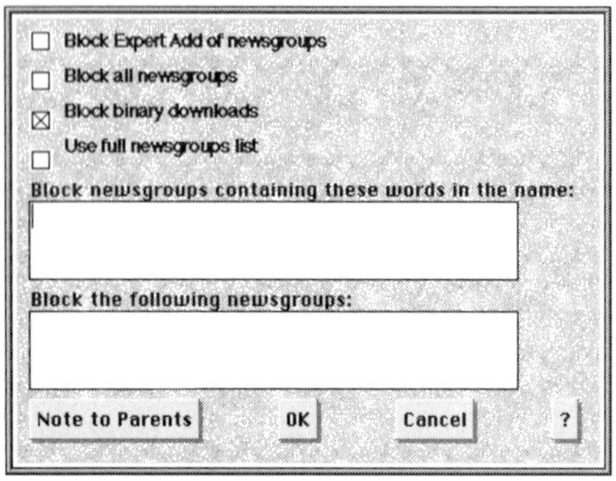


**Figure 51.** *Newsgroup controls restrict access to newsgroups in a variety of ways.*

**Figure 52.** *Mail controls block or allow access to all e-mail or just e-mail from specific addresses.*

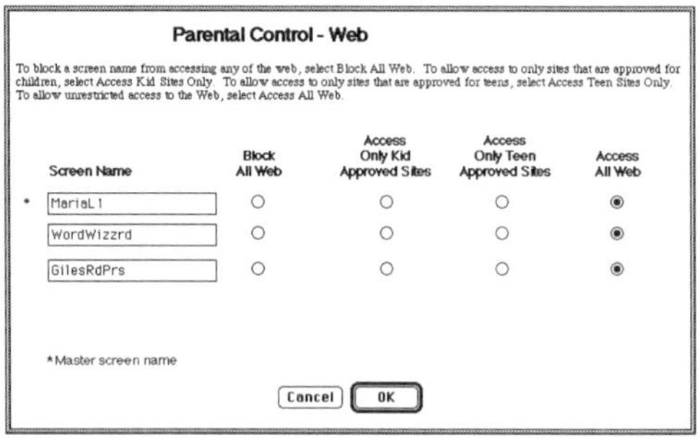


**Figure 53.** *Web controls block or allow access to all or just approved web sites.*

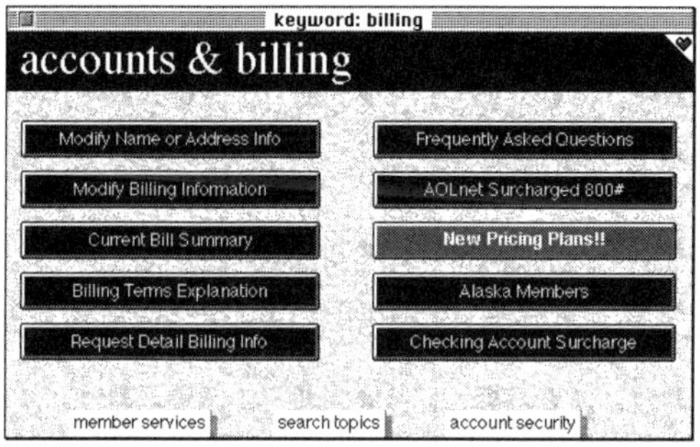


**Figure 54.** *The Accounts & Billing window offers access to several billing options.*

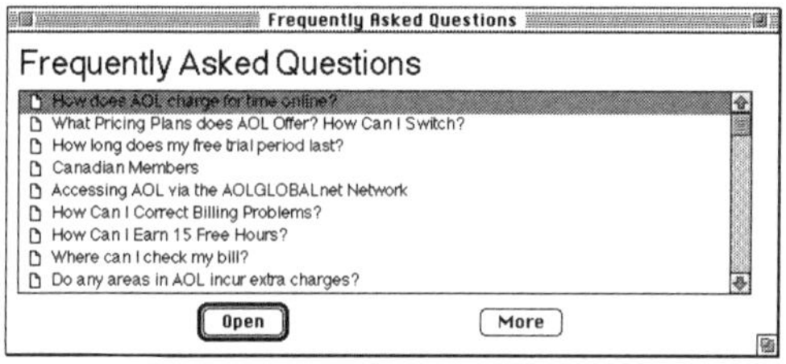


**Figure 55.** *The Frequently Asked Questions window lists questions commonly asked by members.*

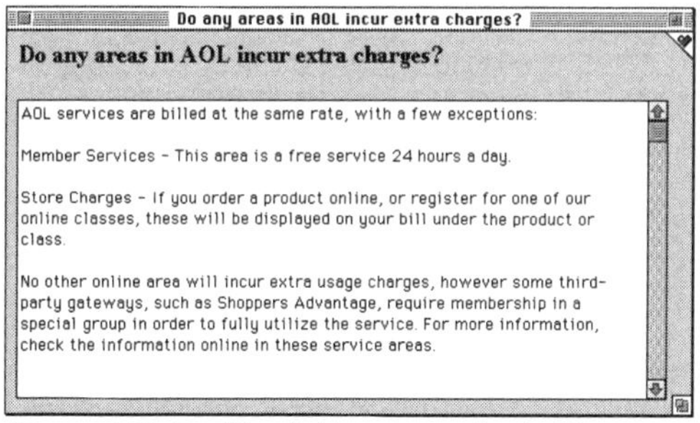


**Figure 56.** *Double-clicking a question in* **Figure 55** *displays its answer in a window like this.*

## About Billing Options

AOL's Accounts & Billing window (see **Figure 54**) offers several billing options, including:

- Learn how AOL bills you.
- Change your account information.
- Select a pricing plan.
- View your monthly bill.

## To open the Accounts & Billing window

Use the keyword BILLING.

The Accounts & Billing window (see **Figure 54**) appears.

## ✔ Tip

- Keywords are discussed in **Chapter 3**.

## To learn how AOL billing works

1. Click the Frequently Asked Questions button in the Accounts & Billing window (see **Figure 54**).
2. A Frequently Asked Questions window (see **Figure 55**) appears. Double-click a topic that interests you to display a window containing more information (see **Figure 56**).

## To change account information

1. To change your name or address information, click the Modify Name or Address Info button in the Accounts & Billing window (see **Figure 54**).

   *or*

   To change your payment information, click the Modify Billing Information button in the Accounts & Billing window (see **Figure 54**).
2. Follow the prompts that appear on screen to enter corrected information in simple forms and save it.

## To select a pricing plan

1. Click the New Pricing Plans!! button in the Accounts & Billing window (see **Figure 54**).
2. A New Pricing Plans window (**Figure 57**) appears. Read the message in the left scrolling list. You can double-click a topic in the right scrolling list to display a text document with more information.
3. When you're ready to select a plan, click the Sign Up! button in the New Pricing Plans window.
4. A Sign-Up! window appears (see **Figure 58**). Click the button for the plan you want.
5. Another Sign Up! window appears (see **Figure 59**). Read the information it displays. Then click the Sign Up Now! button.
6. A dialog box informing you that your request has been sent appears. Click OK or press Enter to dismiss it.

### ✔ Tip

- As pricing plans change, so will the figures and instructions here.

## To view your current bill

1. Click the Current Bill Summary button in the Accounts & Billing window (see **Figure 54**).
2. The Current Bill Summary window appears (see **Figure 60**). It contains information about the current month's bill.

### ✔ Tip

- The information in the Current Bill Summary window (see **Figure 60**) will vary depending on your balances and the billing plan you have selected.

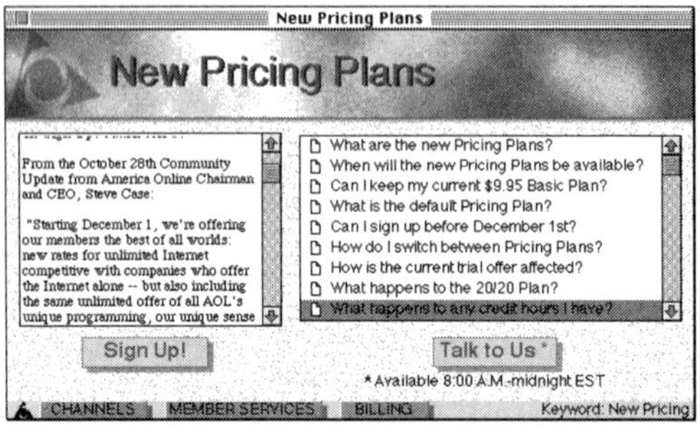


**Figure 57.** *A window like this provides information about AOL's various pricing plan options.*

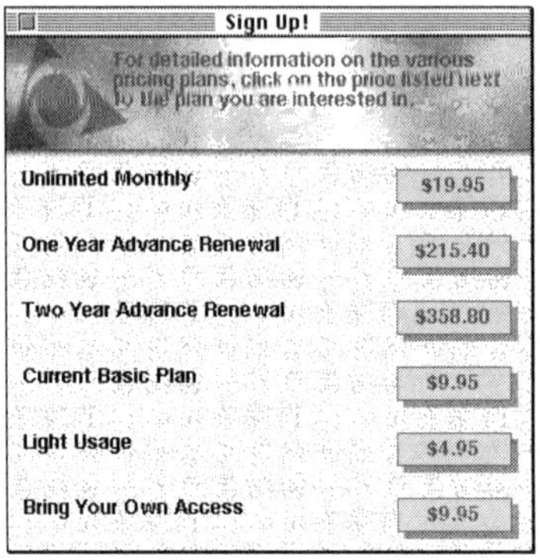


**Figure 58.** *Click the button for the plan you want.*

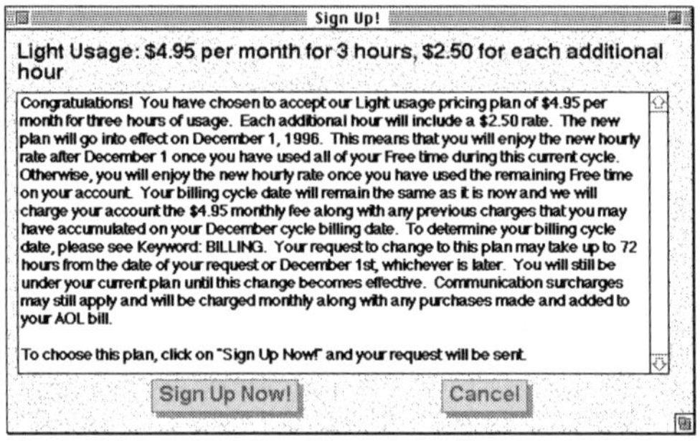


**Figure 59.** *A window like this one explains the billing plan you selected.*

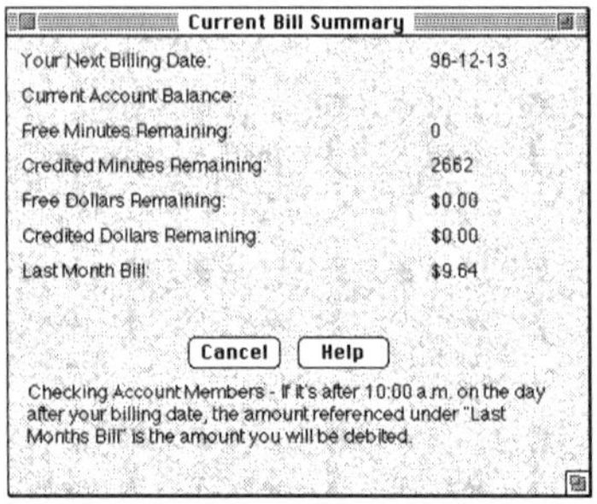


**Figure 60.** *Your current billing information appears in a window like this one.*

# CHANNEL SURFING ON AOL 12

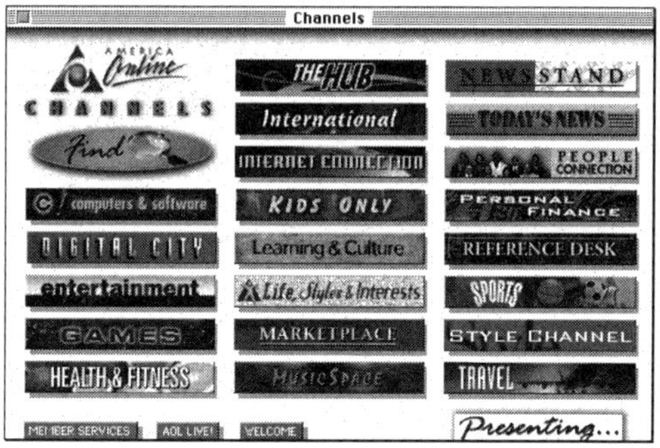


**Figure 1.** *AOL's Channels window is a great place to start your exploration of AOL.*

## About Channels

AOL's content is organized into channels, each of which can be accessed by clicking the appropriate button in the Channels window (see **Figure 1**).

This chapter will give you a brief tour of each of AOL's channels, showing you the main channel window and providing a brief description of the channel's contents. It will also suggest content and features that might interest you while you explore AOL on your own.

### ✔ Tips

- AOL's content is constantly changing and growing. Because of this, the illustrations in this chapter (as well as those throughout this book) may not exactly match what you see on your screen as you open various windows.
- The features covered in this chapter are only a small sampling of what's available on AOL.
- Although some areas or forums are maintained by AOL staff, others are maintained by outside companies. Because of this, AOL content is not representative of AOL's corporate policies and beliefs.
- Consult **Chapter 3** for more information about opening and using the Channels window to navigate AOL's content and features.
- Another way to browse AOL's content and features is to start with the keyword list provided in **Appendix D**.

## About the Computers & Software Channel

The Computers & Software channel (keyword COMPUTERS; see **Figure 2**) offers access to software, computer publications, support forums, and other features of interest to computer users.

**Figure 2.** *The Computers & Software channel offers access to features of interest to computer users.*

### ✔ Highlights

- Check the Software Center (keyword SOFTWARE CENTER) for a wealth of shareware and freeware files.
- Get updates and support from hardware and software vendors in the Company Connection (keyword COMPANY CONNECTION).
- Learn more about the latest electronic gadgets in the Consumer Electronics area (keyword CE.)

## About the Digital City Channel

The Digital City channel (keyword DIGITAL CITY; see **Figure 3**) offers access to news, sports, weather, and chat for cities all over the US.

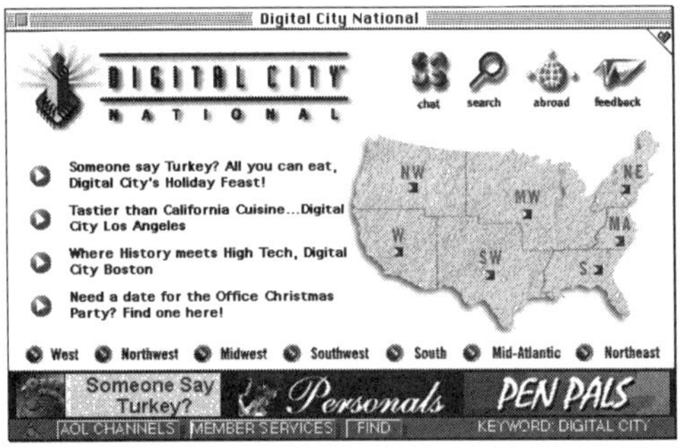


**Figure 3.** *The Digital City channel offers a wealth of information about a number of US cities.*

### ✔ Highlights

- Keep in touch with college classmates in the Alumni Hall (keyword ALUMNI HALL).
- Chat with members in other cities. Click the Chat button in any Digital City window, then double-click the folder for the city with which you want to chat in the National Chat window.
- Do the *New York Times* Crossword Puzzle right on your computer. Click the Northeast button, then click the New York button. Double-click the Crosswords option in the New York Times Online window that appears. You can then download the puzzle and the software needed to complete it.

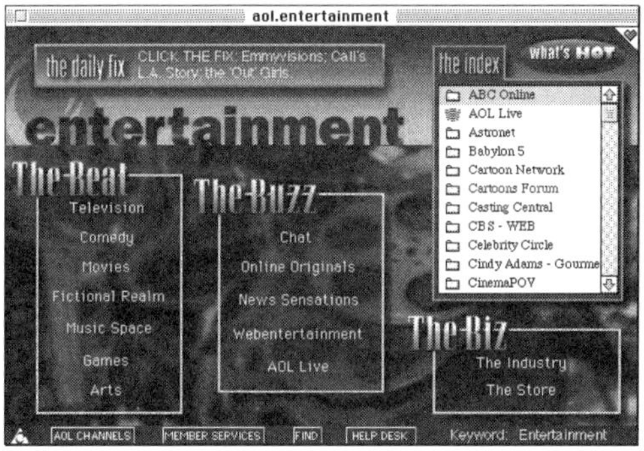


**Figure 4.** *The Entertainment channel helps you keep up with the world of entertainment.*

## About the Entertainment Channel

The Entertainment channel (keyword ENTERTAINMENT; see **Figure 4**) helps you keep up with the world of entertainment, including television, comedy, movies, and more.

### ✔ Highlights

- Find areas devoted to your favorite television shows and movies by scrolling through and double-clicking on options in the Index scrolling list.
- Get TV listings online. Click the Television button, then the TV Listings button. Use options that appear to get the TV listings.
- Read David Letterman's latest Top Ten List. Double-click Letterman's Late Show Online in the Index scrolling list, then click the Top Ten buttons until the most recent Top Ten list appears.

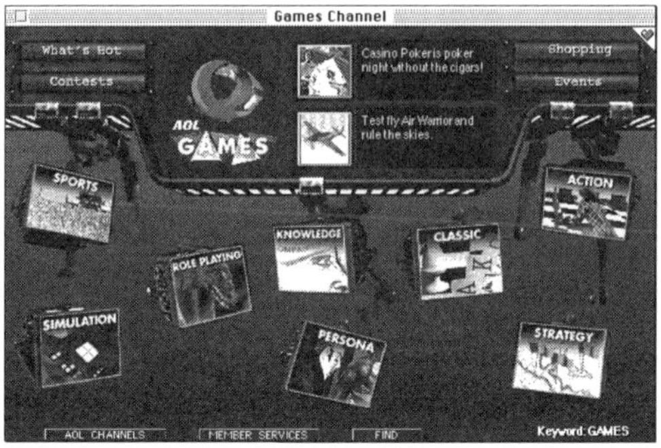


**Figure 5.** *The Games channel is for learning about, downloading, and playing all kinds of games.*

## About the Games Channel

The Games channel (keyword GAMES; see **Figure 5**) lets you learn about, download, and play games.

### ✔ Highlights

- Play Neverwinter Nights (keyword AD&D), a fantasy role-playing game, online with other AOL members.
- Download the hottest shareware and freeware games. Click any of the topic buttons, then click the Software button in the window that appears.
- Enter a contest to win prizes. Click the Contest button in the Games Channel window.

## About the Health & Fitness Channel

The Health & Fitness channel (keyword HEALTH & FITNESS; see **Figure 6**) helps you keep healthy and in shape by providing information about medicines, diet, and exercise.

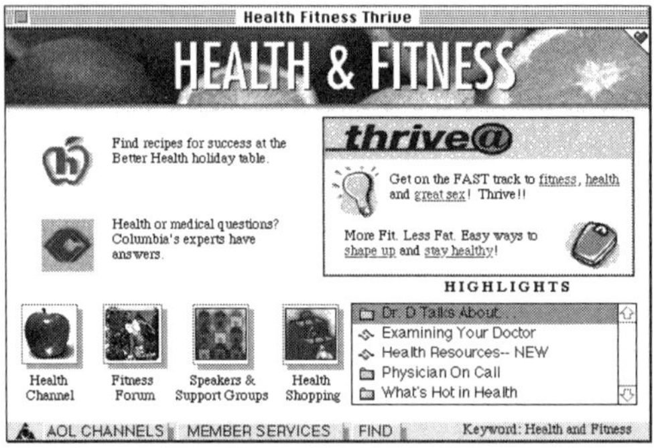


**Figure 6.** *The Health & Fitness channel helps you keep healthy and in shape.*

### ✔ Highlights

- Get information about medicines in the Consumer Reports Drug Reference (keyword DRUG REFERENCE).
- Learn more about alternative medicines in the Alternatives: Health & Healing forum (keyword AHH).
- Access fitness-related World Wide Web sites. Click the Fitness Forum button (or use the keyword FITNESS), then double-click the Web site of your choice in the scrolling list.

## About The Hub

The Hub (keyword HUB; see **Figure 7**) offers a grab bag of unusual and often humorous information, presented as "shows."

**Figure 7.** *The Hub is the place to go for unusual and often humorous information about almost anything.*

### ✔ Highlights

- Read the Other News, "the only news you HAVE" to know (keyword OTHER NEWS).
- Download one of the dozens of letters written by Cyrano for your letter-writing needs (keyword CYRANO).
- Get your fortune told online. Double-click Tarot to Go in the scrolling list (or use the keyword TAROT TO GO).

**Figure 8.** *The International channel is a good source of information about companies worldwide.*

## About the International Channel

The International channel (keyword INTERNATIONAL; see **Figure 8**) offers access to information about cities and countries all over the world.

### ✔ Highlights

- Learn more about almost any country in the world from people who know. Click the name of a continent, then double-click the name of a country in the scrolling list. Click the message boards button to open the message board for that country.
- Shop for products made all over the world in the International Marketplace (keyword INTERNATIONAL STORE).
- Get the latest news from abroad. Click the News & Business button to get started.

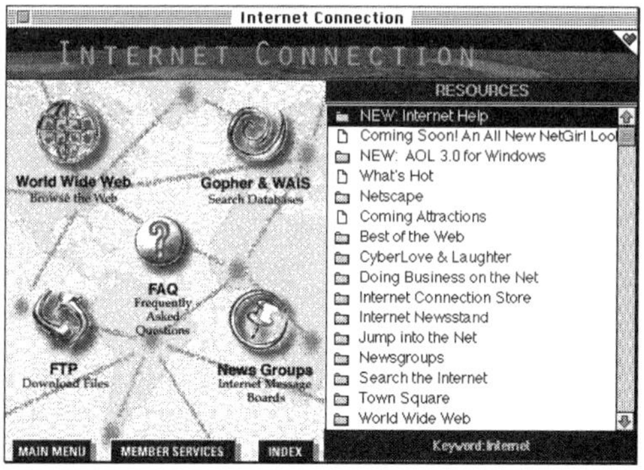

**Figure 9.** *The Internet Connection offers access to the most commonly used features of the Internet.*

## About the Internet Connection

The Internet Connection (keyword INTERNET CONNECTION; see **Figure 9**) is your key to accessing the Internet from AOL, including the World Wide Web (keyword WWW), FTP servers (keyword FTP), Usenet newsgroups (keyword NEWSGROUP), and Gopher and WAIS databases (keyword GOPHER). The Internet is covered in detail in **Chapter 9**.

### ✔ Highlights

- Search the Web for pages that interest you. Click the World Wide Web button (or use the keyword WWW), then enter a search word or phrase in the edit box and click the Search button.
- Browse interesting articles on Gopher servers. Click the Gopher & WAIS button (or use the keyword GOPHER), then click the Gopher Treasures button.

## About the Kids Only Channel

The Kids Only channel (keyword KIDS; see **Figure 10**) is an area designed specifically for children up to 12 years old.

### ✔ Highlights

- Check out your favorite cartoons online. Click the Central button, then double-click the Cartoon Network option in the scrolling list (or use the keyword CARTOON NETWORK).
- Find a pen pal. Click the Clubs button, then click the Pen Pals button.
- Get help for homework. Click the Homework Help button (or use the keyword HH KIDS).

**Figure 10.** *The Kids Only channel is a great place for kids to start exploring the online world.*

## About the Learning & Culture Channel

The Learning & Culture channel (keyword LEARNING; see **Figure 11**) is a source of educational and cultural information for all AOL members.

### ✔ Highlights

- Get career guidance or help in finding a job. Click the Careers button (or use the keyword CAREER).
- Make a virtual visit to the Smithsonian National Museum of American History (keyword NMAH).
- View the web pages of your favorite authors. Click the Books button (or use the keyword BOOKS), then click the Author Pages button.

**Figure 11.** *The Learning & Culture channel offers a wide range of features to expand your horizons.*

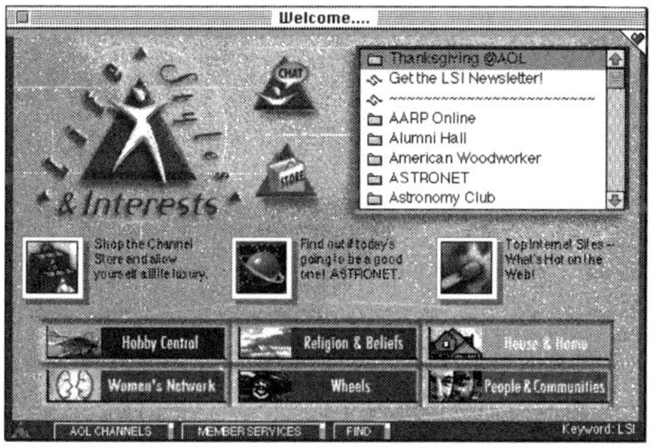


**Figure 12.** *The Life, Styles & Interests channel offers information about things that are important—or at least interesting—to you.*

## About the Life, Styles & Interests Channel

The Life, Styles & Interests channel (keyword LSI; see **Figure 12**) is where you can get information on the things that really matter in your life.

### ✔ Highlights

- Learn more about your hobbies. Click the Hobby Central button, then double-click the name of your hobby in the scrolling list.
- Exchange messages with automobile enthusiasts. Click the Wheels button, then double-click the Automotive Message Center option in the scrolling list.
- Look for a new home in the Real Estate Center (keyword REAL ESTATE).

**Figure 13.** *The Marketplace channel lets you shop for just about anything—right from your Mac!*

## About the Marketplace Channel

The Marketplace channel (keyword MARKETPLACE; see **Figure 13**) is the place where you can shop 24 hours a day, without leaving the comfort of your home.

### ✔ Highlights

- Order books at a discount from Read USA (keyword BOOKS).
- Buy commercial software from atOnce Software (keyword ATONCE)—and get it immediately!
- Find that elusive kitchen gadget you can't live without in the Chef's Catalog Store (keyword CHEFS CATALOG).

## About the MusicSpace Channel

The MusicSpace channel (keyword MUSIC; see **Figure 14**) is where you can get information about all kinds of music, recording artists, and recordings.

**Figure 14.** *The MusicSpace channel offers a wealth of information about the world of music.*

### ✔ Highlights

- Learn where your favorite artists will be playing this season. Double-click the Concert Information option in the scrolling list (or use the keyword CONCERTS), then double-click the name of the artist or band you're interested in seeing.
- Learn what's new in the record stores. Double-click the New Releases option in the scrolling list (or use the keyword NEW MUSIC).

## About the Newsstand Channel

The Newsstand channel (keyword NEWSSTAND; see **Figure 15**) is your source for the electronic version of dozens of newspapers and magazines.

**Figure 15.** *The Newsstand channel is where you can read articles from dozens of top newspapers and magazines.*

### ✔ Highlights

- Read articles from the latest issue of your favorite magazine. Double-click its name in the scrolling list.
- See what *Consumer Reports* magazine says about a product you want to buy. Double-click Consumer Reports in the scrolling list (or use the keyword CONSUMER REPORTS), then click the Search button to search for the product by type or name.
- Find a job or home in another city. Double-click the name of a newspaper in the scrolling list for the city in which you are interested, then click the Classified Ads button to check the classified ads.

**Figure 16.** *The Today's News channel offers up-to-date news and analysis.*

## About the Today's News Channel

The Today's News channel (keyword NEWS; see **Figure 16**) is where you can get up-to-the-minute news, weather, sports, and commentary.

### ✔ Highlights

- See a current weather map for the country. Click the Highlights button under Weather, then double-click U.S. Current Weather Map.
- Get in-depth information about current political issues. Click the Politics button under Politics, then double-click the topic that interests you.
- Search the news for articles that interest you. Click the News Search button, then enter a search word or phrase to begin the search.

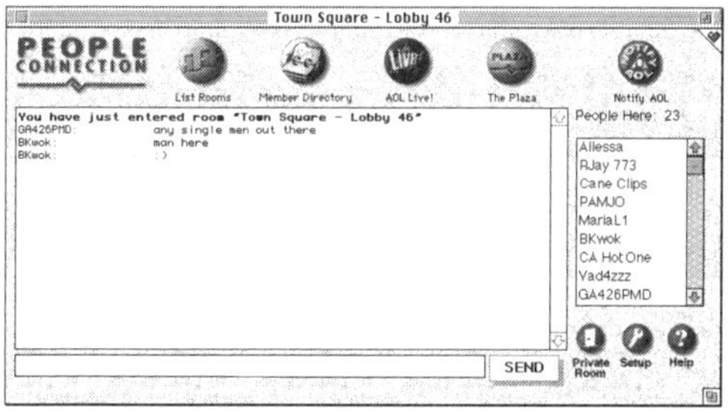


**Figure 17.** *The People Connection offers access to every chat area on AOL.*

## About the People Connection

The People Connection (keyword CHAT; see **Figure 17**) is where you can find AOL members to chat with about almost any topic. The People Connection and its features are discussed in detail in **Chapter 7**.

### ✔ Highlights

- Join an AOL-sanctioned chat. Click the Chat Rooms button, then double-click the name of a room that interests you.
- Find chat rooms that interest you. Click the Plaza button for suggestions.

## About the Personal Finance Channel

The Personal Finance channel (keyword FINANCE; see **Figure 18**) offers access to information to help you make investment decisions and check the status of your investments.

**Figure 18.** *The Personal Finance channel is your source for information about financial matters.*

### ✔ Highlights

- Let AOL track your investments by creating one or more portfolios with AOL's Portfolio feature (keyword PORTFOLIO).
- Create charts of stock quote information in the Historical Stock & Fund Quotes area (keyword HISTORICAL QUOTES).
- Use the Online Investor area (keyword ONLINE INVESTOR) to learn more about investing.

## About the Reference Desk Channel

The Reference Desk channel (keyword REFERENCE; see **Figure 19**) is an online reference library, with dictionaries, encyclopedias, and other reference works.

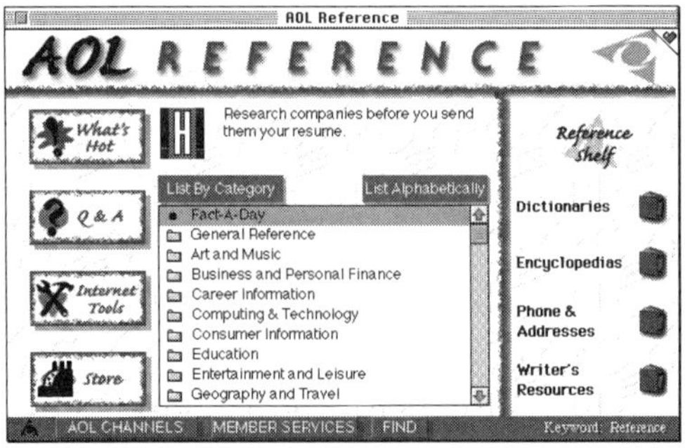


**Figure 19.** *The Reference Desk channel offers a wealth of up-to-date reference materials.*

### ✔ Highlights

- Look something up in an encyclopedia. Click the Encyclopedias button, then choose a specific encyclopedia by clicking its button. Use the search feature to find the information you need.
- Find your high school sweetheart's address in the Pro CD National Telephone Directory (keyword WHITE PAGES).
- Improve your geography knowledge in the Geography and Travel area (keyword REFGEOGRAPHY).

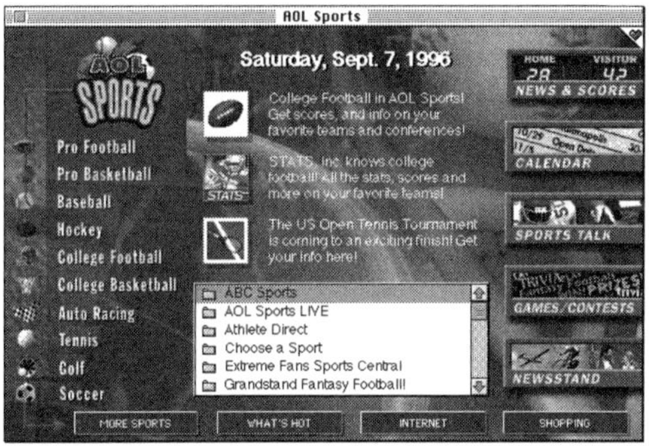


**Figure 20.** *The Sports channel is your source for up-to-date information about your favorite sports.*

## About the Sports Channel

The Sports channel (keyword SPORTS; see **Figure 20**) helps you follow your favorite sports—no matter what they are.

### ✔ Highlights

- Get the score for last night's game. Click the News & Scores button, then click the Scoreboard button. Choose the sport that interests you from the pop-up list and find the score you want in the scrolling list below it.
- Find information about unusual sports like biathlon, lacrosse, and rugby. Click the More Sports button (or use the keyword MORE SPORTS), then double-click the name of the sport that interests you in the scrolling list.
- See who's playing this week. Click the Calendar button to access television listings, sports schedules, and more.

**Figure 21.** *The Style channel helps keep you in vogue.*

## About the Style Channel

The Style channel (keyword STYLE; see **Figure 21**) puts you in touch with the world of fashion and style.

### ✔ Highlights

- Exchange messages with other style-conscious AOL members. Click the Boards button, then locate and open a message board that interests you.
- Find fashion sites on the World Wide Web. Double-click the Fashion Weblinks button in the scrolling list.
- Get information about top models and popular celebrities. Double-click the A-List: Celebrity Central option in the scrolling list to get started.

## About the Travel Channel

The Travel channel (keyword TRAVEL; see **Figure 22**) provides the information you need to plan and book vacations and business trips.

**Figure 22.** *The Travel channel offers all kinds of information for travellers.*

### ✔ Highlights

- Learn more about a travel destination. Click the Research & Plan button, then double-click the scrolling list option for the area that interests you.
- Purchase airline and train tickets and make hotel reservations online. Click the Book It! button to begin.

## About Member Services

Although Member Services (keyword MEMBER SERVICES; see **Figure 23**) is not an AOL channel, it *is* an unlimited use area you may find useful for getting more information about AOL.

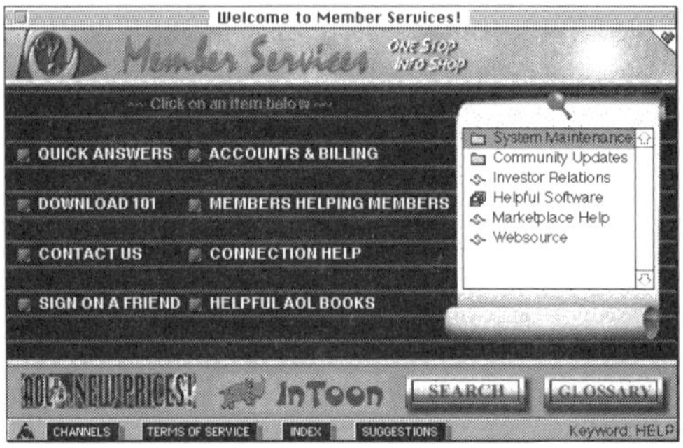


**Figure 23.** *Member Services isn't a channel, but a place to get information about AOL.*

### ✔ Highlights

- Get answers to commonly asked questions. Click the Quick Answers button.
- Contact the folks who run AOL or provide technical support by voice, fax, e-mail, or chat. Click the Contact Us button for options.
- Get a starter kit for a friend and get free time on AOL. Click the Sign on a Friend button.

## To open the Member Services window

Choose Member Services from the Members menu (see **Figure 24**).

*or*

Click the Member Services button on the toolbar.

*or*

Use the keyword MEMBER SERVICES.

**Figure 24.** *One way to open the Member Services window is to choose Member Services from the Members menu.*

# MENUS & SHORTCUT KEYS A



## About Menus & Shortcut Keys

This appendix illustrates all of America Online's menus. It also provides a list of all shortcut keys you can use with America Online.

Using menus and shortcut keys is discussed in detail in **Chapter 2**.

## Modifier Keys

| Key Name | Keyboard Key |
|---|---|
| Command | ⌘ |
| Shift | Shift |

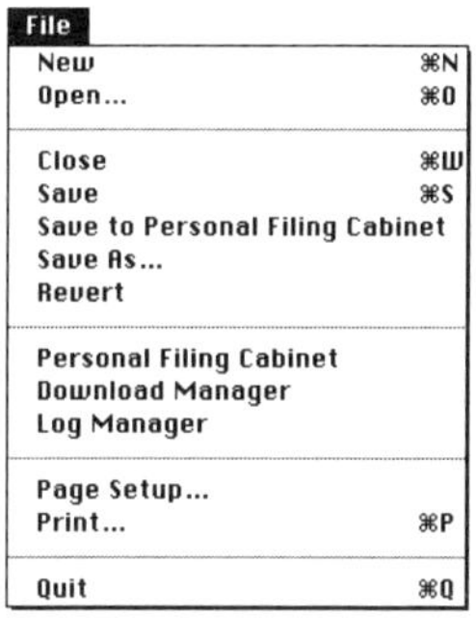


## File Menu Commands

| | |
|---|---|
| ⌘ N | New |
| ⌘ O | Open |
| ⌘ W | Close |
| ⌘ S | Save |
| ⌘ P | Print |
| ⌘ Q | Quit |

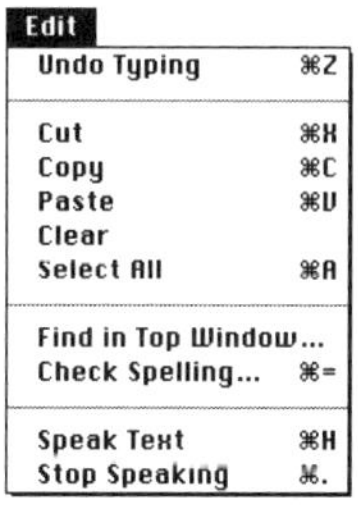


## Edit Menu Commands

| | |
|---|---|
| ⌘ Z | Undo |
| ⌘ X | Cut |
| ⌘ C | Copy |
| ⌘ V | Paste |
| ⌘ A | Select All |
| ⌘ = | Check Spelling |
| ⌘ H | Speak Text |
| ⌘ . | Stop Speaking |

## Format Menu Commands

| | |
|---|---|
| ⌘T | Plain Style |
| ⌘B | Bold Style |
| ⌘U | Underline Style |

**Note:**
*The Insert Favorite Place command turns into the Edit Favorite Place command if a Favorite Place hyperlink is selected.*

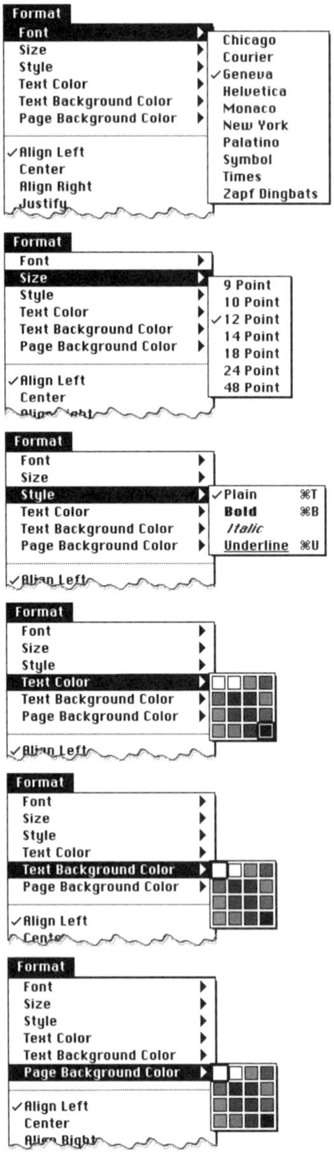

**Note:**
*The Sign Off command turns into the Setup & Sign On command when you are not connected to AOL.*

## Go To Menu Commands

| | |
|---|---|
| ⌘ E | Exit Unlimited Usage Area |
| ⌘ K | Keyword |
| ⌘ F | Find |
| ⌘ 1 | What's Hot |
| ⌘ 2 | Discover America Online |
| ⌘ 3 | Sign On a Friend |
| ⌘ 4 | Top News |
| ⌘ 5 | Stock Quotes |
| ⌘ 6 | AOL Live |
| ⌘ 7 | Internet Connection |
| ⌘ 8 | Reference Desk |
| ⌘ 9 | Entertainment |
| ⌘ 0 | Market Place |

## Mail Menu Commands

| | |
|---|---|
| ⌘ M | Compose Mail |
| ⌘ R | Read Mail |

## Members Menu Commands

| | |
|---|---|
| ⌘ I | Send an Instant Message |
| ⌘ G | Get a Member's Profile |
| ⌘ L | Locate a Member Online |

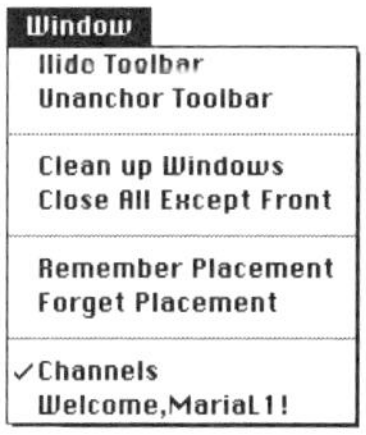


## Window Menu Commands

## ? Menu Commands

| | |
|---|---|
| ⌘ ? | AOL Guide |

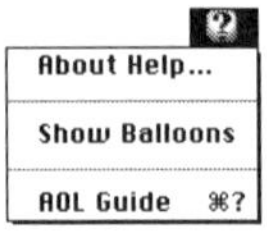

# TOOLBAR REFERENCE B



## About the Toolbar

America Online's toolbar offers quick access to many America Online features. This appendix illustrates, names, and describes each toolbar button. Unless otherwise noted, you must be connected to use each of these buttons.

The toolbar is discussed in **Chapter 2**.

**Online Mailbox**
Click this button to display the Online Mailbox window. This is the same as clicking the You Have Mail button in the Welcome window. See **Chapter 4** for more information about e-mail.

**Compose Mail**
Click this button to write a new e-mail message. This is the same as choosing Compose Mail from the Mail menu or pressing [⌘][M]. You do not need to be connected to use this button. See **Chapter 4** for more information about e-mail.

**Channels**
Click this button to display the Channels window, which offers access to all America Online features by topic. This is the same as choosing Channels from the Go To menu. See **Chapter 3** for more information about the Channels window.

**What's Hot**
Click this button to display the What's Hot window, which offers access to new and exciting America Online features. This is the same as choosing What's Hot from the Go To menu or pressing [⌘][1].

**People Connection**
Click this button to go to a live chat lobby. From there you can go to or create a public or private chat room. See **Chapter 7** for more information about AOL's chat feature.

**File Search**
Click this button to open the Software Search window and search through the thousands of files in the file libraries. See **Chapter 6** for more information about AOL's file libraries.

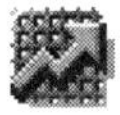

**Stocks & Portfolios**
Click this button to open the Quotes & Portfolios window and get quick access to your personal portfolio(s). This is the same as choosing Stock Quotes from the Go To menu or pressing [⌘][5]. See **Chapter 12** for more information about stocks and portfolios.

**Today's News**
Click this button to open the Today's News window, which offers access to top current news stories. This is the same as choosing Top News from the Go To menu or pressing ⌘4. See **Chapter 12** for more information about using news services.

**World Wide Web**
Click this button to open AOL's browser, Microsoft Internet Explorer, and access the World Wide Web on the Internet. See **Chapter 9** for more information about using Internet features.

**Marketplace**
Click this button to access AOL's online shopping feature. This is the same as choosing Market Place from the Go To menu or pressing ⌘0. See **Chapter 12** for more information about online shopping.

**My AOL**
Click this button to display the My AOL window, which you can use to change preferences and customize AOL. This is the same as choosing My AOL from the Members menu. See **Chapter 11** for more information about setting preferences.

**Online Clock**
Click this button to see the current time and an estimate of the amount of time you've spent online. This is the same as choosing Online Clock from the Go To menu.

**Print**
Click this button to print the currently active file. This is the same as choosing Print from the File menu or pressing ⌘P. You do not need to be connected to use this button. Printing is discussed as it applies throughout this book.

**Personal Filing Cabinet**
Click this button to open the Personal Filing Cabinet window, which lets you view downloaded files and saved messages. This is the same as choosing Personal Filing Cabinet from the File menu. You do not need to be connected to use this button. See **Chapter 10** for more information about the Personal Filing Cabinet.

**Favorite Places**
Click this button to open the Favorite Places window, which offers quick access to your favorite places on AOL. This is the same as choosing Favorite Places from the Go To menu. You do not need to be connected to use this button. See **Chapter 3** for more information about Favorite Places.

**Member Services**

Click this button to go to Member Services, a free area with features to help you learn more about AOL. This is the same as choosing Member Services from the Members menu. See **Chapter 12** for more information about Member Services.

**Find**

Click this button to search for an area or topic on AOL. This is the same as choosing Find from the Go To menu or pressing ⌘F. See **Chapter 3** for more information about the Find feature.

**Keyword**

Click this button to open the Keyword window, which you can use to go to an area by entering its keyword. This is the same as choosing Keyword from the Go To menu or pressing ⌘K. See **Chapter 3** for more information about using Keywords and **Appendix D** for a comprehensive list of AOL areas and their keywords.

# ONLINE SHORTHAND & SMILEYS

C



## About Online Shorthand & Smileys

AOL offers many ways to communicate with AOL members, as well as people and organizations on other online services and the Internet: e-mail (see **Chapter 4**), message boards (see **Chapter 5**), Live Chats (see **Chapter 7**), and Internet Newsgroups (see **Chapter 9**). All of these methods have one thing in common: they rely on typed messages.

AOL members, as well as the users of other online services and the Internet, often use two communication techniques when exchanging messages with each other:

- *Online shorthand* is a method of communicating commonly-used, lengthy phrases without typing in every word. By abbreviating phrases, you can save many keystrokes and still convey the same message.
- *Smileys* are character sequences that, when viewed sideways, resemble facial expressions. They're used in almost the same way people use facial expressions in one-on-one communciation. A smiley representing a wink, for example, can let the person reading your message know that your message's contents should be taken lightly because you're just kidding around.

This appendix lists some of the more widely used online shorthand and smiley sequences on AOL. You'll learn others as you exchange messages and chat with other AOL users. If you're interested in learning more smileys, look for *The Smiley Dictionary*, a Peachpit Press book compiled by Seth Godin.

## Online Shorthand

| | |
|---|---|
| AFK | Away From Keyboard |
| BAK | Back At Keyboard |
| BRB | Be Right Back |
| BTW | By The Way |
| GMTA | Great Minds Think Alike |
| IMHO | In My Humble Opinion |
| LOL | Laughing Out Loud |
| L8TR | See You/Talk to You Later |
| ROTF | Rolling On The Floor |
| ROTFL | Rolling On The Floor Laughing |
| RTFM | Read The Freaking Manual |
| TTFN | Ta-Ta For Now! |
| WB | Welcome Back |
| WTG | Way To Go! |

## Smileys

| | |
|---|---|
| :) | smile |
| :-) | smile (with a nose) |
| ;) | wink |
| ;-) | wink (with a nose) |
| :D | grin |
| :( | frown |
| :'( | crying |
| :P | sticking out tongue |
| :* | kiss |
| :X | my lips are sealed |
| {} | a hug |

# AREA & KEYWORD LIST D

## About Keywords

Keywords offer a quick way to move from one area to another on AOL. Simply choose Keyword from the Go To menu, click the Keyword button on the toolbar, or press ⌘K to display the Keyword dialog box. Then enter the keyword of the area to which you want to go and click Go or press Enter.

This appendix provides a comprehensive list of the keywords you can use on AOL. Keywords are listed in alphabetical order by channel and then by area. The keyword appears in uppercase characters after the name of the area. Area names followed by an asterisk (*) are unlimited use areas.

For more information about using keywords, consult **Chapter 3**. To obtain a copy of the most up-to-date list of keywords, use the keyword KEYWORD while on AOL.

## General Purpose Keywords

AOL Gift Certificates – AOL GIFT, GIFT CERTIFICATE
AOL Highlights Tour – TOUR, AOL HIGHLIGHTS
AOL Press Release Library – PRESS, PRESS RELEASE
AOL Software Shop – SOFTWARE SHOP, AOL SOFTWARE SHOP, SOFT SHOP
AOLsewhere – AOLSEWHERE, AWAY, AWAY FROM HOME
Best of America Online showcase – BEST OF AOL, 25 REASONS, UNIQUE
Buddy Lists – BUDDY, BL, BUDDIES, BUDDY LIST, BUDDY LISTS, BUDDY MAIN
Buddy View – BUDDY VIEW
Edit your member profile – PROFILE, CHANGE PROFILE, EDIT PROFILE, MEMBER PROFILE
Fax/Paper Mail – FAX, PAPER MAIL, US MAIL
Guide Pager – GUIDE PAGER, GUIDE PAGE
Keyword List Area – KEYWORDS, KEYWORD, KEYWORD LIST
Marketing Prefs – MARKETING PREFS, MARKETING PREFERENCES
Member Directory – MEMBERS, DIRECTORY, MEMBER DIRECTORY
Multimedia Preferences – MULTIMEDIA PREFS
New Features & Services – NEW
Online Shorthand – SHORTHAND, SHORTHANDS
Orientation Express – ORIENTATION, DISCOVER, DISCOVER AOL, NEWBIE, NEW MEMBER, NEW MEMBERS, ORIENTATION EXPRESS
Personal Choices area – PERSONAL CHOICES
Time of day and length of time online – CLOCK, ONLINE CLOCK
Top Tips for AOL – TOP TIPS, BEST TIPS, HOW TO, NAVIGATE, TOP TIPS
What's Hot This Month Showcase – HOT, WHATEVER, WHATS HOT
What's Hot Today! – HOT TODAY

## Member Services Keywords

Accounts and Billing* – BILLING
America Online Glossary* – GLOSSARY
AOL 2.6 for Macintosh* – BROWSER FIX
AOLGLOBALnet International Access* – AOLGLOBALNET, GLOBALNET
AOLNET* – AOLNET
Cancel Account* – CANCEL
Change your password* – PASSWORD, CHANGE PASSWORD
Community Updates from Steve Case* – STEVE CASE, LETTER, LETTER2

Credit Request Form for connect problems* – CREDIT, CREDIT REQUEST, DOWNLOAD CREDIT, PC-LINK HOTLINE

Desktop Cinema* – DESKTOP CINEMA

Download Help* – DOWNLOAD 101, DOWNLOAD HELP

ExpressNet Art Download* – AMEX ART, EXPRESSNET ART

France Beta Test* – FRIEND IN FRANCE, FRENCH TEST

GPF Help* – GPF

High Speed Access* – HIGH SPEED, 9600, 9600 ACCESS, 9600 CENTER, MODEM, MODEM HELP

Member Services* – HELP, ASK AMERICA ONLINE, ASK AOL, ASK CS, CS LIVE, CUSTOMER SERVICE, FEEDBACK, FREE, HOTLINE, INFORMATION, SERVICE, SUPPORT, SYSOP, TECH HELP LIVE, TECH LIVE

Member Survey* – MEMBER SUVERY

Multimedia Showcase* – MM SHOWCASE

Newest Version of AOL Software* – NEW AOL

One Stop Infoshop* – QUESTION, QUESTIONS

Parental Controls – PARENTAL CONTROL*

Questions* – WRITE TO STAFF, ASK STAFF, WRITE TO OUR STAFF

Sign On a Friend* – FRIEND

Sound Room* – SOUND ROOM

Suggestion boxes* – SUGGEST, SUGGESTION

System Response Area* – SYSTEM RESPONSE

Terms of Service* – TOS, TERMS, TERMS OF SERVICE, TOS ADVISOR

Upgrade to latest AOL software* – UPGRADE, AOL PREVIEW

Virus Letter* – VIRUS2

## Computers & Software Channel Keywords

3D Forum – 3D, 3-D, 3-D RENDERING, 3D-RENDERING, 3D RENDERING, POV, RAYTRACE, RENDERING

Aatrix Software, Inc. – AATRIX

Abbate Video – ABBATE VIDEO, VIDEO TOOLKIT

Access Software – ACCESS SOFTWARE, LINKS

Accolade, Inc. – ACCOLADE

Acer America Corporation – ACER

Activision – ACTIVISION

Adobe Center menu – ADOBE, ADOBE PHOTOSHOP

Adobe Systems, Inc. – ADOBE, ALDUS

Advanced Color Imaging Forum – IMAGING, COLOR IMAGING, PA

Advanced Gravis – GRAVIS, ADVANCED GRAVIS

Advanced Logic Research – ALR, ADVANCED LOGIC

Advanced Software, Inc. – ADVANCED

Advertising Special Interest Group – AD SIG, ADVERTISING, ADVERTISING SIG

Advisor Software – ADVSOFT

Affinity Microsystems – AFFINITY, AFFINIFILE, AUTOMATION, AUTOMATE, MACRO, MACROS, SCRIPT, SCRIPTING, SCRIPTS, TEMPO, TEMPO II, TEMPO II PLUS

AfterEffects – AFTEREFFECTS, COSA

Aladdin Systems, Inc. – ALADDIN, STUFFIT

Alpha Software Corporation – ASC TECH, ASC TS

Altsys Corporation – ALTSYS

Alysis Software – ALYSIS, SUPERDISK

Ambrosia Software – AMBROSIA

Animated Software – ANIMATED SOFTWARE

Another Company – ANOTHER CO

Apogee/3D Realms Entertainment – APOGEE, 3D REALMS

Apple Business Consortium – APPLEBIZ

Apple Computer – APPLE COMPUTER

Apple System 7.5 Update – APPLE UPDATE, MOS UPDATE

Apple/Macintosh Forums – MAC, APPLE, MAC COMPUTING, MACINTOSH

AppleScript SIG – APPLESCRIPT

Applications Forum – PAP, PC APS, PC APPLICATIONS, PC APPLICATIONS FORUM, APPLICATIONS, APPLICATIONS FORUM, APPS, BUSINESS FORUM, PRODUCTIVITY, PRODUCTIVITY FORUM

Architects, Engineers and Construction SIG – AECSIG
Argosy – ARGOSY
Ariel Publishing – ARIEL
Arsenal Commmunications – ARSENAL
Art Age Software – EPSCONVERTER
Artemis Software – ARTEMIS
Articulate Systems – ARTICULATE, ASI
Artifice, Inc. – ARTIFICE
Artists' Spotlight – ARTISTS SPOTLIGHT, ARTIST'S SPOTLIGHT
Association of Online Professionals – AOP, ASSN ONLINE PROF
AST Support Forum – AST
Asymetrix Corporation – ASYMETRIX
AT&T – AT&T, AT&T, ATT WIRELESS
Atlus Software – ATLUS
atOnce Software – AT ONCE
auto*des*sys, Inc. – FORMZ
Autodesk Resource Center – AUTODESK
Avid Technology – AVID, AVID DTV
Avocat Systems – AVOCAT, AVOCAT SYSTEMS
Awakened Eye SIG – AWAKENED EYE, AE, AWAKE EYE
Baseline Publishing – BASELINE
Baseview Products, Inc. – BASEVIEW
BBS Corner – BBS, BBS CORNER
BeeSoft – BEESOFT, BEE
Bentley Systems, Inc. – MSTATION
Berkeley Macintosh Users Group – BMUG
Berkeley Systems – BERKELEY, BERK SYS, BERK SYS WIN
Best! Ware – MYOB
Bethesda Softworks, Inc. – BETHESDA, BETHESDA SOFTWORKS, BETHSEDA
Bit Jugglers – BIT JUGGLERS
Blizzard Entertainment – BLIZZARD ENT
Blue Ribbon Soundworks – BLUE RIBBON
Boston Computer Society – BCS
Bowers Development – BOWERS, APP MAKER
BPS Software – BPS SOFTWARE, ADDONS
Brainstorm Products – BRAINSTORM
Broderbund – BRODERBUND
Bungie Software – BUNGIE
Byte By Byte Corporation – BYTE BY BYTE
ByteWorks – BYTEWORKS, BYTE
CAD Resource Center – CAD, AUTOCAD
Callisto Corporation – CALLISTO
Capstone Software – CAPSTONE
Cardinal Technologies, Inc. – CARDINAL
Casady & Greene – CASADY
CE Software – CE SOFTWARE
CH Products – CH PRODUCTS
Claris – CLARIS
ClarisWorks User Group – CWUG
Common Ground Software – COMMON GROUND, NO HANDS, NO HANDS SOFTWARE
Compaq – COMPAQ
CompuAdd – COMPUADD
Compukids – COMPUKIDS
Computer Bowl – COMPUTER BOWL
Computer Peripherals, Inc. – CPI, COMPUTER PERIPHERALS
Computers & Software channel – C!, C&S, COMPUTER, COMPUTER FORUM, COMPUTING, COMPUTING AND SOFTWARE, COMPUTING FORUMS, FORUM, FORUMS, PC FORUMS, PC SECURITY, SIFS, SIGS, TECHNOLOGY
Computing & Software – COMPUTING DEPT, Old Style
Computing Company Connection – CCC, CC, COMPANIES, HARDWARE COMPANIES, IC, INDUSTRY, INDUSTRY CONNECTION, PUBLISHERS, SOFTWARE COMPANIES, SOFTWARE PUBLISHERS
Computing News – COMPUTING NEWS
Computing Print & Broadcast – CPB, CP&B, VIENNA, YOUR MOMMA
Computing Spring Fling – SPRING
Connectix – CONNECTIX, RAM DOUBLER
Consumer Electronics – CE, ALARM, AUTO SOUND, BEEPER, CELLULAR, CELLULAR PHONE, CONSUMER ELECTRONICS, HOME AUDIO, PAGER, SECURITY
Corbis Media – CORBIS, CORBIS MEDIA
Corel Special Interest Group – COREL, CORELDRAW
Craig Crossman's Computer America – COMPUTER AMERICA, CRAIG CROSSMAN, CROSSMAN

Crystal Dynamics – CRYSTAL
Database Support SIG – DATABASE, DATABASES
DataPak Software – DATAPAK, DATAPACK
Datawatch – DATAWATCH, VIREX
Davidson & Associates – DAVIDSON
Dayna Communications – DAYNA
Daystar Digital – DAYSTAR
DayTimer Technologies – DAYTIMER
Dell Computer Corporation – DELL
Delta Point – DELTA POINT
Delta Tao – DELTA, DELTA TAO
Deneba Software – DENEBA, CANVAS
Design SIG – DESIGN SIG, DESIGNER, GRAPHIC DESIGN
DeskMate – DESKMATE, DES, PC DESKMATE, PC DM
Desktop & Web Publishing – DWP, MAC DESKTOP, MAC DTP, MAC WORLD PROCESSING, MDP, DTP, DESKTOP PUBLISHING, WORD PROCESSING
Developers Forum – MDV, MAC DEVELOPMENT, PROGRAMMING, MAC PROGRAMMING, ASSEMBLY, BASIC, C, DEV, DEVELOPER, DEVELOPMENT, DEVELOPMENT FORUM
Development Forum – PDV, PC DEV, PC DEVELOPMENT, PC DEVELOPMENT
Dial/Data – DIAL, DD
Diamond Computer Systems – DIAMOND, DIAMOND COMPUTERS
Digital Eclipse – DIGITAL ECLIPSE
Digital Equipment Corporation – DEC
Digital Imaging Resource Center – DIGITAL IMAGING, SCANNERS
Digital menu – DIGITAL
Digital Technologies – DIGITAL TECH
Disney Interactive – DI, DISNEY INTERACTIVE, DISNEY SOFT, DISNEY SOFTWARE
Domark Software, Inc. – DOMARK
Don Johnston, Inc. – DJ, DON JOHNSTON
Downloading Hall of Fame – HALL OF FAME, HOF
Dubl-Click Software – DUBLCLICK
Dynaware USA – DYNAWARE, DYNAWARE USA
Edmark Technologies – EDMARK, KID DESK, PEN PAL
Electric Image – ELECTRIC, ELECTRIC IMAGE
Emigre Fonts – EMIGRE
Equis International – EQUIS
Eric Karros Kronikles – KARROS
Expert Software, Inc. – EXPERT, EXPERT SOFT
Extensis Corporation – EXTENSIS
Family Computing Forum – FC, FCF
Family Computing Forum: Contest Central – CONTEST CENTRAL
Family Computing Forum: Family Games – FAMILY GAMES
Family Computing Forum: Family Room – FAMILY ROOM, FAMILY ALBUM
Family Computing Forum: Life's Workshop – WORKSHOP
Family Computing Forum: Lifestyles & Computing – COMPUTING LIFESTYLES
Family Computing Forum: Maximum AOL – MAX AOL, AOL MAX, CRC, FAMILY RESOURCE, FCRC, MAXIMUM AOL
Family Computing Forum: News & Reviews – FAMILY NEWS, NEWS & REVIEWS, PRODUCT REVIEWS, REVIEWS
Family Computing Forum: The Family Room – FAMILY ALBUM, FAMILY ROOM
Family Computing Forum: Tip of the Day – FC TIPS, AOL TIPS, MAC TIPS, TIP, WINDOWS TIPS
Family Computing Resource Center – FAMILY COMPUTING
Farallon – FARALLON
First Look at How New Products – FIRST LOOK, FIRST
Focus Enhancements – FOCUS, FOCUS ENHANCEMENTS, LAPIS
FontBank – FONTBANK
Forte Technologies – FORTE
Fortner Research – FORTNER, FORTRAN, LANGUAGE SYS
Fractal Design – FRACTAL, FRACTAL DESIGN
France & Associates – FRANCE & ASSOCIATES
Franklin Quest – FRANKLIN
Freelance Artists SIG – FREELANCE
FullWrite – FULLWRITE, AKIMBO

Future Labs, Inc. – FUTURE LABS, TALK SHOW
Galacticomm – GALACTICOMM
Games & Entertainment – MGM, MAC GAME, MAC GAMES, GAMES FORUM, ADVENTURE, ARCADE, SIMULATOR
Games Forum – PGM, PC GAMES, GAMES FORUM, PC GAMES FORUM, ADVENTURE, ARCADE, SIMULATOR
Gametek – GAMETEK
Gateway 2000, Inc. – GATEWAY, GATEWAY 2000, MOO
GCC Technologies – GCC
GDT Softworks, Inc. – GDT, GDT SOFTWORKS
General Magic – GENERAL MAGIC
Geoworks – GEOWORKS
Geoworks Development – GEO SDK
GIF Converter – GIF CONVERTER
Global Software Suport – GSS
Global Village Communication – GLOBAL VILLAGE, GLOBAL, TELEPORT
Graphic Arts & CAD Forum – MGR, MAC ART, MAC GRAPHICS, ANIMATION, ART, CAD, GRAPHICS, GRAPHIC ARTS, GRAPHICS FORUM
Graphic Simulations – GRAPHIC, GRAPH SIM, GRAPHIC SIMULATIONS, GSC, SIMULATIONS
Graphics Forum – PGR, PC GRAPHICS, ANIMATION, PC ANIMATION, ART, CAD, GRAPHICS, GRAPHIC ARTS, GRAPHICS FORUM, PC GRAPHICS FORUM
Graphisoft – GRAPHISOFT
Graphsoft, Inc. – GRAPHSOFT, BLUEPRINT, MINICAD
GroupWare SIG – GROUPWARE
Gryphon Software – GRYPHON, GRYPHON SOFTWARE, MORPH
Hardware – MHW, MAC HARDWARE, HARDWARE, HARDWARE FORUM, SILICON
Hardware Forum – PHW, PC HARDWARE, HARDWARE, HARDWARE FORUM, PC HARDWARE FORUM
hDC Corporation – HDC, HDC CORPORATION
Help Desk – MAC HELP, ABF, AOL BEGINNERS, BEGINNER, BEGINNERS, GETTING STARTED, GETTING STARTED FORUM, HELP DESK, STARTER
Hewlett-Packard – HP
Hewlett-Packard Omni Go 100 – OMNI GO
Hewlett-Packard: Fax Products – HP FAX
Hewlett-Packard: Home Products Information – HP HOME
Hewlett-Packard: Information Storage Products – HP STORE
Hewlett-Packard: Multifunction Products – HP MULTI
Hewlett-Packard: Plotter Products – HP PLOT
Hewlett-Packard: Printer Products – HP PRN
Hewlett-Packard: Scanner Products – HP SCAN
Hewlett-Packard: SCSI Products – HP SCSI
Hewlett-Packard: Server Products – HP SERVER
Hewlett-Packard: Support Information Files – HP FILES
Hewlett-Packard: Vectra Products – HP VECTRA
HyperCard & Scripting Forum – MHC, MAC HYPERCARD, HYPERCARD
IBM Forum – IBM
IBVA Technologies – IBVA, IBVA TECH
IC Hilites – IC HILITES
Inline Design – INLINE, INLINE SOFTWARE
Insignia Solutions – INSIGNIA, INSIGNIA SOLUTION
Intel Corporation – INTEL, CONNECTION, INTEL INSIDE, PENTIUM, P6
InterCon Systems Corporation – INTERCON
Interplay – INTERPLAY
InTrek – INTREK
Intuit, Inc. – INTUIT
Iomega Corporation – IOMEGA
ISDN SIG – ISDN
ISIS International – ISIS, ISIS INTERNATIONAL
Island Graphics Corporation – ISLAND, ISLAND GRAPHICS
JASC, Inc. – JASC, PSP
JLCooper Electronics – COOPER
JLCooper Electronics – JL COOPER
JPEGView – JPEGVIEW

Kasanjian Research – KASAN, KR, KASANJIAN
Kensington Microwave, Ltd. – KENSINGTON
Kent*Marsh – KENT MARSH
Kim Komando's Komputer Clinic – KOMANDO, COMMANDO, KOMANDO CLINIC, KOMPUTER TUTOR, MR SCIENCE
Kurzweil Music Systems – KURZWEIL
Lawrence Productions – LAWRENCE
Leader Technologies – LEADER, LEADER TECH, TECHNOLOGIES
Leading Edge – LEADING EDGE
Library Media Center SIG – MEDIA CENTER
Lind Portable Power – LIND
LinksWare, Inc. – LINKSWARE
Linn Software – LINN SOFT, LINN SOFTWARE
Live Picture, Inc. – LIVE PICTURE
Logicode Technology, Inc. – LOGICODE
LucasArts Games – LUCAS, LUCAS ARTS
Mac Communications and Networking Forum – MCM, MAC COMMUNICATION, MAC COMMUNICATIONS, MAC TELECOM, MAC TELECOMM, MTC
Mac Computing Conference Center – MAC CONFERENCE
Mac Computing News & Newsletters – MAC NEWS
Mac Desktop Video & Multimedia Forum – MMM, MAC MULTIMEDIA, MVD, QUICKTIME
Mac Education & Technology Forum – MED, MAC EDUCATION
Mac Graphics Illustrator SIG – ILLUSTRATOR
Mac Kids World – MAC KIDS
Mac Shareware Awards – MUT AWARDS, MUT AWARD
Mac Software Center – MAC SOFTWARE, MAC DOWNLOADING, MAC LIBRARIES, MAC SOFTWARE CENTER
Mac Virus Information Center – MAC VIRUS
MacApp Developers Association – MADA
MacHack – MACHACK, HACK, HACKER
Macintosh Business & Home Office Forum – MBS, 4DDA ENTRY, MAC BUSINESS, APPLICATIONS, APPLICATIONS FORUM, APPS, BUSINESS FORUM, PRODUCTIVITY, PRODUCTIVITY FORUM
Macintosh Essential Utilities – MAC ESSENTIALS
Macromedia, Inc. – MACROMEDIA, MACROMIND
MacSciTech SIG – MACSCITECH
Mactivity Forum – MACTIVITY
Mainstay – MAINSTAY
Management Science Associates – MSA
Manhattan Graphics – MANHATTAN GRAPHICS, RSG
Mark of the Unicorn – MOTU
Martinsen's Software – MARTINSEN
Maxis – MAXIS
MaxTech Corporation – MAXTECH, GVC
McAfee Associates – MCAFEE
MECC – MECC, TRAILHEADS
Member Scrapbook – SCRAPBOOK
MetaTools, Inc. – METATOOLS, BRYCE, HSC, HSC SOFTWARE, KPT, KPT BRYCE
Metricom, Inc. – METRICOM, RICOCHET
Metrowerks – METROWERKS
Metz – METZ
Micro J Systems, Inc. – MICRO J
MicroFrontier, Ltd. – MICROFRONTIER
Micrografx, Inc. – MGX, MICROGRAFX
MicroMat Computer Systems – MICROMAT
MicroProse – MICROPROSE
Microseeds Publishing, Inc. – MICROSEEDS
Microsoft Knowledge Base – MSKB, KNOWLEDGE BASE
Microsoft Resource Center – MICROSOFT, MS SUPPORT
Microsoft Works Resource Center – MS WORKS
Mindscape – MINDSCAPE, SOFTWARE TOOLWORKS, STW, TOOLWORKS
Mirror Technologies – MIRROR
MobileMedia – MOBILEMEDIA, PCS
Morgan Davis Group – MORGAN DAVIS
Motorola – MOTOROLA, ENVOY, MARCO
MS-DOS 6.0 Resource Center – DOS 6, DOS 60, MS DOS 6, MS DOS 60

Multimedia Forum – PMM, MM
Multimedia menu – MULTIMEDIA
Music & Sound Forum – MMS, MAC MUSIC, MAC SOUND, MUSIC & SOUND, MUSIC AND SOUND FORUM, MUSIC FORUM, MIDI, QMMS
Music and Sound Forum – PMU, PCMU, PCMUSIC, MIDI, MUSIC & SOUND, MUSIC AND SOUND FORUM, MUSIC FORUM, PC MUSIC AND SOUND FORUM, PC MUSIC FORUM, PC SOUND, PC SOUND FORUM
Mustang Software – MUSTANG, MUSTANG SOFTWARE, QMODEM, WILDCAT, WILDCAT BBS
National Association of Quick Printers – NAQP
NEC Technologies – NEC, NEC TECH
NeoLogic – NEOLOGIC
Netscape – NETSCAPE, TO NETSCAPE
New Product Showcase – NPS, IIN, NETWORKS EXPO, NEW PRODUCT SHOWCASE, REDGATE
New Tek – NEW TEK, LIGHT WAVE, VIDEO TOASTER
New World Computing – NEW WORLD
Newsbytes – NEWSBYTES, COMPUTER NEWS
Newton Resource Center – NEWTON, MESSAGE PAD
Next Century Technologies – NCT
Nikon Electronic Imaging – NIKON
Niles and Associates – NILES, ENDNOTE
Nisus Software – NISUS
Nomadic Computing Discussion SIG – NOMADIC
Novell Desktop Systems – NOVELL, DIGITAL RESEARCH, DIGITAL RESEARCH INC, DRI
Now Software – NOW
Object Factory – OBJECT FACTORY
Olduvai Software, Inc. – OLDUVAI
ON Technology – ON
Onyx Technology – ONYX
Opcode Systems, Inc. – OPCODE, OPCODE SYSTEMS
Operating Systems Forum – MOS, SYSTEM 7, MAC O/S, MAC OS, MAC OPERATING SYSTEMS, SYSTEM 7.0, SYSTEM 7.1, SYSTEM 71
Optima Technology – OPTIMA
OPTIMAS Corporation – OPTIMAS, BIOSCAN
Origin Systems – ORIGIN, ORIGIN SYSTEMS
OS/2 Forum – OS2, IBM OS2, OS TWO
P.L.A.C.E.S. Interest Group – PLACES
PaceMark Technologies, Inc. – PACEMARK
Packer Software – PACKER
Palm Computing – PALM, PALM COMPUTING
Parsons Technology – PARSONS
Passport Designs – PASSPORT
PC Applications: Kids on Computers – COMPUKIDS
PC Data Forum – PC DATA
PC Multimedia's Video – VIDEO ZONE
PC Software Center – PC SOFTWARE
PC Virtual Toolbox – PC TOOL
PDA Forum: Development SIG – PDA DEV, PDA DEV SIG
PDA Forum: PDA Shop – PDA SHOP
PDA's Palmtop Paperbacks! – ETEXT, EZINE
PDA/Palmtop Forum – PDA, EXPERTPAD, NEWTONBOOK, PALMTOP, PDA FORUM
Peachtree Software – PEACHTREE
Personal Computer Peripherals – PC PC
Philips Media OptImage – OPTIMAGE
Photodex – PHOTODEX
Photoshop SIG – PHOTOSHOP, PHOTOSHOP SIG
Pictorius, Inc. – PICTORIUS, PEREGRINE, PROGRAPH, TGS
Piereian Spring Software – PIERIAN, PIERIAN SP
Pixel Resources – PIXEL
PKWare, Inc. – PKWARE
PowerBook Resource Center – POWERBOOK, LAPTOP, NOTEBOOK
PowerMac Resource Center – POWERMAC, POWER PC
Practical Peripherals, Inc. – PPI, PRACTICAL PERIPHERALS
Prairie Group – PRAIRIE, PRARIE SOFT

Preschool/Early Childhood SIG – PRESCHOOL, EARLY ED, EARLY EDUCATION
Print Artist Special Interest Group – PRINT ARTIST, IA, INSTANT ARTIST, INSTANT ARTIST 1
Programmer University – PU, PROGRAMMER UNIVERSITY
ProVUE Development – PROVUE
Psion – PSION
Qualitas – QUALITAS
Quantum Quality Productions – QQP
Quark, Inc. – QUARK
Radius, Inc. – RADIUS, SUPERMAC
Ray Dream – RAY, RAY DREAM
Reactor – REACTOR
ResNova Software – RESNOVA SOFTWARE, RESNOVA
Roger Wagner Publishing – ROGER WAGNER, HYPERSTUDIO, STUDIOWARE
Roland Corporation U.S. – ROLAND
Rotunda Auditorium – @ROTUNDA
Rotunda Forum Auditorium – ROTUNDA, FORUMAUD, FORUMAUDITORIUM, FORUMROT, STUMP
Ryobi – RYOBI
Search database of files – FILE SEARCH, QUICK FIND, QUICK FINDER
Serius – SERIUS
Seventh Level Software – 7TH, SEVENTH
Shareware Solutions – SHAREWARE SOLUTIONS
Sierra On-Line – SIERRA, DYNAMIX
SoftArc – SOFTARC
Softdisk Superstore – SOFTDISK, SUPERSTORE
SoftLogik – SOFTLOGIK
Software Center – SOFTWARE CENTER, DOWNLOAD, DOWNLOADING, FILE, FILES, LIBRARIES, LIBS, SEARCH, SOFTWARE, SOFTWARE DIRECTORY, SOFTWARE LIBRARY, SOFTWARE LIBRARIES, SOFTWARE HELP
Software Hardtalk with John C. Dvorak – DVORAK, SOFTWARE HARDTALK
Software Unboxed – SOFTWARE UNBOXED, BROADCAST SOFTWARE
Sony Magic Link – MAGIC LINK, SML, SONY
Sophisticated Circuits – SOPHCIR
Sound & Midi Resource Center – MMS TOOL
Spectrum HoloByte – SPECTRUM
Specular International – SPECULAR
Spider Island Software – SPIDER, SPIDER ISLAND
Sprint Annual Report – SPRINT, Old
SRS Labs – SRS LABS, 3D AUDIO, 3D SOUND
SSSi – SSSI
STAC Electronics – STAC
Staff Development SIG – STAFF, STAFF DEVELOPMENT
Starfish Software – STARFISH
Starplay Productions – STARPLAY
STF Technologies – STF, STF TECHNOLOGIES
Strata, Inc. – STRATA
Strategic Simulations – STRATEGIC, SSI
Sunburst Communications – SUNBURST
SuperCard Scripting Center – SUPERCARD
Survivor Software – SURVIVOR, SURVIVOR SOFTWARE
Symantec – SYMANTEC, 5TH GENERATION, CENTRAL, CENTRAL POINT, CPS, DELRINA, FIFTH, NORTON, PETER NORTON
Synex – SYNEX
Tactic Software – TACTIC, NEW ERA, NUBASE
Take 2 Interactive Software – TAKE 2, TAKE 2 INC
Team Concepts – TEAM CONCEPTS, TEAM
Technology Works – TECHWORKS, TECHNOLOGY WORKS
Tektronix – TEKTRONIX
Telecom/Networking Forum – PTC, PCM, PC TELECOM, PC TELECOM FORUM, COMMUNICATIONS, NETWORKING, NETWORKING FORUM, TELECOM, TELECOM FORUM, TELECOMMUNICATIONS
Texas Instruments – TI, TEXAS INSTRUMENTS
The 3DO Company – 3DO, COMPANY 3DO,THREEDO
The Cobb Group Online – COBB, COBB GROUP

The Filemaker Pro Resource Center – FILEMAKER
The Macintosh Bible/Peachpit Forum – PEACHPIT, MAC BIBLE, MACINTOSH BIBLE
The Voyager Company – VOYAGER
Three-Sixty Software – THREE SIXTY
Thrustmaster – THRUST MASTER
TIGERDirect, Inc. – BLOC DEVELOPMENT
TIGERDirect, Inc. – TIGER, TIGERDIRECT
Time Warner Interactive – TWI
Timeslips Corporation – TIMESLIPS
Tom Snyder Productions – TSP, TOM SNYDER
Trendsetter Software – TRENDSETTER, TS
Trimble Navigation, Ltd. – TRIMBLE, GPS
Truevision – RASTEROPS
Tseng – TSENG
Tune Up Your PC – TUNE UP, AUTOEXEC, CONFIG, TUNE UP YOUR PC
Turtle Beach Systems – TURTLE BEACH, TURTLE SYS
UniverseCentral.Com – UNIVERSE, RALPH Z, RALPH ZERBONIA, UNIVERSE CENTRAL
User Group Forum – UGF, AUG, USER GROUP, USER GROUPS
Userland – USERLAND
Utilities Forum – MUT, MVT, MAC UTILITIES
Ventana Communications – VENTANA
Vertisoft – VERTISOFT
Video SIG – VIDEO SIG
Videodiscovery – VDISC
VIDI – VIDI
Viewer Resource Center – VIEWER, PLAYER, PLAYERS, VIEWERS
Viewpoint DataLabs – VIEWPOINT
Village Software – VILLAGE, VILLAGE SOFTWARE
Virtual Post Card Center – POSTCARDS
Virtual Reality Labs, Inc. – VRLI
Virtual Reality Resource Center – VR, VIRTUAL REALITY
Virtus Corp. – VIRTUS, WALKTHROUGH
Virus Information Center SIG – VIRUS
Vision Video – VV, VISION VIDEO
Visionary Software – VISIONARY
Visioneer – VISIONEER, PAPERPORT
Visual Basic Area – VB, VISUAL BASIC
Voyetra Technologies – VOYETRA
Web Page Clip Art Creation Center – WEB ART
Web Publishing SIG – WEB PUB, WEB PUBLISH, WEB PUBLISHING
Western Digital – WESTERN DIGITAL, WDC
Westwood Studios – WESTWOOD, WESTWOOD STUDIOS
What's Hot in Computing – SCHEDULE, CALENDAR, TITF
What's Hot in Computing – CALENDAR, SCHEDULE, TITF
What's Hot in Mac Computing – MAC HOT, HOT MAC
What's Hot in PC Computing – HOT PC, PC FORUMS HOT, PC HOT
Wilson Windoware – WILSON, WINDOWWARE
Windows Forum – WIN, WIN 95, WIN FORUM, WINDOWS 95, WINDOWS FORUM
Windows News – WIN NEWS
Windows NT Resource Center – WIN NT, WINDOWS NT
Windows Services – WINDOWS
Windows Shareware 500 – WIN 500, WINDOWS 500
Windows Wallpaper & Paint Center – WALLPAPER
Wireless Communication – WIRELESS
Word Perfect Support Center – WORD PERFECT
Working Software – WORKING
Xaos Tools – XAOS, XAOS TOOLS
XCMD SIG – XCMD, XCMD SIG
ZDNet – ZDNET, ZD, ZIFF
Zedcor, Inc. – ZEDCOR
Zelos – ZELOS
Zoom Telephonics – ZOOM TELEPHONICS

## Digital City Channel Keywords

Alaska – ALASKA, ALASKA DC, ALASKA DCITY, ALASKA DIGC, ALASKA DIGITAL CITY, DC ALASKA, DCITY ALASKA, DIGC ALASKA, DIGITAL CITY ALASKA

Albany, New York – ALBANY, ALBANY DC, ALBANY DCITY, ALBANY DIGC, ALBANY DIGITAL CITY, ALBANY NY, DC ALBANY, DCITY ALBANY, DIGC ALBANY, DIGITAL CITY ALBANY

Albuquerque/Santa Fe, New Mexico – ALBUQUERQUE, DC ALBUQUERQUE, DCITY ALBUQUERQUE, DIGC ALBUQUERQUE, ALBUQUERQUE, ALBUQUERQUE DC, ALBUQUERQUE DCITY, ALBUQUERQUE DIGC

Atlanta, Georgia – ATLANTA, ATLANTA DIGITAL CITY, DC ATLANTA, DC HOTLANTA, DIGC ATLANTA, DIGC HOTLANTA, DIGITAL CITY ATLANTA, HOTLANTA

Austin, Texas – AUSTIN, AUSTIN DC, AUSTIN DCITY, AUSTIN DIGC, AUSTIN DIGITAL CITY, AUSTIN TX, DC AUSTIN, DCITY AUSTIN, DIGC AUSTIN, DIGITAL CITY AUSTIN

Bay City, Michigan – BAY CITY, BAY CITY DC, BAY CITY DCITY, BAY CITY DIGC, BAY CITY MI, DC BAY CITY, DCITY BAY CITY, DIGC BAY CITY

Buffalo, New York – BUFFALO, BUFFALO DC, BUFFALO DCITY, BUFFALO DIGC, BUFFALO DIGITAL CITY, BUFFALO NY, DC BUFFALO, DCITY BUFFALO, DIGC BUFFALO, DIGITAL CITY BUFFALO

City Web – CITY WEB, DC WEB, WASHINGTON WEB

Dallas/Ft Worth Texas – FT WORTH, DC FORT WORTH, DIGC FT WORTH, DIGITAL CITY FT WORTH, FT WORTH DIGC, FT WORTH DIGITAL CITY

Dayton, Ohio – DAYTON, DAYTON DC, DAYTON DCITY, DAYTON DIGC, DAYTON DIGITAL CITY, DAYTON OH, DC DAYTON, DCITY DAYTON, DIGC DAYTON, DIGITAL CITY DAYTON

Denver, Colorado – DENVER, DC DENVER, DENVER DIGC, DENVER DIGITAL CITY, DIGC DENVER, DIGITAL CITY DENVER

Detroit, Michigan – DETROIT, DC DETROIT, DETROIT DIGC, DETROIT DIGITAL CITY, DIGC DETROIT, DIGITAL CITY DETROIT

Digital Cities – DIGITAL CITY, DCITY NATIONAL, DCN, DC NATIONAL, DIGC, DIG CITY, DIG CITY NATIONAL, DIG CITY USA, DIGITAL CITIES, DIGITAL CITY NATIONAL, DIGITAL CITY US, DIGITAL USA

Digital City: Entertainment – DC FUN

Digital City: Marketplace – DC MARKETPLACE

Digital City: News/Weather – DC NEWS

Digital City: People – DC PEOPLE

Digital City: The Event Source – DC EVENT

El Paso, Texas – EL PASO, DC EL PASO, DCITY EL PASO, DIGC EL PASO, DIGITAL CITY EL PASO, EL PASO DC, EL PASO DCITY, EL PASO DIGC, EL PASO DIGITAL CITY, EL PASO TX

Eugene, Oregon – EUGENE, DC EUGENE, DCITY EUGENE, DIGC EUGENE, DIGITAL CITY EUGENE, EUGENE DC, EUGENE DCITY, EUGENE DIGC, EUGENE DIGITAL CITY, EUGENE OR

Flint, Michigan – FLINT, DC FLINT, DCITY FLINT, DIGC FLINT, DIGITAL CITY FLINT, FLINT DC, FLINT DCITY, FLINT DIGC, FLINT DIGITAL CITY, FLINT MI

Fresno/Visalia, California – FRESNO, DC FRESNO, DCITY FRESNO, DIGC FRESNO, DIGITAL CITY FRESNO, FRESNO CA, FRESNO DC, FRESNO DCITY, FRESNO DIGC, FRESNO DIGITAL CITY

Ft. Myers/Naples, Florida – NAPLES, DC NAPLES, DCITY NAPLES, DIGC NAPLES, DIGITAL CITY NAPLES, NAPLES DC, NAPLES DCITY, NAPLES DIGC, NAPLES DIGITAL CITY, NAPLES FL

Houston, Texas – HOUSTON, DC HOUSTON, DIGC HOUSTON, DIGITAL CITY HOUSTON, HOUSTON DIGC, HOUSTON DIGITAL CITY

Los Angeles – LOS ANGELES, DC LA, DC LOS ANGELES, DIGC LA, DIGC LOS ANGELES, DIGITAL CITY LA, LA DIGC, LA DIGITAL CITY, LOS ANGELES DIGC

Los Angeles: City Tour – LA TOUR

Los Angeles: Community – LA COMM

Los Angeles: News & Weather – LA WEATHER, LA NEWS

Los Angeles: People – LA PEOPLE

Miami/Ft Lauderdale, Florida – MIAMI, DC FT LAUDERDALE, DIGC FT LAUDERDALE, DIGC MIAMI, DIGITAL CITY MIAMI, FT LAUDERDALE DIGC, MIAMI DIGC, MIAMI DIGITAL CITY

Miami: Community – MIAMI COMM

Miami: News & Weather – MIAMI WEATHER, MIAMI NEWS

Miami: People – MIAMI PEOPLE

Midwest – MIDWEST, DC MIDWEST, DIGC MIDWEST, DIGITAL CITY MIDWEST, MIDWEST DIGC, MIDWEST DIGITAL CITY

Minneapolis/St Paul, Minnesota – ST PAUL, DC ST PAUL, DIGC ST PAUL, DIGITAL CITY ST PAUL, ST PAUL DIGC, ST PAUL DIGITAL CITY

New Bedford, Massachusetts – NEW BEDFORD, DC NEW BEDFORD, DCITY NEW BEDFORD, DIGC NEW BEDFORD, NEW BEDFORD DC, NEW BEDFORD DCITY, NEW BEDFORD DIGC, NEW BEDFORD MA

New Orleans, Louisiana – NEW ORLEANS, DC NEW ORLEANS, DCITY NEW ORLEANS, DIGC NEW ORLEANS, NEW ORLEANS DC, NEW ORLEANS DCITY, NEW ORLEANS DIGC, NEW ORLEANS LA

Philadelphia, Pennsylvania – PHILADELPHIA, DC PHILA, DC PHILADELPHIA, DC PHILLY, DIGC PHILA, DIGC PHILADELPHIA, DIGC PHILLY, DIG CITY PHILLY, DIGITAL CITY PHILLY, PHILA DIGITAL CITY, PHILADELPHIA DIGC, PHILLY DIG CITY, PHILLY DIGITAL CITY

Philadelphia: City Tour – PHIL TOUR

Philadelphia: Classifieds – PHIL MARKET

Register as a Digital Citizen – JOIN DIGITAL CITY, DC JOIN, DIGITAL CITY JOIN, JOIN DC

Reno, Nevada – RENO, DC RENO, DCITY RENO, DIGC RENO, DIGITAL CITY RENO, RENO DC, RENO DCITY, RENO DIGC, RENO DIGITAL CITY, RENO NV

Saginaw, Michigan – SAGINAW, DC SAGINAW, DCITY SAGINAW, DIGC SAGINAW, SAGINAW DC, SAGINAW DCITY, SAGINAW DIGC, SAGINAW MI

San Diego, California – SAN DIEGO, DC SAN DIEGO, DC SD, DIGC SAN DIEGO, DIGC SD, DIGITAL CITY SD, SAN DIEGO DIGC, SD, SD DIGC, SD DIGITAL CITY

San Diego: City Tour – SD TOUR

San Diego: Community – SD COMM

San Diego: News & Weather – SD NEWS, SD WEATHER

San Diego: People – SD PEOPLE

San Francisco, California – SAN FRANCISCO, DC SAN FRANCISCO, DC SF, DIGC SAN FRANCISCO, DIGC SF, DIGITAL CITY SF, SAN FRANCISCO DIGC, SF DIGC, SF DIGITAL CITY

San Francisco: City Tour – SF TOUR

San Francisco: Community – SF COMM

San Francisco: News & Weather – SF NEWS, SF WEATHER

San Francisco: People – SF PEOPLE

Seattle/Tacoma, Washington – SEATTLE, DC SEATTLE, DIGC SEATTLE, DIGITAL CITY SEATTLE, SEATTLE DIGC, SEATTLE DIGITAL CITY

South – SOUTH, DC SOUTH, DIGC SOUTH, DIGITAL CITY SOUTH, SOUTH DIGC, SOUTH DIGITAL CITY, SOUTHEAST

Tampa/St Petersburg, Florida – TAMPA, DC TAMPA, DIGC TAMPA, DIGITAL CITY TAMPA, TAMPA DIGC, TAMPA DIGITAL CITY

Tampa: Community – TAMPA COMM

Tampa: News & Weather – TAMPA NEWS, TAMPA WEATHER

Tampa: News & Weather – TAMPA WEATHER, TAMPA NEWS

Tampa: People – TAMPA PEOPLE

Toronto – TORONTO, DC TORONTO, DIGC TORONTO, DIGITAL CITY TORONTO, TORONTO DIGC, TORONTO DIGITAL CITY

Traffic Center – SHADOW, SHADOW BROADCASTING, SHADOW TRAFFIC, TRAFFIC

Tulsa, Oklahoma – TULSA, DC TULSA, DCITY TULSA, DIGC TULSA, DIGITAL CITY TULSA, TULSA DC, TULSA DCITY, TULSA DIGC, TULSA DIGITAL CITY, TULSA OK

Waco/Temple/Bryan, Texas – BRYAN, BRYAN DC, BRYAN DCITY, BRYAN DIGC, BRYAN DIGITAL CITY, BRYAN TX, DC BRYAN, DCITY BRYAN, DIGC BRYAN, DIGITAL CITY BRYAN

Washington: Personals – WASH PERSONALS

West – WEST, DC WEST, DIGC WEST, DIGITAL CITY WEST, WEST DIGC

## Entertainment Channel Keywords

60-Second Novelist: BOnKeRs Trivia – BONKERS, BONK

90210 Wednesdays – 90210, 90210 WEDNESDAYS, BEVERLY HILLS, BEVERLY HILLS 90210, WEDNESDAYS

@the.movies – MOVIES, @ THE MOVIES, @THE.MOVIES, CINEMA, FILMS, MOVIE, THE MOVIES

ABC Good Morning America – ABC GMA, GMA, GOOD MORNING AMERICA, JOEL SIEGEL

ABC KIDZINE – ABC KIDZINE, ABC KIDS, KIDZINE

ABC Love Online – ABC LOVE, LOVE ONLINE, LUV

ABC Online – ABC

ABC Online Auditorium – ABC AUDITORIUM, ABC EVENTS, ABC GUESTS, ABC TRANSCRIPTS, FRIDAY AT 4

ABC Online Auditorium – FRIDAY AT 4, ABC AUDITORIUM, ABC EVENTS, ABC GUESTS, ABC TRANSCRIPTS

ABC Online Help – ABC HELP

ABC Online: America Out Of Line – AOOL, AMERICA OUT OF LINE

ABC Online: Beta area – ABC BETA

ABC Online: KAAL-TV in Rochester, MN – KAAL TV

ABC Online: KABC-TV in Los Angeles, CA – KABC TV

ABC Online: KAIT-TV in Jonesboro, AR – KAIT TV

ABC Online: KAKE-TV in Wichita, KS – KAKE TV

ABC Online: KESQ-TV in Palm Springs, CA – KESQ TV

ABC Online: KEZI-TV in Eugene, OR – KEZI TV

ABC Online: KFSN-TV in Fresno, CA – KFSN TV

ABC Online: KGO San Francisco Newstalk AM 810 – KGO

ABC Online: KGO-TV in San Francisco, CA – KGO TV

ABC Online: KGTV-TV in San Diego, CA – KGTV TV

ABC Online: KGUN-TV in Tucson, AZ – KGUN TV

ABC Online: KHBS/KHOG-TV in Fort Smith, AR – KHBS TV

ABC Online: KIFI-TV in Idaho Falls, ID – KIFI TV

ABC Online: KIVI-TV in Boise, ID – KIVI TV

ABC Online: KMBC-TV in Kansas City, MO – KMBC TV

ABC Online: KMGH-TV in Denver, CO – KMGH TV

ABC Online: KNTV-TV in San Jose, CA – KNTV TV

ABC Online: KNXV-TV in Phoenix, AZ – KNXV TV

ABC Online: KOAT-TV in Albuquerque, NM – KOAT TV

ABC Online: KOCO-TV in Oklahoma, OK – KOCO TV

ABC Online: KODE-TV in Joplin, MO – KODE TV

ABC Online: KQTV-TV in St. Joseph, MO – KQTV TV

ABC Online: KTBS-TV in Shreveport, LA – KTBS TV

ABC Online: KTKA-TV in Topeka, KS – KTKA TV

ABC Online: KTRK-TV in Houston, TX – KTRK TV

ABC Online: KTVX-TV in Salt Lake City, UT – KTVX TV

ABC Online: KTXS-TV in Abilene, TX – KTXS TV

ABC Online: KVIA-TV in El Paso, TX – KVIA TV

ABC Online: KVUE-TV in Austin, TX – KVUE TV

ABC Online: News Views – ABC NEWS VIEWS, NEWS VIEWS

ABC Online: Rock & Road – RR, R&R, ROCK & ROAD

ABC Online: WZZM-TV in Grand Rapids, MI – WZZM TV
ABC Prime Time – ABC PRIME TIME, ABC ENTERTAINMENT
ABC Radio – ABC RADIO, PAUL HARVEY
Academy Awards – OSCAR, ACADEMY AWARDS, OSCARS
American Entertainment Network – AEN
AOL Contest area – CONTEST, CONTEST AREA, CONTESTS, WINNER
Assassins – ASSASSINS
Babylon 5 – BABYLON 5, BABYLON
Broken Arrow – BROKEN ARROW
Cannes Film Festival – CANNES
Cartoon collection – YOUR TOONS
Cartoon Network – CARTOON NETWORK, TOONS
Cindy Adams: Queen of Gourmet Gossip – CINDY, ADAMS, CINDY ADAMS
CinemaPOV – CINEMAPOV, CPOV
Comedy Central – COMEDY CENTRAL
Comic Strip Centennial – COMIC STRIP, POSTAL STAMPS
Comics Selection – COMICS
CompuToon area – COMPUTOON
Court TV's Law Center – COURT TV, COURTROOM TELEVISION, LAW, LAW CENTER, OJ
Critic's Choice – CRITIC, CRITICS, CRITICS CHOICE
CyberJustice – CYBERJUSTICE
CyberJustice Contests – CJ CONTESTS
CyberJustice's Arch of Public Opinion Polls – POLLS
CyberJustice's Courts of Karmic Justice – COURTS
CyberJustice's Gazette Online/Email – GAZETTE
CyberJustice's Istorian's Time Capsule – TIME CAPSULE
CyberJustice's Kennehora Junction – KENNEHORA, KENNEHORA JUNCTION
CyberJustice's Meet The Locals – LOCALS
CyberJustice's Oasis of Xaiz – DOROTHY
CyberJustice's Record Your Judgment – JUDGMENT
CyberJustice's Reward & Punishment – QUIKJUSTICE
CyberJustice's Worry Free Zone – WORRY
CyberJustice's Worry, Complain & Sob – KIVETCH
Cyberserials – CYBERSERIALS, CYBERSOAPS, SERIALS
DC Comics Online – DC COMICS, BATMAN, DC COMICS ONLINE, MAD, MAD MAGAZINE, MILESTONE, PARADOX, SUPERMAN, VERTIGO
DC Comics Online: Chat Rooms – DC CHAT
Deadly Games – DEADLY
Dilbert Comics – DILBERT, DILBERT COMICS, DILBOARD
Disney Jobs – DISNEY JOBS
Disney Services – DISNEY
DragonRealms – DREALMS, DRAGONREALMS
E! Entertainment Television – E!
Entertainment channel – ENTERTAINMENT, E, GOSSIP, PLAY, REC CENTER, RECREATION, RECREATION CENTER
Entertainment Chat – ECHAT, ENTERTAINMENT CHAT, HOT CHAT
Entertainment Weekly – EW, ENTERTAINMENT WEEKLY
Entertainment [just try it] – SEX
Entertainment's Radio Forum – RADIO, RADIO FORUM, SATELLITES
EXTRA Online – EXTRA, ACE VENTURA, ACE VENTURE STORE
Favorite Flicks! – FAVORITE FLICKS, FAVE FLICKS, OLD FAVES
Ferndale – FERNDALE
Follywood – FOLLYWOOD
Fraiser Tuesdays – FRASIER, FRAISER TUESDAYS
Games & Entertainment Newsletter – NEWSLETTER
Get Movin' With Oprah – OPRAH
Global Challenger Balloon Race – HOT AIR
Good Morning America Recipes – EATS
Hecklers Online – ;, ;- , COMPUTER GAMES, HECKLE, HECKLER, HECKLER ONLINE, HECKLER'S ONLINE, HECKLERS, HECKLERS ONLINE, HO, HOL, JOKE, LIMERICK, WEB COMEDY, WEB HUMOR, WISE GUYS
Hecklers Online: Clubs – HECKLERS CLUBS, HECKLING CLUBS, HO CLUBS

Hollywood Online – HOLLYWOOD, HOLLYWOOD ONLINE
Home Video – VIDEOS, HOME VIDEO
Horoscopes – HOROSCOPE, HOROSCOPES
Hypractv8 with Thomas Dolby – HYPR
Intelligent Gamer Online – IG, IG ONLINE, INTELLIGENT GAMER
Lifetime Television – LIFETIME, LIFETIME TV, LIFETIME TELEVISION
Lois & Clark – LOIS & CLARK, L & C, L AND C, LOIS AND CLARK
Lost & Found TV Shows – LOST TV SHOWS, CANCELLED TV SHOWS, FALL TV, FALL TV SHOWS, FOUND TV, GONER TV, LOST TV, NEW TV SEASON
Lotteries – LOTTERY
Mad About You Fan Forum – MAY, MAD ABOUT, MAD ABOUT YOU, MAD ABOUT YOU SUNDAYS
Main TV Screen – TV, TELEVISION
McLaughlin Group – MCL, GROUP, MCLAUGHLIN, MCLAUGHLIN GROUP, WRONG, WRONG!
Melrose Mondays – MELROSE, MELROSE MONDAYS
Movie Forums area – MOVIE FORUMS
Movie Review Database – MOVIE REVIEW DB, CINEMAN, CINEMAN SYNDICATE, FILM REVIEW DATABASE, FILM REVIEW DB, FILM REVIEWS DATABASE, MOVIE REVIEW DATABASE, MOVIE REVIEWS DATABASE, MRD
Movie Reviews – MOVIE REVIEWS
MovieLink – MOVIELINK, 777-FILM, 777-FILM ONLINE, HOW TIMES
Movies on the Web – MOVIES WEB
MovieVisions – MOVIEVISIONS, FILM STUDIOS
MTV News – MTV NEWS
MTV Online – MTV
MTV Online: Hot Spot – HOT SPOT
MTV Online: Krank – KRANK
MTV Online: News – MUSIC NEWS
Mysteries from the Yard – MYSTERIES, BOOKSHOP, HOLMES, MFTY, MYSTERIES FROM THE YARD, SHERLOCK, SHERLOCK HOLMES
NBC... NOT! – NOT NBC, NBC
New Movie Releases – NEW MOVIES, NEW FILM, NEW FILMS, NEW MOVIE, NEW MOVIE RELEASES, NEW RELEASES, SUMMER MOVIES
NewsGrief – NEWSGRIEF, NG
Nick at Nite – NICK AT NITE, NAN, NICK @ NITE, TV LAND
Nickelodeon: Kids' Choice Awards – KIDS CHOICE
NTN's QB1 – QB1
Parascope – PARASCOPE, ALIENS, CONSPIRACY, PERISCOPE, PS, PSCP, SCOPE, STRANGE, WEIRD, WIERD
Play-By-Mail Clubs & Messaging – PBM CLUBS
Play-By-Mail Forum – PBM, PLAY-BY-MAIL
Playbill Online – PLAYBILL, BROADWAY
Playbill Online: Tony Awards Central – TONY AWARDS, TONYS
Showbiz News & Info – SHOWBIZ INFO, SHOWBIZ NEWS
Sightings Online – SIGHTINGS
Smart Mouths – SMARTMOUTHS
Soap Opera Digest – SOD, DIVA, DIVA LA DISH, SOAP DIGEST
Soundbites Online – SOUNDBITES, SATIRE
Space: Above & Beyond – SPACE A&B, SPACE ABOVE & BEYOND, SPACE ABOVE AND BEYOND, SPACE: ABOVE AND BEYOND
Star Wars Sim Forum – STAR WARS, STAR WARS SIM
Starfleet Online – STARFLEET, ACADEMY
Tell a Story – TREASURES
Telluride Film Festival – TELLURIDE
The ABC Rock & Road Beatles Anthology – BEATLES ANTHOLOGY
The Biz! – HOLLYWOOD PRO, HOL PRO
The Biz! – THE BIZ
The Cartoons Forum – CARTOONS
The Casting Forum – CASTING, ACTING, ACTORS, ACTRESSES, CASTING FORUM
The Comedy Pub – COMEDY PUB, COMEDY, HUMOR, JENNY FLAME, LOL, PUB
The Funny Pages – FUNNIES
The Geraldo Show – GERALDO, GERALDO SHOW
The IMPROVisation Online – IMPROVISATION, IMPROV

The Ricki Lake Show – RICKI LAKE
The Sci-Fi Channel – SCIFI
The WB Network – WB, FROG, MICHIGAN J FROG, THE WB NETWORK, WBNET
Ticketmaster – TICKETMASTER, TICKET
TV Networks area – TV NETWORKS
TV People – TV PEOPLE
TV Quest – TV GUIDE, LISTINGS, TV LISTINGS, TV SOURCE
TV Shows – TV SHOWS
TV Shows Gossip – TV GOSSIP
TV Spoofs – TV SPOOFS, SPOOFS
TV Viewers Forum – TV VIEWERS
VGA Planets – VGAP, VGA PLANETS
VH1 Online – VH1
Virgin Records – VIRGIN RECORDS
Virgin Records -or- Virgin Sound & Vision – VIRGIN
WEBentertainment – WEB ENTERTAINMENT
Weekly World News – WWN, ASK SERENA, BATBOY, BIGFOOT, DEAR DOTTI, ED ANGER, ELVIS, NESSIE, SATAN, SIDESHOW, VAMPIRE, WWN, WEEKLY WORLD NEWS
What's Hot in Entertainment – HOT ENTERTAINMENT, DAILY FIX, ENT SPOT, ESPOT, FIX, HOT ENT, HOT ENTERTAINMENT
WHFS 99.1 FM – WHFS, 99.1, HFS, MODERN ROCK
Wizard World – WIZARD, ANIME, COLLECTING, IQ, MANGA, WIZARD WORLD
WLS Chicago – WLS
WWW Game Sites – GAME SITES, GS
X Files Forums – X FILES
X Files Fridays – XF FRIDAYS
X Files Sim Forum – X FILES SIM

## Games Channel Keywords

Adventures by Mail – ABM, ADVENTURES BY MAIL, MONSTER ISLAND, QUEST
Air Warrior – AIR WARRIOR, KESMAI
America Online Gaming Conference – AMERICON
Boxer*Jam Gameshows – BOXER, BOXER JAM, BOXER*JAM, STRIKE-A-MATCH
ChipNet Online – CHIPNET, CHIP
Collectible Card Games Forum – CCGF, COLLECT CARDS
Computer Gaming World – CGW, CGW, COMPUTER GAMING, COMPUTER GAMING WORLD
Crossword America – CA, XWORDS
Download Online Games* – DOWNLOAD GAMES, GAMES DOWNLOAD
Dr. Gamewiz Online – GAMEWIZ, DR GAMEWIZ, GAMEWIZ INC
Federation – FED, FEDERATION
Fellowship of Online Gamers/RPGA Network – FELLOWSHIP, FOG, RPGA, RPGA NETWORK
Flight Sim Resource Center – FLIGHT SIM, CRASH, FIREBALL, FLIGHT, FLIGHT CENTER, FLIGHT SIMS, FLIGHT SIMULATIONS, FSRC
Free-Form Gaming Forum – FFGF, RDI
Game Base – GAME BASE
Game Designers Forum – GAME DESIGN, GAME DESIGNER, GAME DESIGNERS
GamePro Online – GAMEPRO
Games channel – GAMES, AOL GAME FORUMS, GAME, GAMES & ENTERTAINMENT, GAMES CHANNEL
Games Channel: Action – GC ACTION
Games Channel: Classic Games – GC CLASSIC
Games Channel: Contests – GC CONTESTS
Games Channel: Gaming Information – GC INFO
Games Channel: Knowledge Games – GC KNOWLEDGE
Games Channel: News – GC NEWS
Games Channel: Persona Games – GC PERSONA
Games Channel: Role Playing Games – GC RPG
Games Channel: Simulation Games – GC SIMULATION
Games Channel: Sports Games – GC SPORTS
Games Channel: Strategy Games – GC STRATEGY
Games Parlor – GAMES PARLOR, GAME ROOMS, PARLOR
Gaming Information Exchange – GIX

GemStone III – GEMSTONE, GEMSTONE III

Hecklers Online: Antagonistic Trivia – AT, AI INC, ANTAG, ANTAGON, ANTAGONIST, ANTAGONISTS, ANTAGONIST TRIVIA, ANTAGONISTIC TRIVIA, ATG

Modus Operandi – MODUS, MODUS OPERANDI

Murder Mysteries Online – MURDER, CYBERSLEUTH, I FORSOOTH, MMO, MURDER MYSTERY, MURDER MYSTERIES

Nintendo Power Source – NINTENDO, NOA, NINTENDO POWER SOURCE

Non-Affiliated Gamers Forum – NAGF

NTN Trivia – NTN, COUNTDOWN, NTN TRIVIA

Online Gaming Forums – OGF, GAMING, ONLINE GAMING

President '96 – PRESIDENT 96

RabbitJack's Casino – CASINO, RABBITJACK'S CASINO, RABBITJACKS CASINO

Role-Playing Forum – RPG, ROLE PLAYING

Scorpia's Lair – SCORPIA, SCORPIA'S LAIR, SCORPIAS LAIR

Simming Forum – SIM, SIMMING, SIMS

Sol III Play-by-Email Game – SOL III

Strategy & Wargaming Forum – STRATEGY, CHESS

Trivia Forum – TRIVIA, TRIVIA FORUM

Trivial Pursuit Interactive – TRIVIAL PURSUIT, TPI

TSR Online – TSR, TSR ONLINE

Unlimited Adventures – UA, UNLIMITED ADVENTURES

Virtual Airlines – VIRTUAL AIRLINES, LYNX, LYNX AIRWAYS, SKYLINE, SKYLINE AIRWAYS, SUNAIR, SUNAIR EXPRESS, VAA, VAS

What's Hot in AOL Games – HOT GAMES, GC HOT

Yoyodyne Entertainment – YOYO, YOYODYNE

Yoyodyne Entertainment: Games – YOYO GAMES

## Health & Fitness Channel Keywords

Alternative Medicine Forum – ALTERNATIVE MEDICINE

America Lung Association – ALA, AMERICAN LUNG, AMERICAN LUNG ASSOC

American Cancer Society – ACS, ACS NATL

American Diabetes Association – DIABETES, AMERICAN DIABETES

American Running & Fitness Association – ARFA

Avon's Breast Cancer Awareness Crusade Online – CRUSADE

Better Health & Medical Forum – HRS, BETTER HEALTH

Cancer Forum – CANCER

Children's Health Forum – CHILDREN'S HEALTH

Columbia's Health Today – COLUMBIA/HCA, COLUMBIA/HCA, COLUMBIANET, COLUMBIA.NET, HEALTH TODAY, ONE SOURCE, SENIOR FRIENDS

Dependency and Recovery Issues – DEPENDENCY

Fitness Forum – FITNESS, EXERCISE

Have a Healthy New Year! – NEW YEAR

Health Channel – HEALTH, MEDICINE

Health Focus – HEALTH FOCUS

Health Resources – HEALTH RESOURCES, HEALTH MAGAZINES, HEALTH REFERENCE

Health Speakers and Support Groups – HEALTH LIVE

Health Web Sites – HEALTH WEB

Issues in Mental Health – IMH

Men's Health Forum – MEN'S HEALTH

Men's Health Internet Sites – MENS' HEALTH WEB

Mental Health Forum – MENTAL HEALTH

Mental Health Web Sites – MENTAL HEALTH WEB

Multiple Sclerosis Forum – MULTIPLE SCLEROSIS

National Alliance of Mentally Ill – NAMI

National Multiple Sclerosis Society – NMSS

Personal Empowerment Network – PEN, EMPOWERMENT

Psychology Forum – PSYCHOLOGY

Self-Help area – SELF-HELP

The Health Zone – HEALTH ZONE, CHOCOLATE, CYBERSLIM, IHRSA, HZ, QUALITY, Z, ZONED, ZONIE, <Z>

United Cerebral Palsy Association – CEREBRAL PALSY, UCPA

What's Hot in Health – HOT HEALTH, WHAT'S HOT IN HEALTH

Women's Health Forum – WOMEN'S HEALTH, WOMENS HEALTH

Women's Health Internet Sites – WOMEN'S HEALTH WEB

## The Hub Keywords

The Hub – HUB, THE HUB

The Hub: ArtSpeak – ARTSPEAK

The Hub: Calendar Girls – CALENDAR GIRLS

The Hub: Celebrity Sightings – CELEBRITY

The Hub: Channel Zero – CHANNEL ZERO

The Hub: Click Here – CLICK HERE

The Hub: Cyrano – CYRANO

The Hub: Even More Bridges of Madison County – BRIDGES

The Hub: Fuzzy Memories – FUZZY

The Hub: Get A Life – GET A LIFE

The Hub: Gigabytes Island – GIGABYTES

The Hub: Global Worldwide Pictures International, Ltd. – GWPI

The Hub: Heaven – HEAVEN

The Hub: Index – HUB INDEX, HUB CONTENTS, THE HUB INDEX

The Hub: John the Hitchhiker – HITCHHIKER, HITCHIKER

The Hub: Ken's Guide to the Bible – KENS GUIDE

The Hub: Konspiracy Korner – KONSPIRACY

The Hub: Meanwhile – MEANWHILE

The Hub: Modern Lives – MODERN LIVES

The Hub: Monolith – MONOLITH

The Hub: Sourcerer – SOURCERER

The Hub: Space – SPACEY

The Hub: Susan – SUSAN

The Hub: The Hot Button – HOT BUTTON

The Hub: The Other News – OTHER NEWS

The Hub: Today's Other News – TODAY'S OTHER

The Hub: Useful Things – USEFUL THINGS

The Hub: Useless Things – USELESS THINGS

The Hub: Weird Sisters – WEIRD SISTERS

The Hub: You Are Very Intelligent and Somewhat Artsy – YAVIASA

## International Channel Keywords

AOL Canada – CANADA, AOL CANADA, CANADA, CANADIAN

AOL Canada: Chat – CANADA CHAT

Australia – AUSTRALIA

Austria – AUSTRIA

Belgium – BELGIUM

Bulgaria – BULGARIA

Cameroon – CAMEROON

City Guide to Malta – MALTA

Czech Republic – CZECH REPUBLIC

Denmark – DENMARK

Egypt – EGYPT

Finland – FINLAND

Greece – GREECE

Guam – GUAM

Hong Kong – HONG KONG

Hungary – HUNGARY

Iceland – ICELAND

International channel – INTERNATIONAL, AOL INTERNATIONAL, AOL WORLD, FRANCE, GERMANY, INTERNATIONAL US, INTL, JAPAN

Ireland – IRELAND

Israel – ISRAEL, AOL ISREAL, AOL ISRAEL, ISREAL

Italy – ITALY

Kazakhstan – KAZAKHSTAN

Korea – KOREA

Latvia – LATVIA

Luxembourg – LUXEMBOURG

Malawi – MALAWI

Mexico – MEXICO

Netherlands – NETHERLANDS

New Zealand – NEW ZEALAND

Nigeria – NIGERIA

Northern Mariana Islands – N MARIANA ISLANDS

Norway – NORWAY

Papua New Guinea – PAPUA, NEW GUINEA, PAPUA NEW GUINEA
Philippines – PHILIPPINES
Poland – POLAND
Portugal – PORTUGAL
Puerto Rico – PUERTO RICO
Russia – RUSSIA
Singapore – SINGAPORE
South Africa – SOUTH AFRICA
Spain – SPAIN
Sweden – SWEDEN
Switzerland – SWITZERLAND
Taiwan – TAIWAN
The World – THE WORLD, COUNTRIES, WORLD
Turkey – TURKEY
Ukraine – UKRAINE
United Kingdom – UNITED KINGDOM
Uzbekistan – UZBEKISTAN

## Internet Connection Keywords

Answer Man – ANSWERMAN
AnswerMan: Glossary – AM GLOSSARY
AOL Roadtrips – ROADTRIP, AOL ROADTRIP, BUS, VAN, ROADTRIPS, RT
Companies on the Internet – TOP COMPANY SITES
Computing Internet Sites – COMP SITES, COMPUTING SITES
Cyberlove & Laughter – CYBERLOVE & LAUGHTER
CyberSmith – CYBERSMITH, CSMITH, CYBERCAFE, NET HEAD JED, NET HEAD RED, YBERSMITH
File Transfer Protocol – FTP
GNN Best of the Net – GNN
Internet Chat – INTERNET CHAT, INET CHAT, NET CHAT
Internet Chat – NET CHAT, INET CHAT, INTERNET CHAT
Internet Computing Magazines – INTERNET MAGAZINES, INET MAGS, INET MAGAZINES, INTERNET MAGS
Internet Connection channel – INTERNET, INTERNET CENTER, INTERNET CONNECTION, NET
Internet E-Mail – INTERNET EMAIL, INET EMAIL
Internet Exchange – INTERNET EXCHANGE, INET EXCHANGE, NET EXCHANGE
Internet Gopher – GOPHER, VERONICA, WAIS
Internet Graphic Sites – INTERNET GRAPHICS
Internet Mailing Lists – MAILING LISTS, LISTSERV
Internet Newsstand – INTERNET NEWS, 'NET NEWS, NET NEWS, INTERNET NEWSSTAND
Internet Organizations – INTERNET ORGS, INTERNET.ORGS, INET ORGS, NET ORGS
Internet Questions* – INTERNET QUESTIONS
Internet Software – INTERNET SOFTWARE, NET LIBRARY, NET SOFT, NET SOFTWARE
Internet Suggestions – NET SUGGESTIONS
Internet Usenet Newsgroup area – NEWSGROUPS, KEEPER, NEWSGROUP, USENET
Mail Gateway – MAIL GATEWAY
My Place – MY PLACE, for FTP sites
Navisoft – NAVISOFT
Net.Orgs – NETORGS
NetGirl – NETGIRL
NetGirl: Personals – NETGIRL PERSONALS
Newsgroup Scoop – SCOOP
Personal WWW Publishing area – HOME PAGE, PP
Pro's Corner – PRO'S CORNER, CORNER EARL'S GARAGE, EARLS GARAGE, GARAGE, NET EXPERT, PROS CORNER, PRO'S, PROS
Seven Wonders of the Web – 7 WONDERS, SEVEN WONDERS
The Dead End of the Internet – DEAD END
The Web Diner – WEB DINER, DINER, DINER CREW, HTML HELP, WEB BIZ, WEBD, WEB DINER, WEB HELP, WEBSITE
Top Computing Internet Sites – TOP COMP SITES, TOP COMPUTING SITES
True Tales of the Internet – TRUE TALES
Web Makeover – WEB MAKEOVER
Web Review – WEB REVIEW

Web University – WEB UNIVERSITY
Websource – WEBSOURCE
What is http? – HTTP
Winsock Central – WINSOCK, TELNET
World Wide Web – WEB, WEBCRAWLER, WORLD WIDE WEB, WWW

## Kids Only Channel Keywords

Blackberry Creek – BLACKBERRY, BLACKBERRY CREEK
Club KidSoft – KIDSOFT, CLUB KIDSOFT
Just Books! – BOOKS ON BREAK
Kid's Top Internet Sites – KIDS WEB
Kids Only channel – KIDS, KIDS ONLY
Kids Out: London's Family Events Guide – KIDS OUT, KO
Kids' Guide Pager – KO HELP
Kids' Warner Brothers Online – KIDS WB, KIDS' WB
KidsBiz – KIDSBIZ
KidzBiz' POG Area – POG, POGS
Nickelodeon Online – NICKELODEON, ORANGE, SLIME
Nickelodeon Selections – NICK
The Quest CD-ROM Companion to AOL's Kids Only channel – KIDS QUEST
Weekly Reader News – WEEKLY READER

## Learning & Culture Channel Keywords

Academic Assistance Center – AAC, RESEARCH, TUTORING
Access Excellence – EXCELLENCE, ACCESS EXCELLENCE
Adoption Forum – ADOPTION
Adult Literacy & Education Forum – LITERACY, READ
Afterwards Cafe – AFTERWARDS, ARTS, OPERA, POETRY
Alumni Hall – ALUMNI HALL, ALUMNI
America Online Education Initiative – AOL EDUCATION
American Federation of Teachers – AFT
American Leadership Forum – ALF
AOL Families – AOL FAMILIES, DAD, DADS, FATHER, FATHERS, MOM, MOMS, MOTHER, MOTHERS, PARENT, PARENTING, PARENTS, PIN
AskERIC – ASKERIC, ACCESS ERIC, ERIC
Barrons Booknotes – BARRONS, BOOKNOTES
Book areas – BOOKS
Bookwoman's Literature Game – SN LIT GAME
Bull Moose Tavern – BULL MOOSE
C-SPAN – CSPAN, CSPAN ONLINE
C-SPAN in the Classroom – CSPAN BUS, CSPAN CLASS, CSPAN CLASSROOM, CSPAN SCHOOLS
California State University – CSUC, CHICO
Career Development Training – TRAINING
Career Selections – CAREERS, CAREER
Channel One Network Online – CHANNEL ONE, CHANNEL 1, HACIENDA
Charter Schools Forum – CHARTER, CHARTER SCHOOL, CHARTER SCHOOLS
Child Safety Brochure – CHILD SAFETY
College Board – COLLEGE BOARD
College Selections – COLLEGE
Composer's Coffeehouse – COMPOSER, COMPOSER'S, COMPOSERS
Compton's Education Connection – EDUCATION CONNECTION
Compton's Living Encyclopedia – COMPTONS ENCYCLOPEDIA
Compton's NewMedia Forum – COMPTONS
Compton's Software Library – COMPTONS SOFTWARE
Compton's Study Break – STUDY BREAK
Corcoran School of Art – CORCORAN
CyberLaw/CyberLex – CYBERLAW, COMPUTER LAW, CYBERLEX
Dictionary of Cultural Literacy – DOCL, DCL
Education Advisory Council Online – ED ADVISORY, EDA
Electronic Courseware – COURSEWARE, ECS
Electronic Partnerships – EPARTNERS
Electronic Schoolhouse – ESH, SCHOOLHOUSE
Electronic University Network – EUN, UNIVERSITIES, UNIVERSITY

Employer Contacts Database – CONTACTS
Employment Agency Database – NAPC
Exam Prep Center – EXAM PREP
George Washington University – GWU
Gifted Online – GIFTED
Goals 2000: National Education Act – GOALS 200
Help Wanted Ads – JOBS, HELP WANTED
Home Education Magazine – HEM
Homer's Page at The Odyssey Project – HOMER, HOMER'S PAGE
Homeschooling Forum – HOMESCHOOL, HOMESCHOOLING
Homework area – HOMEWORK, HOMEWORK HELP
Homework Help – HH KIDS
Hot Topics – HOT TOPICS
International Cafe – INTERNATIONAL CAFE, FOREIGN, LANGUAGES
International Languages – LANGUAGE
Kaplan Online – KAPLAN, ACT, GREENBERG, NCLEX, NURSING, TEST PREP
Kaplan Online -or- The Princeton Review – SAT, BUSINESS SCHOOL, GMAT, GRADUATE SCHOOL, GRE, LAW SCHOOL, LSAT, MCAT, MEDICAL SCHOOL
Kaplan Online or The Princeton Review – GMAT, BUSINESS SCHOOL, GRADUATE SCHOOL, GRE, LAW SCHOOL, LSAT, MCAT, MEDICAL SCHOOL, SAT
Kaplan Online or The Princeton Review – GRE, BUSINESS SCHOOL, GMAT, GRADUATE SCHOOL, LAW SCHOOL, LSAT, MCAT, MEDICAL SCHOOL, SAT
Learning & Culture channel – LEARNING, EDUCATION, LEARN, LEARNING & REFERENCE, LEARNING AND REFERENCE, LEARNING CENTER
Learning & Culture Store – L&C STORE
Manager's Network – MANAGER, MANAGER'S, MANAGER'S NETWORK, MANAGING
Montessori Schools – MONTESSORI, MONTESSORI SCHOOLS
NAESP Web Link – NAESP
NAS Online – NAS, AGRICULTURE, ENGINEERING, MATH, SOCIAL SCIENCE, TRANSPORTATION
National Education Association Public Forum – NEA PUBLIC
National Museum of American Art – NMAA, AMERICAN ART
National Museum of American History – NMAH, AMERICAN HISTORY
National Parenting Center – NPC, NATIONAL PARENTING, TNPC
National Principals Center Web link – PRINCIPALS
Nolo Press' Self-Help Law Center – NOLO, NOLO PRESS, LAWYER
Online Campus – CAMPUS, CLASSES, IES, REGISTER, SIGNUP
Online Courses – COURSES, INTERACTIVE ED, INTERACTIVE EDUCATION
Practical Homeschooling – PHS
Princeton Review Informed Parent – PARENT ADVICE
Scholars' Hall – SCHOLARS, SCHOLAR'S HALL, SCHOLARS' HALL, SCHOLARS HALL
Scholastic Libraries – SN LIBRARIES
Scholastic Network Preview Area – SCHOLASTIC
Scholastic Network: Special Guests – SN GUESTS
Scouting Forum – SCOUTING, SCOUTS
Simon & Schuster College Online – S&S, A&B, ALLYN & BACON, COLLEGE ONLINE, KIRSHNER, PH, PRENTICE HALL, SIMON, SIMON & SCHUSTER
Simon & Schuster Online: Biology Dept. – BIOLOGY
Simon & Schuster Online: Criminal Justice Dept. – CRIMINAL JUSTICE
Simon & Schuster Online: English Dept. – ENGLISH
Simon & Schuster Online: Geography Dept. – GEOGRAPHY
Simon & Schuster Online: Health, Pys. Ed. & Rec. Dept. – PHYS ED
Simon & Schuster Online: Human Sexuality Dept. – HUMAN SEXUALITY
Simon & Schuster Online: Mathematics Dept. – MATHEMATICS
Simon & Schuster Online: Political Science Dept. – POLITICAL SCIENCE
Simon & Schuster Online: Social Work Dept. – SOCIAL WORK

Simon & Schuster Online: Sociology Dept. – SOCIOLOGY
Smithsonian Online – SI, MUSEUM, MUSEUMS, SMITHSONIAN
Space and Astronomy – SN SPACE
Student's Election Handbook – ELECTION HANDBOOK
Study Skills Service – STUDY, STUDY SKILLS
Talent Bank – TALENT
Teacher Pager – TEACHER PAGER
Teachers' Forum – T TALK
Teachers' Lounge – TEACHERS' LOUNGE, TEACHER'S LOUNGE, TEACHERS LOUNGE
Teachers' Newsstand – TNEWS
The ABC Classroom – ABC CLASS, ABC CLASSROOM, SMART WATCHING
The Discovery Channel – DSC, DISCOVERY
The Discovery Channel: Chat – DCI CHAT, DISCOVERY CHAT
The Discovery Channel: Education – DSC ED, DSC-ED, DISCOVERY ED, TLC ED, TLC-ED
The Educator's Network – TEACHER, TEACHERS, TEN
The Lab – THE LAB
The Learning Channel – TLC
The Nature Conservancy – NATURE, THE NATURE CONSERVANCY, TNC
The Odyssey Project – ODYSSEY, GEOGRAPHIC, NATIONAL GEOGRAPHIC, NGS, ODY, ODYSSEY PROJECT, THE ODYSSEY PROJECT
The Princeton Review Online – PR, PRINCETON, PRINCETON REVIEW, STUDENT, STUDENT ACCESS, TEST DAY
The Reading Room – READING ROOM
Turner Adventure Learning – TAL
University of California Extension – UCAL, CMIL, UCX
University of Virginia Alumni/McIntire School of Commerce – MCINTIRE, MCINTIRE ALUMNI
What's Hot in AOL Families – FAM HOT
What's Hot in Learning & Culture – L&C HOT, LC HOT, LEARNING & CULTURE HOT

## Life, Styles & Interests Channel Keywords

24 Hours in Cyberspace – CYBER 24
24 Hours of Democracy Web site – 24 HOURS
A Day in the Life of Cyberspace – 1010
AARP Annuity Program – AARP ANNUITY, AARP ANNUIT
AARP Auto & Homeowners Program – AARP HARTFORD, AARP HART
AARP Credit Card Services – AARP BANK 1
AARP Group Health Insurance – AARP PRU
AARP Investment Program – AARP SCUDDER, AARP FUND
AARP Life Insurance Program – AARP NY LIFE, AARP LIFE
access.point – ACCESSPOINT, ACCESS.POINT, CHARITY, CITIZEN, CIVIC, COMMUNITY, DONATION, DONATIONS, NOT-FOR-PROFIT, PHILANTHROPY, VOLUNTEER, VOLUNTEERS
access.point: Nonprofit Professionals Network – NONPROFIT
Advice & Tips – ADVICE, TIPS
Afrocentric Culture – AFROCENTRIC, AFRICA, AFRICAN-AMERICAN, BLACK-AMERICAN, BLACK AMERICAN, BLACKS
AIDS and HIV Resource Center – AIDS, HIV
America's National Parks – PARKS, NCPA
American Association of Retired People – AARP
American Civil Liberties Union – ACLU, CIVIL LIBERTIES
American Dialogue – DIALOGUE, AMERICAN DIALOGUE, BKG
Andy Pargh/The Gadget Guru – GADGET GURU, ANDY PARGH, ELECTRONICS, GADGET, GURU, PANASONIC, PARGH, PRIMESTAR, RCA, RUBBERMAID, TIMEX, TURNER VISION, WAHL
Arizona Central – ARIZONA, ARIZONA CENTRAL, AZ CENTRAL, PHOENIX
Arizona Central: ALT. – AZ ALT, AZ ALT.

Arizona Central: At Ease – AZ ENTERTAINMENT, AZ AT EASE
Arizona Central: Carousing – AZ CAROUSING, AZ CONCERTS
Arizona Central: Computers – AZ COMPUTERS
Arizona Central: Couching – AZ COUCHING, AZ TV
Arizona Central: Destinations – AZ DESTINATIONS, AZ TRAVEL, AZ TRIPS
Arizona Central: Dining – AZ DINING, AZ EATS, AZ PENELOPE
Arizona Central: Films – AZ FILMS, AZ MOVIES
Arizona Central: Golf – AZ GOLF
Arizona Central: House/Home – AZ HOUSE, AX GARDENING, AZ HOME
Arizona Central: KTAR Talk Radio – AZ KTAR
Arizona Central: Newsline – AZ NEWSLINE, AZ NEWS
Arizona Central: Photos – AZ PHOTOS
Arizona Central: Plan On It – AZ CALENDARS, AZ FUN
Arizona Central: Plan On It – AZ SPORTS CALENDARS, AZ SPORTS SCHEDULE
Arizona Central: Preps – AZ PREPS, AZ HIGH SCHOOLS
Arizona Central: Schools – AZ SCHOOLS
Arizona Central: Scoreboard – AZ SCOREBOARD, AZ SCORES
Arizona Central: Small Business – AZ SMALL BUSINESS, AZ BIZ
Arizona Central: Sound Off – AZ SOUNDOFF, AZ BENSON, AZ CARTOON, AZ COLUMNS, AZ EDITORIALS, AZ LETTERS, AZ OPINIONS
Arizona Central: Sports – AZ SPORTS, AZ ASU, AZ CARDS, AZ DIAMONDBACKS, AZ SUNS, AZ U OF A
Arizona Central: Stardust – AZ STARDUST, AZ THEATER, AZ THEATRE
Arizona Central: The Best – AZ BEST
Arizona Central: Volunteers – AZ VOLUNTEERS
Arizona Central: Your Community – AZ COMMUNITY
Arizona Central: Your Life – AZ LIFE
Arizona Central: Your Money – AZ MONEY, AZ BUSINESS
Army and Air Force Mutual Aid Association – AAFMAA
Artists on America Online – ARTISTS, ARTIST
Assemblies of God Online – AGOL
Astronet – ASTRONET, AMERICAN ASTROLOGY, ASTROLOGY, ASTROMATES, CAROLE 2000, CHINESE ASTROLOGY, COSMIC MUFFIN, FINANCIAL ASTROLOGY, GENIE EASY, INTERACTIVE ASTROLOGY, KRAMER, WELCOME TO PLANET EARTH, ZODIAC
Astronomy Club – ASTRONOMY
Aviation Forum – AVIATION, AIRPLANE, AIRSHOWS, AV FORUM, FLY, GENERAL AVIATION, JET, SKY DIVING, ULTRALIGHTS
Baby Boomers area – BABY BOOMERS, BABY BOOMER
Bernie Siegel Online – BERNIE
Bethel College and Seminary – BETHEL
Bethel Theological Seminary – BTS
Birding Selections – BIRDING
Car/Cycle Selections – CARS, AUTOMOBILE, AUTOMOTIVE, CAR, MOTORCYCLE, MOTORCYCLES
Catholic Community – CATHOLIC, POPE
Celebrity Cookbook – COOKBOOK, CELEBRITY
Challenger Remembered – CHALLENGER, ASTRONAUTS, KENNEDY SPACE, KENNEDY SPACE CENTER, SHUTTLE, SPACE SHUTTLE
Chicago Online – CHICAGO, CHICAGO ONLINE, COL
Chicago Online: Business Guide – COL BUSINESS
Chicago Online: Calendar & Almanac – COL CALENDAR
Chicago Online: Chat – COL CHAT
Chicago Online: Education Guide – COL EDUCATION, COL EDUCATE
Chicago Online: Libraries – COL FILES
Chicago Online: Lifestyles – COL LIFESTYLES
Chicago Online: Mall – COL MALL
Chicago Online: Marketplace – COL MARKETPLACE
Chicago Online: Media Guide – COL MEDIA

Chicago Online: News, Business & Weather – COL NEWS
Chicago Online: Planner – COL PLANNER
Chicago Online: Sports – COL SPORTS
Chicago Online: Technology Guide – COL TECH
Chicago Online: Ticketmaster – COL TICKET
Chicago Online: Visitor Guide – COL VISITOR
Christian Books & Culture – BC, BOOKS & CULTURE
Christian Camping International – CCI, CHRISTIAN CAMPING
Christian College Guide – CCG, CHRISTIAN COLLEGES
Christian Community Development Association – CCDA
Christian Education Center – CEC, CHRISTIAN EDUCATION
Christian Media Source – CMS, CHRISTIAN MEDIA
Christian Ministries Center – CM
Christian Products Center – CPC, CHRISTIAN PRODUCTS
Christian Resource Center – RC, CHROL RESOURCES
Christianity Online – CHRISTIANITY, <><, CHRIST, XOL
Christianity Online Chat & Live Events – CO LIVE, CHRISTIAN CONNECTION, CHROL CHAT, FELLOWSHIP HALL
Christianity Online Classifieds – CLS, CHROL CLASSIFIEDS, CO CLASSIFIEDS
Christianity Online Newsstand – CN, CNEWS, CO NEWS
Christianity Online: Associations & Interests – CO INTERESTS, ASSN, CO ASSOCIATIONS
Christianity Online: Campus Life's Student Hangout – CO TEENS, CHRISTIAN STUDENT, CHRISTIAN STUDENTS, CO STUDENT, CO STUDENTS, CO TEEN, CO YOUTH
Christianity Online: Church Leaders Network – CLN, CHURCH LEADERS, CHURCH LEADERS NETWORK, LEADERS NETWORK
Christianity Online: Contest – XCON, CON, CO CONTEST
Christianity Online: Holidays and Contests – CO HOLIDAY, CO HOLIDAYS, H&H, HOLI, HOLIDAYS & HAPPENINGS
Christianity Online: Kids – CO KIDS, CHRISTIAN KID, CHRISTIAN KIDS
Christianity Online: Marriage/Family Forum – CO FAMILY, CHRISTIAN FAMILY, CHRISTIAN FAMILIES, CO FAMILIES
Christianity Online: Men – CO MEN, CHRISTIAN MAN, CHRISTIAN MEN, CO MAN
Christianity Online: Singles – CO SINGLES, CHRISTIAN SINGLE, CHRISTIAN SINGLES, CO SINGLE, CO SINGLES
Christianity Online: Women – COW, CHRISTIAN WOMAN, CHRISTIAN WOMEN, CO WOMAN, CO WOMEN
Christianity Online: Word Publishing – WRD
Consumer Electronics – CE, ALARM, AUTO SOUND, BEEPER, CELLULAR, CELLULAR PHONE, CONSUMER ELECTRONICS, HOME AUDIO, PAGER, SECURITY
Cooking Club – COOKING CLUB
Corkscrewed Online – CORKSCREWED
Craft Selections – CRAFTS
Craig Anderton's Sound Studio & Stage – SSS, ANDERTON
Daily Living – DAILY LIVING
Deaf & Hard of Hearing Forum – DEAF
Department 56 Collecting – DEPT 56, DEPARTMENT 56
Digital Cities -or- DC Comics – DC
Digital City Boston – BOSTON, BOSTON ONLINE
DisABILITIES Forum – DIS, BLIND, DISABILITIES, DISABILITY, PHYSICALLY DISABLED
Do Something! – DO SOMETHING, DS
Earth Day / Environment – ENVIRONMENTAL ED
Electronic Gourmet Guide – EGG, EGG BASKET
Environment Forum – ENVIRONMENT, EARTH, EFORUM

Jewish File Downloads – JEWISH DOWNLOADS
Jewish Food – JEWISH FOOD
Jewish Holidays – JEWISH HOLIDAYS, JEWISH HOLIDAY, PASSOVER
Jewish Isreali Elections – JEWISH ELECTIONS, ISREAL ELECTIONS
Jewish Message Boards – JEWISH BOARDS
Jewish News – JEWISH NEWS
Jewish Singles – JEWISH SINGLES, JEWISH MATCHMAKER
Jewish Store – JEWISH STORE
Jewish Youth – JEWISH YOUTH
Jewish.COMMunity – JEWISH, JCOL, JEWISH COMMUNITY
Jokes! Etc. – JOKES
KidCare – KIDCARE
Kodak Photography Forum – KODAK
Kodak Web Site – KODAK WEB
Korean War Memorial Home Page – KWM WEB
Lambda Rising Bookstore Online – LAMBDA RISING, GAY BOOKS, LAMBDA
LatinoNet Registration – LATINONET
Libertarian Party Forum – LIBERTARIAN, LIBERTARIAN PARTY, LIBERTARIANS
Life, Styles & Interest's Top Internet Sites – CLUBS & INTERNET
Life, Styles & Interests channel – LIFESTYLES, CLUBS, COMMUNITY CENTER, HOBBIES, INTEREST, LIFESTYLES & HOBBIES, LIFESTYLES & INTEREST, LIFESTYLES & INTERESTS, SPECIAL INTERESTS
Love@AOL – LOVE@AOL, AMOR, AMOR, DATE, DATING SERVICE, DATING SERVICES, LOVE, LOVE AT AOL, LOVER, LUST, LUV, MATCHMAKER, MATCHMAKING, PASSION
Mad About Music – MAM, FLASH
Massachusetts Governor's Forum – MASS, MASS., MASSACHUSETTS
Medline – MEDLINE
Men Are From Mars – MARS, MEN ARE FROM MARS, JOHN GRAY
Mercury Center – MERCURY, MERCURY CENTER, SAN JOSE
Mercury Center Bay Area Living area – MC LIVING
Mercury Center Business & Technology area – MC BUSINESS
Mercury Center Communication – MC COMMUNICATION
Mercury Center Communication – MC TALK
Mercury Center Entertainment area – MC ENTERTAINMENT
Mercury Center In the News area – MC NEWS
Mercury Center Sports area – MC SPORTS
Messiah College – MES, MESSIAH
Michigan Governor's Forum – MICHIGAN, MICHIGAN GOVERNOR
Military and Vets Club – MILITARY, VETERANS, VETS, VETS CLUB
Military City Online – MCO, DEFENSE, MC, MILITARY CITY, MILITARY CITY ONLINE
Military City Online: Communications – MCO COMM
Military City Online: Headquarters – MCO HQ
Military City Online: Shop – MCO SHOP
Military City Online: Tour – MCO TOUR
Military City Online: Villains of Fact & Fiction – VILLAINS, SCOUNDREL, SCOUNDRELS, VILLAIN
Military City Online: Worldwide Military Installations Database – MCO BASES
Minirth Meier New Life Clinics – MIN, MINIRTH MEIER, MMNLC, NEW LIFE
Moms Online – MOMS ONLINE, MOM, MOMS, MOTHER
National Network for Youth – NNFY, NNY, YOUTHNET
National Space Society – NSS, SPACE
National Urban League – NUL, URBAN LEAGUE
Neighborhoods, USA – NEIGHBORHOODS, NEIGHBORHOODS, USA
NetNoir – NETNOIR, NET_NOIR, NET_NOIRE, NETNOIR, NETNOIRE, NOIR-NET, NOIRE_NET, NOIRENET
New England Cable News – NECN, CABLE NEWS, NEW ENGLAND CABLE, NEW ENGLAND CABLE NEWS, NEW ENGLAND NEWS
New Product News – NEW PRODUCTS, NEW PRODUCT
Non-Profit Network – NPN, NON PROFIT, NON PROFIT NETWORK

Online Legal Areas – LEGAL, LEGAL SIG, LIN
Outdoor Adventures Online – OAO, ADVENTURE, OUTDOOR, OUTDOOR ADVENTURE
Overseas Brats – BRATS
Owens Corning – OC
Pagan Religions & Occult Sciences – PAGAN, MAGICK, MAGICKAL, WICCA
Parent Soup – PARENT SOUP, IVILLAGE, PARENT'S SOUP, PARENTS SOUP
Parent Soup: Chat – PARENT SOUP CHAT
Parent Soup: Local Information – PARENT SOUP LOCAL INFO
Pet Care Forum – PET, ANIMAL, ANIMALS, PET CARE, PETS
Photography area – PHOTO, PHOTOGRAPHY
Photography Selections – CAMERA
Pictures of the World – PICTURES
Planet Ealing – PLANET EALING
PlanetOut – PLANETOUT, PNO
Politics – CAPITAL, CAPITAL CONNECTION, CONGRESS, DEBATE, GOVERNMENT, ISSUES, POLITICS, PUBLIC POLICY, WASHINGTON
Popular Photography Online – PHOTOS, CAMERAS, POP PHOTO, POPULAR PHOTOGRAPHY
Psych Online – PSYCH ONLINE, ONLINE PSYCH
Public Safety Center – PSC, EMERGENCY, EMERGENCY RESPONSE, ERC, PUBLIC SAFETY, SAFETY
Quilting Forum – QUILTING, QUILT, QUILTERS
Religion & Ethics Forum – ETHICS, ATHEISM, BAHA'I, BUDDHISM, CHRISTIAN, CREED, DENOMINATION, ECCLESIASTICAL, HINDUISM, ISLAM, METAPHYSICS, NEW AGE, PHILOSOPHY, PERSUASION, RELIGIONS, SECT, UNITARIUM
Religion & Ethics Forum – RELIGIONS, ATHEISM, BAHA'I, BUDDHISM, CHRISTIAN, CREED, DENOMINATION, ECCLESIASTICAL, ETHICS, HINDUISM, ISLAM, METAPHYSICS, NEW AGE, PHILOSOPHY, PERSUASION, SECT, UNITARIUM
Religion News Update – RNU, RELIGION NEWS
Ringling Online – RBO, RBO, RINGING, RINGLING BROS, RINGLING ONLINE
San Jose Mercury News – MC NEW
Science Fiction & Fantasy – SF, ANALOG, ASIMOV, FANTASY, HORROR, MYSTERY, SCI FI, SCI-FI, SCIENCE FICTION
Scuba Club – SCUBA, GO SCUBA
Self-Help area – SELF HELP, SELF-HELP
SeniorNet – SENIOR
SERVEnet – SERVENET, SERVENET, YOUTH SERVICE AMERICA, YSA
Sexually Transmitted Diseases Forum – STD
Simi Winery – SIMI WINERY
Sound, Studio, Stage News – SSS NEWS
Spiritual Mosaic – SPIRITUAL
Spiritual Mosiac – MOSIAC
Star Trek Club – TREK, STAR TREK
Taylor University – TAY, TAYLOR UNIVERSITY
Teen Selections – TEEN, TEEN SCENE, TEENS
The Bicycle Network – BICYCLE, BFA, BIKENET
The Book Nook – BOOKNOOK, BOOK
The Civil War Forum – CIVIL WAR
The Exchange – EXCHANGE, BOATS, COINS, COLLECTOR, OUTDOORS, RAILROADING, STAMPS, THE EXCHANGE
The Exchange: Collector's Corner – ANTIQUES, TOYS
The Exchange: Communities Center – COMMUNITIES, AFRICAN AMERICAN, AMERICAN INDIAN, ASIAN, MEN, NATIVE AMERICAN, ORGANIZATIONS, THIRTIES, TWENTIES
The Exchange: Home & Careers – H&C
The Exchange: Interests & Hobbies – GUNS
The Exchange: Outdoor Fun – OUTDOOR FUN
The Image Exchange: Ask Todd Art – ASK TODD ART, ASK TODD, TODD ART
The Love Shack – LOVE SHACK
The Positive Living Forum – PLF, POSITIVE LIVING
The Prayer Network – TPN, PRAYER NET

This Week's Best Cyberviews – CYBERVIEWS, CYBERVIEW

Transgender Community Forum – GENDER, CROSSDRESSER, CROSSDRESSING, F2M, GLCF TCF, M2F, SRS, TCF, TG, TRANSGENDER, TRANSSEXUAL, TRANSVESTITE

Utah Forum – UTAH, UTAH FORUM

Vietnam Veterans Memorial Wall – THE WALL, VIETNAM, WALL

Virginia Forum – VIRGINIA, VIRGINIA FORUM, VA, VA., OLD DOMINION

Virtual Christian Humor – HUM, ;-D, VH, VIRTUAL HUMOR

Vote America – VOTE AMERICA

Wedding Workshop – WEDDING

Wheels Exchange – WHEELS EXCHANGE, CAR PHOTOS, MEMBERS' RIDES, MEMBERS RIDES

White House Forum – WHITE HOUSE, CLINTON, THE WHITE HOUSE

Women's Interests – WOMEN, WOMENS, WOMEN MAIN, WOMEN SPOTLIGHT

Women's Interests: Arts and Letters – WOMAN COLLECTIONS

Women's Interests: Community – WOMEN ROUND

Women's Interests: Educational Opportunities – WOMEN CLASS

Women's Interests: Message Boards – WOMAN BOARDS

Women's Interests: News – WOMAN NEWS

Women's Interests: Organizations – WOMAN VOICES

Women's Interests: Web Sites – WOMEN WEB

World Beliefs – WORLD BELIEFS

World Crisis Network – WCN, WORLD CRISIS

Writer's Club – WRITERS, WRITER, WRITER'S, WRITER'S CLUB, WRITERS CLUB, WRITING

Writer's Club: Chat Rooms – WC CHAT, WRITERS CLUB CHAT, WRITE

Writer's Club: Romance Writers & Readers – ROMANCE GROUP

Young Chefs – YOUNG CHEFS

Your Good Life – GOOD LIFE

Your Mind & Body Online – YMB, MIND & BODY, MIND AND BODY, YOUR MIND & BODY, YOUR MIND AND BODY

Zondervan Publishing House – ZON, ZP, ZONDERVAN

## Marketplace Keywords

800-TREKKER: 24 Hour Sci-Fi Collectibles Hotline – 800-TREKKER, 1-800-TREKKER, 1-800-TREKER, 800-TREKER, TREKER, TREKKER

America Online Store – AOL STORE, AMERICA ONLINE STORE, AOL PRODUCTS, MUG, T SHIRT, TOUR GUIDE

American ExpressNet – AMEX, AMERICAN EXPRESS, EXPRESSNET

AOL Classifieds – CLASSIFIEDS, AOL CLASSIFIED, AOL CLASSIFIEDS, CLASSIFIED, CLASSIFIEDS ONLINE

AOL Enterprise – AOL ENTERPRISE, AOL BUSINESS, AOL ENTERPRISES, ENTERPRISE, ENTERPRISES

AT&T Home Business Resources – FOUR RESOURCES, 4RESOURCES

AutoVantage – AUTOVANTAGE, AUTO, AV

AutoVantage: New Car Summary – NEW AUTO, CAR INFO, CAR SUMMARY, NEW AUTO, NEW CAR

Avon – AVON

Blockbuster Music's Online Store – BLOCKBUSTER

Brainstorms Store – BRAINSTORMS

Cadillac WWW Home Page – CADILLAC

Caffe Starbucks – STARBUCKS, CAFFE STARBUCKS

Checkbook Bargains – BARGAINS

Chef's Catalog – CHEFS CATALOG, CHEF'S CATALOG

Collectibles Online – COLLECTIBLES, COLLECT, COLLECTIBLES ONLINE

Computer Express – COMPUTER EXPRESS

Dinner On Us Club – PREMIER, EAT, EAT OUT, DINE OUT, PD, PREMIER DINING

Downtown AOL – DOWNTOWN, DOWNTOWN AOL, DT, DT AOL

Downtown AOL Message Boards – DOWNTOWN MSG

Eagle Home Page – EAGLE

Eddie Bauer – EDDIE BAUER
Eli's Cheesecakes – CHEESECAKES, CHEESECAKE, ELI, ELI'S, ELI'S CHEESECAKES, ELIS CHEESECHAKES
Eli's Cheesecakes Contest – ELI CONTEST
F.A.O. Schwarz – FAO SCHWARZ, FAO
Family Product Showcase – FAMILY SHOWCASE
Federal Express Online – FEDEX
Felissimo – FELISSIMO
Fossil Watches and More – FOSSIL, FOSSIL WATCHES
General Motors Web Site – GM
Global Plaza – GLOBAL PLAZA
Godiva Chocolatiers – GODIVA
Greet Street Greeting Cards – GREET STREET, GREET ST
Gucci Parfums Counter – GUCCI
Guess, Inc – GUESS
Gwaltney Hams & Turkeys – GWALTNEY, SMITHFIELD, HAMS
Hallmark Connections – HALLMARK, CARDS, HALLMARK CONNECTIONS
Hammacher Schlemmer – HAMMACHER, HAMMACHER SCHLEMMER
Health and Vitamin Express – HEALTH EXP, HEALTH EXPRESS, RX, VITAMIN EXP, VITAMIN EXPRESS
Infiniti Online – INFINITI, INFINITI ONLINE
Internet Connection Store – ICS, IC STORE, INTERNET STORE, NET STORE, NET BOOKS, WOLFF BOOKS
JCPenney – JCPENNEY
KidSoft Superstore – KIDSOFT STORE
Lens Express – LENS, LENS EXPRESS
Lillian Vernon – LILLIAN VERNON, LILLIAN
Mama's Cucina by Ragu – MAMA, ITALIAN FOOD, MAMA'S CUCINA, PASTA, RAGU, SAUCE
Marketplace channel MARKETPLACE, MALL, SHOPPING, STORE, STORES, THE MALL
Marketplace Gift Service – 2MARKET, CD, TO MARKET, TWO MARKET
Marketplace Gift Services – GIFT SERVICES
McFamily Community – MCFAMILY, MCDONALD'S
Moonstone Mountaineering – MOONSTONE
Nissan Online – NISSAN
OfficeMax Online – OFFICEMAX, OFFICE
Oldsmobile/Celebrity Circle – OLDS, CELEBRITY CIRCLE, OLDSMOBILE
Omaha Steaks – OMAHA, OMAHA STEAKS, STEAKS
Omaha Steaks Offer – SWEETHEART
One Hanes Place – HANES, BALI, CHAMPION, L'EGGS, PLAYTEX
Online Bookstore – BOOKSTORE, READ USA
Pangea Toy Net – TOY NET, BEANIE, BEANIE BOY, CRISPY, PANGEA, PANGEA TOYNET, THE TOY NET, TOY, VIRTUAL TOYS, VTOYS
Pangea Toy Network: ToyBuzz – TOYBUZZ, PLAYMATES
Paul Frederick MenStyle – PAUL FREDERICK
Peapod Online – PEAPOD
PictureWeb & PicturePlace – PICTUREPLACE, PIC, PICTUREWEB
Pork Online – PORK
Price Online – PRICE, PRICE ONLINE
PUR Drinking Water Systems – PUR
REI Recreation Equipment, Inc. – REI
Romance Store – ROMANCE STORE
Shopper's Advantage Online – SA, COMPUSTORE, SHOPPERS ADVANTAGE
The Fragrance Counter – FRAGRANCE, COLOGNE, PERFUME
The Fragrance Counter – PERFUME, COLOGNE, FRAGRANCE
The Fragrance Counter: Clearance Counter – CLEARANCE
The FreeShop Online – FREESHOP , FREESHOP ONLINE
The Sharper Image – SHARPER IMAGE, SI STORE
Tower Records – TOWER, RECORD, RECORDS, TOWER RECORDS
United States Postal Service – USPS
Warner Bros. Studio Store – WB STORE, WARNER BROS. STORE, WARNER BROS. STUSTO, WARNER BROS STORE, WARNER STORE
Windham Hill – WINDHAM HILL, WINDHAM
Zima – ZIMA
Zima Events – ZIMA TALK

## MusicSpace Keywords

America Online Guitar SIG – GUITAR, GTR, GUITAR SIG

Chicago Symphony Orchestra Online – CHICAGO SYMPHONY

Coda Music Tech – CODA, CMT, CODA MUSIC

Drum Magazine – DRUM

Grateful Dead Forum – DEAD, :, GRATEFUL DEAD, THE DEAD

Grateful Dead Forum Store – GD STORE

House of Blues Online – HOB, BLUES, HOUSE OF BLUES, JAZZFEST

MuchMusic Online – MUCHMUSIC, MUCHMUSIC ONLINE

Music Media – MUSIC MEDIA

Music Message Center – MMC

MusicSpace – MUSICSPACE

MusicSpace Communications – MUSIC TALK

MusicSpace Studio – STUDIO

MusicSpace WEB TopStops – MUSIC WEB

Rockline Online – ROCKLINE, CRAZY HORSE, HITS

RockNet Information & Web Link – ROCKNET, ROCKLINK

TAXI Information and Web Link – TAXI

Virgin's Virtual Valley – VALLEY, PEANUTS, VIRTUAL VALLEY

Warner/Reprise Records Online – WARNER, REPRISE, WARNER MUSIC

Woodstock Online – WOODSTOCK

## Newsstand Channel Keywords

@times Store – TIMES STORE, NYT STORE, @TIMES STORE

@times/The New York Times Online – @TIMES, AT TIMES, NEW YORK, NEW YORK CITY, NEW YORK TIMES, NYC, NYT, NY TIMES, TIMES, TIMES NEWS

@times: Art & Entertainment Guide – TIMES ARTS

@times: Arts & Leisure – TIMES LEISURE, LEISURE

@times: Books of the Times – TIMES BOOKS

@times: Dining Out & Nightlife – TIMES DINING

@times: Film – TIMES FILM, TIMES MOVIES

@times: Museums & Galleries – TIMES ART

@times: Music & Dance – TIMES MUSIC, DANCE

@times: Page One-Top Stories – TIMES STORIES

@times: Sport News – TIMES SPORTS

@times: The New York Region – TIMES REGION

@times: Theater – TIMES THEATER

American Woodworker – WOODWORKER, AMERICAN WOODWORKER, PLANS, WOOD, WOODWORKING

American Woodworker: Tool Reviews – POWERTOOLS, MACHINERY, POWER EQUIPMENT, POWERTOOL, TOOL, TOOLS

Arizona Central: Cactus League Classifieds – AZ CACTUS

Astrograph – ASTROGRAPH

Backpacker Magazine – BACKPACKER, BACKCOUNTRY, CAMPING, ECOTOURISM, HIKER, HIKING, OUTDOOR GEAR, TRAIL GUIDES, TRAILS, WILDERNESS

Backpacker Online's Marketplace – BP MARKETPLACE

Bicycling Magazine – BIC MAG, BICYCLING, BICYCLING MAGAZINE, MOUNTAIN BIKE

Bicycling Magazine: Tour de France Coverage – TOUR DE FRANCE

Big Twin Online: The All-Harley Magazine – BIG TWIN, HARLEY, HARLEY DAVIDSON

Boating Online – BOAT, BOAT, FISH, FISHING, INBOARD, MARINE, OUTBOARD, POWER BOATS, SPEED BOATS, WATER, YACHTS

Business Week Online – BW, BIZ WEEK, BW ONLINE, BUSINESS WEEK

Business Week: Search – BW SEARCH

Campus Life Magazine – CL, CAMPUS LIFE

Cancer Journal from Scientific American – CANCER JOURNAL, CANCER J SCIAM

Car and Driver Magazine – CAR AND DRIVER, DRIVING

Catholic News Service – CNS, CATHOLIC NEWS, CATHOLIC NEWS SERVICE

Chicago Online: Classifieds – TRIB ADS, TRIB CLASSIFIED

Chicago Online: Columnists – TRIB COLUMNISTS

Chicago Tribune – TRIBUNE, CHICAGO TRIBUNE, TRIB

Chicago Tribune: Election '96 – COL GOVERNMENT, COL GOVT

Chicago Tribune: Local Entertainment Guide – COL ENTERTAINMENT

Chicago Tribune: News Quiz – NEWS QUIZ

Chicago Tribune: Sports Area – TRIB SPORTS

Chicago Tribune: Traffic Updates – COL TRAFFIC

Christian Computing Magazine – CC MAG, CHRISTIAN COMPUTING

Christian History Magazine – CH, CHRISTIAN HISTORY

Christian Reader – CR, CHRISTIAN READER

Christianity Today – CT, CHRISTIANITY TODAY

CNN Newsroom Online – CNN, CNN GUIDES, CNN NEWSROOM, DEMOCRACY, NGUIDES

Columnists & Features Online – COLUMNS, COLUMNISTS, FEATURES

Computer Life Magazine – COMPUTER LIFE, CLIFE, JUST DO IT, LIFE

Consumer Reports – CONSUMER, CONSUMER REPORTS, CONSUMERS, WOMEN ONLY

Consumer Reports Complete Drug Reference Search – DRUG REFERENCE

Cowles/SIMBA Media Information Network – COWLES, COWLES SIMBA, INSIDE MEDIA, MEDIA, MEDIA INFORMATION, SIMBA

Cycle World Online – CYCLE, CYCLE WORLD, CYCLING, HELMETS, MOTORCYCLING

Digizine Sites on the Web – DIGIZINES, CYBERZINES, EZINES

Disney Adventures Magazine – DISNEY MAGAZINE, DISNEY ADVENTURES

Doctor Who Online – DR WHO, DOCTOR WHO

Elle Magazine Online – ELLE, BEAUTY, CLOTHES, CLOTHING, DESIGN, DESIGNERS, FASHION, MODELS, TRENDS

Family Life Magazine Online – FAMILY LIFE

FamilyPC Online – FAMILY PC, GAMESTER, GIGABRAIN, MEGA NEWS, MEGAZINE, MEGAZONE

Flying Magazine – FLYING, AIRCRAFT, AIRCRAFTS, AIRPORTS, FLYING MAG, FLYING MAGAZINE, IFR, PILOTS, VFR

Generation Next – GEN NEXT, GENERATION NEXT, NEXT

Hachette Filipacchi Magazines – HACHETTE, HFM MAGNET WORK, MAGNET, MAGNETO

Health Magazine – HEALTH MAGAZINE

Health Magazine's Current area – HMCURRENT

Health Magazine's Relationships area – HMRELATIONSHIPS

Health Magazine's Remedies area – HMREMEDIES

Highlights for Children – HIGHLIGHTS, HFC, HIGHTLITES, HIGHTS ONLINE

Highlights for Children Catalog – HIGHLIGHTS CATALOG, HFT CATALOG, HFC STORE, HIGHLITES CATALOG

HISPANIC Online – HISPANIC ONLINE, HISPANIC MAGAZINE, LATINA, LATINO

Home Office Computing Magazine – HOME OFFICE, HOC, SOHO

HomePC Magazine – HOME PC

HomePC Magazine: Children's Software – CHILDREN'S SOFTWARE

I-Wire Online – IWIRE, COMPUTE, I-WIRE

Ideas for Better Living – BETTER LIVING, IDEAS FOR BETTER LIVING

Inc Live Conference Room – @INC LIVE

InToon with the News – INTOON, DEPIXION, EDITORIAL CARTOONS, KEEFE, MIKE KEEFE, TOON, TOONZ

Leadership Journal – LJ, LEADERSHIP, LEADERSHIP JOURNAL

Longevity Magazine Online – LONGEVITY, ANTI-AGING, ANTI AGING, ANTI-OXIDANTS, HERBS, HOMEOPATHIC REMEDIES, MASSAGE, PLASTIC SURGERY, SPA, SPAS, VITAMINS, WELLNESS, WORKOUTS, YOUNGNESS, YOUTHFUL

Mac Home Journal – MAC HOME, MAC HOME JOURNAL, MHJ

Mac Today Magazine – MAC TODAY

MacWorld Magazine – MACWORLD

Marriage Partnership Magazine – MARRIAGE, MARRIAGE PARTNERSHIP, MPM
Mercury Center Advertising – MC ADS, MC CLASSIFIEDS, MC MARKET
Mercury Center Newshound – NEWSHOUND, MCPR, MERCPR, PERSONAL REPORTER
Mercury Center Newspaper Library – NEWS LIBRARY, MC LIBRARY, NEWSPAPER LIBRARY
Mercury Center Trivia – MC TRIVIA, GERTIE
Metropolitan Home – MET HOME, METROPOLITAN HOME
Mirabella Magazine – MIRABELLA, MIRABELLA ONLINE
Mobile Office Online – MOBILE, PORTABLE, PORTABLE COMPUTING
Motley Fool's Rogue – ROGUE, JIM'S BRAIN
Multimedia World Online – MMW NEWS, MMW, MMW WORLD
Multimedia World Online – MMW, MMW NEWS, MMW WORLD, MULTIMEDIA WORLD
Multimedia World Online's Clinic – MMW CLINIC
Multimedia World Online's Library – MMW LIBRARY
Multimedia World Online's Office – MMW OFFICE
Multimedia World Online's Pavilion – MMW PAVILION
Multimedia World Online's Test Track – MMW TEST TRACK
Multimedia World Online's Welcome area – MMW WELCOME
National Catholic Reporter – NCR, CATHOLIC REPORTER
Newspaper Association of America – NAA, ASNE, NVN
Newspapers selection – NEWSPAPERS, LOCAL NEWSPAPERS, LOCALNEWS, NEWSPAPER
Newsstand channel – NEWSSTAND, MAGAZINES
Newsweek Magazine – NEWSWEEK
Nutrition Forum – NUTRITION
OMNI Magazine Online – OMNI, OMNI MAGAZINE, OMNI ONLINE
Orlando Sentinel Online – OSO, ORLANDO, ORLANDO SENTINEL
Orlando Sentinel Online: Autos – OSO AUTO
Orlando Sentinel Online: Baseball – OSO BASEBALL
Orlando Sentinel Online: Beach – OSO BEACH, OSO BEACHES
Orlando Sentinel Online: Black Voices – OSO BLACK, BLACK VOICES, BLACK-VOICES
Orlando Sentinel Online: Black Voices' Chat – BV CHAT
Orlando Sentinel Online: Business – OSO BUSINESS
Orlando Sentinel Online: Chat – OSO CHAT
Orlando Sentinel Online: Classified Ads – OSO CLASSIFIEDS, OSO CLASSIFIED
Orlando Sentinel Online: College Football – OSO COLLEGE FOOTBALL, OSO COLLEGE FB
Orlando Sentinel Online: Download Libraries – OSO DOWNLOAD
Orlando Sentinel Online: Entertainment – OSO ENTERTAIN
Orlando Sentinel Online: Government – OSO POLITICS, OSO GOVERNMENT
Orlando Sentinel Online: Homes – OSO HOMES
Orlando Sentinel Online: Hurricane Survival Guide – OSO STORM
Orlando Sentinel Online: Jobs – OSO JOBS, OSO WANT ADS
Orlando Sentinel Online: Living – OSO LIVING
Orlando Sentinel Online: Magic – OSO MAGIC, OSO MAGIC MAG
Orlando Sentinel Online: Merchandise – OSO MERCHANDISE
Orlando Sentinel Online: Movies – OSO MOVIES
Orlando Sentinel Online: OSOnet – OSO NET
Orlando Sentinel Online: Photos – OSO PHOTOS
Orlando Sentinel Online: Predators – OSO PREDATORS
Orlando Sentinel Online: Religion News – OSO RELIGION

Orlando Sentinel Online: Services – OSO SERVICES, OSO SERVICE
Orlando Sentinel Online: Sound Off – OSO SOUND OFF
Orlando Sentinel Online: Space – OSO SPACE
Orlando Sentinel Online: Sports – OSO SPORTS
Orlando Sentinel Online: Theme Parks – OSO THEME PARK
Orlando Sentinel Online: Things To Do – OSO TO DO
Orlando Sentinel Online: Top Stories – OSO TOP
Orlando Sentinel Online: Transportation – OSO TRANS
Orlando Sentinel Online: Weather – OSO WEATHER
Oskar's Magazine – OSKARS, OSKAR'S
PC Today – PC TODAY, PC CATALOG
PC World Online – PC WORLD, PC WORLD ONLINE
PC World: Netscape – PCW NETSCAPE
Road & Track – ROAD, AUTOS, R&T, ROAD & TRACK, TRACK
Saturday Review Online – SATURDAY, CLASSICAL MUSIC, LITERATURE, READING, SAT REV, SATURDAY REVIEW, SOCIETY, SRO, THEATER, THEATRE
Saturday Review Online: Conference Room – SRO SALON
Scientific American – SCI AM, SCIENCE, SCIENTIFIC, SCIENTIFIC AMERICAN
Scientific American Medical Publications – SA MED
Scientific American: Frontiers – SAF, FRONTIERS
Smithsonian Magazine – SM, SMITHSONIAN MAGAZINE
Spin Online – SPIN, SPIN ONLINE
Standard & Poor's Marketscope – MSCOPE
Stereo Review Magazine – STEREO, AMPLIFIERS, AUDIO, CDS, HOME THEATER, SOUND, SPEAKERS, STEREO EQUIPMENT, STEREO REVIEW
Sunset Magazine – SUNSET, SUNSET MAGAZINE
The Atlantic Monthly Online – ATLANTIC, ATLANTIC MONTHLY, ATLANTIC ONLINE, FICTION, IDEAS
The New Republic Magazine – NEW REPUBLIC, THE NEW REPUBLIC, TNR
The New York Times Crosswords – @TIMES CROSSWORD, CROSSWORD, CROSSWORDS, NYT CROSSWORD, NYT CROSSWORDS
Time Message Boards – TIME
TIME Message Boards – TIME DAILY
Today's Christian Woman – TCW
TopModel Online – TOP MODEL
USA Today Industry Watch section – CAREER NEWS
USA Weekend – USA, USA WEEKEND
USA Weekend: News & Views – NEWS & VIEWS, N&V
Washington Week In Review Magazine – WWIR
Windows Magazine – WIN MAG, WINDOWS MAG, WINDOWS MAGAZINE
Wired Magazine – WIRED
Woman's Day Kitchen – WD KITCHEN
WordPerfect Magazine – WP MAG
Worth Magazine Online – WORTH, WORTH MAGAZINE, WORTH ONLINE
Woth Magazine Online: Portfolio – WORTH PORTFOLIO
Your Church Magazine – YC, YOUR CHURCH

## People Connection Keywords

AOL Live Auditorium – @AOL LIVE, @AOL LIVE, AOL DEAD
AOL Live! – AOL LIVE, AOL LIVE!, AUDITORIUM, BOWL, CENTER STAGE, CHAT SCHEDULE, COLISEUM, CS, LIVE, GLOBE, LIVE!, LIVE TONIGHT, ODEON, PC AUD, SHOWS
AOL Live! Event Transcripts – TRANSCRIPTS, TRANSCRIPT
AOL Live! Spotlight – SPOTLIGHT
Baumrucker Conference – BAUMRUCKER, FIRST BYTE
Cyber Rap auditorium – @CYBER RAP
Cyberplex auditorium – @CYBERPLEX
Dalai Lama Conference – DALAI LAMA, DL
LaPub – LAPUB
Main Stage auditorium – @MAINSTAGE
People Connection channel – PEOPLE, CHAT, PC, PEOPLE CONNECTION, TALK

Portrait Gallery – GALLERY
Romance Channel – ROMANCE
Romance Connection – DATING
The Bowl auditorium – @BOWL
The Coliseum auditorium – @COLISEUM
The Crystal Ball Forum – TAROT, CRYSTAL BALL
The Globe auditorium – @GLOBE
The News Room auditorium – @NEWS ROOM, @THE NEWS ROOM
The Odeon auditorium – @ODEON
Today's Events in AOL Live! – EVENTS, EVENT, YUBBA

## Personal Finance Channel Keywords

AIQ Systems – AIQ SYSTEMS, AIQ
American Association of Individual Investors – AAII
AOL Mutual Fund Center – MUTUAL FUND, AOL MFC, MFC, MFC 95, MUTUAL FUND 95, MUTUAL FUNDS, MUTUAL FUND CENTER
AOL's Real Estate Center – MLS, ARM, HOME EQUITY LOANS, HOME REFINANCING, MORTGAGE, MORTGAGE RATES, MORTGAGES, NAREE, REAL ESTATE
Bank of America – BOFA, BA, BANK AMERICA, BANK OF AMERICA, BOFA, HOME BANKING
Block Financial Software Support – TAXCUT, KIP, KIPLINGER
Business Rankings – BUSINESS RANKINGS, RANKINGS
Business Sense – BUSINESS SENSE
Business Strategies Forum – STRATEGIES, BS FORUM, BUSINESS KNOW HOW, BUSINESS STRATEGIES
California Mortgage Bankers Association – MIX CMBA
Chicago Online: Crain's Chicago Business – CCB, CRAIN'S, CRAIN'S SMALL BIZ, CRAINS, CSB
Citicorp Mortgage – MIX CITICORP
Commerce Business Daily – CBD
Company Research – COMPANY, COMPANY RESEARCH, HQ
Company Research Message Boards – BEATY, ACCORDING, ACCORDING TO BOB, BEATY, BOB BEATY, BOBB
Computing Tax Corner -or- Tax Forum – TAXES
Data Track Systems, Inc. – MIX DATA TRACK
Decision Point Forum – DP, DECISION, DECISION POINT, DPA, STOCK CHARTS, STOCK TIMING
Disclosure Incorporated – DISCLOSURE
Disclosure's EdgarPlus – EDGAR
Disclosure's Financial Statements – FINANCIALS, BALANCE SHEET, FINANCIAL STATEMENT, INCOME STATEMENT
Fidelity Online Investments Center – FIDELITY, FID
Fidelity Online's Funds Area – FID FUNDS, FID BROKER
Fidelity Online's Guide Area – FID GUIDE
Fidelity Online's Newsworthy Area – FID NEWS
Fidelity Online's Planning Area – FID PLAN
Fidelity Online's Working Area – FID AT WORK
First Chicago Online – FIRST CHICAGO ONLINE
Fundworks Investors' Center – FUNDWORKS
Genesis 2000 – MIX GENESIS
Harvard Business School Publishing – HBS PUB
Herb Greenberg's Business Insider – BIZ INSIDER, BUSINESS INSIDER
Historical Stock & Fund Quotes – HISTORICAL QUOTES
Hoover's Business Resources – HOOVER, HOOVER'S, HOOVERS
Hoover's Company MasterList – MASTERLIST, COMPANY UPDATES, HOOVERS UPDATES, UPDATES
Hoover's Handbook of Company Profiles – COMPANY PROFILES, CORPORATE PROFILE, CORPORATE PROFIILES
Hoover's Industry Profiles – INDUSTRY PROFILES
How to use StockLink & Gateway Host – TRADEPLUS, ETRADE
InBusiness – INBUSINESS, IBIZ, INBIZ, INTERNET BIZ

Inc. Magazine – INC., INC, INC MAGAZINE, INC. MAGAZINE, INC ONLINE, INC. ONLINE
Industry Insider – INSIDER
Industry Insider or The Cobb Group Online – INSIDE
Investment Lingo – LINGO, INVESTMENT LINGO
Investor's Business Daily – IBD, INVESTOR'S BUSINESS, INVESTOR'S DAILY, INVESTORS BUSINESS, INVESTORS DAILY
Investors' Exchange – IE, ICF, TICF
Investors' Network – INVESTORS NETWORK, IN, INVEST, INVESTING, INVESTMENT, INVESTMENTS, INVESTOR, INVESTOR'S NETWORK, INVESTORS
Mixstar Mortgage Information Exchange – MIXSTAR
Morningstar Mutual Funds – FUND, FUNDS, MORNINGSTAR
Motley Fool: Airlines – FOOL AIR, FOOL AERO
Motley Fool: Ask the Headhunter – HEADHUNTER
Motley Fool: Biotechnology – FOOL BIO
Motley Fool: Chemicals – FOOL CHEM
Motley Fool: Desktop Video – FOOL DTV, FOOL VID, DTV
Motley Fool: Food – FOOL FOOD
Motley Fool: FoolMart – FOOL MART, FOOL STORE, WALMART
Motley Fool: Hardware – FOOL HARD
Motley Fool: Health – FOOL HEALTH
Motley Fool: Networking – FOOL NET
Motley Fool: Oilfield Services – FOOL OIL
Motley Fool: Paper & Trees – FOOL PAPER
Motley Fool: Railroads – FOOL RAILS
Motley Fool: Real Estate – FOOL REIT, FOOL REITTO, REIT
Motley Fool: Semiconductors – FOOL CHIPS, FOOL SEM, SEM
Motley Fool: Software – FOOL SOFT
Motley Fool: Storage Tech – FOOL TECH
Motley Fool: Utilities – FOOL UTIL
NAEA Tax Channel – TAX CHANNEL, NAEA
Omega Research – OMEGA
OSO Classified Real Estate – OSO REAL ESTATE
PC Financial Network – PCFN, PC FINANCIAL, PC FINANCIAL NETWORK
Personal Finance channel – PF, FINANCE, MONEY, PERSONAL FINANCE
Personal Finance Software Center – PF SOFTWARE
Personal Finance Software Support – PFSS, SOFTWARE SUPPORT
Plus ATM Network – PLUS
Quotes Plus – QUOTES PLUS
Real Estate Selections – REAL ESTATE
Real Life Financial Tips – REAL LIFE, FAMILY FINANCES, FINANCIAL PLANNING, INSURANCE, JOB, PLANNING, RETIREMENT, RL, YM, YOUR MONEY
RSP Funding Focus – RSP, SCHOLARSHIP, SCHOLARSHIPS
Small Business Administration – SBA
Stock Reports – STOCK REPORTS
StockLink: Quotes & Portfolios – STOCKLINK, QUOTE, QUOTES, STOCK, STOCK QUOTES, STOCKS
Tax Forum – TAX, TAX FORUM
Taxlogic – TAXLOGIC
Telescan Users Group Forum – TELESCAN
The Apple Citibank Visa Card – CITIBANK
The Kaufmann Fund – KAUFMANN
The Motley Fool – FOOL, COMMONS, COOKIE, COSTARD, FESTE, FOOLISH, LAUNCE, LAVATCH, MFOOL, MOTLEY, MOTLEY FOOL, PORT FOLLY, THE MOTLEY FOOL, TODAY PITCH, TODAYS PITCH, TRINCULO
The Nightly Business Report: Making $ense of It All – NBR
The Nightly Business Report: NBR Online Report – NBR REPORT
Top Advisor's Corner – ADVISORS, ADVISOR, TAC, TOP ADVISOR, TOP ADVISORS
Twentieth Century Mutual Funds – CENTURY, 20, 20TH, 21ST, CENTURY FUNDS,TWENTIETH, TWENTIETH CENTURY, TWENTIETH-CENTURY

U.S. Treasury Securities – TREASURY SECURITIES, NATIONAL DEBT, PUBLIC DEBT, SAVINGS BONDS, TREASURY BILLS, TREASURY BONDS, TREASURY DIRECT, TREASURY NOTES, US SAVINGS BONDS, U.S. SAVINGS BOND, US TREASURY SECURITIES

Vanguard Fund Information – VSTATS

Vanguard Online – VANGUARD, VANGUARD ONLINE, VG

Vanguard Online: Communications – VCOMMS

Vanguard Online: Mutual Funds Campus – VFUNDS

Vanguard Online: Planning & Strategy – VSTRATEGY

Vanguard Online: Vanguard News – VNEWS

Wall Street SOS Forum – SOS

Wall Street Words – WSW, WALL STREET WORDS

Weigand Report – WEIGAND

Your Business – YOUR BUSINESS, BUSINESS CENTER, E-ZONE, ENTREPRENEUR ZONE, EZ, EZONE, MS BIZ, MSBC, SBC, SMALL BUSINESS, THE ENTREPRENEUR ZONE, THE ZONE, YB, YOUR BIZ, ZONE

Your Business Lunch – LUNCH, BUSINESS LUNCH, YOUR BUSINESS LUNCH

Your Government Resources – GOVERNMENT RESOURCES

Your Industry – INDUSTRIES

Your Money – YOUR MONEY

Your Stock Portfolio – PORTFOLIO, STOCK PORTFOLIO

Your Voice – VOICE

## Reference Desk Channel Keywords

AT&T 800 Directory Web Site – 800, 800 DIRECTORY, TOLL FREE

Bartlett's Quotations – BARTLETT, BARTLETT'S, BARTLETTS, QUOTATION, QUOTATIONS

Bartlett's Quotations – QUOTATION, BARTLETT, BARTLETT'S, BARTLETTS, QUOTATIONS

Business Yellow Pages – YELLOW PAGES, ABI, ABI YELLOW PAGES, MAILING LIST

Columbia Encyclopedia – COLUMBIA, CCE

Computer and Internet Dictionary – QUES DICTIONARY

Dictionary of Computer Terms – COMPUTER TERMS

Dictionary Selections – DICTIONARY

Grolier's Encyclopeda – GROLIER'S, GROLIER, GROLIERS, MME, GMME

Hot Reference – HOT REFERENCE, HOT REF, REF HOT

MacMillan Information SuperLibrary – SUPERLIBRARY, MACMILLAN

Merriam-Webster Dictionary – MERRIAM, MERRIAM-WEBSTER, WEBSTER

Merriam-Webster's Collegiate Dictionary – COLLEGIATE, COLLEGIATE DICTIONARY, MW DICTIONARY

Merriam-Webster's Kids Dictionary – KIDS DICTIONARY

Merriam-Webster's Medical Dictionary – MEDICAL DICTIONARY

Merriam-Webster's Thesaurus – THESAURUS

NY Public Library Desk Reference – DESK REFERENCE, NY PUBLIC LIBRARY

Phone Directories – PHONE DIRECTORY, PHONE BOOK, TELEPHONE, TELEPHONE NUMBERS

Places Rated Almanac – PLACES RATED, PLACES RATED ALMANAC

ProCD National Telephone Directory Search – WHITE PAGES, PROCD

Reference Daily Dose – DAILY

Reference Desk channel – REFERENCE, REFERENCE DESK

Reference Desk: Help – REFERENCE HELP

Reference: Web Research – WEB RESEARCH, WEB TOOLS

U.S. Census Information Web Page – US GAZETTEER

Word Histories – WORD HISTORIES

Zip Code Directory – ZIP CODES, ZIP CODE, ZIP CODE DIRECTORY

## Sports Channel Keywords

1995 NBA Draft – NBA DRAFT

1996 Pro Bowl – PRO BOWL

ABC Hockey Trivia – HOCKEY TRIVIA, NTN HOCKEY TRIVIA

ABC Online: Wide World of Sports – WWOS, WIDE WORLD OF SPORTS
ABC SPORT STORE – ABC SPORTS STORE
ABC Sports – ABC SPORTS
ABC Sports College Football – ABC FOOTBALL, ABC COLLEGE FOOTBALL
ABC Sports Figure Skating – ABC FIGURE SKATING, FIGURE SKATING
ABC Sports Major League Baseball – ABC BASEBALL, MLB
ABC Sports Women's Sports – ABC WOMEN, ABC WOMEN'S
ABC Sports' REV Speedway – REV, ABC AUTO RACING, REV SPEEDWAY, SPEEDWAY
ABC Track – ABC TRACK, EQUIBASE, WINNER'S CIRCLE
ABC Triple Crown – ABC TRIPLE CROWN, TRIPLE CROWN
ABC Triple Crown – TRIPLE CROWN, ABC CROWN, ABC TRIPLE, ABC TRIPLE CROWN
America's Cup 1995 – AMERICAS CUP, AMERICA'S CUP
America-3: The Women's Team – AMERICA3, ACUBED
AOL Auto Racing – AUTO RACING, NASCAR
AOL Football – FOOTBALL, COLLEGE FOOTBALL
AOL Golf area – GOLF
AOL Skiing – SKI
AOL Sports Archive – SPORTS ARCHIVE
AOL Sports Live – AOL SPORTS LIVE, LIVE SPORTS, SPORTS EVENTS, SPORTS LIVE
AOL Sports: Running – RUNNING
AOL Tennis – TENNIS
AVP Pro Beach Volleyball – VOLLEYBALL, KING OF THE BEACH, KOB
Baseball Daily by Extreme Fans – HARDBALL, BASEBALL DAILY
Boating Selections – BOATING, SAILING
Burger King College Football – BK, BURGER KING
Choose a Sport on AOL – CHOOSE A SPORT
Extreme Fans: College Hoops – EXTREME FANS, EXTREME FANS, FANS
Extreme Fans: Message Boards – HOOPS BOARDS
Fool Bowl – FOOL BOWL, BOWL GAME, FIESTA BOWL, ORANGE BOWL, ROSE BOWL
Fred Edelstein's Pro Football Insider – EDELSTEIN
French Open – FRENCH OPEN
GolfCentral – GOLF DATA
Grandstand's Sport Trivia Question of the Day – QOTD
Home Team Sports – HTS
Horse Forum's Dressage MiniForum – DRESSAGE
Iditarod Trail Sled Dog Race – IDITAROD
iGolf – IGOLF
iGolf History – IGOLF HISTORY
iGolf: Tour Championship – TOUR CHAMPIONSHIP
Indianapolis 500 – INDY, INDY 500
iSKI – ISKI, MOUNTAIN, MT, SKIING
John Naber – NABER, JOHN NABER
Major League Baseball Team: Atlanta Braves – BRAVES, ATLANTA BRAVES, BRAVOS
Major League Baseball Team: Boston Red Sox – BOSOX, BOSTON RED SOX
Major League Baseball Team: California Angels – ANGELS, CALIFORNIA ANGELS
Major League Baseball Team: Chicago Cubs – CUBS, CHICAGO CUBS, CUBBIES
Major League Baseball Team: Chicago White Sox – WHITE SOX, CHICAGO WHITE SOX, CHISOX
Major League Baseball Team: Cincinnati Reds – REDS, CINCINNATI REDS
Major League Baseball Team: Cleveland Indians – INDIANS, CLEVELAND INDIANS, TRIBE
Major League Baseball Team: Colorado Rockies – ROCKIES, COLORADO ROCKIES
Major League Baseball Team: Detroit Tigers – TIGERS, DETROIT TIGERS
Major League Baseball Team: Florida Marlins – MARLINS, FLOIDA MARLINS
Major League Baseball Team: Houston Astros – ASTROS, HOUSTON ASTROS
Major League Baseball Team: Kansas City Royals – ROYALS, KANSAS CITY ROYALS

Major League Baseball Team: Los Angeles Dodgers – DODGERS, DOGERS, LOS ANGELES DODGERS

Major League Baseball Team: Milwaukee Brewers – BREWERS, MILWAUKEE REWERS

Major League Baseball Team: Minnesota Twins – MINNESOTA TWINS

Major League Baseball Team: Montreal Expos – EXPOS, MONTREAL EXPOS

Major League Baseball Team: New York Mets – METS, NEW YORK METS

Major League Baseball Team: New York Yankees – YANKS, NEW YORK YANKEES, YANKEES

Major League Baseball Team: Oakland Athletics – ATHLETICS, A'S, OAKLAND A'S, OAKLAND ATHLETICS

Major League Baseball Team: Philadelphia Phillies – PHILLIES

Major League Baseball Team: Pittsburgh Pirates – BUCS, PIRATES, PITTSBURGH PIRATES

Major League Baseball Team: San Diego Padres – PADRES, SAN DIEGO PADRES

Major League Baseball Team: Seattle Mariners – MARINERS, M'S, SEATTLE MARINERS

Major League Baseball Team: St. Louis Cardinals – CARDINALS, ST. LOUIS CARDINALS

Major League Baseball Team: Texas Rangers – RANGERS, TEXAS RANGERS

Major League Baseball Team: Toronto Blue Jays – BLUE JAYS, JAYS, TORONTO BLUE JAYS

Matt Williams' Hot Corner – MATT WILLIAMS, MATT

Michael Jordan area – JORDAN, AIR JORDAN, MF, MICHAEL JORDAN

MLB All-Star Ballot – ALL STAR

Motley Fool: The Fool Dome – FOOL DOME, FOOLBALL, FOOL SPORTS, BASEBALL WORKSHOP, BWOL

Motorsport '95 Online – MOTORSPORT, MOTORSPORTS

NBA Basketball – BASKETBALL

NCAA Football Bowl Info – BOWLS, BOWL GAMES

NCAA Hoops – NCAA, HOOPS

NESN: New England Baseball – NESN BASEBALL, AROUND THE HORN, NEW ENGLAND BASEBALL, RED SOX, RED SOX BASEBALL

NESN: New England Baskteball – NESN BASKTEBALL, ABOVE THE RIM, BOSTON CELTICS, CELTICS, CELTICS BASKETBALL

NESN: New England Football – NESN FOOTBALL, NEW ENGLAND FOOTBALL, NEW ENGLAND PATRIOTS, RED ZONE

NESN: New England Hockey – NESN HOCKEY, BOSTON BRUINS, BRUINS HOCKEY, CUTTING EDGE, NEW ENGLAND HOCKEY

New England Cable Network: Sports for Kids – KID SPORTS

NHL Hockey – HOCKEY

NHL Online – NHL, ABC HOCKEY, ABC NHL

NTN Basketball Trivia – NTN BASKETBALL TRIVIA, BASKETBALL TRIVIA, HOOPS TRIVIA, NTN HOOPS TRIVIA

Olympic Festival Online – OLYMPICS, OLYMPIC, OLYMPIC FESTIVAL

On Hoops Basketball Web Page – ON HOOPS

Pro Basketball Center by STATS, Inc – STATS HOOPS, STATS BASKETBALL

Pro Sports Center by STATS, Inc. – STATS, STATS, INC., STATS, INC, STATS INC

Roger Clemens' Playoff Baseball Journal – ROGER CLEMENS

Sailing Forum – YACHTING, BOARDSAILING, WINDSURFING

Ski Reports – SKI REPORTS, SKI CONDITIONS, SKI WEATHER

Snowboarding Online – SNOWBOARDING, ASYLUM, SOL

Sports channel – SPORTS, BOXING, SPORTS LINK

SurfLink – SURFLINK, SURF, SURFBOARD, SURFER, SURFERS, SURFING

The GM's Corner – GM'S CORNER, GMS CORNER

The Grandstand – GRANDSTAND, THE GRANDSTAND

The Grandstand's Baseball Dugout – GS BASEBALL

The Grandstand's Basketball Off the Glass – GS BASKETBALL
The Grandstand's Boxing – GS BOXING, Squared Circle
The Grandstand's Chat Rooms – SPORTS CHAT, SPORTS ROOMS
The Grandstand's Collecting – GS COLLECTING, Sports Cards
The Grandstand's Fantasy & Simulation Leagues – FANTASY LEAGUE, CYBERSPORTS, FANTASY LEAGUES, SIMULATION LEAGUES
The Grandstand's Fantasy & Simulation Leagues – FANTASYLEAGUE(S, SIMULATIONLEAGUES
The Grandstand's Fantasy Baseball – FANTASY BASEBALL
The Grandstand's Fantasy Basketball – FANTASY BASKETBALL
The Grandstand's Fantasy Football – FANTASY FOOTBALL
The Grandstand's Fantasy Hockey – FANTASY HOCKEY
The Grandstand's Football: 50 Yard Line – GS FOOTBALL
The Grandstand's Golf: On The Green – GS GOLF
The Grandstand's Hockey: Blue Line – GS HOCKEY
The Grandstand's Horse Sports: Post Time – GS HORSE, HORCE RACING, HORSE SPORTS
The Grandstand's Libraries – SPORTS LIBRARIES
The Grandstand's Major League Soccer – MLS LIVE
The Grandstand's Martial Arts: The Dojo – GS ARTS, KARATE, MARTIAL ARTS
The Grandstand's Motor Sports: In The Pits – GS AUTO
The Grandstand's Other Sports: Whole 9 Yards – GS OTHER, BOWLING, ROLLERSKATING, SWIMMING
The Grandstand's Sideline – GS SIDELINE
The Grandstand's Simulation Auto Racing – ICRS, SIMULATION AUTO
The Grandstand's Simulation Baseball – GBL, SIMULATION BASEBALL
The Grandstand's Simulation Basketball – SIMULATION BASKETBALL
The Grandstand's Simulation Football – GSFL
The Grandstand's Simulation Football – SIMULATION FOOTBALL, ASFL, CNFA, GCFL, GPFL, GMFL, GSFL, GUFL, NWFL, OFL, RSFL
The Grandstand's Simulation Football – SIMULATION FOOTBALL, ASFL, CNFA, GCFL, GPFL, GMFL, GSFL, GUFL, NWFL, OFL, RSFL
The Grandstand's Simulation Golf – GGL, ALPT, GGL, MAC ALPT
The Grandstand's Simulation Golf – SIMULATION GOLF, ALPT, GGL, MAC ALPT
The Grandstand's Simulation Hockey – GSHL, SIMULATION HOCKEY
The Grandstand's Simulation Wrestling – GWA, SIMULATION WRESTLING
The Grandstand's Soccer: The Kop – GS SOCCER
The Grandstand's Sports Boards – SPORTS BOARDS
The Grandstand's Sports Products: Sportsmart – GS SPORTSMART
The Grandstand's Sports Software Headquarters – GS SOFTWARE
The Grandstand's Sports Trivia – GS TRIVIA, GS SPORTS TRIVIA, GRANDSTAND TRIVIA
The Grandstand's Winter Sports: The Chalet – GS WINTER
The Grandstand's Wrestling: Squared Circle – GS WRESTLING
The Grandstand: Horse Sports & Racing Forum – HORSE SPORTS, GS HORSE, HORSE RACING
The Horse Forum – HORSE, HORSES
The Lacrosse Forum – LACROSSE, LAX
The Olympic Shop – OLYMPIC SHOP, OLYMPIC STORE
The Pat O'Brien Report – PAT O, PAT O'BRIEN, PAT OBRIEN
The Sporting News – SPORTING NEWS, THE SPORTING NEWS, TSN
The Surf Shack – SURF SHACK
Trans-America Footrace – TA FOOTRACE
U.S. Golf Society Online – PLAYWELL
United States Figure Skating Association – USFSA

Washington Capitals – CAPS, CAPITALS
What's Hot in Sports – HOT SPORTS, SPORTS HOT
Wheels – WHEELS, RACING
Wimbledon – WIMBLEDON
Women's Sports World – WSF, WOMENS SPORTS
World Wrestling Federation – WWF, RAW, SUMMER SLAM, SUPERSTARS, WRESTLING

## Style Channel Keywords

Style channel – STYLE, A-LIST, BEAUTY 911, BODY ELECTRIC, CELEBRITIES, DESIGNER STUDIO, FACE, GIRL STUFF, GUY STUFF, MAKEOVER, MAKEUP, MODELS! MODELS!, PARTY GIRL, SCENTS, STYL*E, STYLE, STYLE CHANNEL, STYLE 911, SUIT, UNDIES, VIP, WWWARDROBE

## Today's News Keywords

1995: The Year in Review – 1995, YEAR, YIR, YEAR IN REVIEW, REVIEW
AIDS Daily Summary – AIDS DAILY
Balkan Operation Joint Endeavor – BOSNIA, BALKAN, UNPROFOR, YUGOSLAVIA
Blizzard Fun! – BLIZZARD
Business News area – BUSINESS, BUSINESS NEWS
Color Weather Maps – WEATHER MAPS, COLOR WEATHER MAPS
Congressional Quarterly – CQ, CONGRESSIONAL
Croatia – CROATIA
Entertainment News – ENTERTAINMENT NEWS
Galileo Mission to Jupiter – GALILEO, JUPITER, NASA, STARS
Hillary Rodham Clinton – FIRST LADY, HILLARY
Hot News – HOT NEWS
Main Weather Area – COLOR WEATHERMAPS
Market News – MARKET, MARKET NEWS
Pictures of the Week – EDITOR'S CHOICE, EDITORS CHOICE, IOTW
Search News Articles – NEWS SEARCH, NEWS WATCH, SEARCH NEWS
Sport News – SPORTS NEWS
The Campaign Trail – CAMPAIGN 96, DECISION 94
Today's News channel – NEWS, HEADLINES, NEWS AND FINANCE, NEWS & FINANCE, NEWS ROOM, NEWS TEXT, NEWS/SPORTS/MONEY, NEWSLINK, OUR WORLD, TODAY'S NEWS, TOP NEWS
Today's News: It's a Mad, Mad World... Dispatches from the Wires – MAD WORLD
Tropical Storm and Hurricane Info – HURRICANE, TROPICAL STORM
U.S. & World News – WORLD NEWS, US NEWS
Weather – WEATHER

## Travel Channel Keywords

AAA Online – AAA, 3A, TRIPLE A, A3
Arthur Frommer's Secret Bargains – ARTHUR FROMMER, AF'S SECRET BARGAINS, SECRET BARGAINS
Bed & Breakfast U.S.A. – B&B, BED, BED & BREAKFAST, BREAKFAST
Cruise Critic – CRUISE CRITIC, CRUISE, CRUISE CRITICS, CRUISES, SHIP CRITIC, SHIP CRITICS
Destination Florida – FLORIDA
Destination Florida: Attractions – DF PARKS
Destination Florida: Kennedy Space Center – DF SPACE
Destination Florida: Outdoors – DF OUT
Destination Florida: Places to Stay – DF ROOMS
Destination Florida: Restaurants and Nightlife – DF FOOD
Destination Florida: Shopping – DF SHOP
Destination Florida: Sports – DF SPORTS
Destination Florida: Ticketmaster – DF TICKET
EAASY SABRE Travel Service – EAASY SABRE, AMERICAN AIRLINES, EASY, EASY SABRE, SABRE
Emerald Coast – EMERALD COAST
Family Travel Network – FTN, FAMILY TRAVEL NETWORK, KID TRAVEL
Family Travel Selections – FAMILY TRAVEL
Florida's Space Coast – SPACE COAST

Fodor's Worldview – WORLDVIEW

Frommer's City Guides – FROMMER, FROMMER'S, FROMMER'S CITY GUIDES, FROMMERS, FROMMERS CITY GUIDES

Golfis Forum – GOLFIS, GOLF AMERICA, GOLF COURSES, GOLF INFORMATION, GOLF RESORTS

Inside Flyer – INSIDE FLYER, FREQUENT FLYER

Lanier Family Travel Guides – LANIER, LANIER FAMILY TRAVEL

One World Travel – ONE WORLD, ONE WORLD TRAVEL, RESERVATION, RESERVATIONS

Preview Vacations – VACATIONS, PREVIEW VACATION, VACATIONS

Preview Vacations' Travel Update – PLAY KEYWORD

RPM Worldwide Entertainment & Travel – RPM, RPM TRAVEL

The Florida Keys – THE KEYS, FLORIDA KEYS, THE FLORIDA KEYS

The Ski Zone – SKI ZONE

Travel & Leisure Magazine – TL, TRAVEL & LEISURE

Travel channel – TRAVEL, SHOPPING & TRAVEL, SHOPPING AND TRAVEL

Travel Forum – TRAVEL FORUM, TRAVELER

Travel Holiday Magazine – TRAVEL HOLIDAY

Traveler's Advantage – TA, TRAVELERS ADVANTAGE

Traveler's Corner – TRAVELERS CORNER, WEISSMAN

U.S. State Department Travel Advisories – TRAVEL ADVISORIES

What's Hot in Travel – HOT TRAVEL, TRAVEL PICKS

Zagat Restaurant/Hotel/Resort/Spa Surveys – ZAGAT, ZAGATS

# INDEX

## D



## E

Index

## H



## I



## K



## L



## M

Index